THE JACOBEAN AGE

RICHARD, THIRD EARL OF DORSET, from a portrait by
Daniel Mytens in the possession of MARGARET, COUNTESS
of SUFFOLK AND BERKSHIRE

THE JACOBEAN AGE

By

DAVID MATHEW

With Illustrations

KENNIKAT PRESS
Port Washington, N. Y./London

THE JACOBEAN AGE

First published in 1938
Reissued in 1971 by Kennikat Press
Library of Congress Catalog Card No: 72-118488
ISBN 0-8046-1237-4

Manufactured by Taylor Publishing Company   Dallas, Texas

FOR
GERVASE MATHEW

PREFACE

THIS volume is a study of the historical setting of the first quarter of the seventeenth century in England. The trend of political development, the routine detail of the central administration and the slow movements of Court form the basis of the book. The requirements of a fluctuating taste, the effect of architectural schools and the range of experience of foreign travel are seen mirrored in the life of the rich lords and the landed gentry and the great buoyant middle class. Each change in the structure of the social life is accompanied by the unvarying influence of privilege. Through a comparatively restricted circle there came each change in taste and prejudice and knowledge.

Such a study requires the examination of a mosaic of contemporary record, each detail helping to build up the setting of the Jacobean scene. The political and religious influences, always explicit and sometimes superficial, are found reflected in daily life and casual writing. Depositions, statements and informal notes and letters provide a flood of information on the state of mind of wide sections of the people. The official point of view can often be contrasted with unpremeditated comment. The incidental detail contained in letters thus assumes a new significance. From these and similar sources we can detect those underlying suppositions which were accepted without question, the mutual approach of different classes, the lines of flattery and the clear prejudice. The life of the official world or that of the members of the household of some great manor are each seen protected by their own conventions. The limits within which individual action could find scope can be defined. For an elaborate and insecure

7

political machinery was linked with the character and sanc-
tions of the Stuart kingship. The relationship of the wealthy
landed families with the Court involved not only an acute
and shifting competition but the burden of extravagance and
emulation. The sense of oligarchic dynasty can already be
traced in the embryo.

On account of the nature of the approach this study of the
changing cultural and politico-religious background is chiefly
concentrated upon those sections of the English social scene
which guided and benefited by policy and fostered letters.
Again economic theory lies outside this book's scope.

The volume on *The Jacobean Age* is to be followed by one
dealing with *The Early Carolines* and the two periods, though
so distinct, are so closely interwoven that there must be an
arbitrary element in the selection of any date which is chosen
to divide them. The decade of the Buckingham ascendancy
has a certain unity and the present book closes in 1628 with
the Duke's assassination; an event which had the widest
repercussions on opinion in England. A more detailed appreciation of the Puritan influence is reserved for the later volume
as it is naturally impossible to find a dividing date in the
growth of this religious sentiment.

In the first place I should wish to express my gratitude to
the Marquess of Salisbury for his permission to use the
unpublished and uncalendared Hatfield House MSS. dealing with the years 1606–12 on which the earlier chapters of
this study are principally based. I should also wish to express
my thanks to Lord Arundell of Wardour and the Hon. John
Arundell for the use of the Wardour MSS. which contain so
complete a picture of the life of a great household in the
West of England, to Baroness Beaumont for the use of the
Stapleton MSS. and the Errington MSS. at Carlton Towers,
and to Admiral Lord Stafford for the use of the Sulyard of
Wetherden papers among the MSS. at Swynnerton in connection with which I am particularly grateful to the Rector of

Swynnerton, the Rev. J. B. Frith. I am also anxious to thank Mrs. Andrew Kerr for permission to use the Coke MSS. at Melbourne Hall which are in some ways the most remarkable collection of private letters and memoranda dealing with this period still remaining in private hands. I am grateful to the Duke of Norfolk for permission to use the MSS. relating to Thomas Earl of Arundel at Arundel Castle, and to Lord Sackville for the use of the Sackville and Cranfield MSS. from Knole now deposited at the Public Record Office.

My thanks are also due to the Librarian of Worcester College, Oxford, for the use of Inigo Jones's notes relating to his Italian journeys, to the President of Ushaw College for the use of the Eyre MSS., and to the President of St. Edmund's College, Ware, for the use of early seventeenth-century books from the Douai press in the college library. I must thank the Librarians at the Public Record Office and the Bodleian for their very courteous assistance and especially the Librarians at the British Museum, where I have used both the great collections and MSS. of a more specialized character like the Correspondence of Sir Thomas Edmondes, the Letters of Sir Theodore Turquet de Mayerne and the Letter Book of Sir Richard Norton.

Finally my brother Gervase has worked out with me every portion of this book which I dedicate to him.

DAVID MATHEW

Woburn Square.
September, 1938

CONTENTS

Chapter   *Page*

I. THE JACOBEAN BACKGROUND . . . 1

II. THE CHARACTER OF THE REIGN . . . 17

III. SALISBURY AND THE KING 37

IV. THE ROUTINE OF POLITICS 54

V. THE CLOSE OF THE CECIL INFLUENCE . . 71

VI. A CROSS SECTION IN 1613 . . . 84

VII. VILLIERS AND BACON 108

VIII. ARUNDEL AND ITALIAN TRAVEL . . . 124

IX. THE DIPLOMATIC BACKGROUND . . . 149

X. THE ECLIPSE OF THE HOWARD GROUPING . 159

XI. THE VILLIERS FACTION 178

XII. SPAIN AND VIRGINIA 187

XIII. THE NATURE OF POLITICAL INFLUENCE . 206

XIV. DONNE AND PRINCE CHARLES . . . 216

XV. THE CATHOLIC MINORITY 230

XVI. THE BAROQUE APPROACH 246

XVII. SECRETARY CONWAY 257

XVIII. SECRETARY COKE 281

XIX. THE DUKE'S DEATH 290

XX. EPILOGUE 301

APPENDIX 315

BIBLIOGRAPHICAL NOTE 333

INDEX 338

ILLUSTRATIONS

Facing page

I. RICHARD, THIRD EARL OF DORSET . . 1
From a portrait by Daniel Mytens in the possession of
Margaret Countess of Suffolk and Berkshire.

II. ANNE, LADY MORTON 35
From a portrait attributed to Paul van Somer in the
possession of Mr. Benjamin Guinness.

III. ARCHBISHOP ABBOT 95
From a portrait in the National Portrait Gallery.

IV. SIR EDWARD SACKVILLE 103
From a portrait by Daniel Mytens in the possession of
Margaret Countess of Suffolk and Berkshire.

V. THOMAS, EARL OF ARUNDEL AND SURREY . 141
From a portrait attributed to Daniel Mytens in the
possession of the Duke of Norfolk.

VI. THE DUCHESS OF BUCKINGHAM . . . 181
From a portrait by Paulus Moreelse in the possession
of Mr. Bruce Ingram.

VII. GEORGE, FIRST DUKE OF BUCKINGHAM . . 209
From a portrait in the possession of Mr. T. W. Fitzwilliam.

VIII. PHINEAS PETT 298
From a portrait attributed to Jan de Critz in the
National Portrait Gallery.

CHAPTER I

THE JACOBEAN BACKGROUND

IN spite of the abrupt cleavage between the late Tudor and Jacobean periods it was inevitable that the early years of the Stuart reigns should have been overshadowed by an Elizabethan afterglow, the confused reflection of a Court epoch which had been at once sceptical and aggressive, artificial, tired, prodigal and consciously heroic. The young men, the favourites of a regime, vanish easily as in the brief passage of an Essex or a Buckingham. It is the middle-aged courtiers, less imaginative in outlook, sober, pliable and acquisitive, who strike the deep roots and remain in possession. Among the main purposes served by the reign of James I was the liquidation of the Elizabethan spirit. The sea adventure, heavily capitalized but insolvent, and the remunerative mannered bravura of the sword play, all this was linked with Gloriana. It was not without its bearing on the situation that the new King should have a horror of naked steel.

Yet the full extent of the changes was to some extent masked so long as the guidance of affairs remained in the control of Burghley's son. A study of the Hatfield House papers gives an impression of Sir Robert Cecil as cautious, lavish and ultimately solitary; an overwhelming political personality whose influence was not traceable in its entirety. The general direction of the King's policy and the supervision of domestic matters hinged upon him; he had secured the succession and was alone in a position to carry out his master's wishes. It was a further asset that he represented the mid-

Elizabethan or Burghley period of the late reign. He had remained apart from the euphuistic imperialism and the bombast which had surrounded the Queen's last years and was deeply inimical to Raleigh, who was so magnificent and gallant and financially quite meretricious.

Sir Robert, with his experience of a lifetime in the service of the State, had a profound distrust for rash expedients. The development of his own properties, the quiet acquisition of Cranborne Chase, the surrender of Theobalds to the King, the building of Salisbury House and Hatfield had been attained securely. Proceeding always with high authority through a careful early manhood, he was found at the King's accession wise and mature. And of all qualities King James most prized wisdom. It must have seemed inevitable that this statesman should remain in power and advance to the Treasury and a great earldom. From 1603 until his death in 1612 Cecil, created Viscount Cranborne and then Earl of Salisbury, remained in effect first minister. He was always a little remote from the new Court as from the old; sympathetic to his sovereign's pacific views; patient with his ecclesiastical concerns; clever with the King's unguarded affections.

He has been unjustly described as opportunist, and he certainly abhorred large and windy projects. Also he seems to have enjoyed the labour of mastering the delicate problems which his sovereigns set him. It was, perhaps, in this retention of the perfect confidence of Queen Elizabeth and King James I that he showed his quality rather than in his elimination of his singularly blundering opponents. The articles of his political faith seem to have been deep-rooted and in part unconscious; but the doctrine to which in his actions he adhered most strongly, was that of the inviolable supremacy of the landed interest.

A peculiar difficulty is experienced in attempting to penetrate to the mind of the early seventeenth-century leaders on account of the depth of their reverence for such abstract ideas as sovereignty and possession. Sceptical as they often were and wholly freed from illusion, no alternative presented itself to them: they had a sureness very hard to comprehend in regard to the doctrines on which the then world-order rested.

The social value of landed influence was an axiom; every sentiment of patriotism fed this same belief: it must have been clear to all the rich and ageing men conscious of their civic virtue, that the fortune of the nation was linked up with their own prosperity. The period was fundamentally complacent and there appears to have been a still content among the many who had adequate possessions and were unharassed by a sceptical intelligence. Cecil was particularly clear-sighted; but it seems that for the generality of the second generation of the new lords, there was an element of poetry in their serious labours as they disencumbered their fine properties and raised up their seed to enter into the patrician Promised Land of the eighteenth century.

A certain balance of forces and carefully adjusted division of offices had formed the basis of Cecil's power; for it was his wise practice to propitiate or, if necessary, conciliate all those who disposed of political influence and were prepared to enter into such accord with him. At the same time he fully shared that dislike of minorities and of the improvident and dissident which was characteristic of the nation state. In consequence there stood ranged behind the administration all those who accepted the religious settlement and appreciated the money values of a sound conservative programme in home politics and finance. The idea of a profitable peace was obviously attractive to men who had never been prepared to lock up their capital in the later crazy variants of sea adventure.

In the circle of the politicians moved by these ideas Cecil had not so much quelled as smothered opposition. The Lord Treasurer Dorset was venerable, quiescent and his father's friend, while the peers of the Howard grouping, Northampton, Nottingham and Suffolk, decided to support a statesman whom they could not dominate and whose position they had no immediate hope of undermining. And it was just this form of collaboration which Cecil managed with such skill, soothing them with titles and rewards and deference and preserving for himself his own more private access to the sovereign. It is not surprising that his cousin Bacon was impotent before Cecil's calm and almost phlegmatic talent.

In the new reign it was quiet political support and well-judged loans and money gifts which brought promotion. The day of political meteors was over and it was both easy and essential to be on the right side. The bravura of the Essex Rising seemed impenetrably remote now that it was no longer customary for gentlemen of property to attach themselves to the fortunes of a leader. There were too many earls for any peer of that rank to attain to the perilous isolation of Essex or Leicester. As a consequence the wealthiest lords obtained a measure of privacy surrounded only by their numerous agents and retainers who were hardly expected to share with them their political opinions.

Security and the knowledge of perpetual continuance descended upon the rich landed families as normal and inevitable, and in time as uninteresting, as the autumn mist on their pastures. Burghley House and the transformed abbeys had proclaimed too insistently their owners' rise to wealth. The mind of this generation turned to the building of great country houses which should be expressive of the station of their masters, and of the prestige now carried by the vast and compact properties. In a manuscript left by Anne, Countess of Dorset, Pembroke and Montgomery, who was born in 1590, and thus belonged to the first post-Elizabethan generation, there is a reference which expresses the novel outlook. "So as in both their lifetimes," she writes of her two husbands, "the marble pillars of Knole in Kent and Wilton in Wiltshire were to me oftentimes but the gay harbours of anguish."[1] Change the phrases a little and the sentence will stand for any moment in that period of social history which began with the completion of Knole and ended with the passing of the Tennysonian atmosphere.

At the same time this very prosperity enabled many of the leaders of the landed class to abstain from active politics. There was no considerable war during this reign; the forced atmosphere of the Elizabethan Court had vanished; education in the technical sense was as ever unnecessary. In this connection Lady Dorset's second husband Philip Earl of Montgomery can stand as an example of that privileged and undisturbed possession which very well conveys the sense of the profound peace of country life. "This second lord of mine," Lady Dorset writes of him,[2] "was born a second son. He was no scholar to speak of . . . yet he was of a very quick apprehension, a sharp understanding, very crafty withal, and of a discerning spirit, but extremely choleric by nature. . . . He was never out of England, but some months when he went into France with some other lords in 1625 to attend Queen Mary."

Clarendon refers[3] to Montgomery's "skill and indefatigable industry in Hunting" and to his pretending "to no other Qualifications than to understand Horses and Dogs very well." The type was not yet common, nor is Clarendon altogether trustworthy in his comment. Still, when the necessary transliteration in these phrases has been made, one can trace the line of descent from which would come the unfashionable eighteenth-century peerage and the great landowners of quiet Victorian conservatism. The idea of the transmission of the new-built Tudor properties was now

[1] Cal. Hothfield MSS., in *Ninth Report*, App. Pt. vii, p. 89.
[2] *Life of Lady Anne Clifford*, ed., J. P. Gilson, Roxburgh Club, 1916, p. 55.
[3] *The History of the Rebellion*, ed., 1705, i, p. 59.

established; from the Jacobean watershed there came both Whigs and Tories.

The sense of corporate dynasty is also for the first time apparent, the gradual cohesion of the family unit, the emergence of the principle of co-ordinated leadership as instanced by the Howards and the first elements of that dynastic quality which was to prove so deep an influence on political history in England. The easy opportunity for the buccaneer in politics had now gone by, and the great families were beginning to advance in phalanx to the government of the State. The dominance of interests rather than individuals presaged the slow and heavy rising to power of a plutocratic oligarchy. Although it was still rare for the merchant class to reach the peerage, this reign saw the rise of Sir Lionel Cranfield and Sir Baptist Hicks. Syston, that great Jacobean manor, is typical of the buildings of the city families; while the reserves of the landowners were replenished by marriage with the heiresses of commercial fortunes.

Even now the personality of the head of the house, his strength and weakness, was beginning to be overshadowed by the corporate tradition. The great houses, themselves, lying in their parks under the tempered English sunlight seemed already beyond the reach of danger, assets sometimes unrealizable but in essentials indestructible.

Compared to this reality of the land certain other forms of investment would appear both hazardous and casual. Gifts and the sale of offices at Court, and even the grant of some monopolies, were regarded as subsidiary to this primal ownership; while the voyages to Newfoundland and the Summer Islands seemed at first to offer hardly more than the mirages of fortune.[1] A strain of financial inconsequence was nourished in those about the King on account of their

---

[1] Cf., a letter from Governor Butler at Bermuda to Sir Nathaniel Rich, dated 30 November, 1620, in which he refers to his good hope of silk worms for "our very spiders spin such strong silken webs as to catch birds as big as blackbirds in them," Cal. Manchester MSS., p. 36.

sovereign's easy generosity. It was a change from the old Queen's parsimony and from what was called in the language of that day "this frost in the Exchequer." At the same time the sale of the reversion of offices, though increased by the element of inconsequence, was based in part upon an embryonic system intended to remedy the inadequacy of salaries and the absence of pensions.

There has, perhaps, been a certain exaggeration in the condemnation of this practice. The financial laxity seems inseparably bound up with the coming of the years of peace and the consequent suave methods of acquisition. In this connection a letter from the Earl of Northampton, who was at that time Lord Privy Seal, to Lord Clifford conveys an impression of that atmosphere of the closed Court circle; the serene contentment; the fine rewards; the natural passing breath of anxiety. "In this place," he wrote from the palace,[1] "we enjoye all happiness, under the moste worthy kinge that did ever live, and holde ourselves secure by observinge that all princes in the world, at this day, are desirous to make his m'ty an indifferente umpire in their differences. We lacke nothinge here but money; and that lacke growes out of the bownty of the kinge, which is virtuous so long as it is proportioned to means sutable; but furder it hath no warrant among philosophers."

This is an instructive passage echoing the superficial word play and the wide magnanimous phrasing which indicate a tone of mind very remote from the reactions of the populace. In such sentences words are decked out with ornament not cleared for use, and phrases may attain to an irrelevance so entire as to pass beyond the borders of sincerity and insincerity. A value was placed upon literary artifice as such. Cautious and sober men would often feel it incumbent on them to display their sensitive appreciations by introducing

---

[1] Bolton Abbey MSS., printed in *The History and Antiquities of Craven*, ed. T. D. Whitaker, p. 363.

an element of fantasy into their letters. In a competitive age it was always pleasant to find some forms of homage which could only be practised by a restricted circle.

Besides, few letters written in the official world and concerning the sovereign or his actions, could be regarded as wholly private. As the fine quills traced these phrases and allusions the men of rank could assure themselves that here was no damaging material which might be yielded up to their rivals' agents by the public posts. Again, when writing even to avowed opponents within the grouping of the King's advisers, a high magniloquence would be maintained. The precautionary element in these courtesies is very often overlooked. It is, perhaps, simplest to regard them as two contemporary methods used to express that long tradition of the non-committal which is so deeply ingrained in prudent politics. Surely it was a very polite form of double insurance.

In dealing with the correspondence of all those who come within the range of Jacobean politics, it is necessary to remember that the generation was attracted by and wholly unafraid of overt display. This characteristic extended to their prudence so that light falls on each element in that quality, which they prized so highly, on their fine remote wisdom and their blatant cunning. How hard it is to understand the mood of a generation so entirely unselfconscious?

At that period, too, there was an inevitable discrepancy between the knowledge of affairs possessed by Londoners and that to which the rural population could attain. They were so remote; few could read; they had no free movement. For them the physical presence of the sovereign was essential as they had seen her when they crowded the roads on her slow journeys. The old Queen had gone on constant progresses, and it had been a point of honour with her subjects to foster the gallant extravagance of her legend. The England of the last sixteen years of her reign had been characterized by that war-time mentality inseparable from apparent national peril; the more explicit and vocal patriotism, the contempt and hatred for the Queen's enemies; the unquestioned personal ascendancy of the sovereign confronting danger in defence of her regality. It was not possible for King James to enter into that inheritance, nor did he desire it.

In the first place the new King had little taste for the Elizabethan form of progress. His sense of theatre excluded that element of popular applause on which the Queen had thrived. With the exception of his single journey to Scotland in 1617, he never visited the North, nor did he go into the West of England or beyond the limits of the northern Midlands. Apart from those journeys to Wilton and Woodstock, which were more frequent in his early years, he came in time to settle down to a life which centred on London and the new country palaces of Theobalds and Royston. Beyond the Cotswolds and west of Salisbury the King was but a name.

The new generation of countrymen had never seen him, and there was no war to stir up the rural life. It was only at the very end of this period, when men were being "pressed" for the Duke of Buckingham's expeditions, that the farmer was obliged to turn his thoughts to foreign policy. After the rigid taut Elizabethan sentiment one can almost feel public opinion sagging away. The Puritan influence will be considered later and the effect of the changing religious values on the individual, but it seems well to survey briefly some of those aspects of the national life in which politics and religion overlapped.

At this time a certain lassitude was creeping over the religious scene. The Established Church seemed fortresslike and impregnable; entrenched by statute. Everywhere the Anglican episcopate was accepted as an influential political and social factor. As a body the Bishops had achieved a wide measure of respect due to their administrative competence, their sedate accessibility and their grave proclamation of those maxims in State and Church which in the seventeenth century met with such wide acceptance. They had the advantage of an entirely insular experience and, like all the great corporations of that world, had a profound feeling for their own dignity.

The episcopal bench was reasonably homogeneous; rather closely knit; frequently linked by ties of discipleship or marriage. It was a sphere governed by a code of integrity and courtesy, and its peace was only marred upon occasion by carefully-nourished, muted antipathies. Such a quiet academic bureaucracy offered as good a chance of perpetuating a type as did any other form of association. The Bishops had, indeed, the power to unite extreme loyalism with an accommodating temper. But on account of their entrenched position it was inevitable that the episcopate should suffer from the defects which assail all hierarchies whose members are convinced that they can never be unseated from their privilege. There seems no reason to doubt that their religious reverence for the Crown was as sincere as it was surely fortified by all their learning. Easy manners marked the approach of the Jacobean prelates to their equals and they showed a generous hospitality in their dealings with all persons of low condition who were neither recusant nor nonconformist. The portraits in the college halls of their universities give an admirable impression of these churchmen, with the shrewd inquiring eyes and the pursed lips and the hands folded in their great lawn sleeves.

Into this body there was now to enter a spiritual force of fine strength and lasting influence. It was the succession to the See of Chichester in 1605, which was to mark the moving of the waters. For in that year there came to the episcopate Lancelot Andrewes with his scholarly piety and his keen grave zeal; his attachment to the words of Scripture; his heavy oaken eloquence. At the King's accession he was

Dean of Westminster and a short passage from Bishop Hacket's work will give an impression of a side of Anglican life which must be stressed. "He (Dean Andrewes)," wrote the Bishop,[1] "never walked to Chiswick for his recreation without a brace of this young fry (the Westminster scholars), and in that wayfaring leisure had a singular dexterity to fill those narrow vessels with a funnel." It was such teaching which helped to fashion the strong attachment to the English Church.

The position of the Catholic minority was very different from that of those affected by the Puritan influence. For it was a widespread, loosely organized and gradually receding community, and not a leaven. Although the edges of this allegiance were ill-defined and surrounded by a penumbra of barely discernible supporters, it was still a powerful corporate body. Its weakness as an element of opinion arose from the accessibility of its wealthiest members to Court influence. It was the summit of the iceberg of English Catholicism that was constantly melting away.

There was little in common between the strong north-country Catholics; the squires and their dependents scattered across England; the southern lords; the Londoners and townsmen. And it was only the peers who were exposed in full measure to the suave courtesies of King and minister and prelate alike determined to remain oblivious of the religious idiosyncrasies of those who were worthy on other grounds of high respect. It is this area of privilege, including also the greater landowners and cutting across the English scene, which makes it so difficult to determine the exact position of the Catholics. In the highest reaches of the Court, men like the fourth Marquis of Winchester and the fourth Earl of Worcester, appear to have been almost wholly immune from the operation of the Elizabethan penal statutes. At the same time, the rich squires, especially in the Midlands,

[1] Bishop Hacket's *Life of Archbishop Williams*, Pt. i, p. 48.

could sometimes stave off a conviction even when a prosecutor had appeared.

A letter in the *Montagu Musters Book* throws an interesting light upon this point. "Sir Thomas Brudenell," wrote the justices,[1] "beinge divers times beefore us himselfe, his wife and many of his familie to the number of fifteen Recusantes; when if there had not beene too much regard had of him by some of us, there had passed a conviction before this time." It is not possible to determine how frequently the Catholic squires succeeded in escaping the penalty of recusancy through their neighbours' charity, embarrassment or lethargy. Great wealth was very seldom denied its privileges in a society which was gradually becoming permeated by the oligarchic spirit.

It is worth noting as a transient feature of the beginning of the reign, that there was even a certain boldness in the Upper House. "The Lord Viscount Montague," so runs an entry in the *Journal* for June 1604,[2] "undertook (as it were by way of Apology for all the Sorts of Recusants) the Defence of their Religion, and to inveigh against the whole State of Religion now established in this Realm, pretending the great Antiquity of their and the Novelty of this; saying that we had been misled to forsake the Religion of our Fathers." At this date Mr. Fawkes was still "beyond the seas in the countries of the archduke's abeyance," but the "practice" which is associated with his name was soon to put an end to the possibility of such public freedom of expression.

There can be little doubt that nothing in the King's reign made so deep a stir among the English people as the discovery

[1] Letter written in 1612 or 1613 to the Lords of the Council by the deputy lieutenants and justices of the peace of Northamptonshire in regard to the presentation for recusancy of Sir Thomas Brudenell, afterwards Lord Brudenell of Dene, by the minister of his parish, the constable and church-wardens, *The Montagu Musters Book*, ed. Joan Wake, Northamptonshire Records Society, p. 228.

[2] Details of the debate on the third reading of an Act for the due execution of the Statutes against Jesuits, seminary priests, recusants, etc., *Journals of the House of Lords*, ii, p. 328.

of the Gunpowder Plot and this matter of His Majesty's preservation. The Plot, as revealed, possessed the exciting and dangerous character which in that age alone left a lasting impress. The Old Testament, read painfully at home or heard in the churches as the people sat loyally and stolidly beneath the lectern, had nourished and reinforced the natural expectation of the catastrophic; while the sequence of the published events contained every ingredient of a happily brutal and heroic tragedy. The popular feeling would seem to have been further excited by an element of superstitious dread and the idea of the Papist was soon confused with that of those malevolent biblical figures which now came to fill the background of the imagination of the people.

The sense of righteousness was interlocked with the new-found doctrine of private judgment and all the memories of the Inquisition, St. Bartholomew's and the Marian burnings became fused in the ardour of this discovery. Even the coarse element of the ludicrous, which is so often the salt of enduring legend, was not lacking; Guido Fawkes in his high-crowned hat with the gunpowder beneath the House of Parliament. Few men have ever done a graver dis-service to their co-religionists than those who were consenting parties to the ground plan of this conspiracy.

On 9 November, 1605, King James made his speech from the throne at the delayed opening of Parliament. There were present at least fourteen Catholic peers as he spoke of his and their preservation. The argument he then set forth is well worth pondering. "And now," he began, "I must crave a little Pardon of you, that since Kings are, in the Word of God himself, called Gods, as being his Lieutenants and Vice-regents on Earth, and so adorned and furnished with some Sparkles of the Divinity, to compare some of the works of God the Great King towards the whole and general World to some of his Works towards Me, and this little World of my Dominions compassed and severed by the Sea from the rest of the Earth." These words contained high doctrine and they proved acceptable.

Two expressions of opinion in which the profound public disturbance about the Plot is seen reflected may be recorded. The mind of the Catholic body, far removed from Catesby's raffish circle, found its expression in a ballad composed in the later half of the reign after the execution of John Thules at Lancaster for saying Mass. Two verses from *O God above relent*,[1] the song of the death of Mr. Thewlis, have an especial relevance.

> "Noe Treason I have done
> Against King nor Countrie;
> Christ Jesus, godes owne sonne,
> A witnes take for mee.
>
> It is for his dere sake,
> His Church both meeke and free,
> That I doe undertake
> A true Catholike to dye."

Bishop Andrewes was invited to preach eight sermons before the King on the anniversary of His Majesty's delivery from the Gowrie Conspiracy and ten sermons on that of his preservation from the Gunpowder Plot.

In this connection two qualities characteristic of these years should be recorded, the feeling for temporal dignity and for the Crown as the fount of honour and the strange immediacy of scriptural history. "It should never," declared King James in Parliament after the failure of the Plot, "have been spoken nor written in ages succeeding, that I had died ingloriously in an Ale-house, a Stews, or such vile place, that mine end should have been with the most Honourable and best company, and in that most Honourable and fittest place for a King to be in, for doing the turns most proper to his office."

[1] British Museum Add. MS. 15,225, ff. 22–5, printed in *Old English Ballads*, 1553–1625, ed. Hugh E. Rollins.

It is wholly in accord with the curiously telescoped view of history at that time that we should read in Raleigh's *History of the World*, "of the last acts of King David; his summoning a Parliament." The biblical characters were very close and they overshadowed the chronicles and the heraldry. Camden was Clarenceux king of arms throughout this period, and editions of his *Britannia* were being slowly absorbed into the new private libraries of England. His archæology was satisfying and not recondite, and his maps with the castles, parks and steeples, and the full-rigged ships and dolphins, formed an element in the background of the English mind.

Except in certain sophisticated circles, study of all kinds appears to have been regarded with a high seriousness. The compilation of the heraldic visitations of the English counties was then taking place, and the maintenance of their right to arms weighed comfortably upon the landed gentry. In the country manor-houses the information on these subjects would sink soberly into the mind. "The elephant," the gentlemen would read in their *Display of Heraldry*, "is a beast of great strength, but greater wit and greatest ambition. The beast is so proud of his strength, that he never bows himself to any (nor indeed can he); and when he is once down (as it usually is with proud Great ones) he cannot rise up again. *And to provoke the elephants for to fight they shewed them the bloud of grapes and mulberries*, 1 Maccabees, 6, 34."

They were so constantly brought back to the rock of Scripture. Thus the ninth section of the seventh chapter of the first book of the first part of Sir Walter Raleigh's *History* was entitled "That the Arke was of sufficient capacitie." The information to be credible must be both detailed and exact. "The common crowe and rooke of India," begins Sir Walter in considering the sorts of animals within the ark, "is full of red feathers in the drown'd and low Islands of Caribana; and the blackbird and thrush hath his feathers mixt with blacke and carnation, in the North parts of Virginia. The dog-fish of England is the sharke of the South Ocean."

Supple as they might be in their everyday approach, the politicians of that age paid to the words of Scripture the tribute of a heavily underlined acceptance. "But for my-selfe," writes Raleigh in this preface, "I shall never be perswaded, that God hath shut up all light of Learning within the lanthorne of Aristotles braines: or that it was ever said unto him, as unto Esdras, *Accendam in Corde tuo Lucernam intellectus.*" There is, too, a constant invocation of the justice of Providence. "For that King," declares Raleigh in regard to Henry I in this same preface, "when both by force, craft and cruelty, he had disposed, overreacht, and lastly made blinde and destroyed his elder Brother Robert Duke of Normandy to make his owne sonnes Lords of this Land: *GOD* cast them all, male and female, nephews and neeces (Maud excepted) into the bottome of the Sea."

This last note of the coming of God's justice and his availing wrath was to be sounded again and again throughout this century. The other fresher element in Raleigh came from the late reign with its easy wealth and those doubtful enter-prises which were always lit by his own shattering and unhampered courage. The new age had turned its back on the gold which did not come through chartered companies. One of his phrases in particular brings back the world of that now foundered imagery, "the drown'd and low Islands of Caribana."

CHAPTER II

THE CHARACTER OF THE REIGN

THE varying judgments in regard to the personality of King James I differ chiefly in emphasis and interpretation. There is little dispute as to the facts of the later portion of his life when he had reached that haven of refuge the English throne. He was singularly fortunate in succeeding to the Crown at a period when the cultivated circles were reacting from the hot Elizabethan ardour. In this cooler atmosphere men could attempt to appreciate that quality of conscious wisdom which the King prized so highly. A report sent to the Doge and Senate by the Venetian Envoy in the last years of the reign, gives the impression which the sovereign succeeded in conveying. "But," wrote Signor Valaresso,[1] "no man knows what is really passing in the King's mind: he is sagacious, deep and impenetrable." Certainly the King was sagacious, deep and impenetrable, but he was also eminently safe. His theological interests were of a character to lull the suspicions of all those who were politically significant.

"I reverence and admit,[2]" wrote the King soon after he had come to England, "the four first General Councils as Catholic and Orthodox. And the said four General Councils are acknowledged by our Acts of Parliament, and received for orthodox by our Church." The Counter-Reformation was

[1] Letter from Alvise Valaresso to the Doge and Senate, dated 23 February, 1624, Cal. S. P. Venetian, 1618–25, p. 220.
[2] This passage appears in the King's profession of faith in *A Premonition to All Most Mighty Monarchs, Kings, Free Princes, and States of Christendom.*

17

hardening and the stress was coming to be laid upon a certain civic orthodoxy. The relation between Church and State throughout Europe was gradually becoming stabilized. In the Catholic countries the framework of the decrees of Trent was seen as inevitable and the relationship of the governments with the Holy See and the system of nunciatures had induced the belief in the static condition of organized society in its religious aspect. In the Anglican and Lutheran territories there was, perhaps, an even clearer sense of the respect which religion owed to the dominant and protecting State. Uniformity was so obviously desirable and the attitude towards the favoured creed was frequently an unquestioning and unenthusiastic acceptance. In fact the Erastian spirit was slowly seeping through and had gained a hold upon the ruling classes. Viewed in this light the religious elements were inextricably mingled with the other attributes of kingship. Even on a mild regalian theory it was a part of the King's concern for his loyal subjects that he should take constant thought for that religion "acknowledged by our Acts of Parliament."

As a second passage from his profession of faith makes clear, King James's interests were jumbled together. Words came from him in a spate, and theology and sport were mingled in his mind and united by his easy laughter. "As for Purgatory, and all the trash depending thereupon," he wrote in *A Premonition*, "it is not worth the talking of; Bellarmine cannot find any ground for it in all the Scriptures. Only I would pray him to tell me, if that fair green meadow that is in Purgatory have a brook running through it, that in case I come there I may have hawking upon it. But as for me I am sure there is a Heaven and a Hell, *praemium et poena*, for the Elect and Reprobate; how many other rooms there be I am not on God His Council." These sentences are valuable for they indicate how it was that the coarse young favourites were at their ease with the royal theologian, and how he came

in time to rile the Puritans. Among the Cecil Papers[1] there
is a long prayer in verse eighty lines in length, and addressed
to the King in his last years. It is clearly of Puritan origin
and one couplet apostrophizing the sovereign bears on this
subject.

> "Then let him hear, good God, the sounds
> And cries of men as well as hounds."

In this connection it is worth considering briefly the
strength of Puritanism in its relation to the King's position.
A double trend of opinion can be discerned in the Puritan
element. There were those who traced their spiritual descent
to a Genevan ancestry and were sustained in the *milieu* of the
merchants and in such an academic centre as "the pure
House of Emmanuel." This was the consistent and unbend-
ing Puritanism whose professors were conscious of their
integrity, equally steadfast and upright, and with an acute
awareness of Rome and license. Various circumstances
delayed the impact of this politico-religious force upon the
world of fashion and the Court, and it is, perhaps, first seen
in political action during the opposition to the Duke of
Buckingham.

Meanwhile another section of English opinion was moving
towards a Puritan outlook. The squirearchy had hitherto
shown itself but little affected by godly doctrine and it was
during this reign that a change gradually became apparent.
That section of the country gentry who were markedly sober
in their tastes sought for a life of strictness in which habits of
lifelong bible-reading reinforced an exacting scrutiny of
moral values. This trend was frequently to be discovered
even in those whose doctrinal training had been merely conventional and in persons in whom the gravity always associated with the exercise of parental authority had taken on a
religious colouring.

This Puritanism, when found among gentlemen of rank,

[1] Cecil MSS., vol. 206, f. 100.

was in its earlier manifestations detached from rather than opposed to the Stuart Court. It would be premature to detect in the earlier portion of the reign any Puritan reaction against the Court which was socially significant. All Protestants were obviously prepared to take a lenient view of the intended royal victim of the Powder Plot. The turning point came with the proposals for a Spanish royal marriage for Prince Charles. At the same time it would be giving a disproportionate importance to political changes if it were to be suggested that any specific public event contributed in a marked degree to the slow development of a religious standpoint which for a long time could hardly be dissociated from the general Anglican tradition. It may be noted that the Puritan tendency among the squirearchy had in some respects a parallel in the Jansenist movement in so far as the latter affected the French Court circles. Both were in a sense reactions from the inevitability of conventional religious acceptance. It was a part of the penalty of the close association between Church and State in the seventeenth century that all men were compelled to be technically God-fearing.

King James was very ready to accept the framework of the Established Church which he found in England at his accession. There was a dignity and assurance in its traditions and in the position of its great officers as they moved in harmony beneath the throne. The divines thronged round him only anxious that he should exercise the power of kingship. It was a change from Scotland and the harsh Presbytery. The Hampton Court Conference in 1604 initiated the King into this atmosphere of respectful and reasoned deference and his conversation and correspondence with the Anglican episcopate continued to give His Majesty throughout his reign full scope for the development of his theological interests and acumen. After his years of struggle he found men who very perfectly comprehended his regal office. Mr. Hooker, who had died three years before the accession of

King James, had expressed the matter lucidly. "Our Kings," he had written in regard to the relationship of the royal authority to the law,[1] "therefore, when they take possession of the room they are called unto, have it painted out before their eyes, even by the very solemnities and rites of their inauguration, to what affairs by the said law their supreme authority and power reacheth. Crowned we see they are, and enthronized and anointed: the crown a sign of military, the throne, of sedentary or judicial, the oil, of a religious or sacred power."

The view which James I and Charles I held as to their royal power was the reverse of irresponsible. They recognized the law to which they were subject and through which they ruled. The opposition to their view of kingship did not arise on account of any vagueness but rather because it was so precise, so legalistic.

King James was no innovator and he found the Elizabethan settlement in possession and hallowed by temporal victory. In this connection the suggestion that he was ever likely to become a Catholic is worth a brief discussion. There is a constant tendency among minorities unreasonably to expect some spectacular reversal of their situation. The conversion of the sovereign is the appropriate mirage which rises before the imagination of every dissident religious community.

In the case of King James the Catholics were misled by his manifest interest in the Tridentine polity. Yet this interest arose principally from a concern for the recognition of his place in the comity of sovereigns. It was the monarchical and not the dogmatic conceptions of the Tridentine world which made appeal to him. In his *Premonition* the King sets forth clearly the character of the attraction. "And," he wrote,[2] "for myself (if that were yet the question) I would

[1] *Richard Hooker, The Laws of Ecclesiastical Polity*, Book VIII, Ch. ii, sec. 13.
[2] *A Premonition.*

with all my heart give my consent that the Bishop of Rome
should have the first seat; I being a Western King would go
with the Patriarch of the West. And for his temporal prin-
cipality over the Signory of Rome, I do not quarrel it either.
Let him in God His Name be *Primus Episcopus inter omnes
Episcopus*, and *Princeps Episcoporum*, so be it no otherwise
but as Peter was *Princeps Apostolorum*. But as I well allow
the hierarchy of the Church for distinction of orders (for so
I understand it), so I utterly deny that there is an earthly
monarch thereof, whose word must be a law, and who
cannot err in his sentence, by an Infallibility of Spirit." Such
phrases must have conveyed a deep satisfaction to the royal
mind. Confronted by the entrenched Anglican position,
which gave encouragement to his theological speculations,
the King knew contentment. The fact that his parents had
been Catholics was, under the special circumstances of their
lives, a wholly irrelevant consideration.

King James was a man who very seldom allowed himself
to be deflected in matters of opinion, although he was more
open to persuasion when alternative lines of action were in
question. At the time of his accession he had been married
for some fourteen years to Anne of Denmark, a princess of
Lutheran antecedents and passive character, mentally
lethargic and addicted to the masque and the chase. Her
influence upon her husband seems to have been entirely
negative. She forwarded no policy, nor, with the exception
of George Villiers, the interests of any individual. Her
attitude towards religion remains in doubt, but there is some
evidence that she moved towards and perhaps accepted
Catholicism and that her interest in this matter evaporated
before her death.[1] She bore her husband seven children and

---

[1] According to Gretzer's copy of Fr. Robert Abercrombie's MS. in the
Bibliothèque Nationale, fonds latin 6951, Queen Anne was reconciled to
the Catholic Church in 1600 or 1601 and received Communion nine times
before her departure for England in 1603. She refused to communicate
according to the Anglican rite at her Coronation. The evidence for any

her last pregnancy occurred in 1606. The King was careful to give her the conventional marks of affection and was not unfaithful. The Van Somers portrait gives an impression of the Queen in her last years standing in her spreading far-thingale beside her black-a-moor groom before the royal stables at Theobalds. She was a little self-indulgent; fond of her dwarf greyhounds; tired; extravagant; rather careless. The King might accede to her good nature or less frequently to her hostility. Politically she never counted.

At this point it is well to bring forward a contemporary view of King James which was noted down by Sir John Oglander, a landowner in the Isle of Wight, who had a distant acquaintance with him in the latter portion of his reign. "Secondly," wrote Oglander after describing the King's faults of temper,[1] "he loved young men his favourites, better than women, loving them beyond the love of men to women. I never yet saw any fond husband make so much or so great dalliance over his beautiful spouse as I have seen King James over his favourites, especially the Duke of Buckingham."

This represents the current opinion, but it does not seem to be completely borne out by the facts. In his youth in Scotland the King had had a romantic quasi-filial devotion to the Duke of Lennox, an equivocal friendship for the Master of Gray, and perhaps some other experiences. When he reached England this emotional factor was not considered by the best qualified observers to be of potential political significance. It was rather that a whole category of young

---

practice of Catholicism in England is weaker and she attended the services conducted by her almoner although she does not appear ever to have received the Anglican sacrament. At her death in February 1619, she made a declaration to Archbishop Abbot, which was capable of an Anglican interpretation. Père J. de la Servière rather tends to strain the evidence in favour of the Queen's continued Catholicism in an article on this subject in *Dictionnaire d'Histoire et de Géographie Ecclésiastiques*, III, col. 337–9.

[1] *The Commonplace Book of Sir John Oglander, Kt. of Nunwell*, 1622–52, edited by Francis Bamford, p. 196.

courtiers received favour and attracted vaguely his unguarded and valuable affection. Only very gradually and not fully until 1611 did this absorption concentrate on Robert Ker. In Ker's case the Queen was stung into hostility, while on the contrary she welcomed his supplanter Villiers. This latter fact reinforces the impression that paternalism was the essential quality in King James's attitude towards his last and greatest favourite. He had then grown elderly, fatherly in his love and in the wise counsel he bestowed. But for the first years of the reign there was no such concentration of interest as might disturb the political equilibrium. Until the death of Salisbury the old ministers of the Crown remained secure in their predominance.

In regard to the familiar descriptions of King James's person it is worth noting that too much credence is given to the estimate of Sir Anthony Weldon and other enemies who wrote when it was desirable to make the King ridiculous. Oglander, whose work was apparently free from this motive, may be quoted[1] briefly. "He spoke much and as well as any man, or rather better, but for bodily action—put riding aside —he did not, or could not, use much: his body for want of use growing that way defective. . . . He was an infinite lover of fruit, as grapes, melons and the like, and as free a drinker of sweet wines and Scotch ale." And this is balanced by an account written in later years by Bishop Goodman. "I think," he wrote in his *Memoirs*[2], "that King James every autumn did feed a little more than moderately upon fruits; he had his grapes, his nectarines, and other fruits in his own keeping, besides, we did see that he fed very plentifully on them from abroad. . . . After this eating of fruit in the spring time his body fell into a great looseness." The impediment of speech was real and so was the King's dislike of weapons, and these characteristics entailed a certain loss of

[1] Sir John Oglander (1585–1655), op. cit., pp. 195–6.
[2] Godfrey Goodman, *Memoirs*, i, pp. 409–10. Dr. Goodman was chaplain to Queen Anne and after 1621 Dean of Rochester.

prestige; but it would be a mistake to over-emphasize the importance of the personal qualities of the monarch. Men sought from the sovereign not friendship but opportunity, and this James I was delighted to provide. Much more significant than the King's private qualities were the facts that he was lavish in his expenditure and easily approachable by the wealthier section of his subjects. Thus the King's appreciation of the virile was a matter which was in itself indifferent and only of interest in so far as it widened the area of opportunity and gave men a more equal chance to come close to the bestower of rewards.

The satisfaction which King James's interest in sport gave to the wealthy gentry is very well indicated in the admirable study of Sir Henry Lee by Sir Edmund Chambers. "James's hunting with horse and hound," writes[1] Sir Edmund, "was very different from Elizabeth's lady-like exercise with a bow from a stand in her park, and the memory of his exploits in the field has long been preserved at Ditchley by trophies of stags' heads, with incused tablets of brass beneath them, which thus describe the runs." The author then gives the three inscriptions which he attributes to the year 1605.

24 August, Saturday.
From Foxehole Coppice rouz'd Great Britain's King I fled,
But what, in Kiddington Pond he overtoke me dead.

26 August, Monday.
King James made me run for Life from Dead man's Riding;
I ran to Goreil Gate, where Death for me was biding.

27 August, Tuesday.
The King pursude me fast, from Grange Coppice flying,
The King did hunt me living, the queenes Park had me dying.

It was to some extent an asset for the King that his public relaxations should be concentrated upon sport, while his taste for intellectual exercises was kept for his more private

[1] *Sir Henry Lee, an Elizabethan Portrait*, by E. K. Chambers, p. 210.

life. Masques, too, appealed to him, but he had little interest in the development of taste. His feeling was for ceremonial and not for detail. The collecting of pictures and the search for objects of *virtu* only came into fashion in the second portion of the reign and received their impulse from a later generation.

The tolerant and lavish Court of James I provided in these respects a striking contrast to that of his son and successor. The specialized artistic interests, the careful foreign appreciations, and the admixture of a rather Gallic frivolity with a stringent moral standard which characterized King Charles' Court, were hardly likely to commend themselves to the English gentry. There is little doubt that they preferred the sight of the old King sitting loosely in his open chariot[1] of crimson velvet, bidding a pox[2] on those who flocked about him, while he waited to set out from Royston along the lanes to view his great horses[3] at Newmarket.

If it is true, as Sir John Oglander states,[4] that "he was not popular nor plausible to his subjects that desired to see him," this was an attitude which would be appreciated by men of quality. A last quotation from Oglander will give a singularly clear impression on this subject. King James, he writes,[5] "was excessively taken with hunting, although in his latter time by reason he could not ride fast, he had little pleasure in the chase: his delight was to come in at the death of the deer and to hear the commendations of his hounds."

It is this quality in the reign, the concentration on physical exercises and sport, that has so constantly been overlooked. The number of persons of influence who were directly

---

[1] This chariot is described in a letter from Sir John Davys to the fifth Earl of Huntingdon, dated February 1624, Cal. Hastings MSS., II, p. 63.
[2] *Autobiography of Sir Simonds D'Ewes*, i, p. 170. According to Oglander the King's ordinary oath was "God's Wounds," op. cit., p. 196.
[3] Among the many references to the King's interest in this subject there is a detailed letter from Sir John Throckmorton to Mr. Trumbull, dated 7 December, 1615, and printed in Williams' *Court and Times of James I*, p. 383.
[4] *Commonplace Book of Sir John Oglander*, p. 196.   [5] ibid, p. 195.

affected by the King's theological interests was very restricted
in comparison with that vast grouping which carried through
the invariable succession of accretion and inheritance. The
life of the squirearchy went forward in a profound tranquillity which was deepened by the state of peace with Spain.
The financing of "adventures" to the coast of Virginia now
sank into its place as one among many objects of speculation
and expenditure which might well attract a nobleman in his
leisure. In the rural parts many of the characteristics of the
mid-Elizabethan period survived unchanged; but the sense
of unthreatened contentment was stronger than formerly and
tended to breed that note of truculence which a wide section
among the gentry desired to see imported into foreign policy.

The fevers of the Essex period had passed. These had
stirred the Court, but had left the country unaffected. The
solid squires seem to have shown a profound distaste for the
ephemeral aspects of London life. Shrewd and acquisitive,
they mistrusted and disliked the fantastic mind of Robert
Devereux; the magnanimous and indeterminate intention;
the Italianate pre-occupations; the casual interest in erudition; and, above all, that combination of scepticism with a
desire for ill-founded and personal adventure. In the
country Essex and his followers had left no mark and the
more prudent spirit of an earlier generation was now ascen-
dant. In effect one political group, not large numerically and
entirely urban in its tone, had been eliminated and their
elders entered into a long possession.

A detailed description of the background of the life of a
great property situated in the western counties will serve to
balance the account of the influence of the Court. For
various reasons Wardour provides an excellent example. It
was to stand one of the most celebrated of the Parliamentarian sieges and has an additional interest as the place of
signature of the grant of Maryland. Anne Arundell, Lady
Baltimore was brought up there. Like so many of the homes

of the country peers it remained substantially unaltered
between the late Elizabethan period and the Civil Wars. The
house, the decoration, and the routine, appear to have
changed singularly little since the fifteen-eighties. Its master,
who belonged to a family of distinction and great antiquity,
lived remote from the Court. He was, however, related to
the Howards and thus familiar with the orbit of the ruling
stocks. He had inherited an attitude of subdued adherence
to the ancient faith and determined loyalty to the Crown.
The owners of Wardour were rich; they were successful; in
a measure they were rewarded. Their record is typical of the
mounting years.

In the life of the country the Elizabethan ways and fashions
long survived. The change of sovereign and the impact of
foreign customs would be felt in the Home Counties, within
an easy ride of the Court. The Venetian room at Knole
suggests the repercussions of current taste; but the remoter
countryside in the West and in the Midlands was unaccustomed to change. In addition the power of the father was
very real and authority remained concentrated in the head
of the family. Those who had grown to manhood in the
mid-Elizabethan period not infrequently survived until the
very eve of the civil wars and retained into old age a fulness
of domination and possession. These characteristics were
fully exemplified at Wardour in the early years of James I as
that great estate swung on in the full tradition of the Elizabethan type of splendour.

The inventory at Wardour Castle taken in 1605, and the
very diffuse descriptive wills, give a detailed view of the
surroundings of Thomas first Lord Arundell.[1] His half-

---

[1] Lord Arundell of Wardour was born in 1560, inherited his father's
estates in 1598, was raised to the peerage in 1605 and died in 1639. That
this span of life was not uncommon among the great landowners is clear
from such cases as those of the first Lord Fairfax (1560–1640) Lord
Treasurer Manchester (1563–1642), Lord Treasurer Marlborough (1550–
1629) and Lord Montagu of Boughton (1562–1644). Chief Justice Coke
was born in 1552 and survived until 1634.

length portrait hangs at Wardour, and he is seen wearing a rich black pleated surcoat. His silver-headed staff is beside him. The short black beard curls against the high white ruff and the hair is thick and dark above the lined forehead. Painted in old age it shows the strong nose and the tired and level eyes. He had then been living for many years in Wiltshire, and his service against the Turks, for which he received a Countship of the Sacred Empire, had dated back to his father's lifetime. That father, Sir Matthew Arundell, had given his life to the steady intake of land which was a mark of the Elizabethan families. In 1570 he had re-purchased Wardour, granted in 1547 and lost in 1552. In 1572 he had acquired the neighbouring manor of Semley, in 1575 the manor of Hanley, in 1581 the manor of Keyneston in Dorset, in the next year the manor of Sock Durys in Somerset, in 1588 lands in Margaret Marsh in Dorset and the manors of Clifton and Limbury in Devon, in 1595 Mere Park and the manor of Anstey. All over England it was such dates rather than those of national policy which held significance. The sixteenth century was a good period for the possessors; the rich landowners of whatever faith looked back in gratitude. At the accession of James I Thomas Arundell had entered since five years into his inheritance; the period of consolidation was beginning; those links were already forged which bound Wardour to the Royalism of the Civil Wars.

The social outlook was already marked by an essential conservatism which good fortune had rendered neighbourly and genial. In the will of Sir Matthew Arundell, witnessed in 1598,[1] the generosity towards his equals which was characteristic of the Elizabethan period, is coupled with a provision for the workers on the estate which has all the flavour of Victorian beneficence. The gifts to Francis "my plomber," and William "my gardener," "three quarters of wheat and three of barley and the white spavin mare to

[1] Will of Sir Matthew Arundell. P.C.C. (12 Kidd), 1508–9.

George the cook and to his wife," 40*s.* to Greenhill, Dr. Jessop's man, a year's wages for the household servants, all combine to suggest the rural unit of recent memory. And the directions for the disposal of the Wardour stable indicate the range of one family's friendship.

"To Rt. Hon. Sir Robert Cecill Knt my horse called Otoman desiring him to be good to my son for my sake and for my son Willyam's.

To Lord William Howard £100 and the gelding which I had of Dick Brooke.

To Edward Gage my nag called Bampfield.

To Scipio Coriton my nag called Knapton.

To William Boules my nag called Uvedall and £10.

To Mr. Barnard Greenefield my pied mare colt.

To Ralph Sheldon Esq. my gray nag called Raughley.

To Sir George Trenchard Knt, one mare, nag or colt as my son shall appoint.

To Lord Stourton my young gray gelding.

To Sir George Carew of Cockington my little pied nag.

To Henrie Carew my nag called Fovent.

To old William Monke three quarters of wheat and the same of barley and my nag called Compton.

To Francis Packinge Esq. my bay nag called Raughley.

To Mr. Nicholas Wadham my grey Turkey colt.

To Alexander Brett Esq. my bay colt with white legs.

To Captain Davis my white mare which came from Sir John Peters. All the residue of my horses, not bequethed, I give to my son Thomas Arundell."

It is a list drawn up with an evident mingling of prudence and affection. Under one aspect it is a record in miniature of all those families, Stourtons, Petres, Gages, Sheldons, and Carews, who shared the Arundells' outlook and fortune. The horses' names are interesting. How did they come by them?

There were details of the Wardour entail[1] and some

---

[1] The first provision in this will is worth recording, although unlike the other detail it is by no means typical of the generation. "Whereas," declared Sir Matthew, "it has been my purpose to employ £2,000 whereby the poor of Tysburie, Donhead Andrew, Donhead Marie in Wilts, and of Melburie,

bequests of wearing apparel, a custom surviving from an earlier age. To Lord Henry Howard Sir Matthew left his long velvet cloak; to Master Henry Cary his new grey furred coat; to Christopher Mercer his old furred coat and his night-gown; to Justice Walmeslow his gold spectacles. So much for the immediate background which the inventory of 1605 enables us to complete.[1]

The house at Wardour had been altered in accordance with the new style of building and extensively reconstructed about thirty years before this date. Much of the furniture and decoration was carried out in a style then familiar to persons of rank, while some pieces which were of a more unusual character seem to have been brought back by Lord Arundell from the Turkish wars. One can almost see the interior of the great chamber, the five pieces of tapestry; the walnut table with around it the twelve square stools each covered with a needlework cushion; the tall cupboard with the velvet curtain fringed with gold thread and silk; the two crimson-backed chairs of ceremony. Around the walls of the chamber, away from the fireplace with its copper andirons and the copper hanging candlestick, hung twenty-four pictures of the Popes and Emperors. They were probably a series of conventionalized portraits; small and commissioned from the same source; not unlike the surviving examples in the green gallery at Knole. They were soon to go out of fashion and do not appear to have been regarded as works of art, but rather as a seemly mural embellishment which would adequately suggest the idea of magnificence. In a less conspicuous angle

---

Compton and Fontmell in co. Dorset should be set in work. I direct that Lord Wm. Haward, Lord Harrie Haward and Edward Gage, Esq., and their survivors after my decease shall take out of the manors and lands I have leased upon trust, the sum of £200 yearly, until £2,000 has been levied, from time to time to disburse the same to the said purpose as at their discretion shall seem best."

[1] Arundell of Wardour MSS., endorsed, "An inventorye of all the ornaments, ympedments and household stuff in Warder Castell, Anstey House and Shaston House taken the Xth of August, 1605."

of the room a pallet, a feather-bed bolster and a pair of blankets were arranged beneath a blue silk quilt.

It was in the gallery at Wardour that there were to be found those curios whose counterpart has filled the English country houses until long past the days of Waterton. Here there could be studied to advantage the objects which Lord Arundell had collected in his journeys, a Turkish bow with a quiver of arrows, an Indian weapon, an Indian ruff, an ostrich egg hanging in the middle of the gallery, a shell of the mother-of-pearl, a coker-nut. Francis Bacon's correspondence reveals the immense interest with which gentlemen of this period would pursue their speculations as to the origin and uses of natural objects.

This gallery was not kept with the same ceremony as the great chamber. A small ladder had been left beneath the large looking-glass which swung in its frame against the further wall; there was a series of portraits of the poets, some alabaster cameos and five rather ancient maps.

Throughout the house there were the tapestries and hangings of the old fabrics which had now been known in England for some centuries, the sylvan scenery of the "forest-work," the coloured arras with the story of Troy's destruction, the tapestry of the life of Hercules and in the lesser rooms the worsted dornix and the serge coverings. The old-fashioned names from the Flemish towns, dornix and bridges satin,[1] suggest a remote period, but the great number of the rooms at Wardour and the differentiation in the quality of the furniture indicate that the country house with its complex organization was now in being.

The description of the bedchamber within the gallery, which was apparently Lord Arundell's, will complete the impression of this detailed background. As he sat within his great bed and looked across the crimson satin quilt, which covered the pair of fustian blankets, and through the curtains of crimson

[1] The dornix from Tournai, the bridges from Bruges.

taffeta the owner's glance would fall on the Turkey foot carpet and on the rich carpet with a green centre which was laid, like a cloth, upon the marble table. A crimson velvet hanging covered the livery cupboard and the two window-cloths of the same material and colour were laid about with silver lace. If it is carefully considered the magnificence and the limitations are alike remarkable. In the neighbouring pallet chamber there were two couch bedsteads and no further furniture.

The supply of plate at Wardour was already elaborate; deep silver basins, silver candlesticks and platters, a covered silver sugar box and chafing dishes, three dozen silver spoons. There were marble candlesticks with gilding and Venetian wine-glasses, two large Flanders silver pots for beer, and porcelain cream and salad dishes. So much was provided for the table whose ceremonial was of such importance in the external routine of the wealthy. There was a good supply of linen in the housekeeper's charge. In addition two earthen basins and ewers are specifically mentioned for use in the bedchambers, so that some washing arrangements were provided for the persons of the chief distinction.

There is no reference to family portraits which were at this date not yet common, nor to a library. There was a muniment room with "evidence boxes" and in the withdrawing parlour a standing cupboard for the virginals. Private chambers were allotted to the nine upper servants and the porter slept in his lodge at the entrance to the house where the Wardour woods came down to the great towers.

One detail in the inventory has a specialized interest, the reference to the chapel. For, after the elaborate detail, there is a chilling effect in the entry, "32. In the chapple one white marbell table boorde." The Arundells were Catholics and it is possible that on account of the penal laws the chapel was thus left permanently dismantled, but it is on the whole more probable that the room was used for its original purpose during the calmer years of the seventeenth century. Naturally the Mass vestments would not be mentioned in any inventory however private.

The *lacunae* in the data provided by these lists of furniture are as noticeable as their sudden shafts of illumination. This is well illustrated in the case of the inventory of the contents of Hengrave Hall in Suffolk taken four days after King James's accession. This was a domestic establishment of the larger kind, more considerable in extent than the arrangements at Wardour, but much less rooted in the land. The house was the outstanding example on a grand scale of the architecture of the last decade before the Reformation. It had been built by Sir Thomas Kitson, the founder of a very rich mercantile family which had married in the next generation into the conservative county stock of Cornwallis of Brome. Sir Thomas Kitson the younger had died at the end of the winter of 1602–3, and the property had now come to his daughter, Lady Darcy, afterwards Countess Rivers, a determined, rather shrewish woman, addicted to gallantry and separated from her husband. In a subdued fashion all four, Sir Thomas and Lady Kitson and Lord and Lady Darcy were Catholics.

The chapel in the house had been completed in 1538 and had thus been designed for the celebration of Mass; its contents are described in detail. A stained glass window with twenty-one lights stood above the altar. The kneeling stools are not mentioned, but their valuable coverings are inventoried[1] "one long cushion of white taffita, embroydered with roses of divers colors, one round cushion with the picture of Our Ladye, wrought with gold," nine more cushions and one "payer of little orgaynes." There was "one byble and one service book, one surplesse, one large old Turkye carpet which lyes upon ye aulter." It is clear that the Vicar of

---

[1] All the details of these inventories are printed in John Gage's *Antiquities of Hengrave*, pp. 211–37.

ANNE, LADY MORTON, from a portrait attributed to Paul
van Somer in the possession of MR. BENJAMIN GUINNESS

Hengrave would come here on occasion for a celebration. By contrast with these somewhat staid appointments an impression of real warmth is conveyed by the inventory of the "books of musicke in ye Chamber where ye musicyons playe." Here there is a singular completeness and one can almost see the great volumes with their dull bindings lying about haphazard in the winter firelight.

"vj bookes covered with parchment, contg vj setts in a book, with songes of iiij, v, vj, vij, and viij partes.

v bookes, covered with parchment, with pavines, galliardes, measures and cuntry dances.

v bookes of leavultoes and corrantoes.

v books covered with parchment, with pavines and galliards for the consert.

one great booke which came from Cadis, covered with redd lether and gylt.

v bookes contg one sett of Italyan fa-laes."

These evoke a delightful picture suggestive of the conventional Elizabethan gaiety.

At Wardour, also, the inventories throw light on one of the domestic aspects of the household life. In the Porter's Lodge crowded away against the stone wall spaces stood the superfluous furniture, "one lyverye Bedsteede,[1] one ffeather Bedd and a bolster, a payer of blankettes, and one peece of Hanginges belonginge to Mr. Thomas Arundelles Chamber." The same note recurs in all these lists, a certain sense of confusion, a rather prodigal superfluity of the then-established luxuries, an atmosphere of respectful but light-hearted accountancy.

It was a system under which some of the traditional leaders of the pecrage were now failing for its cumbrous mechanism needed to be assisted by grants and new realizable unfrozen capital. The Radcliffes, Earls of Sussex were among those

[1] Inventory, art. 25, Arundell of Wardour MSS. An entry in the Althorpe MSS. gives a picture of an upper servant's room at this period. "The Butler's Chamber. Impr. a leverye bedstead with a tester of buckram."

who foundered. The honorific proprietorships of honours and knights' fees, fairs and markets were often of little profit but carried, through their very antiquity, that obligation of ostentatious living to which the Jacobean generation fell an easy prey. But the accretions of wealth that have been considered in this chapter were Tudor in origin, compact and valuable; one characteristic united all these families; they had come to their present riches in the new Tudor world.

Naturally these accumulations of property suggested a standard of life which was very different from that of the unpretentious manor houses. Yet within a radius of fifteen miles of Wardour there were other estates built up upon this basis. At Lord Salisbury's house at Cranborne and in a grander way at Wilton, and in a simpler fashion at Sir Anthony Ashley's manor at St. Giles, this system was repeated. Across England the great households were settling to their stride.

CHAPTER III

SALISBURY AND THE KING

I N January 1606, Sir Robert Cecil, recently created Earl of Salisbury, had held the office of Secretary of State for ten years. The Treasurer's staff was at this time possessed by the Earl of Dorset, a man of seventy with that combination of great wealth, defined piety and long-proclaimed integrity which were regarded as the appropriate qualities for an English statesman of the graver sort. He was much bound to Lord Burghley and his great post would come in to Salisbury when he died. This succession would serve to complete the strength of the latter's almost impregnable position; for the other great political family then in office, the Howards, had a reputation which was too doubtful, and a unity which was too precarious to enable them to manœuvre successfully against the Cecils. At forty-two, Salisbury with his swift intelligence knew himself to be politically secure. The Gunpowder Plot had been a god-send for his reputation, but the investigations had proved a severe tax upon his energies. Now the date of the execution of the conspirators was already settled and Salisbury could turn his serene and careful mind to other matters. In his practised awareness of each facet of the public situation, he knew that it was generally conceded that the King's ministers had saved the nation.

In his private life this year marked a period of repose, for the negotiations were already in train which were to lead to the surrender of the great house at Theobalds in Hertfordshire to the King's use. It was not until 1607 that he would receive Hatfield in exchange and settle down to that rapid building which was to occupy, without agitating, his later years. He was curiously and rather attractively devoid of any clear idea of his expenses and his love of restrained gaming often led him to engage himself very deeply when employed upon a great design. To some extent he appears to have been pressed forward in his building projects by the insecurity of his wavering health and the menace of recurrent illnesses. But in this connection it would seem that the influence of his physical under-development, the "crooked back" from which he suffered, has been exaggerated. It was surely jealousy of his predominance that lent its bitter emotion to the rhyme of "little bossive Robin that was so great." Much more significant was the fact that he had risen to power too early. Like the younger Pitt he had never known the freedom of political insignificance. It was perhaps outside the range of his desires even to understand the benefits of a period of free and equal intercourse.

His two elder brothers had died as children and his step-brother, who was later Earl of Exeter, was more than twenty years his senior. In addition Salisbury's conventional and contented marriage had ended with Lady Cecil's death in 1597, and his life was without apparent solace. His only son Lord Cranborne was now fifteen; a slow and idle child; suffering from over-education; not petted. There were also two young daughters to whom their father was attached.

There is no evidence that he ever sought in politically influential circles for that intimacy of which accident had deprived him. So great a contrast to his cousin Bacon, he never seemed to stir but wrung the utmost value from his opportunities. The elaborately staged hospitality on which he concentrated reflected his quality as a politician. It was a little intimidating in its magnificence and in that strength which was built up from the conscious avoidance of all imprudence. This last point has some importance when one is approaching an impression of his character, for he had too great a sense of property to be fanatical, and he stood for the

continuity of a governing class. It was possibly as a result
of this outlook that Salisbury was at times prepared to aid
Catholic recusants, if by so doing he could perform a service
to his colleagues. He had an habitual courtesy of approach
which proved of great value. As Secretary of State the
correspondence of the kingdom flowed in to him, and a
consideration of some sections of his papers will give an idea
of the social background and a view of some of the problems
of that earlier period of King James's reign.

Among the muniments in the possession of the Marquess
of Salisbury at Hatfield House are all those papers which the
first Earl saw fit to preserve. By far the greater part of those
dealing with the reign of James I are still uncalendared, and
there are more than twenty volumes of correspondence
dealing with a single year 1606. All the manuscript material
from which quotations are taken and reference made in this
and the succeeding chapters under the heading of Cecil MSS.,
is therefore unprinted. Some explanation should be given
of the reasons for choosing this particular year for detailed
study and of the general nature of the sources.

The first of January 1606[1] is chosen as the opening date
of a survey because it marks the beginning of what was,
perhaps, the first normal year of the new reign. The Gunpowder Plot, which seems to have seared the King's imagination to a degree which the Elizabethans would hardly have
understood, had now been liquidated. The sovereign's
relations with the English Church were established in their
full contentment and the Jacobean Bible was under way. His
first Parliament was in its second session. A peace with
Spain had been concluded. Attention could be given to
normal administration and appointments, and Salisbury had
by this time evolved that careful technique which he used in
all his dealings with his present King.

[1] For simplification of reference and to avoid the constant use of a
double dating, 1605–6, etc., all years referred to in the text are dated from
the beginning of January and not from March.

In addition the letters under consideration are marked by certain characteristics and the aspects of English life which are revealed fall within defined limits. It is for the most part the incoming correspondence which is in question and matters of political appointment and manœuvre, colonization, private friendship, police methods and local crime are represented. Sometimes the *dossier* of a case will give a vivid impression of a distant rural area; but no information is included unless it would in some way interest the Secretary of State. Above all the letters are marked by seriousness. There is little disposition on the part of their writers to forget that they are addressed to the seat of Government and men acting under this sense of strain will not allow themselves an intentional and misplaced humour. There broods over this correspondence a well-suggested atmosphere of respect.

The variety of subjects treated requires extracts of considerable length if the point at issue is to be made fully and a view given of one phase of the life of Jacobean England. An effect of tedium is, perhaps, inseparable from such a survey. Yet there is something convincing in the effect of ordinariness produced by a correspondence whose subject matter is often so sensational. In general a chronological order has been followed and the letters have been considered one by one as they mounted up upon the Secretary's table.

In the first days of January 1606, Salisbury was returning thanks for the customary series of New Year's gifts to a leading statesman and replying courteously to the offers which were apt to come in about this time from young men of position who wished to have the opportunity of service in his household.[1] The custom of keeping young gentlemen of birth in personal attendance, was now going out of fashion,

---

[1] A letter in the Cecil MSS., Vol. 109, f. 104, dated 6 January, 1605–6, will indicate the nature of this custom. Sir Henry Boteler wrote from Woodhall Lodge to the Earl of Salisbury recommending his son "who by the death of the Earl of Cumberland is at liberty to serve either about his person, or at the table, or in other employments."

but it was a practice which had appealed especially to the great Elizabethan lords since it ministered to the glory of their new peerage.

In the politico-ecclesiastical world one appointment of high consequence would soon be vacant, for Dr. Hutton, the aged Archbishop of York, was dying. He was seventy-five and could not survive the winter. During this new reign he had been merely a cypher and the succession in all its details was already settled. He died on January 15 at the archepiscopal palace of Bishopthorpe, and Salisbury was at once informed by Sir John Ferne, the joint secretary and keeper of the signet in the North. The letter is interesting both on account of its Puritan phrasing and outlook, and because it contains suggestions for filling the vacancy which were in fact to be made effective. It seems probable that Sir John Ferne had a shrewd idea of what the King intended and hoped to establish himself in favour with the new prelates by setting on record his hopes that the promotions would fall upon them.

"In whose place," wrote Sir John in reference to the late Archbishop,[1] "I beseech God to bless the Church with a zealous, painful and preaching successor." He proceeded to enumerate the present evils of "defection to popery and also an apostacy from all religion to impious atheism and profanity" and continued in the strain of exhortation, "You know well what means are best for redress of this mischief. To this province of York, so overpestered with popery and not with 'purinisme,' I beseech you such a one may succeed as is zealous and that will be industrious against Papists and attentive to his function both in preaching and government. Such a one as I hold the Lord Bishop of Durham, who has long experience of this northern country."

"If," continued Sir John considering the vacancy at

---

[1] Letter of Sir John Ferne at York to the Earl of Salisbury, dated 16 January, 1605–6, Cecil MSS., vol. 109, f. 145.

Durham thus envisaged, "you will commend the Bishop to this See, a fitter successor than Dr. James, the Dean of Durham, I suppose cannot be, learned, very grave, wise and of honest conversation unreprovable, a stout oppugner of Papists, and dare in person search their houses and apprehend the most insolent of them. He is an excellent magistrate in that country. The *Jura Regalia* annexed to that bishopric makes that Bishop a principal civil governor in that country and I know the said Dean in matters of justice most upright and sincere."

The President of the Council of the North also sent in his opinion upon this matter, writing direct to the King and giving Salisbury the gist of his comment. "Not being able," wrote Lord Sheffield,[1] "to attend upon him (the King) by reason of my sickness, I have written to him to this effect; that Durham were fit to succeed the Archbishop; the Dean him; and Mr. Ubanke the Prebend the Dean. These are all very sufficient for the places; but the especial motive to me is their long acquaintance with the affairs of that country." It will be noticed that Lord Sheffield, being anxious that men acceptable to the North should be appointed, made suggestions as to the succession, not only to the bishopric, but also to the deanery of Durham.

But in this new reign the Sovereign had a watchful care for episcopal appointments, and everything to do with the great ecclesiastical machinery which he had inherited, gave him pleasure. Not only had the succession of Bishop Mathew to the archbishopric of York and Dr. James to Durham, been determined, but the King had eighteen months ago made a promise of the deanery of Durham which this contingency would render vacant. On 23 January Salisbury received an agitated letter from a Scottish layman, Mr. Adam Newton, the tutor to Henry Prince of Wales. Rumours had reached

[1] Letter of Lord Sheffield to the Earl of Salisbury undated, vol. 114, f. 140. The transcript in the Record Office is placed among the Cecil Papers for January 1605–6.

him of the attempt to secure the deanery for a north countryman and he did not hesitate to use his royal pupil, then aged
eleven, on his behalf.

"His Majesty's promise of the deanery of Durham,"
began Mr. Newton,[1] "made unto me at Hampton Court in
the hearing of the Prince (then aged nine), and my Lord of
Canterbury the very same day he was nominated archbishop
made me so secure of the obtaining of that deanery when-
soever the archbishop of York should die that I did not
imagine any opposition or dream of any difficulties." A note
was added in the handwriting of the young prince. "My
Lord," it ran, "this your resolution I doubt not will make
you continue your former purpose towards my master."
This reminder was as successful as it was ably couched, and
in due course the three promotions were effected.

And then in contrast to these urbane developments there
comes a vivid picture of Yorkshire Catholicism. The life of
the labourers in the depth of the countryside, is, for a moment,
illumined. Throughout this period it is interesting to notice
how the inquiries into Popery cut down through the social
levels to the cottages and the farmsteads. The docquet in
question, which also reached Salisbury in January, contained
depositions relating to the movements of the Inglebys of
Ripley, a recusant family whose counsinship to the Winters
had involved them in that mesh of informations which had
been stimulated by the Powder Plot. There was question of
the "reconciliation" of an old countryman named Gudgeon,
living near Knaresborough, by John Ingleby, a suspected priest.

"Peter Gudgen," deposed[2] Thomas Atkinson, "fetched in
John Ingilbie when old Gudgen lay a dying and Wheelhouse
the tailor came with him, and a stranger, and they prayed

---

[1] Letter from Adam Newton to the Earl of Salisbury dated 23 January,
1605–6, and endorsed "Mr. Newton the Prince's Schoolmaster," Cecil
MSS., vol. 109, f. 40.

[2] Deposition of Thomas Atkinson against John Inglebie, dated 9
January, 1605–6.

with Gudgen till he died. Leonard Smyth, John Ingilbie's chief man, persuaded old Gudgen in his sickness that his religion was not good, and that they be all damned body and soul to the devil that go to Church. . . . When old Gudgen 'drew awayward' John Ingilbie used speeches and reading on his knees till he died, and caused many crosses of wax candles to be made and sewed within the winding sheet. Also that when his father lay a dying, John Ingilbie came to him with hallowed candles, and water, and books, and laboured curiously to reconcile him to the Romish religion, for which his father gave him 10/- and great thanks, and so he died."

There followed the deposition of William Wheelhouse of Windesley Garth dealing with this same subject. "William Wheelhouse, the tailor," so ran the statement,[1] "works to all the great recusants, and can make vestements. He was brought up with Samuel Thackwrey and Robert Suttill, great recusants. John Saunders, my Lady Anne's man, is a con-triver of caves, and Edward Ledger a carrier of messages." Finally on a separate sheet the examination of the tailor was enclosed.[2]

"William Wheelhouse, tailor deposes. He heard there was a meeting at the Lodge of friends, but heard not of any meeting at Plumton. He was at Gudgeon's death with his master (John Ingleby) and Alexander Vavasor of Spalding-ton. They did only kneel down and prayed by him, as the country fashion is, and he knows not whether he died a papist or a protestant." The story carries a complete con-viction with its accusations and its half-evasion. It is the other side of that problem which Sir John Ferne touched on.

To Salisbury such statements were familiar enough[3] and

---

[1] Deposition of William Wheelhouse of Windesley Garth, Cecil MSS.
[2] Deposition of William Wheelhouse, tailor, ibid.
[3] An interesting and detailed account of Catholic customs in Yorkshire, which was forwarded to Salisbury in December 1606, is printed *in extenso* in the appendix, p. 315.

indicated the normal submerged functioning of the Catholic life which the penal laws had made so vulnerable. It was of a great value to the Government to have the power to strike and to gather in a weight of information: to *know* rather than to use its own blunt weapons. Besides, there often seemed no valid reason for interference since the recusancy fines were harvested with regularity. In this particular case Lady Anne Ingleby was a recusant and a daughter of the last exiled Earl of Westmoreland, safeguarded by the solid position of her husband's stock among the rising Yorkshire squires and additionally secured by the fact that her mother was a determined Protestant and by birth a Howard. It was a weakness for the Howards that they should have had so many doubtful relatives. There were no dubious associates who were able to press their claims upon the Earl of Salisbury.

By a coincidence, shortly after the arrival of the docquet in which Lady Anne Ingleby's affairs were mentioned, a request came in to the Secretary from her mother who was anxious to obtain the profit from the "fees" for the creation of a peer. "I formerly commenced," wrote Lady Westmoreland on this occasion,[1] "a suit to His Majesty that he would grant the creation of a baron, such an one as for his religion, conversation and ability as almoner of ways shall seem fit to you his honourable councillor. This is to the King no charge, but honour profitable to the Commons." In effect Salisbury was asked to persuade the King to hand over to her a goose trussed for the plucking. No action was taken on this letter.

A more sympathetic appeal was that of Sir Thomas Knollys, who asked for a commission for twenty-one years

---

[1] Letter from Jane Neville to the Earl of Salisbury, dated Aldarsbroke, 27 January, 1605–6, and endorsed "the pretended Countess of Westmoreland," Cecil MSS., vol. 109, f. 150.

Lady Westmoreland was a sister of Lord Northampton and her husband had been attainted after the Rising of the North.

"to survey furniture and arms for service within this realm:
by himself or his deputies." With his request a memorandum
was enclosed which gives an excellent idea of the older type
of military officer of distinguished birth who survived from
the Elizabethan Age to give a somewhat discontented service
to King James.

"I think,"[1] wrote Sir Thomas Knollys, "it is not unknown
to your Lordship how . . . I have performed honest and true
service in the wars. I first commanded Osteande in the
absence of my brother, where by mine own industry I
suppressed a great mutiny, whereby the town and garrison
were preserved, which otherwise had been lost long ago.
After that I was sent to Lockum . . . where for the safeguard
of the town my troop of horse was quite overthrown, whereof
I yet feel the smart." He then details his services at Tilbury
and at the relief of Bergen-op-Zoom, where he was knighted,
and under Sir John Norreys in the wars of Britanny. "At
the siege of the Spanish fort by Brest," he continued, "(I)
was blown up at the assault with 22 barrells of gunpowder
whereof yet I carry the unfortunate marks about me. After
that I went and was Colonel with my Lord of Essex in the
Island journey and had a ship furnished at my own charges
which stood me in very near £1,000, where attempting to
take the island of Porta Sancta I had my jawbone broken
and 7 of my teeth stricken out. Lastly, I was commanded
to conduct 2,000 soldiers into the Low Countries, whereof
I was promised a regiment: but the States determining and
disposing otherwise of them I was utterly frustrated of any
such command. For my 23 years true and loyal service I
never received any manner of reward either at home or
abroad, whereby now in my declining time I am altogether
destitute of means to maintain myself, my wife, and poor
children. Wherefore, pardon me, if being brought so low,

---

[1] Letter of Sir Thomas Knollys to the Earl of Salisbury, undated, except
for the year, Cecil MSS., vol. 119, f. 19.

that I am almost buried before I am dead, I do presume to appeal to your Lordship for grace and favour."

This was the spirit and manner of the late reign and it was indeed out of favour. The wording which has now a pleasant and archaic ring could then have suggested only tedium. The air of bravado was out of place in addressing a statesman whose way of life was wholly civilian. For more than two centuries an excessive courtesy would still surround the vocabulary of demand and supplication; but by the reign of James I the actual statement of the claim itself was beginning to assume that appearance of sober accuracy which later generations would find essential.

A claim for a recusant, based on the same principle as the claim for the creation of a peer, which was sent in to Salisbury by one of the King's new Scotsmen was more attuned to the current fashion. It was marked, too, by that financial clarity which was gradually coming to be associated with the transaction of all serious business. Sir William Anstruther declared[1] that he had never had any suit since his coming into England, except the pension which he had had by his Honour's means in recompense for the loss of his recusant, Master Talbot.

Such dislocation was typical of the age. The milking of a Catholic recusant would be granted to some courtier, and then the recusant would make a direct composition with the Crown over the head of his beneficiary or worse still would die, and all the trouble had been wasted. Unimportant as is Anstruther's letter, it will serve to introduce the question of the Scottish favourites and the King.

The problem of how to cope successfully with the new King was one which Salisbury was eminently qualified to solve. King James was kindly with a long and generous memory and, above all, predictable. It was not for nothing that Robert

---

[1] Letter from Sir William Anstruther to the Earl of Salisbury among undated papers, 1606, Cecil MSS., vol. 118, f. 106.

Cecil had studied him during the last years of the old Queen's reign. He had a liking for close personal relationships and Salisbury was prepared to accept and, within the limits set by his cool mind, to respond to the royal advances. The situation was easier since the King seemed to have outlived the need for youthful favourites; his chief friend Sir Thomas Erskine of Gogar was his exact contemporary and became the Captain of the Yeomen of the Guard. Since his accession to the English throne he had been attracted by the virile qualities of the young Philip Herbert, whom he created Earl of Montgomery at twenty-one, but the boy's high rank and a certain personal toughness seem to have saved him from sentimental passages. With James Hay, perhaps the most talented of his Scottish adherents, the King's relations were always decorous and it must have seemed to the minister in this quiet year of 1606 that his sovereign was settling down. And if he was settling down it was a small price to pay to have to submit to being called his "little beagle."

It was characteristic of Salisbury that he was not accustomed to fail in carrying through the details of a policy. With Sir Thomas Erskine he was on excellent terms and he would enter diligently but a trifle laboriously into the humour which amused his Scottish master. If the King would only indicate the tone of their relations he was always ready to respond. A letter, probably dating from this year, will suggest the situation. "My little beagle," began the King writing about some trouble with Lord Dunbar,[1] "whether Home will continue in this negative resolution or not, God knows; but sure I am that as none can touch pitch but will be filed with it, so honest men can never deal with inconstant and coy fools, but it will plunge them in a marvellous fashery; and so farewell." The chaff was accepted and the

[1] Letter from the King to the Earl of Salisbury, Cecil MSS., vol. 134, f. 99. It is endorsed 1606?, and the Record Office transcript is placed among the undated years letters for this year, but internal evidence suggests that it should be placed at an earlier date.

pleasant windy phrases repaid by flattery. In February of 1606, Salisbury back at Theobalds after a sitting of the House of Lords wrote to Erskine for the King's perusal. "My Lord," he began,[1] "being newly come home from a long and late session in Parliament, and being close by my chimney's end, a proper place for beagles, I was in dispute whether I should trouble His Majesty with this day's journal." The letter was now well under way, and he remembered to quote a statement that he had made that afternoon in the Upper House. "I daily discerned," Salisbury had told the peers, "how great an advantage we had that lived at the feet of Gamaliel in respect of others more removed."

Then Gamaliel was fond of food and the custom of the age permitted much frank discussion upon this subject.[2] And Erskine would keep Salisbury informed of all that passed, and the King's moods and pleasures. "His Majesty," he wrote to Theobalds from Royston,[3] "minds by the grace of God the morrow to make for Newmarket, because the very day before he came to this town, there died an old man and a child. For Montgomery's match he got the forfeit of 100.1., and then as I think for 40/– the horses ran. But my fellow Montgomery did go before ever . . His Majesty is well pleased and has had good sport at the hunting this morning."

So the situation was in good trim and it was aided by the fact that Salisbury really did share with the King an appreciation for the more civilized forms of the latter's humour. "At one thing ye will smile," wrote the King to his minister,[4]

[1] Letter from the Earl of Salisbury to Lord Dirleton dated 6 February, 1605–6, Cecil MSS. Sir Thomas Erskine was created Lord Dirleton in 1604, Viscount Fenton in 1606 and Earl of Kellie in 1619. As he held the captaincy of the Yeomen of the Guard from 1603 until 1632 he was a stable factor in the life of the Court.

[2] In this connection Sir Anthony Ashley wrote from St. Giles' to the Earl of Salisbury on 21 April, 1606, offering to send him shortly "young pheasants cut and crammed like capons, whose taste very much differs in daintiness from their own nature." Cecil MSS., vol. 116, f. 15.

[3] Letter of Lord Dirleton to the Earl of Salisbury, dated 30 April, 1606, Cecil MSS., vol. 116, f. 26.

[4] Letter of the King to the Earl of Salisbury, undated. Cecil MSS., vol. 134, f. 147.

"he (Hay) advised me not to sell the bear's skin before he was slain." All was well for Salisbury in those peaceful years, and Robert Ker had not yet come to Court, and George Villiers was still a boy. It could not be foreseen that the King's affections would soon be concentrated successively on these young men.

Meanwhile there was another personality of steadily increasing significance at the Court, the King's young son, the twelve-year-old Prince of Wales. As far as the older statesmen were concerned there was nothing that they could do for the lad except to play the jovial and respectful uncle; but Cranborne was fifteen, an age more suitable for gaining the Prince's friendship. An interesting exchange of letters of uncertain date throws a pleasant light on the situation. It opens with a letter from the tutor, Mr. Newton, to the Earls of Salisbury and Suffolk. "His Highness," the note begins,[1] "hath desired your Lordships to be suitors to Their Majesties in a matter which was forgotten by himself, being at Windsor, but the memory whereof was refreshed by the heat of this season, that his highness may have leave to learn to swim. . . . The presumption that his Highness hath by your Lordship's own children going into the water makes him expect your approval. ps., " added the Prince in his own hand, "My Lords, I commend me and my suit unto you. *Coelum et dies mutant, tempus omni labitur, ideo maturatum opus est.*"

In his reply Salisbury struck a suitable and merry note. It was easier at any rate than playing the little beagle. "We remit it unto you," he began the joint letter,[2] "whether it be not a pretty device between a politique young Prince and his master to pick out two plain honest men for an employment to cut our throats with the King, our master. . . . The

---

[1] Letter from Mr. A. Newton to the Earls of Salisbury and Suffolk, Cecil MSS., vol. 134, f. 157.
[2] Letter from the Earls of Salisbury and Suffolk to Mr. Newton, Cecil MSS., vol. 134.

comparison holds not between our boys and sons of Kings: they are like feathers as like as things of nought: Princes are things of weight and consequence and eminent expectation: do not think (we pray you) that the chancellor of Cambridge and the steward want so much Latin as not to remember that *omnia levia sursum tendunt, gravia deorsum.*"

In the autumn of 1606 Sir David Murray of Gorthy, the Scottish poet, whose name is associated with Prince Henry, wrote to Salisbury to ask for aid. Difficulties had arisen between the poet and certain of his countrymen who desired[1] to be placed about the Prince's person. It is always pleasant for a statesman to observe the falling out of thieves, and Sir David received his due encouragement.

Meanwhile, midway between Salisbury's political and domestic life, there was the permanent question of Cranborne's education. At regular intervals there came the reports from Mr. Roger Morrall, who had secured control of his studies, of how he was faring at St. John's, his father's college. Salisbury had foreseen his future. It was all planned; a marriage to the daughter of his colleague Suffolk;[2] a close friendship with the Prince; a clear intellect to carry him through the higher reaches of politics. And then he would sit in his father's seat sifting material and weighing the policies with a smooth competence, the third of his line. This was in the future, but first he had concentrated on his education.

The Lent Term of 1606 was drawing to a close when Mr. Morrall wrote to ask if his charge might "leave his book"

---

[1] Letter of Sir David Murray to the Earl of Salisbury, dated 16 November, 1606, at Richmond. Cecil MSS., vol. 118, f. 56.

[2] A letter of Lady Frances Cecil to the Earl of Salisbury written in 1606, Cecil MSS., vol. 193, f. 8, indicates the close relationship between the two families. "I most humbly intreat you," Lady Frances wrote to her father, "I may continue still with my Lady of Suffolk, for there is no place I desire so much to be in as with her and my Lady Kathren and the rest, so I might with your good will; but, if you have otherways determined of me, I ever rest at your command." Two years later in 1608, Cranborne, then aged seventeen, married Suffolk's daughter, Lady Catherine Howard.

and return to Theobalds for the vacation. Lord Cranborne, his tutor explained,[1] would like a holiday, "as a little intermission would very much refresh his wit and revive his spirits." He was now being taught Latin and logic, and Mr. Morrall was very ready to have him instructed in any other art or tongue either by himself or by some other "prime man" of the University. And, whatever Mr. Casse might say[2] about his being "something alienated from study," his tutor was satisfied with his most important pupil. Possibly he was hardly able to express dissatisfaction without endangering the links which bound him to this great connection.

"My Lord Cranborne," wrote Mr. Morrall from Cambridge in the autumn,[3] "for bodily health was never better since ever I knew him, and for going to his book I find as His Lordship grows in years so his love of learning and liking of his book doth daily increase." But it increased without avail and neither Salisbury's son nor Suffolk's established themselves in a political career. The hopes of a royal friendship did not prosper. As he grew older, Prince Henry's mind tended to romantic and warlike notions, perhaps a little febrile in their quality, but far removed from any sympathy with the silent and unenterprising mood[4] of the son of King James's careful statesman. Salisbury was wise to keep up his good relations with the Scots; for it was Sir David Murray who alone really gained the Prince's confidence.

Even these few extracts from the Hatfield Papers make it clear how prudently the Secretary had built up his position with a calm which would not betray him into anger and a

---

[1] Letter from Roger Morrall to the Earl of Salisbury, dated 9 April, 1606, Cecil MSS., vol. 115, f. 134.
[2] Letter from Edmund Casse to the Earl of Salisbury, dated 9 October, 1606, Cecil MSS., vol. 117, f. 170.
[3] Letter from Roger Morrall to the Earl of Salisbury, dated 11 November, 1606, Cecil MSS., vol. 118, f. 49.
[4] Some credence must be attributed to Clarendon's statement that "he (Cranborne) was a man of no words, except in Hawking and Hunting," *History of the Rebellion*, II, p. 209.

political tolerance instinct with courtesy. Perhaps it is not unfair to attribute to him that gift for the appropriate which makes men successful, but not loved. There was something alarming in his self-command and in that clear vision with which he swept the nearer landscape. Yet it was this efficiency that secured Salisbury in his power which was aided by the royal lethargy and only menaced in a slight degree by the slow ebbing of King James's gratitude.

CHAPTER IV

THE ROUTINE OF POLITICS

SOME space has been given to Salisbury's relations with the King and with the Prince of Wales, and to the manœuvres by which he placated opposition in the highest quarters and neutralized and cancelled his rivals' influence. It has been necessary to discuss these points because the position of the Crown at this period made it essential that the sovereign should not withdraw his confidence. The minister, who had been accustomed from childhood to the atmosphere of the Court, was always perfecting that technique of intercourse with the King which was of an inestimable value. If the pre-occupation with the sovereign and his family seems excessive, it is worth remembering that nothing could replace the capacity for confidential communication with his royal master. Once this was lost political extinction was inevitable.

The weakness in Salisbury's position was precisely this, that his virtuosity was seen to best advantage in his capacity to retain power indefinitely under a sovereign who was alien to him. A study of his period of office gives the impression that he was in some sense exhausted by this effort. At the same time it was not merely fatigue which led him to adopt a passive attitude since he appears to have seen only too clearly the dangers which would attend upon the development of a constructive policy. Francis Bacon's bitterness towards his cousin was possibly increased by Salisbury's talent for keeping the machinery running and maintaining the equilibrium of the *status quo*; for Bacon wholly lacked such static power.

In the handling of the general matters which came before him Salisbury displayed a competence and a quiet shrewd resolution. Balanced and calm, his methods do not appear to indicate any very definite pre-occupation with colonization or on the other hand with the administration of justice, with piracy or crime or local law. His decisions bear the mark of a subdued efficiency which was only saved from grimness by his strange pacific courtesy. It was not the routine labours but the actions of his rivals and colleagues which really disturbed him, and he could suddenly be stirred into a transient yet acute concern by some letter from Lord Dorset or by an effort of Lord Chancellor Ellesmere's to hold the weather gauge in his manœuvres.

Still these were rare alarms and through 1606 the Secretary sat with his meticulous personal plans upon his table while behind them broke the long surge of his despatches. Sir Thomas Edmondes, for instance, the ambassador in Brussels, was sending him letter after letter; while a more hesitant and intermittent correspondence came in from Sir Thomas Glover "at the Vines of Pera." In connection with the agency at Constantinople it is worth mentioning that explicit details of commercial traffic appear infrequently among the Secretary's papers. The agents would correspond[1] with London merchants about "what sorts of stones will sell best (in Pera)" and "the valewe of pearle and unicornes horne, currall and ruffe amber"; but these were matters for the Turkey Company and just over the horizon of Salisbury's responsibility. It was rather disputes and infringements of the law, piracy and the legislation for Virginia which were laid before him.

It is of interest to consider how far the idea of the colonies in North America impinged upon Lord Salisbury's tranquil wisdom. And here it seems not unreasonable to detect a

---

[1] Cf., *Correspondence of John Sanderson*, ed. Sir William Foster, Hakluyt Society, 1930, p. 128.

certain reserve in the minister's attitude towards a project which had been so closely associated with the tempestuous mentality of Sir Walter Raleigh.Since the Virginia settlements of 1585 and 1587 had not survived, the project still lay at the mercy of that untrammelled private initiative which could not but prove unwelcome to the sober statesman. There had been Captain Gosnold's voyage to Northern Virginia, as New England was then called, in 1602, and more recently Captain George Weymouth's expensive enterprise. The latter journey suffered the additional disadvantage that Papists had had a great share in the undertaking. "Therefore," declares William Strachey in a contemporary account of these adventures,[1] "would His Lordship (the Earl of Southampton) well be concurrent the second tyme (after Gosnold's report) in a new survey and dispatch to be made thither with his brother-in-law Tho. Arundell, Baron of Warder, who prepared a ship for Capt. George Weymouth, which set sayle from Ratcliff in March, anno 1605." After describing the journey the same writer gives a clear impression of its effects.[2] "Upon his return his goodly report joyning with Captain Gosnold's shewed the busines with soe prosperous and faire starres to be accompanied, as it not only encouraged the said Earl (the foresaid Lord Arundell[3] being by this tyme engaged so far to the Archduke . . . that he no more thought upon the accion) but likewise called forth many firm and harty lovers."

Arundell was soon to reappear among the number of Salisbury's personal concerns, but there were always drawbacks attaching to private power or an individual religious approach among prospective colonists. The threatened development of such enterprises powerfully aided the move-

---

[1] *The History of Travails into Virginia Britannia.* By William Strachey. Ed. R. H. Major, Hakluyt Society, 1849, p. 159.
[2] ibid., p. 161.
[3] In regard to this enterprise S. R. Gardiner confuses Lord Arundell of Wardour with the Earl of Arundel, *History*, ii, p. 51.

ment for the establishment of a chartered company. In the obtaining of this charter, which was granted on 10 April, 1606, Lord Salisbury took an active share. It was inevitable that he should desire the court of a Company in London where the meetings and business would be centralized beneath the Crown's prevailing influence. All his last years Salisbury was to attempt to canalize or to deflate the old flamboyant forms of irresponsible Elizabethan enterprise. Quietly and with a still grave courtesy he pruned and curbed.

It was in the early days of February that this matter of Virginia came before him in an urgent message from Captain Tomkyns. "My Lord," wrote that seaman,[1] "I understand that two knights, Sir Robert Mansfield and Sir John Trevver, have authority to apprehend me. Upon my return from out of the Levant seas in August 1603, the Lord High Admiral's officers pillaged me of more than 4,000 l. in money and other goods; next I and all my company were proclaimed pirates in every city and haven town of England. . . . Six of my mariners were hanged at Southampton for the sins of the people. All these extremities passed against us upon my enemies' report only."

This letter must have produced some good effect, for Captain Tomkyns is found writing to Salisbury on February 12 in a more hopeful strain. After recalling that he had suffered much from his action in the Levant Seas he proceeded to an explanation. "That argosy," he wrote,[2] "which hath been the cause of my troubles, gave me 200 great shot, and intended to take my ship before ever I fought with her neither putting forth their colours or once speaking to us. The goods I had of that ship belonged to Jews and Armenian

[1] Letter from Captain Tomkyns to the Earl of Salisbury, dated 1 February, 1605-6, Cecil MSS., vol. 109, f. 153.
[2] Letter from Captain H. Tomkyns to the Earl of Salisbury, dated 12 February, Cecil MSS., vol. 104, f. 21. The year 1607-8 has been suggested as a date, but it seems much more probable that it was written a fortnight after the letter of 1 February, 1605-6.

merchants whereof I have good proof."Later he went on to explain that he would like to be helped to Virginia. "Now my request is," he continued, "that your Lordship would favour my cause whereby you shall ever bind me to you. I have a desire to spend my time in Virginia or in the discovery of the North-West passage for the rich kingdom of China, wherein I will willingly adventure my life and fortune." Now that peace had been made with Spain, and since diplomatic incidents were, above all, to be avoided, there was much to be said for passing on the mariners of the old tradition to the New World.

It was an opportune suggestion for the Lord Chief Justice was exercising himself about Virginia. Some time in March a letter on this subject came from Sir Walter Cope, a wealthy man, financially adventurous, who owned the great estate of Kensington, near London. "My Lord Chief Justice (Popham)," wrote Sir Walter,[1] "foreseeing in the experience of his place the infinite numbers of cashiered captains and soldiers, of poor artizans that would and cannot work, and of idle vagrants that may and will not work, whose increase threatens the State, is affectionately bent to the plantation of Virginia; in which he has already taken great pains, and means to disburse 400 1. *per annum* for five years, if the action prospers."

To Salisbury these matters were not of immediate concern; but the increasing power of the City in these adventures was not to be accepted in the West Country without a protest. "The Lord Chief Justice," wrote the mayor of Plymouth to Theobalds,[2] "has recommended to us an enterprise for establishment of a Plantation in the parts of America; whereunto we were drawn to assent upon hope to obtain such free and reasonable conditions as has had in former times

[1] Letter from Sir Walter Cope to the Earl of Salisbury, dated March, 1605–6, Cecil MSS., vol. 191, f. 120.
[2] Letter from the deputy mayor of Plymouth and his brethren to the Earl of Salisbury, Cecil MSS., vol. 116, f. 39.

been granted by the late Queen to certain gentlemen. But it appears that it has been thought more convenient . . . to assign us to be directed (under His Majesty) by a Council of divers, some very worthy and worshipful persons, others of the same rank and quality ourselves are, the greater part strangers to us and our proceedings." This statement was immediately followed up by a letter from the governor of Plymouth, Sir Ferdinando Gorges.

"Some things there are" wrote Sir Ferdinando plunging into the heart of the subject,[1] "whereunto they (the citizens of Plymouth) find themselves tied, which has exceedingly cooled the heat of their affections that at first made proffer of their adventures. . . Besides, for them here (at Plymouth) to be tied upon all occasions to post it to London is a matter so tedious and chargeable as they are wholly distasted with the imagination thereof." These letters make tedious reading and it should have been obvious that, when the great London merchants were entering into competition, the men of the western seaboard could no longer expect their former freedom. Conditions had gravely changed since those dangerous war-time adventures of the sixteenth century.

In this month, too, Salisbury had been installed as High Steward of Portsmouth, a post he had accepted on Lord Devonshire's death.[2] As a consequence a correspondence at once began with Captain Ersfield, the deputy governor of the town, who was anxious for confirmation in his post. The first letter contained a report calculated to display the officer's zeal in a good light. "Near the Isle of Wight," wrote Captain Ersfield,[3] "in a little harbour called Mead-

[1] Letter from Sir Ferdinando Gorges to the Earl of Salisbury, dated 10 May, 1606. Cecil MSS., vol. 116, f. 40.

[2] On 8 April, 1606, the mayor and burgesses of Portsmouth wrote to the Earl of Salisbury to express their great grief at the death of the Earl of Devonshire, their most loving Lord and High Steward, and begging him to accept their choice of him for that office, Cecil MSS.

[3] Letter from Anthony Ersfield to the Earl of Salisbury, dated 19 April, 1606. Cecil MSS., vol. 116, f. 12.

hole, there are associated 20 or 30 seafaring men that rob and spoil by sea whom they can catch, and have taken a Frenchman loaden with wines and other commodities. The chief is one Turnor a Suffolk man." He asked for instructions to assist him in the restoration of order, and sent copious detail of the foreign vessels entering Spithead. But in June Sir Francis Vere, a distinguished officer in command of the garrison at Brill, was appointed to the governorship of Portsmouth and Ersfield was "threatened in his place." The letters from Portsmouth ceased to accumulate upon Lord Salisbury's table.

With Sir Francis Vere there seems to have been little correspondence. But one letter written by him at this time has an especial interest owing to the light which it throws on an aspect of the outlook of the wealthy Englishmen. "I received a letter from the Council," wrote Sir Francis in May 1606,[1] "concerning the licensing of the Graymes to depart hence, but what through mortality and running away few of them are left."

Parallel to this casual reference to "mortality and running away" is a statement by a Hertfordshire widow, Mrs. Margaret Clarke. The Earl's officers, she declared,[2] gave orders that no cottages should be erected in the parish of Hatfield because the poor would much abound thereby. It is not the accuracy or otherwise of the allegations which is important so much as the frame of mind that is revealed.

It is customary to describe the Englishmen of the early seventeenth century as callous and indifferent to suffering; and the burning of witches, the harsh references to vagabonds and rogues, and the provisions of the penal code are held to bear out this accusation. Nevertheless, it would seem

[1] Letter from Sir Francis Vere at Brill to the Earl of Salisbury, dated 31 May, 1606. Cecil MSS., vol. 116, f. 77.
[2] Letter from Margaret Clarke to the Earl of Salisbury. Cecil MSS., vol. 196, f. 10. Undated but placed among the papers of 1607–12 owing to the reference to Hatfield.

to be more accurate to regard the matter not so much as a question of conscious cruelty as of a strict limitation of sympathy. Among men of birth and persons of substance without that title there was a marked considerateness towards their equals which was only blunted by the inevitable pressure of competition. And it was in accordance with the tradition of the period that the merchant should have a care for his industrious apprentice and that the landowner should protect the countrymen actually bred up on his estates. The dispensing of charity was usually prudently restrained within these limits, and Salisbury was following a well-established custom when he provided for the teaching of "the art of clothing or weaving . . . or any other suchlike commendable trade" to fifty poor persons dwelling within the parish of Hatfield to be chosen by himself. Already the idea of the deserving poor was taking root. As for the rest it was difficult for gentlemen of consideration to bend their attention to the "abounding vagabonds." They really did not come within the scope of the accustomed human relations.

This matter of the immense security and strength of the social hierarchy is very seldom fully realized. The cry against "new men" which had a certain actuality in the days of the Pilgrimage of Grace had come by the good years of the seventeenth century to be merely a tribute to the desirability of high position. The English ruling classes have nearly always been lateral in their emphasis; that is to say that it is the high connections rather than the ancestry that has counted. In the reign of James I the Tudor peerage was fully established; they had great transmitted wealth and the lustre of Elizabethan sovereignty. It was only in the nineteenth century that men began to concern themselves about the Plantagenets.

This social outlook transmuted the whole sphere of personal relations. The first question for consideration was the rank and worth of the applicant, and the case of the recusancy fines illustrates this contention. For offences short of treason, and Salisbury knew how peaceful was the state of the country, there was always the possibility of accommodation. A letter from Lord Southampton, who had the merit of having himself conformed to the Established Church, will suggest the position. "Yet must I," wrote Southampton this same summer,[1] "now of necessity renew an old suit in the behalf of my poor aunt Katherin Cornwallis, who by your Lordship's favour, hath hitherto lived free from trouble for her recusancy, but is now by malice likely to be indicted if your Lordship interpose not some mean to help her. She is an old woman that liveth without scandal, and I am in the expectation of some good from her. I assure myself she will take nothing so kindly of me as to preserve her from this danger. If, therefore, your Lordship will hold it fit and will help me it will be to me, I think, a very good turn." This was a well set out argument based on a solid financial advantage, and Salisbury had already shown himself ready to help.

Within a week a letter arrived from Southampton's friend, Lord Rutland, about a similar matter. An apparently unfounded report had reached the King that Sir Oliver Manners was staying in a Jesuit college abroad. "Both he and I," wrote Rutland,[2] "crave this favour from you that His Majesty may be satisfied in the report of his being among the Jesuits in their college, and I hope this bruit will make him careful to avoid this sort of people." Sir Gamaliel Capel

---

[1] Letter from the Earl of Southampton to the Earl of Salisbury, dated 28 September, 1606, Cecil MS., vol. 118, f. 104. The third Earl's mother, the old Countess of Southampton, was still surviving and a Catholic. Lady Catherine Cornwallis was a woman of advanced age since her father, the first Earl of Southampton, had died in 1550.

[2] Letter from the Earl of Rutland to the Earl of Salisbury, dated at Garradon, 4 October, 1606, Cecil MSS., vol. 117, f. 1161. Roger fifth Earl of Rutland who died in 1612, was an Anglican, but his younger brothers, Francis later sixth Earl of Rutland and Sir Oliver Manners, had become Catholics.

had written[1] for some mitigation of the law in the case of his recusant brother-in-law, but manifestly his claims to attention were much less considerable.

In connection with these religious matters, Salisbury had been carrying on through this year a long correspondence with Lord Arundell of Wardour, whose imprudence in taking service in the Spanish Netherlands, could hardly be condoned on the score of the command which he had held in the Imperialist armies against the Turks. He had fallen into positive disfavour through accepting the colonelcy of one of the Archduke's regiments at Brussels, and although he was stationed in a technically friendly capital he realized that it was essential to resume his place in English life. And Salisbury was an adept in the arrangement of reconciliation to the existing power, for he seems to have had a real pleasure in the smooth conquest of refractory opinion. "If my state," wrote Lord Arundell from Brussels,[2] "were not so decayed, and so far indebted, that without some help from His Majesty's bounty, I cannot maintain myself in that reputation as were fitting, I would not at this time importune his Majesty.

"In my first travels,"[3] Lord Arundell continued as he began a recital of his services, "I was persuaded by the duke of Guyse that then was to offer my services to his Majesty's

[1] In a letter to the Earl of Salisbury, dated 27 July, 1606, Sir Gamaliel Capel pleaded the cause of his brother-in-law Nicholas Waldegrave of Essex, a convicted recusant who had paid two parts of his living to the King. Sir Gamaliel who was an Anglican stated that he was "of a quiet and peaceable disposition no meddler in matters offensive." Cecil MSS., vol. 116, f. 64.

[2] Letter of Lord Arundell of Wardour to the Earl of Salisbury, undated 1606. Cecil MSS., vol. 197, f. 78.

[3] The sequence of events can be traced in the despatches sent by Nicolo Molin, the Venetian Ambassador in London, to the Doge and Senate. On 14 September, 1605, he wrote that "the Spanish Ambassador resolved to take out with him Lord Arundel, the man who had raised 2,000 English troops for service in the war (in Flanders) as well as other officer." On 28 September that Lord Arundell had been refused leave to go to Flanders, but on the same day he reported that "he had hired a merchantman, put on a false beard and crossed over in company with the Ambassador." Cal. S. P. Venetian, 1603–7, pp. 416, 426, 427.

mother (Mary, Queen of Scots), which I did, yet with a reservation of my allegiance to our late Queen. Which offer being graciously accepted, and a letter of thanks with promise of advancement returned, it happened that that letter was intercepted by Sir Francis Wallsingam; whereupon I was banished out of the Court for thirteen months, and the displeasure which ensued thereof was so great, that still being reputed Scottish, I was debarred from all this favours whereby I might have advanced my fortunes had not my zeal for his Majesty's title procured me this disgrace.

"My uncle, Sir Charles Arundell, lost his country and all his hopes therein, by whose fall myself (as being his next heir) suffered the greatest loss.

"Immediately upon the death of our late Queen, I caused King James to be proclaimed in Shaftesbury on a market day, eight days before any neighbour town durst do the like.

"In my last voyage into Flanders, how firmly I stood to my obliged duty, how many and great offers of advancement I refused I had rather time manifest than I report."

And then there came a letter to explain his recent actions. "Though I be but newly come out of a fit of burning ague," wrote Arundell,[1] "yet I could not but salute your Lordship with a few lines. None must stand here (in Brussels) that stand not by the favour of Owen and the Jesuits. Against whom because I have stiffly opposed myself permitting none (as near as I could) to bear office in the regiment that dependeth of them, first, they suborned the Sergeant-Major against me and that in so foul treasons and mutinies as that it makes all men here to wonder that there is no justice done upon him; secondly, they left the regiment destitute of any priest (which to this time hath been a thing unseen) by reason that I would not admit any of the Jesuited sort, they would not give maintenance to any other." It

---

[1] Letter from Lord Arundell of Wardour to the Earl of Salisbury, undated 1606. Cecil MSS., vol. 118, f. 107.

must have been satisfying to Salisbury to receive such avowals.

Sir Thomas Edmondes, the ambassador in Brussels,[1] vouched for the accuracy of Arundell's statements. Burghley's work was, indeed, drawing to its conclusion. The condemnation of Fathers Garnett and Tesimond, and the execution of the Gunpowder plotters had made laymen chary even of using the name of Jesuit. Salisbury had great experience of the wealthiest Catholics,[2] and, as they bent towards a close support of the Stuart monarchy, it seemed reasonable to suppose that England was drawing nearer to a secular peace. But to the seventeenth century secular peace was to prove a mirage.

All the correspondence tended to support the justified impression of the security of Salisbury's position. The Earl of Dorset, who would permit himself a little decorous comment[3] in regard to their royal master, was wholly bound to him and a letter commenting on the affairs of government gives a most reassuring glimpse of political unity. "Your care for the King," wrote the Lord Treasurer in an account of the calm unfolding of affairs,[4] "and to be the mean of his preservation, is furthered by God Himself. Therefore I pray you may never die as long as His Majesty lives, which I beseech the Lord may be forever. And I am very glad his Majesty doth like so well our proceeding for the currants.

[1] In a letter dated 28 June, 1606, Sir Thomas Edmondes wrote to Salisbury to assure him that he believed that "Arundell and Sir Griffin Markham who have been chief officers of the regiment, have carefully and dutifully opposed themselves against the lewd proceedings of the ill instruments here."

[2] Lord Stourton had married Salisbury's sister-in-law Frances Brooke, while the fourth Marquess of Winchester had married his niece Lady Lucy Cecil. Salisbury was on most intimate terms with Lady Winchester, who was the mother of the Catholic leader, Lord Winchester of the Siege of Basing House.

[3] "This money for Ireland," write Lord Treasurer Dorset on 10 June 1606, "is to be sent thither by midsummer day. I have told them that there is a loan of £2,000 more for a knight greatly affected by his Majesty named Sir Richard Weston, which they may not deny." Cecil MSS., vol. 116, f. 95.

[4] Letter from the Earl of Dorset to the Earl of Salisbury, dated July 1606. Cecil MSS., vol. 118, f. 143.

Certainly it will prove the best judgment and clearest for the Crown that ever was."

And even the greatest men were prudent in asking his aid for their promotion. "Now Christenmas is done," wrote Lord Chancellor Ellesmere in July 1606,[1] "it is time for those that durst not presume to the feast to seek some part of the fragments.. I find nothing in myself worth valuing . . . save love and fidelity only. This made me, being bashful by nature and lame in limbs, to lie still as the poor lame man by the Pool of Bethesda, hoping that after the Angel's moving of the water some would help to put me in."

"Gifts given to old men" he continued serenely, "serve but as Mary Magdalene's ointment to bury them. Yet that comforts age and in the end serves for good and necessary use. On Sunday last *obiter*, and upon an occasion un-expected, I cast out some few words to his Majesty as a preparative of my suit."

Then there was the Bishop of Exeter lying off in the wind not speaking of office as was fitting among laymen, just touching very quietly on his merits. The immediate occasion of the letter was a dispute with Sir William Stroud over the workings of the Ecclesiastical Commission in Devon, and he first disposed of the matter in hand. "Within these ten days," he went on in a more intimate vein, "I have brought 8 or 9 recusants to the Church; and within one year I hope to clear my diocese of that Popish faction, as I have done of the peevish. I am an honest man, and have lived hitherto without touch, and I am in the midst of a tough and unruly people." Each expression of desire among the civil and ecclesiastical hierarchies came in time to Salisbury.

The Secretary of State was not to follow the Court that summer in its western progress; but his leisure was fully

---

[1] Letter from Lord Ellesmere to the Earl of Salisbury, dated 16 July, 1606, Cecil MSS., vol. 116, f. 151. The reward in question may have been the earldom of Bridgewater for which he worked so perseveringly and eventually successfully; though it came as a posthumous honour.

occupied with the entertainments for the King of Denmark's visit. Varying his own long despatches to the English envoys on the Continent and their careful dignified replies, there came in the plans for the expenses for King Christian and the heavy drift of police reports. In the mass of these papers one fact emerges very clearly. It was a great part of the Minister's duty to protect the person of his sovereign. While his secretaries would scrutinize the postal endorsements[1] of the letters from Dover and the North to test the efficiency of the service, the entry and departure of suspected persons was Salisbury's personal responsibility. Details of doubtful characters crossing the English Channel were brought before him by Sir Thomas Fane, who combined the offices of deputy warden of the Cinque Ports and lieutenant of Dover. For years now the minister had been familiar with all the regulations governing entry to the kingdom; the control exercised by the deputy warden over the owners of the passage boats; the respective functions of the searchers of the customs and the clerk of the passage; the time taken by the messengers in foul or fair weather on the ride between the capital and Dover harbour.

It is interesting to note how rapidly Salisbury's mind seems to have worked when he was dealing with these personal problems. Yet when concerned with matters of financial practice he appears to have accepted the current practice. In this field he was not ready to initiate. Thus the drafting of the patent for white mulberry-trees and the renewal of Sir Michael Stanhope's grant[2] for the importation of

---

[1] The endorsements on a letter sent to Theobalds by the mayor of Chester on 5 January, 1605-6, will give an impression of the rate of travel. "At the citie of Chester of Januarye the Vth at viij of the clocke at night. At Namptwiche at xij the same nighte. Stone at iiij in the morning. Litchfield at viij in the morning. Coleshull at xj. Coventrye paste on after nowne the 6th of Januarie. Daventre at v the afternone the same day. Tocester at 8 the same day. Brickhill at xj. Saint Albans at 4 in ye morning. Barnet past 6 in the morning," Cecil MSS., vol. 109, f. 133.

[2] Letter from Sir Michael Stanhope to the Earl of Salisbury dated 31 May, 1606. For the mulberry patent cf., Cecil MSS., vol. 193, f. 28.

Spanish hat wools went forward normally. There was no need for innovation. To the wealthy men of this elder generation the system of monopolies and patents appeared to be a satisfactory method of distributing the profits of new trade so that persons of worth could benefit by the progress of the nation's commerce.

In this connection gifts were sent in to Salisbury as evidence of the enterprising character of native industry. "Because," wrote Lord Shrewsbury in a typical letter,[1] "you may see what excellent varieties my poor town of Sheffield can afford, my wife sendeth you a case of knives made there representing the figure of Christ with his 12 apostles." It was appropriate to the spirit of the age that these knives should have been brought to Salisbury's notice not by the manufacturer, but by the lord of the soil.

It was the privilege of the greater gentry and the country peers to keep the Secretary of State supplied with game in season and among his presents was "a tassell of goshawks well fore-angled" from Lord Errol.[2] The curiosity which was then a polite accomplishment was ministered to by "a pair of tortoises and a glass of balsam" from Sir Walter Cope.

In conclusion three requests made to Salisbury may be mentioned since they covered diverse fields of his interests and duty. "It may please you," Mr. Nicholas Hillyarde, the painter, wrote to him, "to remember that about 5 years agone, when I drew your picture, I found that favour with you accepted my humble offer of my son Lawrence, his service, and called me to retain him still to perfect him more in drawing, which I have done, and he does His Majesty now good service both in limned pictures and in the medallings of gold."

[1] Letter from the Earl and Countess of Shrewsbury to the Earl of Salisbury placed among the undated letters of the year 1606.
[2] Letter from the Earl of Errol to the Earl of Salisbury, dated at Edinburgh, 9 March, 1606. Cal. S. P. Dom.

And then the recurrent factor of the Catholic problem was once more before him. In a petition Mr. Alban Doleman explained that he was now seventy-six years of age, had been made priest in Queen Mary's reign, was in body very corpulent, huge and most unwieldy, tormented with gout and not able without extraordinary help to move himself. He stated that he was now bound to forsake his friends rather than that they should incur the danger of the last Statutes. He begged that he might be confined to the house of Mr. William Greene of Samford, Essex (who was bound by his father's will to maintain him) there to remain upon His Lordship's command. It was a well conceived letter and a pendant to the grim reminder which Mr. Ralph Dobbinson now submitted.[1] Mr. Dobbinson required payment from the Council of twenty-three shillings and ninepence the sum "expended upon ironwork in setting up the heads of Thomas Pearcye and Robert Catesby upon the Parliament House."

In the heats of August a letter came from Sir Walter Cope who had dealt with Salisbury in the question of the Plantation. "My Lord," began Sir Walter,[2] "you said I should have two lines to Vanlore for credit in the Low Countries. The Scots creditors offer my Lord Daubeney's warrants and others for rectories and chantries about the town." Daubeney was the careless phonetic rendering of Stuart d'Aubigny and this note throws a light upon the manner in which the King's plans for pensioning his Scottish friends by giving them charges against the former chantry lands were faring. But later in this same month Salisbury fell ill and the current interests receded from his mind as his delicate constitution bore the weight of that strain under which it would eventually succumb. Still this year he rallied and the letters in their

---

[1] The letters from Cope, Hillyarde, Doleman and Robinson are preserved respectively in Cecil MSS., vol. 117, f. 29; vol. 115, f. 130; vol. 196, f. 125 and vol. 190, f. 47.

[2] Letter from Sir Walter Cope to the Earl of Salisbury, dated 12 August, 1606. Cecil MSS., vol. 117, f. 29.

Byzantine phrasing lay thick upon his table. "I have to my grief," wrote Sir Edward Wotton,[1] "heard of your indisposition. Your little finger cannot ache but the whole State hath cause to be sensible."

It was naturally only a limited section of English life which was reflected in these papers, but politically it had profound significance. For the possessors of wealth and those who moved in the circles of a flowing expenditure would gravitate towards this centre. As for the mass of the people and the farmers and the smaller merchants, their habits of thought were quite distinct. Personal poverty and an outlook radically dissimilar from that of the ruling classes would exclude them from intimate association with the moulders of policy.

On the other hand the heads of the great political families conceived of financial stringency rather in its corporate than in its personal aspect. The companies in which they ventured might be threatened by a bankruptcy which seldom overtook their private fortune. One of the intimate notes sent to Salisbury by Dorset, is significant. "I return you your papers," wrote the Lord Treasurer who had accumulated a princely fortune,[2] "having read them all in which I see the anatomy of many miseries for lack of money." There was in the high places of the State an enclosed contentment bred of peace. It was in circles far removed from Hatfield or from Knole that one could study in its personal application "the anatomy of many miseries for lack of money."

[1] Letter from Sir Edward Wotton to the Earl of Salisbury, dated 21 September, 1606. Cecil MSS., vol. 117, f. 130.
[2] Letter from the Earl of Dorset to the Earl of Salisbury, dated 11 June, 1606. Cecil MSS., vol. 116, f. 96.

CHAPTER V

THE CLOSE OF THE CECIL INFLUENCE

THE influential elements in the State maintained a fairly stable political balance in the six calm years between 1606 and 1612. The proposals for a union with Scotland had been discussed; the project for a Great Contract in settlement of financial claims had been introduced and then abandoned; there had been various forms of opposition to the levying of impositions; the dissolution of Parliament in 1611 had been marked by bitterness. Nevertheless, except in regard to these legal and constitutional matters and that section of the country actively interested in such dispute, there was an element of dullness in the nation's life. Dorset had died in 1608 and Salisbury had inherited the Lord Treasurer's staff. For most of this period Archbishop Bancroft still ruled at Lambeth; the lines of access to the sovereign changed very little.

The type of entrenched political influence built up by the first minister was for practical purposes impregnable, but there is little doubt that his personal relations with the King were now less cordial. It was not easy for an exhausted statesman to play the "little beagle," and to maintain the appearances of spontaneity. And then in the last three years the King had become absorbed in his affection for Lord Jedburgh's stepbrother, young Robert Ker. The Lord Treasurer was only in middle life, but his health was a doubtful factor and he seems to have felt the need of that retirement which he was in no position to achieve.

Hatfield was now completed, the palace of a great officer

71

of State and in no sense a place for quiet withdrawal as it
stood high and spreading and magnificent, right in the track
of all King James's movements. The building was finished
and all was hoisted into place. It was eighteen months since
"the content of 30 marble stones provided at Carera in the
Prince of Masse his country, and transported into Leghorn
and shipped for England" had been laded and erected in
position. The fireplaces were masked by those great chimney-
pieces which are rightly described with such pomp in the
detailed accounts at Hatfield House. "One chimney-piece,"
so runs the note of the expenses, "with fower dorrick
columns upon 2 pedestals with 2 wide panels between
supporting a vase with a frieze and swelling panels under it
with 4 great curbs bearing 4 Ionic columns with pedestals
and wide panels between and a compt swelling panel in the
middle with small cartooses round about."

It is in this strain that the accounts for the expenditure in
1611 are all conceived; painting the timber work of the great
stairs; working the naked boys and lions standing upon those
stairs; gilding the great pendants from the ceiling; complet-
ing the frieze in gold and walnut-tree colour. It does not
sound restful for a tired man.

The glass of the chapel windows were now in place with
the intertwining legends like *Dauid Goliam superat*. The
designs were realistic with troops marching like the army of
the Prince of Parma. The young David held aloft the Giant's
head transfixed on a broad sword while the sunlight came
through the sharp colours and the forest of spears. On the
right Naaman the Syrian stood dignified and composed in
the blue water, as the biblical scenes unfolded themselves in
an incontestable rotation.

From beyond the chapel there stretched the new long
gallery with its conscious vista. The pictures in the house
were in position as was the mosaic with its conventionalized
likeness of Lord Salisbury sent from Venice by Sir Henry

Wotton. A small portrait represented that wife whom Salisbury had lost, Frances Cecil with the great pearl guard above
her hair and the powdered silver on grey satin. Her triangular
face, remote and unaustere, looked pale and satisfied and
Elizabethan.

Out through the high windows, and in contrast to the oak
and the new bright golden paint, lay the garden with its
terraces and parterres and the mown green walks and the
borders set with pinks. There was the new vineyard and the
nectarines and plum-trees. There would soon be so much
more when the lavish planning had matured; the four
hundred sycamores from the Low Countries; the tulip bulbs
from Leyden; the rose-trees; the melon plants; the Flemish
cherries. Hatfield roofed and glazed and furnished lay spread
across the unfinished landscape. In the east garden the men
were colouring the rocks in the great cistern. It seems that
the Lord Treasurer only spent eight nights in his new palace.

It was in the early months of 1612 that Salisbury's health
finally began to break. "It is on all hands considered,"
wrote Sir John More in this year, "that his lordship must
shortly leave this world, or at least disburden himself of a
great part of his affairs. In this short time of his lordship's
weakness almost all our great affairs are come to a stand,
and his hand is already shrewdly missed; *carendo magis quam
fruendo quod bonum est perspicimus.*" A certain depression
of spirit settled upon him, and the religious phrasing which
had been kept restrained during the years of his political
experience rose to the surface. It had come down from Lord
Burghley and his childhood days. "Ease and pleasure," he
said to Sir Walter Cope, "quake to fear death, but my life
full of cares and miseries desireth to be dissolved." He
seems to have seen by now that his son would never do
work of value. He was bequeathing to his heir Hatfield and
his debts, but the greatness of the line was dying with him.
Court life had been fatiguing since the King's absorption in

his youthful favourite. There was nothing in Salisbury's personality capable of transmuting his master's rather tired regard for him.

For the last few years the minister's life had moved slowly against the set of the tide. Now in the spring of 1612 he made his will and set down in due order the official theology in its uncompromising simplicity, desiring to go "as a man that hath long been satiated with terrestrial glory, and now contemplates only heavenly joy."

Among his papers there is a note written in Italian, dated December 1611, and described as a letter of consolation from an unknown person to the Cardinal of Nazareth. There is no indication of how it came to Salisbury; but it may have had a passing interest for him in these last months; at least he preserved it. "I believe," runs the conclusion,[1] "this misfortune of yours will prove to be a good touchstone to distinguish the true gold from the false. Those who love the great are mostly like the flower called heliotrope, which while the sun shines looks towards it with flowers alive and open, but when the sun sets closes them and looks another way."

Salisbury had always been a little melancholy and his illness was gaining on him.[2] In April the dropsy became more serious, and he was driven down to the Bath in his Emden coach with the white horses. "We went," wrote Mr. Bowle, his chaplain,[3] "to Cowson (Caversham) my lord Knowles his house, where, in the waie, my lord was something moved because his close chaire did not follow him; and because the coach was not so easie as it might have been." He settled with more comfort at the Bath, and the letter

---

[1] Letter in the Cecil MSS., vol. 129, f. 83, translation among the Record Office transcripts.

[2] Lady Russell in one of her exaggerated letters to Robert Cecil had declared that yielding to melancholy will "make you a surly, sharp, sour plum, no better than in truth a very melancholy mole and a *misanthropos* hateful to God and man." Cal. Hatfield MSS., vii, p. 38.

[3] MS. observations of the Rev. John Bowle on the Earl of Salisbury's sickness, *Desiderata Curiosa*, p. 206.

which he wrote to his son is pathetic in the suggestion of lassitude underlying the brave phrasing. "It is vanity," he explained,[1] "for a man to expect to see anything if his eye look upon me before I have made up twelve days trial here counting from my first going in, which you must reckon to be from Tuesday at 3 of the clock; since which time I have been thrice, that is to say Tuesday and Thursday after dinner being driven away on Wednesday by the wind which whenever it riseth driveth all men from all the baths in the town. This day Friday I go in again, for I desire to neglect no time and the sun shines." The cure was unsuccessful, and as he drew near to death, Salisbury's remoteness from those of the Jacobean Court became apparent.

It was on the spiritual plane that he now thought of his unhopeful son. "I love him," Salisbury had said of Cranborne,[2] "more because he is religious than because he is my son." It was at the close of this same Bath journey, when visiting the palsied Sir John Harington, that he gave vent to that copious and tortuous sentiment which sounds like the Elizabethan manner slipping to the ground. "Sir John," he began,[3] "nowe doe th'one creple come to see and visite another, this it is; death is the centre to which wee all do move, some dynameter wise and some circularly, but all men must fall downe to the center."

Salisbury set out homewards with his chaplain and his son and daughter. He was joined at Laycock on Thursday, 21 May, by his chief Scottish friend, Lord Hay. From Lady Stapleton's manor at Laycock he was moved to Marlborough and there in the parsonage house the great Earl of Salisbury died on 24 May, "the sabaoth day."

The passing of the leading statesman of the Elizabethan

---

[1] Letter from the Earl of Salisbury to Lord Cranborne, dated 8 May, 1612. Cecil MSS., vol. 129, f. 106.
[2] Statement of the Earl of Salisbury formerly among the Westmoreland MSS. at Apethorpe, Hist. MSS. Commission's Reports, *Tenth Report*, Appendix II, i, p. 14.
[3] ibid., p. 16.

tradition provides an occasion to consider briefly some aspects of that Anglican position with which the Cecils were already linked so intimately. There is evidence that Salisbury held to his religious standpoint with that assurance which characterized the ethical and political conceptions which to his contemporaries appeared immutable. It was clear to that generation that the link between the secular and ecclesiastical authority was only rendered the stronger by the doctrinal changes. The acceptance of these postulates assisted the development of a calm outlook devoid of rigour and with none of the Puritan distaste for gauds and images. The lavish decorated chapel at Hatfield House had been hung with French pictures upon cloth of the Salutation of the Virgin and the Angel appearing to the Shepherds. The feeling for decorum had effectually separated Salisbury, as it had separated so many of his world, from the uncompromising sternness of Geneva. In external matters the influence of the Tridentine world came in by many channels.

The canopy and vallance of crimson and violet paned damask above the Bishop's seat in Dr. Andrewes' chapel suggested the way of life of the chastened and decorous Tridentine episcopate as did the story of Absalom and Melchisedec worked on the hangings above the altar. The material background was appropriate to the weight of the Anglican tradition, and one can note the stirrings of the Laudian world. In religious questions there was already established in English life that almost Biblical gravity which was to mark the Englishman's approach to holy things. Bishop Andrewes was indeed in many ways the fitting prelate to officiate at the interment of Lord Salisbury's generation. Two phrases from Bishop Hacket's biography of Archbishop Williams give a singularly lifelike impression. "He (Andrewes)," he wrote,[1] "was the most apostolical and primitive-like divine, in my opinion, that wore a rochet in

[1] *Life of Archbishop Williams*, i, p. 45.

his age. Himself," the biographer continued in speaking of his hospitality at Farnham Castle, "seldom knowing what meat he had till he came from his study to dinner, at which he would show himself so noble in his entertainment and so gravely facetious." And in Bishop Buckeridge's funeral sermon we find this note repeated.[1] "He (Dr. Andrewes) was always a diligent and painful preacher. Most of his sermons he was most careful of and exact."

To that age he gave consistency quoting copiously from the Old Testament which the lords of the Protestant ascendancy had learned from the ministers in their childhood. Slowly the more abstruse references in the Bible were finding their way into common speech. Dr. Andrewes spoke of the grapes of Gomserah and enshrined King James's glory in the parallels of David and Saul and Ahasuerus. But it was his solid spirituality, allied to a great confidence in the religious values of the national temperament, which was to make him so determining an influence on Anglican development. He was not to attain to Canterbury and the effect of his personality never stood higher than in these first ten years of his episcopate. He belonged to the passing age which had grown long accustomed to the Cecilian government and had yet to experience the effect of Buckingham's advance in favour and John Donne's entry into the sacred ministry. At fifty-seven he had still fourteen more years of life and was to survive his present sovereign; a great and reverenced ecclesiastical figure aloof from politics. Existing portraits give a clear impression of Bishop Andrewes; the hazel eyes, very shrewd and untroubled; the long thin nose; the full curving grey moustache; the white hair escaping from beneath the prelate's cap. In his life of scholarship and preaching he was without those worldly and frivolous contacts with which Laud was to find himself involved. Something of this is indicated in Dr.

[1] *Bishop Andrewes' Minor Works and Life*, Library of Anglo-Catholic Theology, pp. 295–6.

Andrewes' clothes and manner; the flaps of the black cap
closing down upon the narrow pleated ruff of an earlier
convention; the full linen surplice with the worked design
at the throat, so neat and proper.

He was a wise commentator to accompany the slow and
moulding force of King James's Bible. It is worth pondering
on the words in this translation's preface. "Great and
manifold were the blessings (most dread Sovereign)" began
the translators, "which Almighty God, the Father of all
mercies, bestowed upon us the people of England, when first
he sent Your Majesties' Royal Person to Rule and Reign
over us. For whereas it was the expectation of many, who
wished not well unto our Sion, that upon the setting of that
bright Occidental Star, Queen Elizabeth of most happy
memory, some thick and palpable clouds of darkness would
so have overshadowed this land, that men should have been
in doubt which way they were to walk, and that it should
hardly be known, who were to direct the unsettled State: the
appearance of Your Majesty, as of the Sun in his strength,
instantly dispelled those supposed and surmised mists." As
the words wind in and out in their careful sequence, it seems
almost impossible to disentangle the intertwined and branch-
ing roots of the English Church and Monarchy. These
phrases, too, indicate that object to which Lord Salisbury's
political life had been devoted, the dispelling of "supposed
and surmised mists."

With him there passed perhaps the last English statesman
who both understood and used the Elizabethan language, that
curious unashamed alliteration which the last generation had
so much enjoyed. Salisbury, eminently practical, could yet
understand those who spoke and wrote without fear of
ridicule. But now the whole method of application and
address was changing. Among the associates of his later
years was Sir Thomas Bodley, a diplomat of experience at
this time engaged in establishing the famous library. A letter

written at the end of 1606 and forming part of their correspondence will indicate the literary manner and the form of approach which were passing away.

"There was never," Sir Thomas wrote to Salisbury,[1] "suitor dismissed with greater amazement than I was from your lordship at my last access unto you. So passing strange I found it, in your lordship in especial, and in a matter importing my total ruin, to be so easily rejected. Yet . . . you will never give your voice that any advantage shall be taken to the quite undoing of any person, upon the doubtful understanding of a dark proviso, that for many hundred years was never hitherto construed to any tenants' detriment." It was not the subject matter, which dealt with a dispute with Lord Montgomery, that was significant, but rather the whole tone of mind. Salisbury knew well the custom by which private wrongs were translated into public injuries. More than any other single factor it was his disappearance which severed the link with the actual government of the sixteenth century.

In a certain fashion the life of the young Prince of Wales, which was also drawing to its close, was bound up with Salisbury's; for, as the future sovereign grew to manhood, the attention of the chief minister was bent upon one whose point of view was to be of such cardinal importance in a monarchy where the personal confidence of the King was still a pre-requisite for smooth administration. Actually, in so far as it can be determined, it would appear that the Prince harked back to earlier models and to the figure of Sir Walter Raleigh in the Tower. To a hot young man the Earl of Salisbury was too successful to be likely to prove appealing.

But so much turned upon the personality of the heir to the throne that an added significance is attributed to the year 1612 which saw not only Salisbury's disappearance, but also

[1] Letter from Sir Thomas Bodley to the Earl of Salisbury dated at Fulham, 18 December, 1606. Cecil MSS., vol. 118, f. 88.

the premature death of the Prince of Wales, who only survived the Lord Treasurer for five months dying of typhoid fever in the November of that year. In his family circle King James was left solitary, for his only daughter the Princess Elizabeth sailed for Germany with her husband the Elector Palatine in the following spring and the surviving son, Prince Charles, was a mere child, and a rather backward one, who had been born in the winter of 1600. It is worth considering the consequences of this change in the succession, and some extracts will convey the impression that a further cleavage was now developing between the Elizabethan and Stuart worlds.

The death of Prince Henry had disappointed innumerable place-hunters as well as those who saw advantage in the revival of the traditions of the previous reign. The data is really insufficient to enable us to form a sound impression of the way in which his outlook would have developed. He did not live to reach his eighteenth birthday and there is a rather legendary quality in the atmosphere which so soon came to surround his name, as if he had been a new King Henry V, generous and martial.

The eager Protestantism was possibly exaggerated in a later day when it was sought to free the monarchy from those suggestions of Laudian sympathies with which King Charles was associated in the public mind. Again Prince Henry is always represented as seriously pre-occupied by concern for the national glory, and in Parliamentarian circles there was a certain political advantage to be obtained by contrasting his supposedly aggressive patriotism with that cultivated and hesitant approach which was to lay his successor open to so much misunderstanding. At the same time he definitely does appear to have been insular in the sense that Drake and Raleigh and later Pym and Cromwell were insular, that is to say he was not accessible to Continental influences. On the political side his father King James was always aware of the

Tridentine world and the great European monarchies, while Prince Charles was to prove profoundly sensitive to European cultural movements. But it is clear that at eighteen the Prince of Wales was open, rather autocratic and, above all, accessible. It was principally on account of this last quality that the effect of his death was so disastrous in the *milieu* of the Court, for it deprived half a generation of possible intimates of the Prince of their opportunity and in later years the contrast was often stressed between the elder brother's noble candour and the reserved nature of Charles I.

Anne, Lady Fanshawe in her *Memoirs*, written in 1676, crystallized the legend which had been handed down in her husband's family. "And your grandfather (Sir Henry Fanshawe) was the favourite of Prince Henry," she wrote for her son's benefit,[1] "and had the Prince lived to be King, had been Secretary of State, as he would often tell him. Mr. Camden speaks much in praise, as you may see, of Sir Henry Fanshawe's garden, of Ware Park, none excelling it in flowers, physic herbes and fruit; also he was a great lover of music, and kept many gentlemen that were perfectly well qualified both in that and the Italian tongue, in which he spent some time. He likewise kept several horses of *manège* and rid them himself, which he delighted in, and the Prince would say none did it better." It is a delightful impression but possibly a period miniature rather than truth.

In another way an artificial atmosphere pervades a contemporary account of the spiritual ministrations at the Prince's deathbed. "Finding that Dr. Milbourne, dean of Rochester, was there present," wrote[2] the Bishop of Ely in a contemporary account, "hee (the Prince) willed the said deane to be called; as being one, whom for his learning and carriage and profitable teachinge, above all the rest, hee ever affected and respected." It is difficult to imagine a boy of seventeen

[1] *Memoirs of Anne Lady Fanshawe*, ed. Nicholas, 1829, pp. 13–4.
[2] MS. account of the death of Prince Henry by John More, Bishop of Ely printed in *Desiderata Curiosa*, p. 202.

respecting a clergyman for his "carriage," and the effect of
both these extracts is imprecise. But there is, however, one
passage which carries immediate conviction to the reader.
"This daye," wrote Bishop More of Prince Henry's[1] last
hours, "and at sundrye other tymes since his confusion of
speech he would many tymes call upon Sir David Murraye,
Knt (the onely man in whom he had always putt chiefe trust)
by his name David, David, David." This was Salisbury's
dependent, Sir David Murray. It is not possible to predict
how the reign of Henry IX would have developed.

There is in the autobiography of Sir Simonds D'Ewes a
strangely convincing account of a childhood passed in the
manor house of Coxden at the western end of Dorset. Looking back on a rather lonely and self-conscious childhood
Simonds D'Ewes, then a Parliamentarian of wealth and
position, recalled the mourning at Prince Henry's death.
Puritan in his habit of thought, and depressed at the political
developments of later years, he threw into his account that
nostalgic regret which the dead Prince's name was to awaken.
Interesting in itself it serves to reveal how the moderate
Puritans looked back to the Elizabethans across the unsym-
pathetic reign of Charles I. "The first public grief that ever
I was sensible," wrote[2] Sir Simonds in reference to the events
of his eleventh year, "was at Wambroke, after the death of
England's joy, that inestimable Prince Henry on the 6th day
of November. . . . He was a prince rather addicted to martial
studies and to exercises than to golf, tennis or other boys'
play; a true lover of the English nation, and a sound Protestant, abhorring not only the idolatry, superstitions and
bloody persecutions of the Romish synagogue, but being
free also from the Lutheran leaven. . . . He esteemed not
buffoons and parasites, nor vain swearers and atheists, but
had learned and godly men, such as were John Lord Har-

[1] The Bishop of Ely's account, *Desiderata Curiosa*, p. 202.
[2] *Autobiography and Correspondence of Sir Simonds D'Ewes*, edited by
James Orchard Halliwell, 1845, pp. 46–8.

rington of Exton and others, for the dear companions of his life; so as had not our sins caused God to take from us so peerless a prince it was very likely that Popery would have been well purged out of Great Britain and Ireland by his care; and that the Church of God had not suffered such shipwreck abroad as hath done for near upon the sixteen years last past. Charles, Duke of York, his brother, our present sovereign, was then so young and sickly as the thought of their enjoying him did nothing at all alienate or mollify the people's mourning."

On the next page Simonds D'Ewes reflects on the death of Lord Salisbury. Writing thirty years after the event the ideas which he expresses are naturally the current views of the moderate Parliamentary opposition of the next generation and not the reflections of a child of ten. Yet there is an interest in his conclusion. "The times since," wrote[1] Sir Simonds of Lord Salisbury, "have justified this man's action, that howsoever he might be an ill Christian . . . yet that he was a good statesman and no ill servant of the commonwealth." It is not marmoreal but still an epitaph.

---

[1] *Autobiography*, p. 50. It is not necessary to quote in the text D'Ewes' assertion that Salisbury "might be an ill Christian, in respect of his unparalleled lust and hunting after strange flesh." There is little evidence to form an opinion on the subject of the many attacks upon this isolated man. It is perhaps unlikely that he led a celibate widowerhood after the death of his wife when he was thirty-four; but Salisbury's surviving personal correspondence was eminently decorous. He caused no scandal and there appears to be no record of his rewarding either a mistress or a favourite. Under these circumstances the prudent statesman has surely a right to his privacy.

CHAPTER VI

A CROSS SECTION IN 1613

BEFORE discussing the political situation in the period
following Lord Salisbury's death it is as well to consider
the general situation in the country and perhaps this can
be suggested by a comparatively minute examination of
episodes which reveal the character and *tempo* of the English
life. For this purpose the autobiography of Sir Simonds
D'Ewes, which has just been quoted, provides an impression
of the country life in Dorset, while the examinations of Mr.
Cotton of Warblington very well convey the manner in which
a squire of moderate wealth would approach the unquiet
capital.

Simonds D'Ewes was brought up in the western parts, the
son of one of the six clerks of the Chancery and heir to his
grandfather, a lawyer whose property in lands, leases, goods
and ready money was valued at about £10,000. There was
no profit from nor concern with the recent wars, and no
military connection. "I was born," Simonds D'Ewes relates
contentedly,[1] "through the mercy and providence of my
gracious God (who hath hitherto preserved me) at Coxden
in the parish of Chardstock in the county of Dorset upon
Saturday the eighteenth of December, about five of the
clock in the morning in the year of Our Lord 1602. . . . I was
baptized upon the 29th day of the same month being Wednesday in the open gallery of Coxden aforesaid (in respect
of the extreme coldness of the season) by Mr. Richard White,
the vicar." And then he describes his grandfather,[2] "a

[1] *Autobiography of Sir Simonds D'Ewes*, pp. 1–2.   [2] ibid., p. 29.

great house keeper and having his cellars replenished with
cider, strong beer and several wines," and the dining-room
at Coxden with the coat of arms of Simonds impaling Lovelace and Ensham quarterly on the wainscot above the
chimney. And then he tells us the misadventures of his
childhood when the family went to London in the first year
of James I. "From Coxden," he records,[1] "they travelled
the first day into Dorchester being about twenty miles
whither my tender grandfather accompanied them, in all
which passage, though it was a short day's journey, I never
almost ceased from crying by reason of the continual jogging
of my father's coach in those craggy and uneven ways."

There is another picture equally and suddenly distinct of
the child playing at home in Dorset. "The other danger,"
wrote D'Ewes who is here describing the mercy of Providence
in his escapes,[2] "was not much inferior to some others into
which I actually fell; for the store horses being brought into
the courtyard at Coxden to water, which my father used for
his coach, and myself playing a little behind them with a
ball, it chanced to run under one of them which stood a
little straddling with his hindlegs." The story fades, for its
value lies in the moments when the descriptive detail breaks
through his didactic mind, and he is soon off on a tale of
his first journey to the capital. "In our passage towards
London," he wrote describing an episode in 1610, "we lay
at Blandford at the sign of the *Red Lion*, where shortly after
we had alighted, I desiring to walk into the gardens, took
with me one of my grandfather's clerks named Thomas
Tibbs. We first passed through the stable yard, where I,
seeing divers fowls picking upon a dunghill, like a true child
ran presently towards them to have catched them; but the
place where they stood, being a shining puddle and only
covered over with some dry litter, not long before thrown
out, I sunk into it suddenly above my knees." The touches

---

[1] *Autobiography of Sir Simonds D'Ewes*, p. 29.   [2] ibid., p. 32.

are very characteristic; they are too unadventurous for the Elizabethans; they had not the air of the early Carolines; they suggest irresistibly that peaceful haphazard reign of James I.

The second series of connected statements are much more detailed and belong to a period some three years later. Mr. John Cotton, with whose journey the depositions deal, was a recusant accused of propagating a forbidden work styled *Balaam's Ass*; but in this case the matter of the charge is irrelevant and it is the detail of the journey as it is revealed in the depositions which indicates the spirit of the time. To convey the impression it is essential to quote at some length the passages of the depositions now preserved among the Ancaster manuscripts which have a bearing on this point. In the first place Thomas Critch, innholder, at the sign of the *King's Head* in Southwark deposes.[1] "Hewell remembers that a Hampshire gentleman called Mr. John Cotton was at his house in Easter term last, and he believes he came in a Tuesday about two o'clock in the afternoon, having with him only a young man who attended him. Has conferred with his chamberlain who has known Cotton long, and they both verily believe that his coming was on a Tuesday and not a Wednesday, for they perfectly remember that the house was quiet and had little company in it, whereas on a Wednesday there is much concourse of people, by reason of a market of cloth which is held there, and the repairing thither of many carriers from Godleming (Godalming) and Farnham."

This was followed by the deposition of James Downing,[2] tapster at the *King's Head*, whose statement was borne out by Mr. Cotton's admission that he had supped in that inn in Mr. John Lane's chamber. "Saith that the day when Mr. Lane supped at his master's house in Easter term was a Tuesday, for there was 'a buck washed' in the house which

[1] Cal. Ancaster MSS., pp. 366–7.
[2] Deposition of James Downing, dated 23 June, 1613. Cal. Ancaster MSS., p. 367.

is always done upon the Tuesdays. And the same night there supped in Mr. Lane's chamber a gentlewoman and four men, whom the deponent did not know. A young man with no hair on his face attended them at supper, servant (as it seemed) to one that sat at table. By sun-set their supper was ended."

The next stage of the journey was described by Mr. Cotton in one of his examinations.[1] He declared that "after supper with Mr. Lane, Mrs. Middlemore and others (at the *King's Head*) about sunset he took boat at St. Mary Overies with Mr. Pound and Gimman (his servant) and landed either at Bridewell Dock or the Whitefriars. They went together to the Conduit in Fleet Street, where this examinate stood at the door of one Abbott, a grocer, while Mr. Pound went into Shoe Lane to seek him a lodging. Not speeding there he came back again and went up Fleet Street, but where he lay examinate knoweth not. Examinate lay that night at the house of one Lachy (the house of one that selleth silk stockings) at the *Eagle and the Child,* and his man lay in the same house, and as he thinketh at his bed's-foot."

Examinations of William Jenman and Edward Lachy were put in as support. The statement of William Jenman of Wabberton in Sussex was taken down under heads.[2]

1. Saith he is of the age of twenty years and something past.
2. Hath served Mr. Cotton almost three years.
3. Came to London with him on a rainy day; lodged at the *Eagle and Child* in Fleet Street; stayed there three, four or five days, was in London on May day and after.

Edward Lachie and his wife were examined at Lincoln's Inn.[3] "He saith that John Cotton came to his house in Fleet Street on the Tuesday night and there lodged. And the wife

[1] Examination of John Cotton, dated 20 July, 1613. Cal. Ancaster MSS., pp. 369–70.
[2] Examination of William Jenman, dated 20 July, 1613. Cal. Ancaster MSS., p. 370.
[3] Examination of Edward Lachie and his wife, dated 23 August, 1613. Cal. Ancaster MSS., p. 373.

of this examinate saith that he did not stir forth all Wednesday morning, as she verily believeth, for that he could not pass but through the shop where she was. And they both say that he dined there, and had mutton and porridge and a piece of beef bought by his man at a cook's in Shoe Lane."

Finally, there was the evidence of Mrs. Mabell Anthony, wife of John Anthony, innholder of the *King's Arms* at Godalming, where Mr. Cotton and his man had stayed on both the outward and the homeward journey. Rafe Whytmore, servant at the *King's Arms*,[1] deposed that they returned that way and that Mr. Cotton's man told him "that his master had spent thirty shillings at London those five days." William Dorye of Godalming, shoemaker,[2] "saith that he doth not well remember Mr. Cotton, but being at the *King's Arms* in the company of Richard Cowper and others strangers playing at shovelboard for beer the said Cowper blaspheming God very much, Mr. Cotton came out of his chamber and reproved him."

It is strange how these two accounts dovetail into one another. They both give an impression of an ordered life untroubled by foreign wars, with the gentry already dealing with their innkeepers and tenants in that spirit of genial tolerance which was to mark the eighteenth century. The Puritanism which was already making headway in the towns and in certain districts had hardly yet affected either the landholders or the class which lived upon their needs. It was a period without landmarks and it seems unnecessary to read into the spirit of this time any anticipation of future peril.

During this same year, 1613, a tale of quite another character from that of Mr. Cotton's journey circulated in the Southwark hosteiries, although this recital found less

---

[1] Deposition of Rafe Whytmore, dated 20 June, 1613. Cal. Ancaster MSS., p. 368.
[2] Deposition of William Dorye, same date. Cal. Ancaster MSS., p. 369.

favour at the *King's Head* than at that humbler house, the
White Horse, where the carrier from Horsham used to lie.
It is, perhaps, simplest to present this account in the form
in which the story was published in a brief pamphlet entitled
True and Wonderfull and printed in 1614. The sub-title, "A
discourse relating a strange and monstrous Serpent (or
Dragon) lately discovered," succinctly describes the subject
matter. "In Sussex," the account begins,[1] "there is a pretty
market towne called Horsam, neare unto it a forrest, called
St. Leonard's Forrest, and there, in a vast and unfrequented
place, heathie, vaultie, full of unwholesome shades and over-
growne hollowes, where this serpent is thought to be bred;
but, wheresoever bred certaine and true it is that there it yet
lives. . . .

"This serpent (or dragon as some call it) is reputed to be
nine feete, or rather more, in length, and shaped almost in
the forme of an axeltree of a cart; a quantitie of thickness in
the middest, and somewhat smaller at both ends. . . . He is
of countenance very proud, and at the sight or hearing of
men or cattel will raise his neck upright, and seem to listen
and looke about with great arrogancy. There are likewise
on either side of him discovered two great bunches so big
as a large foote-ball, and (as some thinke) will in time grow
to wings; but God I hope, will (to defend the poor people
in the neighbourhood) that he shall be destroyed before
he grow so fledge. . . .

"A man going to chase it, and as he imagined, to destroy
it with two mastive dogs, as yet not knowing the great
danger of it, his dogs were both killed, and he himself glad
to returne with hast to preserve his own life. Yet this is to
be noted, that the dogges were not prayed upon, but slaine
and left whole: for his food is thought to be, for the most
part, in a conie-warren, which he much frequents; and it is

---

[1] *True and Wonderfull*, printed in the Harleian Miscellany, vol. III,
pp. 109–12.

found much scouted and impaired in the encrease it had woont to afford. These persons, whose names are hereunder printed, have seen this serpent, besides divers others, as the carrier of Horsam, who liethe at the *White Horse* in Southwarke, and who can certifie the truth of all that has been here related."[1] It was a pleasant tale and, in the circles in which it aroused an interest, must have satisfied that taste for monsters[2] which is found among communities still rooted in the land and safe and secure.

It is not surprising that these tales should bring to mind the fireside seat and the well-stocked cellar, and the ripened wit, a trifle hazy and bucolic. And in this connection a curious inventory has survived from the previous year which helps to provide the physical background to much enjoyment. The house in question, the *Mouthe Tavern* without Bishopsgate, was a prosperous one in this year 1612, although its proprietor Mr. George Hitchcock, had unfortunately fallen into litigation. The inventory of the stock-in-trade is most illuminating. The list begins[3] with four pipes of white wine and continues with two hogsheads of old Graves wine, seven hogsheads of Orliane wine, one butt of Malligo wine, one ranlett of Sherry sacke, containing sixteen gallands, a pipe of old Malmsey, three gallands of Alligante,[4] one hogshead of old clarrett and a hogshead of clarrett Graves." Somehow

---

[1] Endorsed John Steele, Christopher Holde, and a Widow Woman dwelling near Faygate.

[2] A passage written half a century later in 1677 by Dr. Robert Plot very well indicates this point of view. "And amongst the *Quadrupeda*, or cloven-hooft Beasts, there was a Hog at Upper Tadmerton, of as strange a stature as they were of age; being fed by one Pargiter to so extravagant a greatness, that he came at last to be near 13 hands high, as it was testified to me by the Reverend Mr. Whateley, Rector of the place, and several others who had carefully measured him." *The Natural History of Oxfordshire*, p. 188.

[3] Inventory of the stocke in trade and furniture of a tavern in Bishopsgate Street in 1612. Contents of the cellar of the defendant, George Hitchcocke's dwelling-house called by the name of the *Mouthe Taverne* without Bishopsgate.

[4] It is interesting to note that the Greek wine Malmsey from the neighbourhood of Monemvasia was still drunk in England at this date. The current variants for Orleans, Malaga and Alicante explain themselves.

the lavishness of the period and its inconsequent expenses seem well suggested by this stock taking.

Beginning with the journey up from Coxden to the Six Clerks Office and continuing with Mr. Cotton's approach to London and the Horsham carrier's it is, perhaps, appropriate to close this section with an episode from a more serious western journey, that of Sir Walter Raleigh on his return from the Orinoco going up to London in custody. The brief account by his gaoler Sir Lewis Stukeley, is valuable not on account of any light which it might throw on Sir Walter's character (for it is an entirely partisan production), but because of the vivid impression which it conveys of social habit. The slight episode also introduces in its final sentence one of the bogeys of the West Country gentlemen of this period, a factor which seems to have inspired a sometimes jocose but constant fear.

"Certainly," Sir Lewis began in his brave account of Raleigh's journey,[1] "perjury was but a peccadillo with this man, which he shewed also towards me, when he protested that I persuaded him to go to Sir Edward Parham's father's house, which is most untrue. For Sir Walter Raleigh (having a secret intention, which afterwards appeared, to play the mountebank at Salisbury, to pretend the taking of a dose of poison, by which he deceived me first that by me he might deceive others,[2] which was a most base, unmanly part) thought Sir Edward Parham's father's house, whom he thought to be a papist, to be a fit subject for suspicion, which he meant to cast upon his friend who had so lovingly and worthily entertained us. 'For,' said Sir Walter, 'though this gentleman would not hurt me, yet there might be priests or Jesuits there that did it. For I remember, after my morning's

---

[1] Sir Lewis Stukeley's *Petition* printed in Harleian Miscellany, III, p. 67.

[2] Sir Lewis asserts in this connection that "not having as yet made him any semblance of condescent, so that I almost came upon him (Raleigh) unawares, even at the moment that he was putting on his false beard and his other disguisements, which declares he did still distrust your (Majesty's) goodness," ibid., p. 65.

draught of a cup of ale, which Sir Edward Parham offered me in the hall, I felt presently a kind of excoriation in my entrails, as if some jesuit had been my butler.' "

One characteristic is seen to recur in these depositions although they are drawn from varied sources; we meet again and again a profound distaste for, and to some extent a dread of, Popery. It is difficult to analyse this feeling which was to sink so deep into the memory of the nation. In the first place the identification of Catholicism with Spanish sympathies was firmly rooted in the popular imagination, and, now that the recollection of the war was fading, there was a widespread conviction that the Stuart government was too weak towards the national enemy. The King's secular appreciation of the Spanish monarchy was beyond the grasp of the country squires and each *rapprochement* with Spain was set down to secret Catholic sympathies. It was in this year, 1613, that Count Gondomar first came to England.

Again the memory of the Gunpowder Plot affected the nation profoundly and for some years increasingly. After all it was not a matter which admitted of defence, and the story as presented possessed that quality of reckless wrongdoing which has always been most repugnant to the English sense. Among the mercantile class the dread of Rome was fanned by the members of the foreign colonies who were predominantly Calvinist. Besides, one element in connection with the Gunpowder Plot was supremely unfortunate for the Papists. The memories of Smithfield and the Inquisition made it essential that the name of Catholic should not again be connected with powder or with fire.

To the Puritan mind Rome stood as the symbol of a sacerdotal tyranny and no attack on the practices of the more rigid members of the Anglican episcopate could be complete without a trumpet call against the Pope and a charge of Romish tendencies. Wherever Calvinism seeped, and in whatever form, it became inevitable that Rome should be the enemy. At the same time the nature of the hatred of Popery in those circles which were open to the Puritan influence was determined by the quality of Puritanism whether in its English or in its Scottish dress. For there was a lucid quality in Puritan thought, fostered by the adherence to each sentence of the Bible, strengthened by their sense of justice and condemnation and rendered adamant by meditation. They were given to abiding and unmuted antipathies and the egalitarian element in their thought structure enabled each Puritan to determine as well as any other man the "marks of the beast" and where lay "Babylon."

Besides, in many circles which were hostile to the ideas of Calvin, a profound dislike for the notion of dogma and for dogmatic utterance had now developed. A great mass of the Elizabethans had freed themselves from the conception of an Universal Church and their children were in no mood to accept an authoritarian interpretation of Christian teaching. The Laudian divines were to arouse the same hostility as Rome not by any means on account of ceremonies but because of the traditionalist and dogmatic element in their religious ethos.

Furthermore, the whole current of seventeenth-century nationalism in England was antipathetic to the very idea of a supra-national organization. In England the moral and ethical background shared by patriotism and religion; the strong feeling for the country churches and for that religious observance which was sunk into the rural life; the *pietas* of the soil and the coming of the Jacobean Bible, the dislike for exclusive and explicit doctrinal statement; perhaps even more significantly the changing pulsation and alternate predominance of ethical and religious values all combined to form in the English mind an uncomprehending distaste for the somewhat gaunt structure of Tridentine Catholicism.

The fact that the fortunes of the Catholic Church appeared to be linked so closely to the Spanish and Imperial branches of the Hapsburg dynasty excited further prejudice, nor were even experienced Englishmen capable of discerning between the ultimate intentions of the Holy See and those of the Cæsaro-Papism from whose upholders she obtained support. It was not to be expected that the insular mentality would make the effort to disentangle the elements in that struggle in which the Roman See was endeavouring to keep herself free from the great authoritarian State who stood sentinel at the Vatican and supported the Church with smothering courtesy. In England each facet of this continental life was uncongenial; the complicated diplomatic procedure; the negotiations about benefices and preferments with the courts of Southern Europe; the grave outward reverence for the Holy See; the strong presentation of the rights of the Papacy, and Bellarmine and his august phrases.

Antipathy to Rome sprung from such diverse causes was naturally to be found in different strata of the English population, and, of course, in varying degrees. Still it is remarkable how many of these factors seem to have played their part in forming the thought of Dr. Abbot, who had been promoted two years earlier to the See of Canterbury. An amalgam of the most profound anti-Roman sentiment went to the moulding of his outlook. The effect of Dr. Abbot's line of thought within the borders of the Church of England made his appointment to the primacy one of the most significant decisions of King James's reign. It seems reasonable to conclude that his installation at Lambeth delayed and at the same time made inevitable Laud's ultimate triumph.

The Archbishop was a man of no concealments and it was from the first clear that he was wedded to that semi-Calvinist interpretation of Augustinian thought from which the King himself had never wholly broken free. The new primate held the moderate Puritan position from which the reign of the late Queen would still be looked upon with favour; his

ARCHBISHOP ABBOT from a portrait in the
NATIONAL PORTRAIT GALLERY

background was the anti-sacramentalist Oxford of the mid-Elizabethan period; his preferment had been for the most part academic and he had become Master of University College at thirty-five. Personally he was a little gloomy; full of kindness; unascetic; a divine of manifest integrity with that consciousness of right which was found so often in his school of thought. It is said that he was not ambitious, but he could not divest himself of his instinctive knowledge of each rung on the ladder of success.

As a young man Abbot had won the affectionate patronage of the chancellor of his own university, Lord Treasurer Buckhurst. The latter had made him his domestic chaplain, procured for him the mastership of the senior college, and the favour from this exalted quarter had been recognized in his three elections as vice-chancellor. Abbot, now Dean of Westminster, had preached the panegyric at his patron's funeral. Then he had been sent on a mission to Scotland by the King whom he had won by his tact with the Scottish prelates; in 1609 he had been consecrated Bishop of Lichfield and Coventry; in 1610 came his translation to the See of Lincoln, and in March 1611, King James appointed him as successor to Archbishop Bancroft.

A picture in the National Portrait Gallery gives an impression of George Abbot in his episcopate; the great billowing sleeves; the small determined hands, the right resting upon a Bible; the chair with the deep embroidery on the red velvet; the cared-for whitening beard; the prelate's atmosphere of long-accustomed dignity, very taut and amenable. The face is drained and white with the effect of a transparent marble faintly flushed and there is a little sensual mouth which humanizes his too-composed figure. Thus Dr. Abbot sat at Lambeth.

The appointment seems to have been a fruit of that lassitude which would overtake the King with increasing frequency in his later years. In this instance he was sufficiently careless of English sentiment to announce that he had chosen the new primate partly on the recommendation of his Scottish friend, Dunbar. It had been expected that the choice would fall upon Lancelot Andrewes; but it seems probable that it was the Bishop of Ely's very assets, his piety and defined theological erudition, and perhaps most of all a certain delicate and permanent seriousness of approach, which made his sovereign hesitate. Possibly, since the relations with Lambeth were so important to him, the King felt that he must have there a prelate who, like Abbot, would be companionable.

Certainly the Archbishop was most friendly to all those who were not Papists or suspect through an undue insistence upon Church order. He would correspond with the foreign Protestants, con over his public lectures on the book of Jonah and take satisfaction in the Princess's marriage to the Palatine. On his desk at Lambeth in this summer of 1613 there lay the reports sent in by Lord Southampton[1] who had gone recusant-hunting in the southern shires with the Primate's keen encouragement. The details of the reliquary of crimson damask found at Warblington with the relics of Barkworth and Rigby, pseudo-martyrs, could not fail to rouse his Puritan contempt for all such "toys."

Dr. Abbot was not without his charity and his shrewd connections. His brother, Sir Maurice, had been for long a promoter of the Indian trade and the Primate himself had held a suitably heavy allotment among the adventurers to Virginia,[2] representing the more explicitly Christian angle of that sound enterprise. He was a bachelor and could be humoured, and a few years later Bacon considering on what sources he might rely for financial assistance in his experi-

---

[1] Report on correspondence sent in by the Earl of Southampton and the subsequent examinations. Cal. Ancaster MSS., p. 365.
[2] In a list of the Adventurers to Virginia the Archbishop of Canterbury is set down as holding seventy-five shares. *The Records of the Virginia Company of London*, iii, pp. 80–90.

ments had written against Archbishop Abbot's name the comment "single and glorious." His easy carriage and familiarity, no less than his unexacting respect for kingship, made him the typical prelate of the Jacobean Court, and even the unfortunate accident which clouded his political influence was singularly in keeping. In July 1621, the Archbishop shot and killed a beater when out after wildfowl with Lord Zouche at Bramshill. In any case his prestige could hardly have survived under that hard clear light which was to mark the ecclesiastical polity of Charles I.

At this date the reign of James I was half complete, Prince Henry was dead and the new heir to the throne was still a child. Coming in his early middle age from the very different conditions of his northern kingdom, James I did not scrutinize or demand exacting standards of professional conduct. It was a consequence of this relaxation and of the absence of inquiry into private standards that originality could flourish in the royal favour, and that in many respects these last years should form a decade of tolerance. In their different ways John Donne, Sir Tobie Mathew and Bishop Williams of Lincoln, could hardly have come so easily to their assured influence under another sovereign.

It is on the other hand remarkable that young George Herbert, who had been for some years in residence at Cambridge and was to become Public Orator of the University, should have looked to this Court for his preferment. Izaak Walton has stated that[1] "with King James died all Mr. Herbert's Court-hopes." It may be true or George Herbert may have changed or, in his youth and under the careful innocence of his mother's tutelage, he may have greatly mistaken the character and interest of his sovereign's circle. There was little in his precise and gentle mind soon turning to devotion which could approve of the old King's disordered luxury.

[1] Izaak Walton, *Life of Mr. George Herbert*, ed. George Saintsbury, p. 276.

Whatever the advantages of freedom the drawbacks appeared most plainly in the brief episode of Robert Ker. The fall of this favourite, now Viscount Rochester and soon to be Earl of Somerset, is so familiar a subject and has received so much concentrated attention on account of its obvious dramatic qualities that it is only necessary here to make a cursory reference to some aspects of his period of authority. This was shorter than has frequently been supposed and was masked by the continuance of the Howards in the great offices of State. Rochester's political significance can only be conceived as beginning with Salisbury's death in 1612 and it can hardly be said to have had importance until after Northampton died in April 1614.

At the same time the predominance of the Howards (if that is not too vigorous a term) did not eclipse nor was it very closely identified with Rochester's influence. Northampton would seem to have guided him, but the connection with Lord Suffolk, who became Lord Treasurer in 1614, was much less close. Their names were, however, to become associated in the public mind through the Essex Divorce, a political manœuvre occupying the summer of 1613, by which Lord Suffolk's daughter, the Countess of Essex was set free to marry the favourite. It appears rather to have been a question of two independent parties, neither of them vitally effective in the political sphere, acting in a temporary alliance. The Howards utilized the influence of a favourite whom they did not create and in whose ultimate fall they were not immediately involved.

Sir Thomas Overbury seems to have acted as Rochester's mentor, but they quarrelled early in 1613, and in April of that year Overbury was arrested. He died in the Tower in the following September, and in October 1615 the favourite, now Earl of Somerset, was accused of poisoning him. He and his wife were found guilty in the next spring. Already in August 1614, the young man who was to become the unique object of the King's affection was presented to his sovereign. These dates are introduced to indicate the narrow limits within which such power as Robert Ker possessed could find exercise. It was an influence never untrammelled and hardly possessed of direction, conditioned by Overbury in its earlier stages and by the Howards at every point. Even the illusion of stability was not conveyed, while the years surged with *epithalamia*.

There was Somerset's own wedding and the King's daughter's marriage with the Elector Palatine. This introduces another facet of that winter of 1613. After the survey of the country life some account of the background of the Princess's wedding will suggest the atmosphere of the English Court.

The warrant to the Great Wardrobe on the occasion of these celebrations gives the impression of lavish uncontrolled expenditure illumined by an interest in a neat invention. From the white baize "masking sutes" and Orpheus in "his antique coate armour" and Entheus and Prometheus in their robes and mantles, making their entrances from behind the holland curtains, attention was drawn to the stars "which mouved in an exceeding strange and delightful manner." "I suppose," runs a contemporary account,[1] "fewe haue ever seene more neat artifice than Master Innigoe Jones shewed in continuing their Motion, who in all the rest of the workmanship which belong's to the whole invention shewed extraordinarie industrie and skill."

In the bride chamber there were hangings embroidered with Venetian gold twist and gold chain lace, and coloured Naples silk, and curtains of yellow Spanish silk. There was varied detail in the great procession, the Florence cloth of silver for the bride-maidens, the pages with gold-edged roses on their shoulders and doublets of cloth of gold and tawny hose, and

---

[1] All these details are from British Museum Add. in MS. 5751 printed *Archæologia*, vol. xxvi, pp. 380–91.

the ladies with their farthingales of taffeta and damask "with wire and silke to them." An exact precedence is reflected in the material and its ornament, the fine black cloth for teachers and the French grey for footmen, the black wrought velvet for the Queen's physician, the livery cloaks of incarnadine French plush, the outfits of the sarcenet for the coachmen and the black Perpetuana "for a madman's sute." Mr. Inigo Jones walked in a retired position in a broad cloth gown with "furr of budge."

The crown jewels were brought forth on these occasions, "the faire great pearle pendante called the Bretherin, the Portugall Dyamond and the great table diamond sett in gould called the Mirror of France."[1] And all this appealed to the King, the jewellery and the new-fashioned ropes of pearls, as he moved forward with the light falling on his black velvet hatband on which shone twenty-five diamonds set in the Spanish manner in buttons of gold. King James was the last English sovereign to love such a riot, a legacy from the Elizabethans. He shambled on contented and insolvent, the ideal royal patron for Ben Jonson; but there were always the Puritans.

Among those who composed *epithalamia* on this occasion was Mr. Donne, not yet in holy orders and living semi-permanently at Drury House with Sir Robert Drury. At this time John Donne, a deeply sensitive man, already middle-aged and with many children, was only gradually finding his way forward after the setbacks that he had encountered once his imprudent marriage had led to his expulsion from Lord Ellesmere's service. His poems were still in manuscript and he had won the King's favour with the *Pseudo-Martyr*; he would soon join the royal chaplains.

It was still some years before Donne was to be discovered as a great preacher and his influence in the moulding of

[1] A detailed inventory of that section of the jewels which was in constant use in 1623 and noting such matters as which of the diamond hatbands had been Prince Henry's is printed in *Archæologia*, vol. xxi, pp. 151-4.

Anglican opinion must be discussed at a later stage. For the
moment it is sufficient to note that a hampering sensitiveness,
from which he never freed himself, served to impede his
progress.   There was in his mind an absence of fanaticism
and a hesitant and questioning sincerity.   In addition he
possessed an appreciation of verbal magnificence and of
grand conceptions and a pliability in inessentials.   These,
indeed, were qualities likely to appeal to his royal master.
Reading Spanish fluently and long accustomed to studying
divinity, Donne seems to have been without desire for the
Roman Church of his childhood and with an entire detachment from the Puritan values.   In many ways he was well-
suited to be the King's interpreter when the latter allowed his
mind to range upon religious subjects.

There were, however, aspects of his mental approach into
which his sovereign could not enter such as that exposed in
the agonized, half-sceptic balance of the XVIIIth Divine
Poem. But it is perhaps the third portion of *A Hymne to
God the Father* which gives the clearest impression of this
divergence.

> "I have a sinne of feare, that when I have spunne
>   My last thred, I shall perish on the shore;
> Sweare by thyselfe, that at my death thy sonne
>   Shall shine as he shines now, and heretofore;
> And, having done that, Thou hast done,
>   I feare no more."

These, surely, are not conceptions which were familiar
to King James whose life moved in a more complacent
setting and was attuned to a somewhat unduly convinced
assurance of Divine protection. Again, Dr. Donne's outlook
was deeply separate from that of his wealthy contemporaries
among whom he had with some difficulty pitched his tent,
Inevitably his concentration on worldly advancement had
betrayed him. Yet alone, and in the realms of the spirit,
he would attempt with a tortured candour to keep the fine

web of his thought cleared from his scepticism and then penetrate towards his difficult God.

It is a corollary to such a standpoint that he should prove to be indifferent to Bacon and in general matters his tentative and doubt-swept mind would hardly have been likely to accept Sir Francis' assurance. Yet, for the carving out of his career, Donne was obliged to depend upon some patron although he was without the toughness which is needed by those who must haul themselves up rung by rung. A letter which he wrote in 1612 on hearing a false report of the death of Bacon's friend, Tobie Mathew, gives an impression of that over-delicate perception which was so out of place in his class and generation.

"You have lost," ran Donne's letter to Sir Francis, "a gentleman whom, in good faith, I ever loved well, out of those things which were within my comprehension which were his wit and applicableness; but, since his death, I hear of one exercise of his judgment which I knew not before, which is that he loved not me. This is Mr. Mathew." Such sensitiveness, which at times approached the morbid, was rare in Donne's *milieu*; but a man who suffers from this frame of mind must always rely on others for his promotion.

It is characteristic of the Jacobean Age that so many distinguished men were first brought forward through dependence on a very few great families. The Cecils naturally were responsible for the largest group of those actually concerned with public life; but Ellesmere had had Donne for his secretary and the future Bishop Williams for his private chaplain. And Ellesmere's son was to play his part in Milton's history. The first Earl of Dorset had been Abbot's patron and now his grandsons, the third and fourth Earls were to prove John Donne's protectors. After his ordination they befriended him and, like the Archbishop of Canterbury before him, he went down to Knole to the dignity of that private chapel. It was a fostering and appraising friendship of the kind which

SIR EDWARD SACKVILLE from a portrait by Daniel Mytens
in the possession of MARGARET, COUNTESS OF SUFFOLK and
BERKSHIRE

his sheltered talent called for, and Edward Sackville was to give him the living of St. Dunstan-in-theWest.

At this stage it is, perhaps, worth considering the ramifications of the Sackville patronage which was so typical of one aspect of that period, heedless, catholic, extravagant and almost non-political. The situation of Knole on the slopes south of Sevenoaks and so close to the stream of London life was well suited to its exercise. Possibly it is sufficiently accurate to detect in Knole the beginning of that influence in English life which was to be exercised by the great house and its now gathering traditions; the carefully graded hospitality; the chapel sealed in its Erastian calm; the ordered ceremony.

It was typical of such an influence that it touched ambassadors rather than the reigning king and that it derived its independence, in part at least, from its complete dissociation from the cruder phases of political manœuvre. None of the inheritors of Knole under the Stuarts were really close either to the sovereign's intimacy or to the machinery of government. Here, unswayed by the prepossessions which would lead the Russells and their like into opposition to the Crown, they maintained the loyalty of an inviolable privilege. One of the State rooms at Knole very well suggests this spirit with its great gilded bed and the gold and green moulded fittings and the thick sage Genoa velvet. Its very name the bedchamber of the Ambassador of Venice, seems to suggest the characteristic of a luxury without ulterior motive.

Something must be said about the Sackville family, and their reactions to the current controversies. The first Earl of Dorset had been Catholic in his younger days, then for decades Elizabethan and in his last years rather astringently Puritan within the framework of the English Church. His political good sense had been exacerbated by the obstinate recusancy of his daughter-in-law, Lady Margaret Sackville, the elder Arundel's sister. With his grandsons the family

type had been matured, personally reckless, generous, a little
aloof, careful neither to offend nor to solicit a minister,
politically prudent, A King's Friend. They were joint lords
lieutenant of Sussex, stewards of the honours of Aquila and
Pevensey, masters of Ashdown Forest; very rooted and
confident. It is from this period in the second decade of the
century that the Gheraerdts portrait of the third Earl dates,
the tall bearded figure with the hat with the cream white
feather and the great gold pompons on his shoes, while
behind him lies the lightness of the stone gallery and the
stone garlands around the coat of arms.

But the younger son of the first Earl, Thomas Sackville,
was a Catholic living at this time in Padua and there he met,
at Santa Guistina, Dom Augustine Baker, who was perhaps
as remote from the spirit of King James's Court as any of
that sovereign's subjects. This convert from the Welsh
Marches was almost without contact with his contemporaries
save for those who were members of his Order or bound to
it by friendship. Fr. Baker's life was encased within a
Benedictine tradition which he had recently attempted to
absorb. He possessed a concentration upon the various
doctrines of spirituality; a personality most engaging,
opinionated, rather querulous; a detachment from other
values than those of prayer. His interests were bounded by
the impact of the Tridentine generations on the earlier streams
of spiritual teaching and experience. His withdrawn calm
was only disturbed by the surface friction of a monastic
community and by the divergent methods of his brethren
in guiding those convents of nuns which were the satellites
of the English Congregation.

In 1619, Fr. Baker lodged with Mr. Sackville in his house
in London. The protection of the Dorsets' family roof tree
thus sheltered Archbishop Abbot and John Donne, and the
author of *Sancta Sophia*.

One characteristic of this English patronage was the

remoteness of the life of the patrons from that of those whom they maintained. Thomas Sackville, for instance, was so little affected by Fr. Baker that he slipped away from Catholicism altogether. The third Earl of Dorset lived for the playing-tables and his wife moved in an agony of law-suits. In this case the portrait at Knole gives a very clear impression; Anne Lady Dorset still very young with an attitude carefully composed, with dark brown hair and a pearl necklace and three roses in a bowl beside her. It is easy to imagine her sitting at the table with its green-fringed cloth, finishing her long cushion of Irish stitch as she listened to her attendants reading Montaigne's essays.[1] The quiet manner, alien to all that we know of her history, has been stressed by Mytens in his picture. One is compelled to believe that she was familiar with the conception, later so powerful, of the necessity of performing the minor duties of her state.

Beyond the relationships which centred about such a house as Knole there stretched the literary affiliations of this period in a criss-cross of changing patronage. As a rule the contact was essentially monetary but frequently disguised by hospitality. It was only the dependent who had a vital interest in the relationship and in consequence the claims of the great families on an especial author waned and waxed rather than conflicted. The Dorsets and Lady Bedford and the Haringtons and, on a lower financial level, Sir Henry Goodere and the Herberts and in Scotland Drummond of Hawthornden were among those principally involved as literary patrons at this date. Michael Drayton's position is, perhaps, typical of that of the more fortunately placed writers who depended on support of this nature.

Down in Warwickshire, Mr. Drayton with his little firmament of patrons, published in this year 1613 the first part

---

[1] These details from her MS. diary come from a slightly later date, November 1616.

of his *Poly-Olbion*, a work which was by far too encyclopædic
to come forth in later times, a chorographical, historical and
geographical account of England, etc. The Elizabethans had
left behind them a desire for length and numbers as is clear
in the train of prefaces to Coryatt's *Crudities*. The pursuit
of a trail of complex allusions remained in fashion and the
legend still subsisted that authors composed their works
solely for their friends' private pleasure.

A study of *The Owl* makes it clear that some such assumption was supposed to underlie Drayton's relations with his
patrons. Certainly it seems improbable that any contemporary, who was out of touch with the politics of favouritism,
could ever have successfully understood *The Owl* or ploughed
past the fauna in that privileged jungle. There is in the
longueurs of these *romans à clef*, a sharp contrast to th
spirit of the succeeding generations and it is possible that
this tendency was preserved by the presence of a sovereign
who was prepared to be lengthily and elaborately amused.
The tone of these grandiose works was too magniloquent for
acerbity and, in general, letters tended to reflect that un-
energetic peace which the King had succeeded in importing
into the main lines of the nation's life.

In these quiet years the administration was almost without
an overt opposition except for the occasional criticism of
financial courses. Under one aspect the appointment of
Archbishop Abbot had been prudent for he had calmed the
moderate Puritans. Fairly recently a small community of
Separatists had crossed from the eastern Midlands and East
Anglia first to Amsterdam and then to Leyden; a move which
appeared both suitable and insignificant. They were to
provide the company of the *Speedwell* and the *Mayflower*.
Meanwhile a spirit of accommodation marked those of a
Puritan temper who remained in office.

In the next winter and in the following spring, the King
came to Cambridge on state visits. Phineas Fletcher wrote

Sicilides in his honour and showed the loyal adherence of the men of strict views at the high tables. Emmanuel College, which had been founded thirty years earlier to keep a guard on prelacy, was prepared to enter into the mood of a sovereign who had Dr. Abbot as his archbishop, and the words of the Cambridge Madrigal would satisfy any peace-maker.

> "But th' pure House of Emanuel
> Would not be like proud Jesabel,
> Nor shew herself before the King
> An hypocrite or painted thing."

What words could better suggest such a delightful lightness of touch in controversy? In another way, too, this verse is characteristic of the period. Unlike his younger son, King James I was not afraid of flippancy.

A framework of dates may help to fix this period of the mid-reign. The men who had been young at the accession had now matured. Southampton, Donne, Inigo Jones, Carleton and Ben Jonson had been born in 1572-3 and were now forty; Sir David Murray, Michael Drayton, Goodere and Sir Henry Wotton rather older. These men would miss their tide with any other sovereign. Dr. Williams, who was thirty-one, and Sir Edward Herbert, who was thirty, although younger in point of age had sprung from the same background. They were linked with the last years of James I and belonged essentially to that period of transition. Prince Charles was now only thirteen, but as the years passed it was not difficult to detect that moral severity which encased him and was to prove so disenchanting to the free-spoken courtiers of his father's day. Only one of the elder men was to penetrate the barrier of the generations and pierce the reserve of their future king. He, too, had been born in 1573 and had waited long and without patience; he was the antithesis of all that the old King enjoyed; his name was Laud.

CHAPTER VII

VILLIERS AND BACON

SUDDEN favour has very seldom fallen to the lot of those who have come to exercise supreme political power in England. To this rule the career of the young English squire who was to become successively Sir George Villiers, Viscount Villiers, then Earl, Marquis and Duke of Buckingham, forms no exception. His introduction to the inner life of the Court was carefully planned, but his rise was gradual and his favour for some time appeared precarious. In the earlier stages of his career he was aided and indeed overshadowed by powerful backers. For more than two years after his introduction to the King, his influence was not predominant either in appearance or in fact. Although he was supported by sections unfriendly to the Howards, Villiers' rise to power was not inconsistent with their continuance in office and the Treasury and Admiralty remained in their hands. For so young a man and of a spirit so adventurous, Buckingham moved very quietly to his great place. There was nothing cataclysmic about Buckingham's career except his end.

It seems to have been during the summer progress of 1614, and according to Dugdale's tradition at Apethorpe in August of that year, that George Villiers was first presented to his sovereign. He was then twenty-two years of age, the portionless younger son of a Leicestershire knight now dead. Sir George Villiers, the father, a substantial squire of sound family, had lived at the manor house of Brooksby near the turnpike road, nine miles from Leicester and six from

Melton Mowbray. He had held the four manors of Brooksby Howby, Goadby and Marwood, all in his native county and this compact property had passed to his eldest son. His widow, who was devoted to her son George, had the dower house of Goadby for life. She was by birth a Beaumont of Cole Orton and a distant cousin of her husband's. A will proved in 1559 gives the property of the Villiers of Brooksby at that date, as rather more than three thousand five hundred acres. They had held for some generations the presentation to the advowsons of the churches of Brooksby and Howby; they were definitely Anglican and without any trace of recusancy in their male line.

George Villiers was young, courageous and open minded, but it is perhaps unlikely that his political influence would have developed had the now ageing King not wished to teach his new disciple and then later on desired to raise to power the "scholar"[1] whom he had moulded. There had been no serious attempt to teach Ker, but the character of Villiers' training, a superficial knowledge of France[2] based on a very ordinary English grounding, made him an excellent subject for the exercise of the King's wisdom. A convincing impression of this state of affairs is conveyed in Sir Henry Wotton's *Short view of the life and death of George Villiers, Duke of Buckingham*. In this case Wotton's own elaborate education particularly fitted him for such descriptive work. "He was nurtured," he begins in reference to the favourite,[3] "where he had been born, in his first rudiments, till the years of ten; and, from thence, sent to Billisdon school in the same county, where he was taught the principles of musick, and other slight literature, till the thirteenth of his age; at which

[1] In 1623 the King justified Buckingham in Parliament. "First, because he being my Disciple and Scholar, he may be assured I will trust his own Relation," printed in Rushworth, *Historical Collections*, i, p. 127.

[2] In the days of his greatness Buckingham received a letter from Charles Maupas, Bishop of Blois who reminded him of his long stay in the town and offered him a *Grammaire et Syntaxe de la Langue Française*. Cal. Drummond Moray MSS., p. 116.

[3] Wotton's *Short View* printed in the Harleian Miscellany, viii, p. 614.

time his father died." Considering that Villiers was so pliant and so fresh, it is not surprising that in time the King resolved in Wotton's words "to make him a masterpiece, and to mould him, as it were, platonically to his own idea."[1]

In the public career of the new favourite there were four distinct stages; first, the eighteen months between his knighthood and reception into the Bedchamber in April 1615,[2] and his creation as Earl of Buckingham on 1 January, 1617; then the period of assured but not undisputed ascendancy which lasted until the beginning of the Spanish journey early in 1623; then the eighteen months between the Duke of Buckingham's return to England in October 1623, and the death of James I in April 1625; finally, the three years of King Charles' reign until the Duke's assassination. The first of these periods was marked by the growth of a hesitant and tentative influence, accommodating and friendly, an increasing affection on the part of the King and hostility from the Prince of Wales. After 1617 the position was consolidated and Prince Charles had been converted; during the last months of the old King's life Buckingham's ascendancy was complete owing to the hold which he now possessed upon the Prince and his sovereign's fatigue and weakness; in the reign of Charles I the Duke was grimly impregnable. It was this last factor which was responsible for the profound bitterness with which the mass of the peers, no less than the great squires, came to regard the favourite who had been at first so easy and accessible. Slowly they realized that they could *never* remove him.

[1] Wotton's *Short View* printed in the Harleian Miscellany, viii, p. 614.
[2] Mr. George Villiers was sworn a Gentleman of the Bedchamber on 23 April, 1615, and knighted the next day at the Queen's palace, Somerset House. A letter from Sir Thomas Somerset dated at London on 12 December, 1614, and preserved among the State Papers and Correspondence of Sir Thomas Edmondes, gives an indication of the approach of this favour. "Great speech there is of a new favorett (viz. George Villiers) and that he should be sworne of the bedchamber ere long; for my part when it is done I will beleave it," Stowe MSS., vol. 175 (24), f. 128.

It is, perhaps, as well at this stage to consider the difficult question of the character of George Villiers' relations with his two sovereigns. The matter must remain unsettled and will depend ultimately on a balance of probabilities, but it has significance since it affects not only the characters of the three principals, but also in a lesser degree the reputation of all those who were close satellites of the favourite's rule. The case against Buckingham is stated in its most reputable form by that sober Parliamentarian chronicler, Sir Simonds D'Ewes. "The King's Majesty," he wrote in his auto-biography in regard to the new favourite,[1] "having at that time fixed his eyes upon the delicate personage and features of Mr. George Villiers." Seeing him in after years at Cambridge with this same prejudice, D'Ewes sets down the impression which the then Duke of Buckingham made upon him. "I saw," he writes,[2] "everything in him full of delicacy and handsome features; yea, his hands and face seemed to me, especially, effeminate and curious."

The King at the time of their first meeting was forty-eight and there is no doubt of the profound and lasting character of the affection which seized him, not in the first months of their acquaintance, but certainly during his fiftieth year. Yet there is reason to suppose that his attitude towards his *protégé* in this the last period of his life, was marked by paternalism. In the first place the Queen, who was jealous of Ker, never withdrew her favour from Villiers. Again any other theory of their relationship would seem most improbable in the light of the romantic friendship which the restrained and isolated Prince was soon to feel for the favoured courtier. Finally, a letter written to Sir George Villiers in December 1615 by the Archbishop of Canterbury, seems to support the same contention. "My George," wrote the Archbishop to the young man for whose new position he

[1] *Autobiography of Sir Simonds D'Ewes*, i, p. 69.
[2] ibid., i, p. 167.

was largely responsible,[1] " be wary that, at no man's instance, you press him (the King) with many suits, because they are not your friends who urge these things upon you, but have private ends of their own, which are not fit for you. So, praying God to bless you, I rest. Your loving father, G. Cant." All that is known to us of the characters of the Queen, Prince Charles and Archbishop Abbot, makes it simpler to suppose that George Villiers' relations with his royal protector were technically innocent. This last consideration would however have proved wholly irrelevant to those most closely connected with King James's Court. Certainly Villiers amply carried out the duty which his supporters required of him, for he completed the disintegration of the King's affection for Robert Ker and he filled the void thus created by himself absorbing his weary master's mind and leisure. It was evidently intended that he should not rule the King, but should occupy him.

In these days Villiers was a great receiver of advice. But it was just because he was in his early twenties so unformed and transparent, in fact so malleable, that he was able to accept with such completeness the Stuart doctrine with which the old King impregnated his unsubtle mind.

The feeling against the Scots had been gathering strength and Ker's position, which had been gradually weakening, was soon to be made untenable by the outbreak of the scandal of Sir Thomas Overbury's death. In consequence there were several different political circles whose members were ready to welcome and to teach an English favourite. The administration was in slack water; Lord Chancellor Ellesmere was very aged and his health was failing, but he still clung to office; the Treasury moved slowly under Suffolk; the work of the Secretariat of State was now disorganized. After Salisbury's death the King had nominally taken this office

---

[1] Letter dated 10 December, 1615, and printed in Bishop Goodman's *Memoirs*, ii, pp. 160-1.

into his own hands and the work was in arrears.[1] Since
Northampton died there had been no minister of rank and
experience who was able to control the management of
home affairs. The appearance of Villiers thus synchronized
with the coming to power of men who might use him.

Two full Secretaries of State, Sir Ralph Winwood and
Sir Thomas Lake, were appointed about this time.[2] The
heads of the great families of the last generation, Pembroke
and his brother Montgomery, Derby, Dorset and Edward
Sackville were readier to play an active part than they had
been during Ker's brief interlude. In the wings the rich
peers waited prepared to receive the offices which the
Howards held, when King James should tire of that tenacious
family. It seems likely, as an historian of the seventeenth
century in England has recently pointed out,[3] that the
Overbury trial with all its sordid detail, the love philtres and
the trafficking and the blackening poisoned tarts, had
aroused a mood of the most profound disgust. A cordial
transient friendliness surrounded the man who could supplant the Earl of Somerset and his entourage. The Archbishop of Canterbury began to play his role, and even Queen
Anne moved out towards the foreground. But much more
significant than any Court manœuvre was the presence of
Sir Francis Bacon rising steadily to the office of Lord
Chancellor. And, together with Sir Ralph Winwood and the
King himself, Bacon now joined the ranks of those instructors
who were prepared to mould and utilize the young Sir George
Villiers.

A great mass of material has been published dealing with
the different aspects of Bacon's life and work. In con-

---

[1] Ker, then Viscount Rochester, had been acting Secretary for a period.
The much less considerable office of second Secretary had been held by
Sir John Herbert from 1593 until his death in 1614. He had been wholly
overshadowed by Lord Salisbury.
[2] Winwood was appointed in 1614 and Lake two years later on the
liquidation of Ker's responsibilities.
[3] Godfrey Davies in *The Early Stuarts*, p. 19.

sequence it is scarcely profitable to go over once again this trodden snow. It is necessary to note some elements in his political position and to attempt to gauge the relationship in which the great man stood to the Court factions of his later years. Since 1613 Sir Francis Bacon had held the attorney generalship, and once this initial advantage had been gained, his smooth progress could almost be forecast. Together with his rival Sir Edward Coke and his enemy Sir Walter Raleigh, Bacon represented the last phases of the Elizabethan Age. His spirit of magnificence, the very conscious magnanimity and that high learning, which he wore with as little concealment as a diamond, were not qualities calculated to ease his personal relations with his colleagues. In the long series of his letters there is no touch of the ordinary and he never possessed that gift of being commonplace which was so essential for the reassurance of his equals in high politics. That lack of intimacy, which is so marked a feature of all his correspondence that has a direct political bearing, was the cause rather than the effect of his protracted disappointments. As the son of Lord Keeper Bacon and the nephew of Burghley, he was too close to the seat of power to prove a congenial colleague for those lawyers who were less well placed. He extended to all men that mixture of irony and didactic metaphor which was only relished by his private friends. Above all he never made explicit compacts. Certainly in the political field Sir Francis Bacon was an uncomfortable man. His manner was too grand for this later time and few men could bear the sudden irony or his great swinging and didactic paragraphs.

The irony was probably responsible for that chilled friendship with which King James continued to regard him, and it can hardly be supposed that Villiers found his lesson palatable. "You are now the King's Favourite," wrote Bacon, "remember well the great trust you have undertaken. You are as a continual sentinel, always to stand upon your watch to give him true intelligence. If you flatter him you betray him. Kings must be answerable to God Almighty (to whom they are but vassals) for their actions, and their negligent omissions. But the Ministers to Kings, whose eyes, ears and hands they are, must be answerable to God and man for the breach of their duties, in violation of their trusts whereby they betray them." And then again Bacon would remind King James and Villiers of his devotion to the Crown, a devotion which appeared to render the Attorney General almost painfully indispensable. "Nevertheless I walk in *via regia*," he wrote to Viscount Villiers.[1] "I rest," he then concluded, "your Lordships trew and most devoted servant Fr. Bacon." The drift of their correspondence shows that Villiers remained grateful, but it is difficult to imagine that he was at ease.

Bacon's profound experience and the panoply of his learning were singularly daunting, and even his relaxations and the pleasures with which he would refresh his most poised mind, were beyond the range both of the favourite and of his royal master. The Attorney-General was at no pains to conceal his sensitiveness and his delicate perceptions, nor their corollary of intolerance. It was not encouraging to hear of the great sweep of his inquiries, the seed plot of the *Novum Organum*, that only too open effort, "to bring in estimation Philosophy or Universality name and thing."

In this connection it may be noted that the increasingly accurate definition of Bacon's position in the development of science, makes it easier to understand the resounding nature of his public fame. In a masterly essay in *Seventeenth Century Studies presented to Sir Herbert Grierson*, Dr. Rudolf Metz shows how much more strongly Bacon was in fact imprisoned in the universal ideology of Aristotelian thought than has

---

[1] Letter from Sir Francis Bacon to Viscount Villiers, dated 14 October, presumably in the year 1616. Cal. Drummond Moray MSS., p. 99.

previously been supposed. "He was not," writes Dr. Metz,[1] "acquainted with the mathematical nature of modern science like Aristotle and the scholasticism and medieval alchemy which developed from him, he was acquainted only with things and their qualities." It was just this factor, however, which contributed to the contemporary recognition of his tremendous stature, and he had the immensity of the familiar.

The very name of Verulamius seems to preclude the possibility of patient and unrequited labour, and of that form of quiet endeavour which in the next reign was to characterize the work of William Harvey. As a figure of the end of the high Renaissance he was incapable of curbing his display. His subtle vital energy was bent upon the attainment of public ends and in the realm of knowledge it was his lucid and unquestioning purpose to make all things manifest. Here again Dr. Metz has an admirable comment. "Typical Renaissance traits in Bacon's intellect," he continues,[2] "are his inordinate scientific ambition, his indomitable zest for life, for organizing and reforming, his disregard of tradition and lack of historical sense, the new attitude to life which seeks expression throughout his work, his Utopian schemes, his rhetorical gestures, his Machiavellism, his many-sided interests and activities, his Utilitarianism, the restlessness of his life. . . . Like almost all Renaissance thinkers, he was inspired with the Faustian urge. In this context may be mentioned one of the most significant and impressive elements of his doctrine; whose motto is 'Knowledge is power,' and its aim the *regnum hominis.*"

This builds up a picture of an age which was passing away, and it seems unlikely that the young cavaliers in their simplicity could have been at home with this Faustian urge. It is perhaps not over fanciful to suggest that in this transition age the figure of Bacon hung in the sky like a Parnassus with

[1] *Seventeenth-Century Studies presented to Sir Herbert Grierson.* Oxford University Press, 1937, p. 28.
[2] ibid., pp. 29–30.

all the cloud effects of a Jacobean masque and the "glory" of the late Elizabethans. He had little in common with Harvey's methods and nothing of that cool thought which was to mark the early Carolines and the world of Chillingworth and Falkland. The new generation was to be in its wide acceptances theological; but Bacon's mind was freed from the element of devotion. In addition it was inevitable that the fierce and the unsophisticated should alike repel him and that in consequence he could never really gain the King's young friends, not even Villiers.

Besides, all the detail of Bacon's private life was unaffected by that recognition of the conventional which had been the saving of his cousin Salisbury. His tastes were so careful and his courtiers intellectual. "Mr. Thomas Hobbes," relates Aubrey in a familiar passage,[1] "was beloved by his lordship, who was wont to have him walke with him in his delicate groves, when he did meditate: and when a notion darted into his minde, Mr. Hobbes was presently to write it downe." Before him was "the stately walke of trees,"[2] planted with elm and hornbeam and Spanish ash and cervices, that led to his country house at Gorhambury where the marble statues of the Claudian Emperors looked south across that tamed and undulating landscape. In the coppices and other boscages there were paths "most ingeniously designed:[3] at severall good views were erected elegant summer houses well built of Roman architecture."

At every meal Bacon is said to have had his table strewn with sweet herbs and flowers and "musique in the next room, when he meditated" and as he sat designing the islands in his garden with their tritons and the musk roses. He found it difficult to bear the smell of neats-leather; he disliked the small beer in Gray's Inn Hall; he was lavish and magnificent. Later when he became Lord Chancellor, he maintained a great

[1] John Aubrey, *Brief Lives*, i, p. 70. Aubrey was born in 1626, but most of his observations regarding Bacon can be confirmed from earlier sources.
[2] ibid., i, p. 79.　　　　[3] ibid., i, p. 83.

household. But there was always a certain aloofness, a concentration, according to report,[1] on his ganymedes and favourites and a perpetual readiness to enter into such large discourses as that on "the benefit of irrigation . . . because of the nitre in the air and the universall spirit of the world." It was, perhaps, the recurrent meditations which proved most disconcerting to young George Villiers and his contemporaries. "In a coppice wood,"[2] declared Aubrey, "his lordship much meditated, his servant, Mr. Bushell, attending him with his pen and ink-horn to sett downe his present notions."

It must have been a great contrast for the favourite to return to the cheerful tone of the King's instructions. The mood of the sovereign's early treatise, the *Basilikon Doron*, was very different from Sir F. Bacon's work; it was straightforward and most easily apprehended. One passage of this book, which had been composed in Scotland for Prince Henry's guidance in his government, was particularly appropriate in this connection. "In your language," wrote the King,[3] "be plaine, honest, naturall, comely, cleane, short and sententious, eschewing both the extremities, as well as not using any rusticall corrupt leide, as booke-language, and pen and ink-horne termes."

Much of King James's success with those of his English circle who came in close contact with him depended upon this friendly, rough, jocose approach. A sentence from the *Basilikon Doron* will make this clear. "And the Craftesmen thinke," wrote the King,[4] and it is probably the personal touches in these treatises that can be most safely attributed to his own pen, "we should be content with their worke, how bad and deare soeuer it be: and if they in any thing be

---

[1] According to Aubrey, ibid., i, p. 71.   [2] ibid., i, p. 83.
[3] *Basilikon Doron* printed in the Political Works of James I, Harvard University Press, 1918, i, p. 46; the most accessible edition. It is interesting to note that King James warns his son to avoid drunkenness and "mignard and affoeminate termes," ibid., pp. 44-6.
[4] *Basilikon Doron*, pp. 22-7.

controlled up goeth the blew-blanket." Another passage
from a speech made in the Court of Star Chamber twenty
years later in the early days of Villiers' favour bears out the
same impression. "Another sort," the King had been speaking of the use of ale-houses for receiving stolen deer,[1] "are
a kind of Alehouses, which are houses of haunt and receipt
for debaushed rogues and vagabonds, and idle sturdie
fellows; and these are not properly Ale-houses, but base
victuallers, such as haue nothing else to liue by, but keeping
houses of receipt for such kinde of customers. I haue discovered a strange packe of late, That within tenne or twelue
miles of London, there are ten or twelue persons that liue
in spight of mee, going with Pistols, and walking up and
downe from harbour to harbour killing my Deere, and so
shift from hold to hold that they cannot be apprehended.
For Rogues, you have many good Acts of Parliament." Thus
easily he conveyed to Buckingham his stores of knowledge.

These years were very peaceful, for Raleigh had not yet
set out on his last voyage and the Spanish ambassador,
Count Gondomar (so courteously acceptable to King James)
had not at this date roused the public hatred. There was
peace in Europe and the Thirty Years' War had not begun.
The favourite forged forward constantly, very open and
secure. As far as domestic customs were concerned this was
the high period of the Jacobean masque, those vast Court
entertainments which were especially characteristic of the
reign. Their scene, from the staging of Ben Jonson's *Black-
ness* in 1605, was usually the old Banqueting House in
Whitehall until it was destroyed by fire. *Tethys' Festival* had
been staged in 1610, Ben Jonson's *Oberon* in 1611, while,
apart from the festivities for the Palatine marriage in 1613,
there had been at least two masques produced in each
succeeding year. To the King these were especially grateful

---

[1] *A Speach in the Starre-Chamber*, 20 June, 1616, Political Works of
James I, i, p. 342.

as he sat on his chair of estate beneath the canopy, divided from the guests by palisades, with the intricacies of the wooden machinery to please him, and the details copied from the Court of Mantua and the Italian *intermezzi* and the new proscenium arch which Inigo Jones had introduced to the stage fixtures. These masques were to grow in elaboration for the sovereign's pleasure, and in some way seem especially to belong to the carefree post-Cecilian decade.

The costume of the courtiers, too, carried with it more extravagance than in King James's earlier period; the shoes with their silk roses; the elaborately slashed and hanging sleeves; the wide paned breeches. The whisk had now come into fashion, that wired-out collar with its elaborate lace edging as seen in the full length of Buckingham. Court dress had reached those final stages of elaboration, the complex detail of the worked silk flowers upon the cloak, the pattern repeated on the shaped doublets and the turned back sleeves, the lace above the over cuffs and the great sewn jewels which shine in the two Sackville pictures. In a portrait of Lady Morton, the wife of a contemporary Dorset squire, there is clearly visible a black silk finger band carried as a distinctive detail. In that still world there seemed no limit to the inventiveness of ornament. The sumptuous plainness of the later Vandyck era and the high boots of the Cavaliers were far away.

Even the trouble in these quiet years was often to prove illusory. Thus an opinion put about at the end of 1616 to the effect that Villiers was declining in the King's favour and that Lord Mordaunt was likely to succeed him, proved to be without foundation. In the following March Bacon became Lord Keeper and was soon raised to the chancellorship and to the peerage as Lord Verulam. And always the King instructed his "disciple," and Secretary Winwood would explain the simpler aphorisms of the foreign policy.

There is a danger that any selection of quotations on this

subject may seem to over-simplify the situation, but the information which the Secretary appears to have imparted was certainly of a devastatingly elementary character. "The howse of Austria," he declared,[1] "for many yeares together interchangeably hath married in their own tribe." On other occasions he would enter into further detail sending Buckingham a copy of a letter written in Italian by the Spanish viceroy of Naples to the Pope against the Venetians and justifying the Spaniards' entry into the Gulf of Venice. "I feare," wrote Winwood,[2] "the Insolencye of thys letter will make hys Majestye, when he shall reade yt, lose all patience." Few men realized how strong was the hold which the favourite had obtained upon his master. He was now laying the foundations of his knowledge of home politics and gathering that insular and wholly inadequate impression of foreign governments which was the only equipment in this field which ever came to him.

In these early days there was a generous courtesy in Villiers' approach which smoothed his ways for him. He was mindful of rank[3] and the consciousness of power had not yet come to destroy his youthful gratitude. Political office had not fallen to him and he had thus the power to ask without the responsibility for refusal. Jealousy was hardly yet aroused. He was fortunate and contented and had undermined no man's position; so that even the Howards were still secure in their entrenchments. Positions of honour rather than of profit, like the lord lieutenantcy of Buckingham, came to him almost unasked.[4] The King gave him a

[1] Letter from Secretary Winwood to the Earl of Buckingham, dated 29 July, 1617. Cal. Drummond Moray MSS., p. 102.
[2] Letter from the same to the same, dated 22 May, 1617, ibid., p. 100.
[3] Letter of Sir George Villiers to Lord Howard de Walden, dated at Newmarket, 4 February, 1616. "The notice your Lordship takes of my service done to your sister (Lady Essex) is beyond my meritt." *Fortescue Papers* (printed by the Camden Society, 1871), p. 12.
[4] Letter of John Chamberlain to Sir Dudley Carleton, dated 8 February, 1616. "The Lord Chancellor begins fairly and softly to resign some of his offices, as the lieutenantcy of Buckinghamshire to Lord Villiers," printed in *Court and Times of James I*, p. 391.

viscountcy and then an earldom; an easy praise surrounded him. A letter from Sir Tobie Mathew asking the favourite's aid in gaining the royal permission for his return to England, after "so many yeares out of my countrey, in suche conversation as your Honours sawe in Paris (and I have cause to glory in such a witnes),"[1] sets the tone of this auspicious period; while the ending is cloying in its quiet assurance. "Yet," concludes Buckingham's correspondent,[2] "it is in my power to give you the glory of praise and you feede not that mouthe in the worlde which shall open itself to your Honour with more appetite of affection than this of mine."

At this stage of his career it is fortunately possible to check from the Hatfield House papers, the impression which Buckingham had made on the great world. The second Earl of Salisbury was now twenty-six, son-in-law to Lord Treasurer Suffolk, and anxious to obtain a Court appointment. The correspondence relating to his ultimately unsuccessful attempt to secure the post of Captain of the Guard, which had been held throughout the reign by Sir Thomas Erskine of Gogar at this date Viscount Fenton, will serve to elucidate the favourite's position. The first letter is written to Lord Salisbury by Lord Gerard, who was employed as a go-between in this affair. "In answer to your Lordship's letter," wrote Gerard, in April 1617,[3] "I must and will ever affirm this that upon the proffer I made from you of 6,000 pieces to my Lord Fenton for his Captain's place of his Majesty's Guard, his Lordship replied it was a great deal, and seemed satisfied for the value. Only he said it should be no act of his to part with an office under so gracious a King and master. I replied your Lordship and your friends would undergo that burthen if his Lordship would be pleased."

But, although the retirement of Lord Fenton was in fact

---

[1] Letter dated 16 July, 1616, and printed in *Fortescue Papers*, p. 16.
[2] ibid., p. 17.
[3] Letter from Lord Gerard to the Earl of Salisbury, dated 18 March, 1617. Cecil MSS., vol. 129, f. 134.

assured, another candidate had appeared in the person of
Sir Henry Rich, who was favoured by the Queen. Salisbury
explained this to Gerard in a return letter, and made it clear
that it was upon Buckingham's power of recommendation
that he now based his hopes. "I presume" wrote Salisbury,[1]
"so much upon my Lord of Buckingham's noble dealing
with me as that he would never have brought my name thus
far upon the stage . . . but that his Lordship was very well
assured that I should be fully satisfied to my content, and the
rather because all men receive courtesies from him, at least
none can challenge him of breach of promise, which I am
confident I shall never have occasion to do."

The King was about to set out on his Scottish journey and
Buckingham, who was with him, wrote to Salisbury from
Hexham where the royal party halted on the northern road.
It is interesting as marking a stage of development, for it
shows Buckingham still hesitant and tentative, frank and
impressionable. "I have so much assurance in his Majesty's
promise," he wrote in reference to the Captaincy,[2] "that I
know there is no cause of doubt. The only uncertainty is
whether I shall have so much of his Majesty's favour till that
time when it should be despatched as to urge it. If it should
so fall out, I know your Lordship will expect no more than
is in my power; but, if it please God to continue the favour
of his Majesty to me, I am confident all shall be done to your
contentment." This is one of the last letters in which
Buckingham sounds the note of uncertainty. His attractive
hesitation alone preserved him from that quality of arrogance
which all favourites succumb to and none can afford.
Throughout the next eleven years he was constantly to receive
but very seldom to bestow, the milk of courtesy.

[1] Letter from the Earl of Salisbury to Lord Gerard, dated March 1617.
Cecil MSS., vol. 130, f. 68.
[2] Letter from the Earl of Buckingham to the Earl of Salisbury, dated
27 April, 1617. Cecil MSS., vol. 129, f. 131.

CHAPTER VIII

ARUNDEL AND ITALIAN TRAVEL

THE gradually increasing power of Buckingham represented only one among a number of political trends which could be discerned in English life during the second decade of King James's reign. The first stages in his career have been considered, but he was only moving very slowly from personal intimacy with the sovereign to an interference in matters of public policy. The Howard peers, Nottingham and Suffolk, were still entrenched in the great offices of State controlling the Admiralty and the Treasury, while the head of their family the Earl of Arundel was coming to occupy a position as a patron of the arts which was to have in certain fields a decisive influence on English life.

The blurred edges of the Court factions and a rather intricate confusion of interests are characteristic of the high politics of these years. Slowly the idea of the political clan was emerging, although it would be fifty years before the country as a whole would recognize the presence of these noble factions. The peers in the reign of James I were equally remote from the sharp and lonely individualism of Norfolk or Northumberland or Somerset under the Tudor sovereigns, and from that developed Georgian system which was to be exemplified in the control of the political chessboard by the great Whig families. In politics the ordered grouping based upon blood relationship and connection, was present only in an embryonic stage. A nebulous alliance was now forming which in the eighteenth century would become a phalanx.

Throughout the period of the Civil Wars the greater

houses increased; split up; re-formed. Thus by 1679, when Lord Stafford's trial concentrated public opinion upon them for a moment, the Howards were widely ramified and disunited; but in the later years of the reign of James I they were still few in number and closely related. Politically the key position was held by Lord Suffolk, who had been Treasurer since the death of his uncle, Northampton, in 1614. Suffolk's two elder sons, Lords Howard de Walden and Andover, sat in the upper house. His brother, Lord William Howard, lived in Cumberland. There was only one junior branch, that represented by the first Earl of Nottingham and his son and nephew. The head of the senior line Thomas, Earl of Arundel, stood remote from his relatives, through the accident of quarrel, through religion and in his tastes. This completed the entire Howard family.[1] The present chapter is devoted to Arundel and to the nature of his influence.

A study of his upbringing and character will make clear the isolated and yet powerful position which the head of the Howards held in the social and politico-religious scene. His mother, Anne, Countess of Arundel, had all the qualities of a matriarch. Remote from politics, she had yet played a considerable part in attaching the sympathies of the Catholics to her husband's family and in fostering the sense of gratitude with which the privileged circles of that persecuted minority were to pursue the House of Norfolk. She was the eldest of the three co-heiresses of Lord Dacres of the North and had been the chief stay of the stricter Recusants since her husband's imprisonment by the Elizabethan government in 1585. Since the death of Lord Arundel in 1595, her only son Thomas, had remained under her control.

---

[1] They had thus five peers at this date, Arundel, Suffolk, Howard de Walden, Andover and Nottingham. In 1626 the Howard de Walden peerage was merged in that of Suffolk, in 1625 Viscount Andover was created Earl of Berkshire, and in 1628 the first Earl of Suffolk's youngest son became Lord Howard of Escrick.

Profoundly religious, her sympathies leaned to the Society of Jesus, and she had the deep sense of obligation, the continuous piety, the generosity and the strain of autocracy which characterized the great lady of the Tridentine tradition engaged in safeguarding the soul's welfare of her dependents. When duty required she could be chill even towards the ministers of her own religion.[1] A description composed in her last years by the author of her biography, who seems to have been a priest residing in the house, will complete the impression. "She was," runs this account,[2] "taller of stature than the common sort, and towards the end of her life something corpulent, but without deformity, it adding a kind of graceful comeliness and majesty."

Her gowns were commonly of ordinary black stuff, but on the principal holy-days she wore a cross of gold, "an agatt in which was the picture of the Blessed Virgin's Assumption, or els a plain pair of beads sent unto her by Father Claudius Aquaviva."[3] It is not difficult to imagine Lady Arundel with her considerable household under the control of Mr. Robert Spiller, "her steward for many years,"[4] the sober state and the private chapel with "every day . . . Masse, Evensong, Litanies and the like."[5] In the chapel of her manor house at Shifnal, there was kept "a hallow'd Candle brought from the holy City of Jerusalem"[6] which she could hold lighted, in token of her faith, in her last hours. She could be merry and was constantly thoughtful for the

---

[1] In *The Life of the Right Honourable Lady Anne Countesse of Arundell and Surrey*, edited by the Duke of Norfolk in 1857, there is reference to her generosity. "And first to begin with Priests, altho' she had little or no acquaintance with any of the Secular Clergy; yet at several times to my knowledge she has given good summes of money for their relief, and would have done more had not the less discretion of some made abate something of her acccustom'd liberality towards them," p. 216.

Later a gift of £2,500 to the Jesuits is mentioned. "But to none, nor to all the rest together was she so beneficiall and bountifull as to those of the Society of Jesus." *ibid.*, p. 218.

[2] *ibid.*, p. 270.   [3] *ibid.*, pp. 271–2.   [4] *ibid.*, p. 240.   [5] *ibid.*, p. 254.
[6] *The Life of the Right Honourable Lady Anne Countess of Arundel and Surrey*, p. 257.

poor.[1] Well past seventy, she belonged to a remote age.
There was a strain of the implacable in her religious con-
victions,[2] and her character was too dauntless for the
Jacobean world.

In Lady Arundel's case the memory of the misfortunes
with which she had been obliged to cope single-handed,
seems to have separated her from her husband's kinsmen as
surely as her intransigent religious outlook. For it had been
a hard struggle to gather together again the lands which
had been her husband's before his condemnation. At the
accession of King James she held only the entailed FitzAlan
land in Sussex which had been her jointure, and in 1604 her
young son was restored in blood as Earl of Arundel and
Surrey. But Lord Northampton and Lord Suffolk had
obtained all the estate that was forfeited to the Crown and
"the Earle of Nottinghame, one of his owne family, begged
his (the young Earl's) house in London."[3]

In time this situation was rectified and Arundel House
in the Strand was re-acquired in 1607 by the Dowager. But
it was difficult for Northampton and Suffolk to be entirely
friendly to the nephew whose property they had gathered in.
It is never very easy for the wicked uncle to appear unselfconscious. The curious character of Lord Arundel, his lack
of normal contacts and his aloof pride, appear to have been
affected by his harsh youth. When he grew up he was to

---

[1] In regard to Mr. Blackwell the archpriest, "she was so well pleased
with the officer who permitted his escape that besides a good summe of
money given at that time, she sent him every year as long as he lived a
venison pasty to make merry with his friends at Christmas," *ibid.*, p. 217.

[2] Her biographer states that her charity extended "yea even to Heretical
Ministers, whom of all sorts of people she seem'd least to love as esteeming
them the Devil's chief instruments in the seduction of souls," *ibid.*, p. 307.
Independent evidence of neighbourly relations with the Anglican clergy is
provided in a letter from Thomas Pierson, minister at Brampton, dated
16 February, 1628, and preserved in the Harley Correspondence among
the Portland MSS.

[3] Quoted from an *Historical Account of Thomas Howard, Earl of Arundel*,
written by his son William Viscount Stafford. This MS. fragment of
twenty-nine pages is printed in Miss Harvey's *Life and Correspondence of
Thomas Earl of Arundel*, p. 464.

react against the influence of his devout mother, and he had no close male relatives to counsel him save these detached and acquisitive peers.[1]

Even in the future there was little to hope for from that quarter. Northampton, who was unmarried, was closely attached to Suffolk and his children, and neither would cast a favourable eye on the education which Arundel was receiving. The open Popery of Lady Arundel and her household must have been uncongenial both to Northampton, who in public bent with the times, and to Suffolk whose religious outlook was Elizabethan. There was also a marked divergence of temperament between the elder Howards and the young head of the family.

Suffolk, himself, was in some respects rather colourless in spite of the great posts to which he had attained, and the elaborated scandal which was to accompany his loss of the white staff. He was primarily concerned with the development of his private fortune and with the management of these accumulated properties which were the patient gathering of thirty years. The other brother, Lord William Howard, was a man of very different character, a powerful administrator on the Scottish Border where he had inherited his wife's share of the Dacre property, including Naworth Castle.[2] After a rather vague Elizabethan upbringing he had become a Catholic as a young man, but in later life held to this faith with a singularly accommodating temper.[3] As

---

[1] The atmosphere is well conveyed in a letter written in June 1603, by Lord Howard de Walden, later Earl of Suffolk, to Robert Buxton. "I am very anxious to understand truly both the means and values of such lands as my brother did lose wherein I am in remainder. My meaning is not to prejudice my nephew in anything; but happily to help myself a little without his harm." Cal. Buxton MSS., Var. Coll., ii, p. 249.

[2] The fourth Duke of Norfolk betrothed his three sons, Philip Earl of Arundel, Lord Thomas later Earl of Suffolk and Lord William to his wards Anne, Mary and Elizabeth Dacre, the three surviving children of Thomas Lord Dacre. Mary Dacre died childless in 1578, and Suffolk then married Catherine daughter of Sir John Knevet of Charlton.

[3] It is worth working out the religious affiliations of the family. Lady Arundel was a strict Catholic and brought up her son in her faith. Lord William was an Erastian Catholic, and his wife and children belonged to

the leader of those who were ready to accept the Oath of Allegiance, he was far removed from Lady Arundel's standpoint. He was a man of some antiquarian tastes; uninterested in politics; seldom at Court. Far away in Cumberland he neither molested, nor protected the young head of his family.

Both Lord William and Suffolk were set in the mould of the late reign, and were thus separated from their nephew by a divergence of outlook strengthened by apathy. Northampton and Suffolk had found themselves concerned with appointments and the political chessboard; but Arundel's views were quite different. Refusing the role of a politician, he preferred the privileges of a great officer of state. While Suffolk was absorbed in the perquisites of the Treasury, his nephew concentrated on the opportunities of the Earl Marshalship during a fresh period of sophisticated decoration. A man of the new age, Arundel was able to realize himself fully as a grandee and a patron.

From his youth Thomas, Earl of Arundel and Surrey seems to have been aware of the greatness of his position, the duties and obligations of what he conceived as a somewhat lonely state, and those lines of conduct and interest which were consonant with his rank. He was without friends of his own rank to counteract his enhanced views of his prerogative, and his great riches were in sight for a number of years before they actually came into his possession. Lavish as he became, there was nothing youthful in his way of spending. An over-careful attention to his delicate health placed him farther apart from other men, and he had a clear conception of affairs and high notions as to the propriety of lines of conduct without any great measure of vitality. Few

---

the old religion. Lord Suffolk seems to have been an Erastian Anglican. His sons were Anglicans, but his daughter Lady Banbury became an ardent and disreputable Catholic. His grandson the second Earl of Berkshire became a Catholic on marrying the daughter of Lord Savage. Lord Northampton avowed himself a Catholic on his deathbed. Both the lines of the Howards of Bindon and the Howards of Effingham were definitely Protestant.

men have been so clearly marked out as patrons of the arts upon the grand scale. He had those gifts of spectatorship which the grandees of the seventeenth and eighteenth centuries were alone able fully to indulge.

In appearance Arundel was impressive rather than attractive, and it is alleged that Elizabeth's Essex had described him, when a child, as a "winter pear."[1] A description of the Earl at a rather later date has been left us by one of his dependents, and suggests the general effect which he created. "His countenance," wrote Sir Edward Walker who entered his service in 1633,[2] "was majesticall and grave; his visage long; his eyes large, black and piercing: he had a hooked nose, and some warts or moles on his cheeks: his countenance was brown; his hair thin, both on his head and beard: he was of a stately presence and gait." There is reason to suppose that the young Arundel mildly repelled his sovereign, who was so susceptible to the physical attractions. There was nothing to arouse his affection in such a figure as Arundel's, with his old-fashioned vaguely senatorial garb, his incipient but controlled phthisis, and his "beard in his teeth."[3]

On the other hand the young peer's circumstances, his view of his ancestry and his early and great marriage separated him from the world of those who were pliant towards their royal master. On this point the evidence of Arundel's correspondence confirms Sir Edward Walker's testimony. "He was," wrote Sir Edward,[4] "a great master of order and ceremony, and knew, and kept greater distance towards his sovereign than any person I ever observed, and expected no

---

[1] By Sir Edward Walker in his *Historicall Discourses*, ed. 1705, p. 210.
[2] *ibid.*, p. 221.
[3] *Historicall Discourses*, Sir Edward Walker, ed. 1705, p. 221.
[4] *ibid.*, p. 222. In this connection reference should be made to the too frequently quoted statement of Clarendon, which bears all the marks of that historian's literary artifice. "The Earl of Arundel . . . resorted sometimes to the Court, beçause there only was a greater man than himself; and went thither the seldomer because there was a greater man than himself." *The History of the Rebellion*, i., p. 55.

less from his inferiors"; and again he "was not so complaisant as other persons that had more of ends."

Arundel was only eighteen, and he appears to have
developed slowly, when his mother definitely broached the
project of his marriage with Lady Alathea Talbot. She was
the greatest heiress of her generation and had been brought
up in the state and the retirement of the great Catholic-
minded household at Sheffield Manor. Her mother, Lady
Shrewsbury, was by birth a Cavendish, in religion a Catholic
and by temperament rather ardent and unbalanced.[1] Her
father, the seventh Earl of Shrewsbury, kept aloof from both
the Elizabethan and Jacobean Courts and was an affectionate,
quarrelsome, litigious man, who was equally remote from
political and religious interests. Lady Alathea had no
brothers and her two sisters were married and, so far, childless.[2] Ultimately she was destined to bring to the Howards
the greater part of the long-accumulated Talbot properties.

Arundel's marriage took place in 1606, and for the next
nine years he was initiated under his father-in-law's tutelage
into the duties of a man of rank. It was a tradition in his
family that Prince Henry was much attached to him,[3] and he
had a certain loftiness of outlook which accorded with those
imperial conceptions which had a marked attraction for the
heir to the throne. An instance of such an almost arrogant
sense of duty is seen in Arundel's visit a few years later to
Raleigh, then about to set sail in the *Destiny* on his last

[1] In August 1618 Chamberlain wrote to Carleton that Lady Shrewsbury
had refused the Oath of Allegiance and had incurred a *præmunire*, Cal.
S. P. Dom. 1611–8, p. 565. A letter in the Hothfield MSS., dated 8 December, 1615, provides a specimen of the pious tone of Lady Shrewsbury's
correspondence.

[2] Neither of these sisters played any part in the Howard grouping.
Elizabeth Countess of Kent was the patron of Selden; Mary Countess of
Pembroke was unhappily married. Clarendon states with his sedate malice
that Pembroke "paid much too dear for his wife's fortune by taking her
person into the bargain," *History*, i, p. 58.

[3] In the MS. fragment relating to Lord Arundel and already mentioned,
his son Lord Stafford states that "he was most particularly favoured by
Prince Henry that then was."

voyage. On this occasion he took him by the hand and asked him to give his word that, however his voyage turned out, he would return to England. Neither then nor at his death, after the disastrous ending of the expedition, did Sir Walter fail to realize the discrepancy of rank between himself and the young peer.

Meanwhile Arundel had developed that taste for foreign travel which was to carry in its train an accumulation of patronage and the intake of those *objets d'art* on which his famous collections were to be founded. His ill health quelled any inclination towards adventure,[1] but, by the orders which flowed from his progresses, he set in motion some of the more important of the cultural contacts between England and the Continent. Abroad, all knew of the great patron and his approach was never unheralded. Personally, he might be listless and in some respects uninstructed, but he was the very first of what was to become a familiar English species, the rich travelling *milord*.

This is a point which is worth developing and a fairly detailed description of the most celebrated of Arundel's journeys will give a suggestion of the influence which his way of life exerted upon the polite circles in London. In the first place the line of European travel, which had been so circumscribed during the years of the war with Spain, was only now being gradually traced out. It was to be a characteristic of the Grand Tour that those embarking on this prescribed and fashionable journey kept so strictly to the beaten track, and this tendency could be discerned in the first tracing out of the conventional English path of travel.

At this period in the seventeenth century Spain and Portugal were hardly visited save by the official English

---

[1] His first serious journey was to the baths of San Cassiano near Padua and Lord Stafford states that in 1612 "the Earl of Arundel grew to be in a consumption, for which the phisitions helde it fit that hee should goe into Italy for the recovery of his healthe," Harvey, *op. cit.*, p. 465. There is a suggestion of the valetudinarian about his journeys.

envoys, and the ignorance about these lands enhanced the general opinion as to the foolhardiness as well as the political unwisdom of Prince Charles's journey to Madrid.[1] On the other hand the Low Countries, both the territories ruled by the States General and those under the governorship of the Archdukes, were beginning to be frequented by visitors to Brussels and The Hague and to Spa. The Chamberlain Letters suggest that, after about 1610, a number of wealthy Englishmen and their wives were accustomed to go in summer to drink the waters at "the Spaw." France and the Rhineland would come within this circuit and the limit of such journeying would be fixed by the cities of northern Italy. The tension between the Venetian Republic and the Holy See came to reassure the Protestant traveller, and throughout the reign there were resident ambassadors at Venice. It was during Sir Dudley Carleton's tenure of this post that Arundel embarked on his second journey.

Occasional Court duty suited Arundel and at the end of April 1613 he crossed to Holland with his wife in attendance upon the Electress Palatine, who was making her first progress to Heidelberg with her husband. Their travelling carriage could not be accommodated in the *Princess Royal* and was despatched from the Tower Wharf to Rotterdam two days later. One of Arundel's stewards and Lord Shrewsbury's coachman accompanied the vehicle. The carriage curtains, which had not been made in time, were sent on later.[2] Thomas Coke, a Derbyshire gentleman formerly in the Talbots' employment, was attached to the Arundels as a

---

[1] An impression of the lack of contact with Spain and Portugal and the continuance of the Elizabethan legend is provided in *Travels describing divers parts of Africk and Asia the Great*, by Thomas Herbert who set out in 1626 on leaving Trinity College, Cambridge. "The seventeenth of November," he wrote, "to our comfort we descried the coast of India . . . that very place where Goa is seated; the bravest, best defended Citie in the Orient; the Magazeen, refuge, seat of Justice, of the insolent and gold thirsty Portugall," lib. i, p. 33.

[2] These details are contained in a letter from Lord Shrewsbury to Coke, dated 29 April, 1613, among the Coke MSS. at Melbourne Hall.

confidential secretary. He spoke and wrote Italian and had managed the Earl's journey to the baths near Padua in the previous autumn.[1] The Arundels' two young sons were at home in England with their grandmother, and Shrewsbury undertook a certain charge of their interests.

The first difficulty that arose on this journey concerned their attitude in religious matters. "It is by four of our Court Bishops much noted," wrote Lord Shrewsbury to Coke,[2] "that neither Lord Arundel nor my daughter have at any time been at prayers with her highness since they went there (The Hague). I have not heard that the King hath heard thereof." But there is no further reference to this complaint and the party moved down from Heidelberg to Strasbourg and thence to Italy. During this second portion of their travel, Arundel had accepted into his *entourage* an architect of forty, who had attained some repute as the deviser of the Twelfth Night masques and had acted as surveyor of works to Henry, Prince of Wales. It is, primarily, this architect, Inigo Jones, who has kept alive the memory of Arundel's journey.

They came to Venice and Vicenza and then, working westward, to Milan. It appears to have been on this elaborate passage through Venetia and Lombardy that Inigo Jones first studied the works of Palladio at Vicenza,[3] and he was lucky to have with him the greatest of his private patrons, a *magnifico* very far above him and aloof, but fortunately ready to pay. Mr. Jones would go about pacing distances and measuring and preparing a detailed analysis,[4] and then

---

[1] Letter from the same to the same dated 22 November, 1612.

[2] Letter dated 26 May, 1613, in the Coke MSS.

[3] The dates of his journey are recorded in Inigo Jones' copy of *Il Quattro Libri dell' Architetture*, by Andrea Palladio, now preserved in the library of Worcester College, Oxford.

[4] On the seventh flyleaf in Book I there are notes of the length of the great court at Windsor, the great court at Theobalds, the front court of Northampton House, the first court at Hampton Court as well as the second fountain court and the green court. In regard to Windsor he mentions "this I measured by paces ye 5 of December, 1619," at Theobalds, "ye 20 of June 1621," at Hampton Court "September ye 28, 1625, Worcester College MSS.

in the cool of the day, for they were travelling in the heats
of an Italian summer, he could draw his patron's attention to
the various grandiose effects. Certainly some of the notes
on the fly-leaves of the architect's Palladio seem to have
been inserted in order to stir the English lord to emulation
rather than for any technical information which they convey.
"On the piaza," writes Inigo Jones of Vicenza,[1] "over
against ye Bassilica is the Captaynes house and a great lodge,
the room aboufe this lodge is adorned with Paintings in ye
roofe of Paulo Verro: and ther is a small Cornish for ye
hangings, another Payntedd, betwene which ar armor
halberds and suchlyke, aboufe quadros paynted."

Again he would make comparison between the French
and Italian conceptions of grandeur in regard to the setting
of entrances and stairways. His notes contain a reference
to Chambord and a little discourse on the Roman spirit.[2]
"Likewise," he writes at a later stage of the journey,[3] "at
ye Thearmi at Baia thear ar many wales with more courses of
Brick and some great Bricke amongst, for ye Romans varried
the things according to thear *Cappriccio* mingling on with
another, so yt sheawd well." This question of the effect of
Cappriccio would have sounded very grateful to the rich
travelling lords. A little note on Vicenza gives an impression
of the desires which must have stirred the minds of patrons.
"The Theater," it runs,[4] "of Palladio's ordering the front
. . . of Bricks covered with stucco full of ornament and
statues." These words were thcmselves adequate and
required no respectful transliteration. The term of the

---

[1] On the tenth flyleaf *verso* in Book I, Worcester College MSS.
[2] "The stairs at Shambourge I saw being in Fraunce, and they are but
2 wayes to assend and ye Nuell hath a waal with windowes cut oute, but
this yt seames was discovered to Palladio and he invented of him sealf
thes staires," note opposite p. 64, Book I, Palladio, Worcester College
MSS.
[3] Notes on p. 11, Book I, headed, "1614, Baia: 17 January." Worcester
College MSS.
[4] Note on tenth flyleaf *verso* of Book I of *Il Quattro Libri dell' Architetture.* Worcester College MSS.

desire of a great nobleman seems here expressed, a front of brick covered with stucco full of ornament and statues.

There was in Arundel's approach to the Arts a singular receptivity to the taste favoured by men of birth and judgment. Clarendon puts it crudely,[1] and probably unjustly, in the phrase that "as to all parts of learning he was most illiterate," while Walker concedes that the Earl was "more learned in men and manners than in books."[2] But, whatever the cause, he was free from preconceptions and was ready to command the purchase of statuary and pictures or the construction of galleries and pavilions, anything, in fact, which seemed to accord with the idea of decorous magnificence.

A brief intercourse was sufficient to make it clear that he had no conception of money values, although he had not yet entered fully into his inheritance, since his father-in-law was still alive. On reaching Milan the secretary of the embassy at Venice[3] wrote to Coke offering to arrange the advance of money, "as such great merchants as Burlamachi forget sometimes sums which are not in the thousands." And then, there was always Arundel's health and his doubts as to whether he should try the waters of San Cassiano again this year.[4] But the season seemed to him too far advanced and the party moved southward to Florence and Siena.

It was when they were at Siena that old Lady Arundel wrote to them about their children a letter which gives an excellent impression of the contrasted interests of the two generations and their outlook upon expenditure. "God His holy and blessed will be fulfilled," began the Dowager,[5] and continued to inquire, "if there be any good pennyworth of

---

[1] *History of the Rebellion*, i, p. 56.   [2] *Historical Discourses*, p. 222.
[3] Letter of Isaac Wake to Thomas Coke dated 10 July, 1613.
[4] Letter of Arundel to Dudley Carleton, dated 16 July, 1613, "som advise me to trye the waters of St. Cashan; & for phisicke at Padoa, I knowe the yeare is too far spent till the fall."
[5] Letter of Anne Dowager Countess of Arundel to Alathea Countess of Arundel dated 8 December, 1613.

tafitiss and tafita sarsnetts that I shall have use for curtains for beds and windows and making of quilts; the colours crimson, yellow, green, blue. . . . Sweet Will, I assure you, is the liveliest merry child that ever you had of his time and looketh well coloured and will be forward in his going. God Almighty bless them all and send you and them a happy meeting. My son doth mention silks to be good in Sienna if twisted silks be good cheap, I think for fringe and embroidery one may do well to buy some store, for here (in London) we pay 3 shillings or eight groats the ounce if the silk be anything good." Neither the carefulness nor the piety meant anything to her only son. Meanwhile Arundel had reached Rome, and, in January, had sent his first series of statues back to London for Arundel House. The collection of the marbles had begun.

The Rome to which he came had already settled down to that long tranquillity which was to remain unbroken till the French Revolution. The austerities of the Tridentine reforms had been assimilated, and the Borghese and Barberini pontificates were opening with their greedy and comparatively irreproachable Cardinals and the train of new Roman princes. Arundel's private views were of less concern than his position, and it was counted to his credit that he had a nobleman's sympathy for Antiquity. His manner was intimidating in its detached courtesy, and it would appear to have been assumed that he took such measures for the due exercise of his personal religion as accorded with his generous blood. Under the circumstances it is not surprising that this Roman visit was insufficient to confirm him in his adherence to his ancestral Faith.

Arundel's attitude appears to have been similar to that which became prevalent in the period of nationalism which is associated with the name and policy of Richelieu. Had he been an Austrian or Italian nobleman he would inevitably have remained a Catholic; but in England such

profession was hampering to his freedom and had an
adverse effect on his prestige. Obtruded religion of whatever
colour was now hardly consonant with the conception of a
great lord. King James had consented to stand godfather to
his son Maltravers, and in consequence the child had been
christened with Anglican rites. Little as Arundel valued
direct political action, which was a sphere more suited to his
inferiors, he felt deeply the curtailment of his privilege and
those petty and unworthy disputes as to his child's religious
education. He had a dislike for the Jesuits and for those
strict Catholics who would intrude outmoded points of
dogma upon the attention of a man of rank who was pre-
occupied with questions of taste and feeling.[1]

In this matter Walker appears to convey the atmosphere
with justice. It is clear how much he venerated that remote
high-minded generosity which served his master's reputation
so faithfully: "Neither," he wrote in his *Discourses*[2] of the
Earl Marshal, "was he of any faction in Court or Council,
especially not of the French or Puritan. . . . He was in religion no bigot or Puritan, and professed more to affect moral
virtues than nice questions and controversies." In Rome
Arundel is seen as a spectator, the first of many English
milords, who were to follow in complacent and decorous
procession, to enjoy that entertaining spectacle.

One of Arundel's letters to his wife gives his point of
view. He had gone on ahead of her to Naples for a short
visit. "All that is here to be seen," he wrote,[3] "you may see
in a short time of despatch. I would wish you to see Rome
well and that you would have been there in the Settimana

[1] A letter from the Earl of Arundel at Venice to Sir Robert Cotton very
well conveys his instinct for decoration which would subserve the prestige
of his family. "If," he wrote, "you could picke out some story of my
ancestours, which would do well in painting, I praye send me itt in writinge,
and directe it to Mr. Richard Willouby, in case I bee not heere," *Letters*,
edited by Sir Henry Ellis, Camden Society, 1843.
[2] *Historicall Discourses*, p. 222.
[3] Letter of Thomas Earl of Arundel to his wife, dated 14 March, 1614.
Cal. Coke MSS., i, p. 83.

Santa. In your way hither you shall find vile hosterias, one mattress, one blanket, no bolster or anything else. At Gæta is a rock which they say clove at Christ His death. In the Castle, Bourbon's body to be seen, asking leave as strangers from Florence. Mr. Coke should put all his money in pistoles. He may hear from us at Fontana dei Serpi or at the Orso del Oro."

Two years after his return from this Italian journey, Arundel brought himself to accept the Anglican Communion. He received with the King on Christmas Day and two sermons were preached on the occasion.[1] His mother was very difficult about the matter and did not forgive him; his wife retained a subdued Catholicism; he was always perfectly friendly to his Catholic dependents. In later years he made many visits to Italy where he was received with the same amity and distinction. He corresponded with Cardinals as before. In a sense his attitude suggested the eighteenth rather than the seventeenth century, for he was the first of the great lords to profess indifference.

Naturally, even in 1614, there was no real anxiety felt by King James's ministers on the score of Arundel's presence in the Papal city. Sir Dudley Carleton made ready a villa at Padua to receive him and reported in reference to his retinue that the Earl's "great family was spread between Siena and Lucca." At the same time Sir Dudley made considerable and successful efforts to induce Arundel to use him as an intermediary in his art collecting. For it was then customary for the English envoys, and especially those in Venice, the Low Countries and Constantinople, to procure works of art and objects of *vertu* for patrons of distinction.

The immediate bearing of this practice on the political background of the time is frequently overlooked. The com-

---

[1] A letter from Chamberlain to Sir Dudley Carleton, dated 4 January, 1616, states that "the Earl of Arundel received the communion on Christmas day in the King's chapel," printed in William's *Court and Times of James I*, p. 385.

mission to be gained was of secondary importance beside the value of establishing a link of rather subservient friendship with a nobleman who might be in a position to aid advancement. The envoys were frequently candidates for the secretaryships of state (an office which was the goal of Carleton's ambition) and their distance from home made it difficult to play a decisive part in the preliminary manœuvres. The lesser political figures seem to have worked on a not very well-founded theory of obligation. There were always posts or even disconnected emoluments for which a great man could recommend them, and this was a very crucial matter when there was no regular diplomatic service and certainly no system of pension.

Finally, it was the illness and death of Arundel's granduncle Lord Northampton, which brought him back to England. It interrupted the elaborate excursions to Trevi, the examinations of the Temple of Vesta and the drawings of antique statues made at his command, while Inigo Jones offered respectful comment and employed himself in measuring the marble draperies. On his return it appeared that Arundel had received considerable legacies, including Northampton's house by the riverside at Greenwich and landed property with an annual rental of £3,000. This was, indeed, an incentive to his chosen work.

During the years which succeeded his return, Arundel rebuilt his mansion in the Strand in accordance with the modern notions. A new Italian gate was built in the garden at Arundel House, and a long gallery on the entrance floor to receive his statuary. The rather limited space was laid out with a straight walk leading to ornamental gateways and a head of Jupiter was "placed in his utmost garden opposite the doores of the gallery."[1] It was not usual at this period to be damped by the thought of the incongruous and Arundel

---

[1] Letter from Edward Shireburn to Sir Dudley Carleton, dated 9 April, 1616, printed in *Original unpublished papers illustrative of the life of Sir Peter Paul Rubens*, collected and edited by W. Noel Sainsbury, 1859.

THOMAS, EARL OF ARUNDEL AND SURREY, from a portrait
attributed to Daniel Mytens in the possession of the
DUKE OF NORFOLK

steadily developed the ground lying between his house and the river in the formal Italian manner suited to Vicenza and the champaign lands along the Brenta. Undoubtedly, it must have been a satisfaction to be the first to propagate this mode.

In general he was much occupied with decorative detail, with "chaynes of gold" and the working in of his colours which were red and yellow.[1] His sequestered interests were very different from the Elizabethan bravery with its sometimes raucous magnificence. "I pray," Arundel wrote to his wife during the time of the rebuilding,[2] "buy Robartes his 2 carpettes and his blewe quilt, for that will serve yr bedde of Japan exceeding well, and fitte it for the collor." But the chief concern was the pictures and the statuary.

During the late Queen's reign there had been a certain amount of collecting, but it seems then to have developed only from a genuine interest. And in that earlier generation the patron had the tastes of an antiquary rather than those of a connoisseur. This is well borne out in the catalogue of the pictures which Arundel's uncle, old Lord Lumley, had gathered together by 1590. It included some pieces which were eventually to be among the gems of the Arundel collection, but the whole attitude was one of naïve and unsophisticated accumulation. The change had come with King James's insistence on learning and in his desire to "educate" his sometimes brutal young favourites.

Thus, when Arundel had been in Italy, Carleton had been engaged in purchasing pictures and statues for the favourite Somerset, who was quite unskilled in these matters, but knew that the King would expect him to have a collection. In September 1615, Somerset and his wife were accused of poisoning Sir Thomas Overbury, and in the course of the following winter and spring he was politically ruined. Imme-

---

[1] Details from correspondence in the Arundel Castle MSS.
[2] Letter written in 1615 preserved among the Arundel Castle MSS., autograph letters No. 193.

diately his collections came into the market, the works of Veronese and the pictures of Susanna and the Queen of Sheba by "Tintoret" and well-chosen heads of Cicero and Brutus and Germanicus. But before this occurred a consignment of pictures, which Carleton had bought on speculation from Daniel Nys at Venice, was purchased by Arundel for £200. Lord Shrewsbury was dead and Arundel had come into his fortune, and in October 1616 the King granted him Somerset's pictures including his Titian and his set of drawings by Leonardo da Vinci.

A few months earlier Lord Roos, a young peer of fantastic tastes, had gone abroad and given his pictures to Arundel. A letter to Carleton from one of his agents gives an admirable impression of the way that this deplorable habit of *giving* had spoiled the middlemen's market. "I omitted in my last," wrote Edmund Shireburn to Carleton,[1] "to let you know that my Lord Rosse (Roos) hath spoiled the sale of your Statuas, because after all his pains and chardges bestowed in collecting and gathering together such antiquities. . . . he hath nowe in an humor (and I may say an ill one) given them all to my Lord of Arundell, wch hath exceedingly beautified his Long Gallery." Roos had obviously collected his "antiquities" in a mood somewhat similar to Somerset's.

The atmosphere was to change again with the influence of Rubens' painting and the coming of Vandyck to England, and the accession of King Charles I. But, before coming to this later period, the question of how far Arundel possessed developed taste is worth discussing. The evidence is not considerable, since his letters on this subject are naturally composed rather of instructions to purchase than of appreciation. There is, however, one letter extant on this point which it would be best to quote in full so that an independent judgment can be formed. It was written to Carleton in 1621

---

[1] Letter from Edmund Shireburn written in London and dated 13 July, 1616, printed by Sainsbury, *op. cit.*, pp. 272–3.

and gives the patron's estimate of Gerard Honthorst's painting of *Aeneas flying from the sack of Troy*, a subject which
Carleton had suggested as elegant and original. "I thinke,"
wrote Arundel,[1] "the painter hath expressed ye story with
much arte & both for the postures and ye colourings. I have
seene fewe Dutch arrive unto it, for it hath more of ye
Italian than ye Flemish and much of ye manner of Cara-
vagioes colouringe, wch is nowe soe much esteemed in
Rome." If studied carefully this letter will be seen to suggest
a power of assimilation, but hardly an independent mind.
So much of his correspondence seems to have in it not only
the assurance and security, but also the rather dead quality
of patronage.

The very search for these works of art separated Arundel
from the peers settled in the English counties, and placed
him on a level with the heads of the great European houses
with their galleries and their groves of statuary. In this
matter, too, his personal attendants, like Francis Junius his
librarian and Signor Vercellini his secretary, suggested the
European range of his tastes and interests. There is at Knole
a painting ascribed to Vandyck[2] which represents Lord
Arundel in his maturity. The Earl in his robes is seated
beside his wife, while behind him holding a scroll stands
Junius (the adopted name of this Heidelberger from Leyden
is in itself of interest), a tall soberly clad bearded figure
with a high forehead beneath his dark cap. In front of Arundel is a great globe with the continents showing in the dim
colouring.

Arundel's interest in eastern antiquities seems closely
linked with this conception. He was anxious to search out for
objects which would be recognized as curious or elegant.
These searches, pursued with a sufficient ardour, were con-

---

[1] Letter of the Earl of Arundel to Carleton, dated 20 July, 1626, printed
in Sainsbury *op. cit.*, p. 291.
[2] The composition of this picture is interesting and tends to mark a
new development in the "conversation piece."

centrated upon the recovery of the rare and strange for the purposes of domestic ornament. The statues and the columns would grace the Palladian entrance halls, then under construction, or perhaps the gravelled prospect in the garden attached to a great house. The flavour of antiquity appealed to those who were beginning to look for a classic proportion in their buildings. The requirements of the patrons were transmitted to the ambassadors who would frequently themselves initiate inquiries as to the interests of the chief patrons. Thus, Sir Thomas Roe, the English envoy in Constantinople, approached Arundel on this matter. It was clearly to the advantage of the ambassadors to use their best endeavours to satisfy their King's favourite and his counsellors. Nevertheless, it was the taste of the English Court which was always dominant; the new mode gathered in. the spoil that it required; Constantinople was merely a digging ground.

The eastern shores of Europe were of interest to the connoisseurs at the Courts of the western sovereigns in so far as they might yield those classical exemplars which Palladio and the tradition of the late Renaissance had taught them to appreciate as the accessories of a taste which appeared to them as at once calm and impregnable. To manifest an interest in Mohammedan art, for instance, would sin against these canons and deprive the patron of that assurance of correct feeling which was an essential adjunct to an interest in artistic matters.

Thus the fact that a period of building was then in progress in Constantinople was a consideration which was wholly irrelevant. When Arundel and Roe were corresponding the six minarets of the mosque of Ahmed had been but recently completed; the gilding shone on the great columns and the blue faience work of the containing walls stood out sharp and bright on the white background. In the lower portion of the city, close to the Golden Horn, the decoration of the Rustem Pasha Djami had been finished a generation earlier.

Here the faience work rose hard and clear above the rich
floor carpets and the opaque colouring of the cut stalactite.
The mosque of the Yeni-Valide was still in construction.
A new delicacy was apparent in the faience of the wall spaces,
The blue designs were paler and merged in the background,
where a faint blue foundation showed through the white
enamelling, very calm and lovely against the scrolls and
borders and the marble flowers. But the distance between
these designs and the lines of taste in Western Europe, was
at that time too considerable. The men who guided and
formed opinion in Rome and Paris and London had not
travelled to these remote regions, and curiosity about the
modern infidel was not yet stirred. Instead, they made search
for classical heads and antique pillars. It was to these
objects that Sir Thomas Roe confined his attention when
he wrote to Arundel from Constantinople in the spring of
1622.

"Concerning antiquities in marbles," he explained to his
distinguished patron,[1] "there are many in divers parts, but
especially at Delphos, unesteemed here. . . . Coynes wilbe
had from Jews, but very dear when inquired for. I have also
a stone taken outt of the old Pallace of Priam in Troy."
The envoy was professedly unskilled in these matters, and he
mentioned a gold coin of Alexander and a brass coin of a
Syrian Queen. The atmosphere of the embassy at Constantinople was one of courteous solicitude while calm
selection reigned at Arundel House. Gradually it became
clear what precisely was required.

"Antiquities," wrote Sir Thomas in 1623,[2] "in gold and
silver of the antient Greeks from Alexander downward . . .
are here to be gathered, but so deare by reason the last
French Ambassador made great search. I may also light of

---

[1] Letter of Sir Thomas Roe, dated 27 January, 1621-2, printed in
Sainsbury, *op. cit.*, p. 281.
[2] Letter dated 1-11 May, 1623, *ibid.*, p. 282.

some pieces of marble by stealth; as now I am offered a lyon to the wast, of pure white, holding a bull's head in its claws. . . . On Asia side, about Troy, Zizicum, and all the way to Aleppo, are innumerable pillars, statues and tombstones of marble which with inscriptions in Greeke may be fetched at charge and secretly."

This showed a sound understanding of the character of the rape required, and Arundel is found writing[1] to the envoy that his own agent, Mr. William Petty "hath certified me of sixe fine pieces of stories in a wall at Constantinople. . . . I knowe eyther for some crowns to the Bashawe, they may be had, or els stollen for money by ye Turkes." The reply to this letter well indicates both the grandiose character of Arundel's conceptions and the meekness with which his suggestions were received. "Your Lordship," began Sir Thomas,[2] "beleeve an honest man and your servant. I have tryed the Bassa, the captyane of the castle, the overseer of the Grand Signor's works, the soldiours that make that watch, and none of them dare meddle: they stand upon two mighty pillars of marble, in other tables of marble, supported with lesse pillars, upon the chiefe porte of the citty; the entrance by the castle called the Seaven Towers."

This letter might have proved a valuable lesson in the use of the globes, and the sculptures from the Golden Gate at Constantinople were not added to the Arundel marbles. It was a habit of the seventeenth century to ransack for its palaces, and by King Charles' accession Arundel's house in the Strand had been completed, with the great hall paved with Purbeck, and the green gallery with its chiming bells and clock, and the garden with its meanders, and in the black and white marble basin of the fountain, the Thames water splashing.

These conceptions were to have their own significance for

---

[1] Letter dated 10 May, *ibid.*, p. 284.
[2] Letter to the Earl of Arundel, dated 20–30 October, 1625.

the development of English planning in the grand manner. From them descended Chesterfield's strictly limited awareness of values; the vast Italianate English houses; the modish collecting of statuary; the Grecian temples and the sylvan glades. These were most often the accompaniments of an outlook remote from politics, marked by a certain element of detached scepticism and conditioned by great wealth. It was no accident that the disciple of Arundel's old age was John Evelyn, the diarist.

In the last months of his life Arundel penned some remembrances on Italy for his young neighbour. They are marked by the assurance which characterized his generation and station. "At Milan," he began,[1] "the Domo, the prime church, is of an infinite charge and will hardly ever be finished, but hath the misfortune to bee done in an ill designe of Gothick Architecture. . . . The church of Saint Celso is not greate but a delicate peice done by the design of that great Architect Bramante, and the carvinge of the facciata are of marble made by that rare Sculptor Hannibale Fontana, whom they esteeme there beyond all Sculptors." And at the same time Evelyn in his diary was describing his father's house at Wotton in terms which indicate how well he was assimilated to this turn of mind. "I should speake much," Evelyn begins in regard to Wotton,[2] "of the gardens, fountains, and groves, that adorned it, were they not as generally known to be amongst the most natural, and (till this later and universal luxury of the whole nation, since abounding in such expenses), the most magnificent that England afforded, and which indeed gave one of the first examples to the elegancy since so much in vogue, and follow'd in the managing of their waters, and other ornaments of that nature." The concerns of the leisured eighteenth century indeed derive from these lines of interest which

---

[1] Remembrances at Milan now among the Arundel Castle MSS. and printed in Harvey, *op. cit.*, p. 451.
[2] *Diary of John Evelyn*, ed. Henry B. Wheatley, 1879, i, pp. 3–4.

persisted through the alien spirit of the Civil Wars. A taste
for the classical mould allied with fantasy was foreshadowed.
The shape of the great world of the eighteenth century could
be discerned, the severe elevation and the pilasters and the
ornamental waters.

CHAPTER IX

THE DIPLOMATIC BACKGROUND

THE contact between England and the Continent depended chiefly upon the intercourse of the merchants and the journeys of gentlemen of leisure. The rich peers were only occasional travellers. Their expenses were too considerable and the circumstances of their journeying too elaborate. They could obtain but little knowledge of the countries visited; their functions were frequently, as in Lord Carlisle's case, ambassadorial; there was always the danger that they might be too far from home at some turn of politics. Even Arundel's travel had more resemblance to a royal progress than to an expedition with exchange of views. Sir Edward Walker cites with approval two traits in his character which indicate very clearly an inhibiting sense of separateness. "He was," writes Sir Edward of the Earl Marshal,[1] "not popular at all, nor cared for it, as loving better by a just hand than flattery to let the common people know their distance and due observance." And again:[2] "He had not many confidants or dependents, neither did he much affect to have them, they being unto great persons both burthensome and dangerous." The ungenial atmosphere thus generated was hardly suitable to ordinary intercourse abroad.

It was in fact the lesser men, the gentlemen of substance with cosmopolitan tastes, the heirs to rich houses, the young men with political ambitions, who found their way to France and Italy in search of instruction and diversion. They were

---

[1] Sir Edward Walker, *Historicall Discourses*, p. 222. [2] *ibid.*, p. 223.

accustomed to travel in companies of three or four, each gentleman attended by his body servant. Those who were prudent notified the English envoys of their movements, and the embassies could gauge the ebb and flow. In the house on the Canareggio at Venice, Sir Henry Wotton penned his invitations and received information about the travellers in the form of letters of honeyed compliment and the more specific memoranda which were submitted by his ill-paid and vaunting spies. If Spain was at peace, Rome was always suspect.

Lord Cranborne, travelling in Italy in 1611 in the last year of his father's life, was required as an exercise to keep a note[1] for Lord Salisbury's use of the "sundry knights and gentlemen" whom he met with on his road. He himself was journeying with Sir Edmund Hampden and five other gentlemen of unimpeachable political discretion.[2] As much could not be said for all the thirty odd Englishmen of quality whom he encountered.[3] This paper gives a vivid impression of such a journey, the young man minutely controlled, tied to his bear leaders and schooled in the avoidance of equivocal hospitality. It was just this hospitality which had ensnared one of the travellers enumerated in his careful list, Mr. Toby Mathew, Sir Francis Bacon's friend. Under these circumstances it is not surprising that the Venetian embassy, which was so close under the lee of the Counter-Reformation, should have acquired a new significance. There the disturbed traveller would meet with the life with which he was familiar, an Italian setting but an English judgment.

Sir Henry Wotton was a man of forty-eight, an experienced and rather anxious diplomat, when he returned in 1616 to

[1] This memorandum is among the Cecil MSS. at Hatfield House, vol. 197, f. 3, and is printed in the appendix, p. 317.

[2] Lord Cranborne adds the following note to the list of his immediate companions. "With these I kept company at Rome and at Naples, never being out of their company, night nor day."

[3] Among the total of thirty-eight names Sir George Petre, Sir William Dormer, Mr. Giffard, Mr. Eyston and Mr. Gage were certainly Catholics.

the embassy in Canareggio, near the Porta degli Ormesani, to commence his second term as ambassador in Venice. He was well suited to such a life, rather over-sensitive to the social nuances, a little extravagant and haphazard, with an eye to the main chance and the gift of fantasy. The embassy was furnished in the modern style with pictures and armour and gilded leather on the walls, a ground carpet in the dining-room and appropriate arras, the whole acquired at a low rate from Venetian Jews.[1] Sir Henry was fond of new devices and had constructed a billiard table. Within the house he diverted himself with an ape upon a chain. He was ready to provide suitable entertainment, duck shooting on the lagoons in winter. In the summer he retired to his villa on the Brenta, staying through the vintage and playing at bowls in the cool evenings. He was interested in the florists' gardens at Chioggia, and sent rose cuttings and melon seed to the King and "finocchio" to John Tradescant. His taste for music was delicate and he himself played on the *viol di gamba*. In questions of architecture he had a solid appreciation of the Palladian manner. Pictures he knew and loved and turned to profit. A certain assured dignity enabled him to carry through to satisfaction that English policy in which he believed wholeheartedly.

In many respects he was the ideal representative of a friendly power. He was, however, at times too sensitive for contentment and he was aware that his connections in England were not strong enough to be subjected to great strain. This he was at pains to avoid, and his correspondence was perhaps too careful in its sincere parade of friendship. His fantasy seems, as in the case of so many Englishmen, to have received encouragement from his profound assurance in the company of foreigners. His knowledge of Italian was very perfect. Verse and conversation and the domesticities

---

[1] A detailed inventory of the contents of the embassy was made in 1610 at the end of Sir Henry's first term in Venice. Cal. S. P. Venetian.

of the rich all came to him as though by nature. No Englishman in his generation had a clearer appreciation of those means by which his countrymen gained some knowledge of their Europe than Sir Henry Wotton as he sat in his green velvet armchair looking out on the canal, fingering a roll of architectural drawings and discussing the "extraordinary greatness" of the dolphins in the Giudecca. Casting his mind back to England, offering his guests a glass of Barolo and a dish of olives, he stood as an early type of the foreigner at home with the intimate customs of a strange city: the first Englishman in Venice.

In Wotton's writings there is noticeable at times that curious pedantry of approach which marked this period. A description of Venice, composed towards the end of his Venetian embassy and apparently addressed to Buckingham, bears out this point. "The general position of the city of Venice," began Wotton, "I have found much celebrated, even by the learnedest of the Arabians, as being seated in the very midde point between the equinoctial and the northern Pole. . . . The circuit thereof, through divers creeks, is not well determinable, but as astronomers use to measure the stars we may account it a city of the first magnitude, as London, Paris, Gaunt, Millain, Lisbon, etc."

On the other hand it was through the diplomatic envoys that the architectural fashions and the new ordered luxury of the Tridentine world were best interpreted in London. Wotton, whose work on the *Elements of Architecture* was published in 1624, could speak upon these subjects with an authority which the casual travellers lacked. He moved, too, in the world of the patrons and was thus held to possess a detachment to which the mere artificers, like Inigo Jones, could not attain. It was clear that he made no profit from the adoption in his own country of those noble and regular styles which he appreciated. A character of Ferdinand, Grand Duke of Tuscany, composed during his later years, conveys the gist of Wotton's standpoint. His "Palace of Pitti at Florence," runs the smooth phrasing,[1] "I came often to review, and still methought with fresh admiration; being incomparably (as far as I can yet speak by experience or report) for solid architecture the most magnificent and regular pile within the Christian world."

He (the Grand Duke) was in his civil regiment of a fine composition between frugality and magnificence; a great cherisher of manual arts, especially such as tended to splendour and ornament, as picture, sculpture, cutting of crystals; inlaying of marbles, limning of beasts, birds and vegetables, embossing and the like." This preference is seen again in Wotton's description of the *Alte Residenz* at Munich where he stayed when on a special mission to the Emperor and the German states. "The Duke Maximilian," the envoy explained,[2] "sent singly for me . . . offering me, after I had passed the Alpes, a little commodity of repose in that poor house (his new palace) as he was pleased to term it; being otherwise one of the most capable, magnificent and regular fabrics of Christendom, and all of his own device and erection within five years."

It is, perhaps, appropriate at this point to consider the nature of the official English contact with these States of the centre and the south of Europe. The constituted order of these governments and their authoritarian quality appealed to the King of England, but it would be of interest to examine the effect which James I and VI himself produced. The influence of the King's writings upon his prestige at foreign courts has hitherto been seldom stressed.

It was to the grave-minded rulers and their advisers, those inured to the Hapsburg governments by long practice, that King James had sent his *Premonition*. The enthusiasms of the Counter-Reformation were now waning and a sober

---

[1] *Reliquiae Wottoniae*, 1st ed., p. 359.
[2] Report to King James I dated June, 1619, and printed in *Life and Letters of Sir Henry Wotton*, ii, p. 175.

concentration on the national and religious aggrandizement had replaced them. A determined doctrinal and political conviction moved the southern sovereigns; an approach which was circumspect and astute; a state in which formalism was beginning to film over the religious values. There was something Palladian about the architecture and conception of the royal authority. Above all the governments reposed on solid bases and their mood was serious, and King James approached them with his heavy lumbering flippancy and his northern wit. "These spirits," he wrote in the *Premonition*[1] in a laboured passage bearing on the Jesuits, "indeed thus sent foorth by this threefold authoritie for the defence of their Triple-crowned Monarch, are well likened to frogges; for they are Amphibions, and can liue in either Element, earth or water; for though they be Churchmen by profession, yet can they use the trade of politique Statesmen; going to the Kings of the Earth, to gather them to the battell of that Great day of God Almightie. What massacres haue by their perswasion bene wrought through many parts of Christendome, and how euilly Kings haue sped that haue bene counselled by them; all the unpartiall Histories of our time doe beare record. And whatsoeuer King or State will not receiue them, and follow their advise, rooted out must that King or State be, euen with Gunpowder ere it faile." There was little in this harangue to commend the King's wisdom to his brother sovereigns.

And then he wandered on in an insecure and rickety parallel between the Pope and Anti-Christ and the succession to "Ethnicke Rome." The Fourth Evangelist, King James explained,[2] "described all sorts of rich wares, whereof that great Citie (of Papal Rome) was the Staple; for indeed shee hath a necessary use for all such rich and glorious wares, as well for ornaments to her Churches and princely Prelates,

---

[1] *A Premonition* printed in its most accessible edition in the *Political Works of James I*, Harvard Political Classics, i, p. 146.
[2] *ibid.*, i, p. 148.

as for garments and ornaments to her woodden Saints; for the blessed Virgin must be dayly clothed and decked in the newest and most curious fashion, though it should resemble the habit of a Curtizane. And of all those rich wares, the most precious is last named, which is the Soules of men: for so much bestowed upon Masses and so much doted to this or that Cloyster of Monkes or Fryers, but most of all now to that irregular and incomprehensible order of Jesuites; shall both redeeme his owne Soule, and all his parents to the hundredth generation, from broyling in the fire of Purgatory. And (I hope) it is no small merchandise of Soules, when men are so highly deluded by the hopes and promise of Saluation, as to make a Frier murder his Soueraigne (Henry III of France); a young knaue attempt the murder of his next Successor (Henry IV); many one to conspire and attempt the like against the late Queene; and in my time to attempt the destruction of a whole Kingdom and State by a blast of Powder."

Then, after returning to the Powder Plot to which King James was accustomed to refer so frequently, the argument shambled forward.[1] "Thus hath the Cardinals (Bellarmine's) shameless wresting of those two places of Scripture, *Pasce oues meas*, and *Tibi dabo claues* . . . animated me to prooue the Pope to bee THE ANTICHRIST, out of this foresaid booke of Scripture; so to paye him in his owne money againe. And this opinion no Pope can euer make me to recant; except they first renounce any further medling with Princes, in any thing belonging to their Temprall Jurisdiction." It was an age which valued balanced statement and a rather over-serious exaltation of authority. The Lutheran princes were calm towards the Church of Rome; the fire had gone from royal controversy. King James desired to be valued for his wisdom; he had dedicated this particular work to

---

[1] *A Premonition* printed in its most accessible edition in the *Political Works of James I*, Harvard Political Classics, i, pp. 149–50.

the Emperor Rudolf and had had it distributed through his ambassadors. At Gratz in Styria, the Archduke Ferdinand now knew that the imperial crown would devolve upon him. He had been brought up by the Jesuits to whom he paid a somewhat exclusive devotion. Authoritarian, full of dignity, his mind marked by a certain stiff and unimaginative rectitude, he examined these pages as they were laid before him. Beside him stood the grave and reverend fathers.

These writings may well have had some bearing on the development of the intransigent attitude which the Emperor Ferdinand II was to maintain towards the later policies of the English king. It was not easy for a seventeenth-century sovereign to forgive levity or to value King James's merry tumbling. It was something of a triumph for Wotton and Carleton and the other envoys that their decorous and careful statements could serve to shield their garrulous master.

The link between diplomacy and preferment in home politics was very close in the Jacobean Age, and those who could shield their sovereign's reputation had a fair chance of English office. Thus, for years Sir Dudley Carleton had observed carefully and hopefully each vacancy in the secretaryship of State, and Sir Henry Wotton was in the same position. These envoys' literary efforts, like their despatches, had in view no foreign public. Embedded as they were in the tradition of the Court, the English trade was for most ambassadors a matter of very minor interest except in so far as it might touch upon the imposts and monopolies of the world of privilege.

From the embassy in Canareggio the thread of Wotton's cultivated personal concern ran through the machinery of the State and its manifestations; through architecture and the masque to that other sovereign power in Whitehall. The embellishment of the Court from which he came preoccupied him. He was without a pension and his future lay in England. The senators of the Serene Republic: the

Venetian envoys to the Stuart Court; the English visitors of rank had all some bearing upon his livelihood. The one matter which must have appeared supremely indifferent was the detail of the cargoes which the English captains landed on the quays of Venice.

There were few periods in which the social cleavage between the Court circle and the merchant seamen has seemed so deep as in those decades which preceded the outbreak of the Civil War. In contrast to the just evaluation of Palladio and Wotton's delicate salesmanship there stands *The Seaman's Song of Captain Ward*. We cannot forget the rugged directness of this chorus which comes ranting into that courtly world of profitable undertones. It, too, deals with Candia and the Cretan territories of Venice, but from what a different angle!

> "Golden-seated Candy,
>   Famous France and Italy.
> With all the countries of the Eastern parts,
>   If once their ships his pride withstood,
>   They surely all were cloath'd in blood,
> Such cruelty was placed within their hearts."

It was a good opening for the description of "the famous pyrate of the world and an English-man born," and the ballad element is introduced in the later verses entitled *The Famous Sea-Fight between Captain Ward and the Rainbow*. A brief quotation will suggest their approach and quality.

> " 'O nay! O nay! then said our King, 'O nay, this may not be,
>   To yield to such a rover myself will not agree;
>   He hath deceived the French-man, likewise the King of Spain
>   And how can he be true to me that hath been false to twain?'
>   'O Royal King of England, your ship's returned again;
>   For Ward's ship is so strong it never will be ta'en.'
>   'O everlasting!' says our King, 'I have lost jewels three,
>   Which would have gone into the seas and brought proud Ward
>   to me!'

'The first was Lord Clifford, Earl of Cumberland;
The second was the Lord Mountjoy, as you shall understand;
The third was brave Essex, from field would never flee;
Which would 'a gone into the seas and brought proud Ward
    to me!' "

These were words which Raleigh would have understood,
but not his careful enemies.

CHAPTER X

THE ECLIPSE OF THE HOWARD GROUPING

FEW processes throw a clearer light on the alternations in political power during the first half of the seventeenth century than that tranquil dissolution of the Howard influence which is associated with the trial of the Earl of Suffolk. Speculation was so rife in the idle circles about the Court that the fall of each great officer was heralded by rumour. But at this period the magnitude of the disaster is less remarkable than the assurance and speed of the recovery of the distressed statesman.

Thomas Earl of Suffolk was fifty-three years of age when the death of his uncle Lord Northampton opened his path to the post of Treasurer. Sir Roger Wilbraham in his journal gives an impression of the situation at this time with the pieces set, as it were, for a losing game. "Julie 1614," the entry runs,[1] "Erle of Suffolk made Lord Tresorer. In October after 1614 . . . the howse of Suffolk was at the highest pitche: himself Lord Tresorer; his son-in-law the Erle of Somersett lord high chamberlain and the most potent favorite in my tyme: Lord Knollys another son-in-law Tresorer of the howse-hold and by his favor made Master of Wards." Studied carefully this list does not appear to indicate a strong position. It seemed that the new Lord Treasurer had almost drifted into power, sponsored by the wealth he had built up and aided by his long experience.

---

[1] *Journal of Sir Roger Wilbraham*, Camden Society Miscellany, p. 115. An entry in the same journal under 24 May, 1612, gives Sir Roger's political affiliations. "Death of the Erle of Salisbury: depe secrett and prudent in Councell: and quid non: *deo servus mihi patronus*", *ibid.*, p. 106.

In religion Suffolk's preferences were Erastian; politically he was unadventurous; his principal concern appears to have been centred on the development of his private fortune. Northampton House in the Strand, which he had inherited from his uncle,[1] made an impressive setting for his astute and cautious action, and he used the prestige of his great name to advantage in his careful intake of landed property. In this matter he had been unfortunate in the early and childless death of his first wife since he had in consequence lost her third share of the inheritance of the Dacres of the North. He had now been married for more than thirty years to Catherine Knevet, a beauty spoiled by small-pox, determined and acquisitive. Through his second wife he had acquired the estates of Charlton in Wiltshire and Escrick in Yorkshire. The property of Audley End and the town of Saffron Walden had been inherited from his maternal grand-father Lord Chancellor Audley, who had garnered them in King Henry's reign. More recently Suffolk had accumulated the Dorset manors of his cousin, the last Viscount Howard of Bindon. The lord lieutenantcy of the counties of Dorset, Cambridgeshire and Suffolk reflected this accretion. He held, suitably enough, the chancellorship of the University of Cambridge. The whole movement of his life was slow, and his public career was marked by a hesitant tenacity. He has left singularly little correspondence and a curiously vague impression. Audley End is his monument. In English legend he is only remembered by one unimportant episode of his early manhood. He was Sir Richard Grenville's last commander.

---

[1] Sir Henry Wotton writing from London on 16 June, 1614, to give Sir Edmund Bacon an account of Lord Northampton's death, remarked: "To my lord of Suffolk he (Northampton) hath left his house, but hath disposed of all the movables and furniture from him. And it is conceived that he died in some distasteful impression, which he had taken against him upon the voices that ran of my lord of Suffolk's likelihood to be Lord Treasurer, which place will now assuredly fall upon him," printed in Logan Pearsall Smith's *Life and Letters of Sir Henry Wotton*, ii, p. 39.

Much more significant than any of Suffolk's personal actions, and giving a suggestion of cohesion to his vacillating public record, is the great house that he created at Audley End. It was the fruit of his maturity; wholly Jacobean in its period, built between 1603 and 1616; settled in that quiet East Anglian landscape; immense and grand and tranquil. "The river," wrote Evelyn after a visit in 1654, "glides before the palace, to which is an avenue of lime trees but all this is much diminished by its being placed in an obscure bottom. For the rest, it is a perfectly modern structure, and shows without like a diadem by the decorations of the cupolas and other ornaments in the pavilions."

This last sentence well describes the house as it appealed, with its security and fantasy, to the seventeenth-century mind. Very briefly it conveys the whole, the great expanses of the rooms, the oak screens overlaid with carving, the dolphins on the ceilings and the careful plaster work and the elaborate stucco pendants. Through the porches with their Ionic and Corinthian columns lay the arched loggias. The sculpturing around these entrances was almost lost in the long high mass of the house front, which rose to the strap-work balustradings with above them the clustered chimneys and the copper-roofed towers and turrets and the metal pennons. The age was attuned to this conception of the great mansion, profuse in its detail, without restraint and unclassical. The pale English sun fell on the acres of stone work and lit the windows and cupolas.

There is little evidence from which to trace the connection between the house and its prosaic and uneasy builder. He had moved from the Charterhouse to his new dwelling at Charing Cross, and he was constantly building both on his wife's estate at Charlton and, apparently, on his new property of Lulworth Castle. Throughout the financial troubles, which are to be described, Audley End was the background of his life; an immense palace conceived perhaps in that spirit of emulation which surged through the richest families; an exhausting expenditure with which he could never draw level; a house laden with carvings and sculptured panels and debts. The light fell upon Lord Suffolk's diadem.

From his first days at the Treasury, Suffolk was anxious to accept the money presents which were offered to him, hopeful of extracting benefit from the contracts which lay upon his desk and possessed by a distant fear of Parliament. A letter among the Longleat MSS. addressed to one of his cousins in the early period of his tenure of office, gives his point of view. "My place," wrote Suffolk,[1] "enforceth me to foresee evils before they fall, which lyberty I hope wylbe geven me, otherwyse my office must of necessitye prove unfortunate to me. Your Lordshipe is near about hys Majestie by whose meanes I desyre to delyver to hym in hys absence that which my duty commands me to do. In the change of the company of the new marchant adventurers to the owld as yet but doubtfully depending I fynd cause of fear, for the owld company who now hath the trade begynnes to complain of the falling of the pryce of cloath beyond the seas by reason that Low countrymen hold them to hard conditions." Then, after discussing an expedient, he continues, "Your Lordship may also remember another offer made by them to Lord Fenton for a yearly sum to be payed, which for my parte I dare not advyse because yt may geve occasion to the marchant for the raysing of the pryce of cloath upon the subject which wyll give an yll taste with yt and no dowbt geve cause for a parlement to question." Every sentence indicates a burdened man.

Even before he was Lord Treasurer it appears that Suffolk had attempted to relinquish to the King[2] his patents for

---

[1] It is suggested that Francis Earl of Cumberland may have been the recipient of this letter. Cal. Bath MSS., ii, p. 63.

[2] Letter of Chamberlain to Carleton dated 25 March, 1613. "The Master of the Rolls withstands the proposal of the Earls of Suffolk and Salisbury to relinquish to the King their patents for currants and Venice

currants and Venice glass and silks, because they would be grievances complained of in the next Parliament. He had other matters to disturb him, his responsibilities as an under-taker[1] for the plantation of Ulster and a dispute with Lord Dunbar's executors[2] about Lady Howard de Walden's mar-riage portion. There had been trouble, too, in acquiring Lord Northampton's minor places and preferments and re-distri-buting them among the family.[3] At the Treasury itself two factors complicated the situation. In his period of office Northampton had written to the King[4] alleging that "the two last Treasurers pared down the robe imperial for their own profit," an unwise accusation calculated to cause enemies to examine the Howards' own imperfect practice. Established at the Exchequer and in control of the machinery sat Mr. Bingley.

From the very beginning of Suffolk's Treasurership, Mr., later Sir John Bingley, pursued his superior with his quick invention. What was required from Suffolk was not planning but consent. He was not molested and was permitted to take the profit in his cautious way. The general line of action is well described by a correspondent of Sir Dudley Carleton's, who was present at the proceedings which followed upon the removal of the white staff four years later. "In divers parti-culars," runs this account,[5] "they found him (Sir J. Bingley)

---

glass and silks because they will be grievances complained of next Parlia-ment," Cal. S. P. Dom. 1611–8, p. 177.

On 30 June, 1611, a re-grant had been made to the Earl of Suffolk of a moiety of all seizures of Venice gold and silver, the same as by a former privy seal passed in the fifth year of the King, S. P. Dom. Jas. I., LXIV, 66.

[1] Register of the Council of Scotland, 1607–10, pp. 793–4.

[2] King James had defended Lord Suffolk in the dispute following the marriage of his eldest son Lord Howard de Walden to Lady Elizabeth Dunbar, *ibid.*, 1610–3, pp. 613, 617, 542–3.

[3] The reversion of the keepership of the tower of Greenwich and the moiety of the manor of Clun, Cal. S. P. Dom, 1611–8, pp. 52 and 137, and the manor of Bishop's Castle, Cal. Corporation of Bishop's Castle MSS., eighth report, pp. 401–3.

[4] Letter from Northampton to James I, dated 8 October, 1612, Cal. S. P. Dom., 1611–8, p. 150.

[5] S. P. Dom. Jas. I, CXI, 18. A portion of the account is printed in Stebbing's *Life and Letters of Sir Francis Bacon*, vii, p. 57.

a great scraper in his office, or as they called it *colore officii*:
a taker of bribes, a broker for my Lord and Lady of Suffolk,
and a manifest dealer in most of these extorting affairs; this
by my Lady of Suffolk's letters . . . he appeared no less: as
also by a book of particular bribes, receipts and disburse-
ments kept by Humphreys, my Lord's servant, and recovered
out of my Lady's hands, being after the greatest evidence
and telltale against them.

And for the Earl, that although in many of these mis-
employments and extortions he had no immediate finger, yet
it was very apparent that he gave way underhand to all the
business: for, when my Lady and Sir John Bingley had made
their bargains, my Lord was ready to subscribe and not
before. Then upon a sudden my Lord became tractable to
deal with, and would give fair language. The Chequer door
was open, and the men they dealt with had their moneys
paid them according to their bargain agreed upon. Before
they had concluded, no business could be suffered to pass:
his Lordship was not to be moved upon any condition."

A note of the Attorney-General's speech on this occasion
confirms the same impression.[1] "He (Sir H. Yelverton)
insisted," the paper runs, "upon their ways of taking and
drawing in of profit, by bargaining, delaying, persuading,
threatening, etc., saying no door could be opened without a
golden key." Now the curious point about this whole
process is the length of time that the golden key was allowed
to remain, however insecurely, in Suffolk's possession.

Bingley had for some years borne an unsatisfactory financial reputation. Even as early as 1614 the agents of the
diplomatic envoys had found the Sub-Treasurer hard of
access. He would subject the warrants from the Exchequer
to an unfriendly scrutiny and the ambassadors themselves

---

[1] This sentence appears in the letters of Sir John Finet to the second
Earl of Salisbury which are preserved in the Cecil MSS., v. 129, ff. 160–73,
and transcribed in the appendix to this volume dealing with the Earl of
Suffolk's case, pp. 319–31.

found,[1] like Sir Thomas Edmondes, that interviews with him were heavy and fruitless. As a result the letter writers seethed with rumours of his impending exposure and of his peccadilloes[2] in managing his sovereign's moneys. But such predictions[3] were premature. Whatever the lesser men might say about the Sub-Treasurer, there were few who would attack his great bland lord.

By the summer even the suggestions of difficulty had passed and Bingley was able to give his attention to his new marriage,[4] a prudent alliance with the mother of the young Lord Grey of Groby. In August, however, the secretaries of State, Lake and Winwood,[5] complained to one another that the Lord Treasurer kept the Court too short of funds. It was even said that the royal huntsmen and the menial members of the household were in want. In October Winwood died suddenly, and by Christmas a rumour had developed[6] that "next term the Earl of Suffolk and Secretary Lake are to receive their doom." But in the New Year all was peaceful as the funds slowly drained away with hardly a gurgle. Sherburne wrote[7] that he was unable to obtain Sir Dudley Carleton's allowance as envoy at The Hague, and that Sir William Zouche could do no better, although he had been authorized to offer a heavy bribe to the Sub-

[1] As early as 23 June, 1614, Alexander Williams had failed to get money for Carleton from Mr. Bingley, although he had an Exchequer warrant. He declared that Sir Thomas Edmondes, the envoy to Brussels, stayed merely for want of money. He wished that there were no worse paymasters than Burlamachi. Cal. S. P. Dom., 1611–8, p. 438.

[2] Letter from Chamberlain to Carleton, dated 18 January, 1617, *ibid.*, p. 428.

[3] Letter from Edward Sherburne to Carleton, dated 21 January, 1617, *ibid.*, p. 429.

[4] Letter from George Gerrard to Carleton, dated 22 July, 1617. *ibid.*, p. 477.

[5] Letter from Sir Thomas Lake to Sir Ralph Winwood, dated 16 August, 1617, at Houghton Tower, *ibid.*, p. 481.

[6] Letter from Sir Edward Harwood to Carleton, dated 3 December, 1617, *ibid.*, p. 501.

[7] Letter from Edward Sherburne to Carleton, dated 4 January, 1618, *ibid.*, p. 511.

Treasurer. A fortnight later the King knighted Sir John Bingley.[1]

There appears to be some doubt as to the extent of King James's knowledge of the situation for in many respects he was well protected from the truth. It seemed unlikely that the uneasy equilibrium would be overset since the Howards' position was guarded by the King's passivity. The young Buckingham had not yet reached the stage at which he himself would suggest decisive action. Two new factors operating simultaneously brought down the house of cards.

In February some members of the Suffolk faction introduced a young connection of the Nottingham Howards, John Monson, to the King's notice in the hope that he might supplant the present favourite. It was a clumsy manœuvre, ill-timed and wholly unsuccessful. And it seems improbable that there was ever a moment when the King could have been attracted away from George Villiers who was so gay and filial. But very likely this episode served to harden the favourite's outlook.

At the same time Sir Thomas Lake, the Secretary of State who had owed his promotion to the Howard influence, now found himself in the gravest trouble. Two years earlier Lake's daughter had married Lord Exeter's grandson, the young Lord Roos, a man of wavering tastes, generous and extravagant.[2] He had hopes but no achievements, strongly desiring that political influence which might have come to the heir of the elder line of the Cecils. The marriage was unhappy and Roos was unsuccessful and dissatisfied; his outlay had been to no purpose; he had won no influence; the King was cold towards him. His case was fairly common at the Jacobean Court: that of a young peer who could not

---

[1] Letter from Chamberlain to Carleton, dated 17 January, 1618, Cal. S. P. Dom., 1611–8, p. 514.

[2] When quite a youth Lord Roos had written to his grand-uncle, Lord Salisbury from Paris, asking his assistance in his suit to marry the Duchesse de la Trémouille. Cecil MSS., vol. 116, f. 84.

make headway against the Herberts and Sackvilles, and the thronging Scots who had won the sovereign's easy confidence. Essentially it was not greatly different from that of his cousin the second Earl of Salisbury, but the head of the younger line held Hatfield and, as long as Exeter sat at Burghley, Roos had to be contented with his failure and his debts.

It was at this stage that Lake had offered a considerable advance in consideration of a mortgage on his son-in-law's property in Essex. On Lake's part this move appears to have been a final effort to salvage a marriage which was valuable to him, and Roos' grandfather, perhaps not unnaturally, withheld the required consent. The Earl of Exeter was an ageing man, cautious and without talent, religious in an old-fashioned way and moving to that transient conventional support which so many peers still gave to Buckingham. Lady Exeter envisaged the favourite as the husband of Lady Diana Cecil, the marriageable daughter.

Into this situation Lady Roos, encouraged by her mother, launched a charge accusing her husband of incestuous relations with Lady Exeter, his grandfather's second wife. Roos himself had left England and become a Catholic,[1] and within a few months was to die in Naples. But Lady Lake's connection with the accusation was fatal, and from the moment of the bringing of the charges the Lakes were doomed. The slander case in the Star Chamber drew nearer with its burden of damages and its inevitable verdict. The secretaryship was irretrievably lost, and the Howards were deprived of their most considerable supporter in official life. There is no evidence that Suffolk himself was interested in Mr. Monson, and it is improbable that he gave any thought

[1] A letter from Sir Thomas Lake to Buckingham, dated 27 January, 1616, gives the Secretary's view of his son-in-law. "I received," he wrote, "these inclosed from Mr. Trumbull, bringing me the discomfortable newes of my Lord Rosse coorses, who is now certainly at Rome, and what further so unsettled and inconstant a brayn as he hath will doe I know not." *The Fortescue Papers*, p. 35.

to Sir Thomas Lake's unpleasant difficulties, but as a result of the coincidence of these two cases he found himself exposed to a hitherto unexpected prosecution. The Suffolks were stripped of that protection which a minion in the secretary-ship of State had long afforded. They were not penalized; they were only aware that they were no longer safeguarded from their enemies. They could perceive that the favourite had changed his stance. It was the first of Buckingham's major interventions in public life. Very slowly the law was set in motion.[1]

But by April there was still no prospect of the affair advancing. "You shall hear nothing this term," wrote Sir Lewis Watson to Sir Edward Montagu in an accurate fore-cast,[2] "of the great business in the Star Chamber." In August the question of these delays was raised at a meeting of the Privy Council,[3] and it was argued that they had been caused in part by the necessity of sending into Ireland one of the officials of the Court with a commission for the examina-tion of certain witnesses. Eventually on 14 October, 1619, the second day of the Star Chamber term, Lord Suffolk appeared before the Court. Two and a half years had already passed since the first explicit rumours.

Wallingford and Salisbury stood by their father-in-law, and Hatfield was the headquarters from which efforts were made to stave off the condemnation. That desire for place in which the younger Salisbury had been bred was farther than ever from its fulfilment. His hesitant offers had been

---

[1] There is a brief account of the Star Chamber Proceedings against the Earl of Suffolk and others, contained in an MS. volume formerly in the possession of Henry John Pye of Clifton Hall, near Tamworth. The first portion of the MS. is in the hand of Sir Robert Pye of Farringford, Remem-brancer of the Exchequer in 1618. The account was printed in the *English Historical Review*, xiii, pp. 716–28. Sir John Bingley is here described as "writer of the tallyes and counter tallyes in his Majesties Receipt of Exchequer," *The Fortescue Papers*, p. 717.

[2] Letter from Sir Lewis Watson to Sir Edward Montagu, dated 21 April, 1619. Cal. Montagu of Beaulieu MSS., p. 96.

[3] At the meeting held on 24 August, Acts of the Privy Council, 1617–2, p. 25.

refused; the attempt to purchase the Captaincy of the Guard two years before was unsuccessful; the elimination of the Howards would place him finally beyond that orbit on which the royal favour fell with profit. He depended upon his father-in-law and the hope of all this grouping lay in corporate action. They appear to have understood that office would never come to them as the reward of ability and talent, but, if it came at all, as a recognition due to the inheritors of accumulated rich endowments and landed power. Even in this decline of their fortune men realized that the Suffolks, Nottinghams and Salisburys moved on a different plane and were answerable to a different set of laws and compensations from those which were applicable to the mere country gentlemen of busy energy who strove for the secretaryships and in diplomacy. It was a member of this lower order Sir John Finet, Master of the Ceremonies at Court, whom Salisbury now called upon to report to him on the progress of the Treasurer's matter.

The five letters on this subject, which were written after the rising of the Star Chamber Court and posted down to Hatfield, appear to form part of a series which has not survived in its entirety. The first is dated 21 October and the earlier letters would seem lost, but a vivid impression is conveyed of a profound outward respect and an apparent obsequious surprise at my Lord's trouble. Sir John Finet begins with a smooth description of the method of evading the charges in regard to losses in the Jewel House. "The part," he writes,[1] "first in question of deceit of trust committed among the Jewels was not so much as mentioned, since my lord and ladys pleading of their discharge under the Great Seal expressly freeing them from ever being molested, impeached or sued to that purpose, served them for an armour of proof (which as Mr. Attorney said the

[1] Cecil MSS., vol. 129, ff. 160, 161. The letters are described more fully in the appendix, pp. 319-31.

other day, the King had given them and they had now put
on) and kept them from all further question." The matters
in regard to the Alum Contract and the Ordnance Office
were, however, more disquieting and Finet was forced to
admit[1] that "the weather grows more and more foul for
this unhappy lord's business, and if the sun of the King's
Grace or the wind of his gracious favour dispel or blow not
away the storm threatened, there is nothing but ruin to be
expected, which God turn away."

The next letter, written three days later,[2] was equally
respectful but still more unhopeful. There was question of
£3,000 taken out of the Receipt of Exchequer, part of the
moneys paid in to His Majesty for the Dutch cautionary
towns. Again there were the moneys charged upon the old
debt of Ireland "for which Sir J. Bingley had a privy seal
in 8 Jas. I. & which as an *abissus* or gulf swallowed store of
treasure never in danger to be accounted for," and there
were the tiresome sums of £100 and £40 said to be taken
by my Lord "out of the Exchequer and paid to Mr. Carter,
the first for his building at Newmarket and the latter for his
stable at Charing Cross." On the following day Finet wrote
again for the matter had indeed gone badly. There was
reference to the £3,000 demanded from Corten by Sir John
Townsend[3] on the Lord Treasurer's behalf, to the £1,500
per annum contributed by the farmers of the leases of
Oswestry, the 3,000 pieces taken from the Merchant Adventurers for confirming or renewing their charter, Sir David
Murray's composition and Sir Miles Fleetwood's gifts.[4] It
was said that Lord Suffolk had retained a portion of the
sum of £2,800 paid to the Sub-Treasurer to distribute
amongst certain pirates to keep them honest men after their

---

[1] Cecil MSS., vol. 129, f. 161.   [2] *ibid.*, vol. 129, f. 162.
[3] Corten (Courteen) was suing for his debt of £18,000 from the King
and Sir J. Townsend was reported to have said: "What is it to give £3,000
to such a man as my lord be it but to purchase his favour?"
[4] In the Pye MS. Sir Miles Fleetwood is described as "Receiver of the
Court of Wards and Liveries." E.H.R., xiii, p. 727.

reclaiming. One Captain Boghe, who should have had £1,100, never could get more than £40 and died in a debtors' prison of discontent. There were many other cases of this description.

It is interesting that this evidence did not deter Finet, who within twenty-four hours had regained his optimism. "This day," he wrote on 29 October,[1] "the defendants came to their answer, which was first taken in hand by Sergeant Richardson, and carried with that strength of wit and argument as hath shaken much the world's opinion concerning the guilt of my Lord in the two charges of the Ordnance and the alum business." In regard to this first matter the Sergeant took the line that the Lieutenant and not the Lord Treasurer was responsible for the payment of the officers of the Ordnance and that such guilt as might exist must rest only upon Sir Roger Dallison. He also brought forward arguments in connection with the granting of the alum contracts and finally disposed of a small question in regard to a gratuity alleged to have been transmitted to Sir Thomas Howard.

Nevertheless, the general argument was more intricate than hopeful. "Many other reasons," concludes Finet at the end of his lengthy letter, "passed *pro* and *contra* to prove and disprove the difference of gain and loss to the King in the time of the agency and of the contract, which was intricate to me to conceive and out of my distance to hear by reason of the then tempestuous noise of my Lord Mayor's shot, drums and trumpets at the landing at Westminster." Through the afternoon of Lord Mayor's day the case went ploughing on.

Down at Hatfield, Lord Salisbury came to a decision when he received in the evening the least discouraging of Finet's letters. Obviously the closing of the speech for the defence was the most favourable moment to take action. It would be premature to approach the King, since his intervention

[1] Cecil MSS., vol. 129, f. 167.

was best secured at a later stage of the process whose inevitable end was clearly envisaged by all the family. On the other hand the appropriate time had now been reached at which the strength of the argument for the defence could be laid before the Secretary of State, who was deeply indebted to the Suffolk-Salisbury connection.

On the resignation of Sir Thomas Lake his place had been granted, a little unexpectedly, to Sir George Calvert, who had served in earlier days as one of Sir Robert Cecil's private secretaries and had retained a close connection with the family. He was now wealthy, prudent in his investments and with an increasing interest in the plantations in America. It seems possible that he had guided the young Lord Salisbury in the matter of the purchase of shares in the Virginia Company.[1] Certainly he was prepared to offer deferential but explicit advice[2] to the master of Hatfield whom he had known as a slow and stubborn boy. This very week-end he was expected to come down to Hartingfordbury to stay with Mr. Mynne, his brother-in-law. A suitable gift of venison from Hatfield had been sent to welcome him.[3] He was at the moment sitting as one of the judges in the Star Chamber and Salisbury wrote to point out the weakness of the case against the Treasurer. The letter does not seem to have been preserved, but it was presumably written on 30 October.

The reply was not encouraging, for it was long since Calvert had had any political connection with the outgoing faction and it was essential that the Secretary's actions should

[1] In a list of adventurers to Virginia, ascribed tentatively to 1618, but perhaps more probably dating from the following year, the names of Sir George Calvert, Lord Cranborne and the Earl of Salisbury occur. *The Records of the Virginia Company of London*, ed. S. M. Kingsbury, iii, pp. 80–90. It seems likely that Salisbury had taken out a block of twenty-five shares in the name of his infant son.

[2] Cf., a letter to Salisbury in regard to young Lord Cranborne's christening, dated at Greenwich 24 June, 1619. "I think if my Lord Marquis (Buckingham) be godfather another godmother would be better than she (Lady Hatton)." Cecil MSS., vol. 129, f. 152.

[3] This information was conveyed in a postscript to Sir J. Finet's letter of October 29.

not be misconstrued either by his sovereign or by the favourite. He was careful to write not from his private house in St. Martin's Lane, but from Whitehall. "Your Lordship," he began,[1] "needs not to make any apology for your freedom with me in anything that you shall desire at my hands, having justly so great interest as you have to command me. And for this particular of my lord of Suffolk's you may assure yourself that I having ever honoured and loved his person shall never be a hindrance of any mercy or favour that his Majesty shall intend towards him. God forbid I should, though I must deal plainly with Your Lordship in this that if it comes to sentence, howsoever Sergeant Richardson did as much for my Lord's defence as possibly the cause would bear, yet in good faith My Lord, *bona fide*, I do not understand that the discharge is so clear as you have heard it be." In this instance the decision to abstain from aiding the fallen peer was as clear as the sentences, which expressed it, were confusing and involved.

When once the attack upon the Howards had commenced, it would have been suicidal folly on the part of the promoters to permit its failure. An acquittal would have been fatal to Suffolk's enemies and it was essential to press the prosecution home. In the Jacobean Age it was especially dangerous for any personage in public life to inflict a light wound upon the powerful.

Besides, Calvert was obliged to remember Buckingham and as long as he was Secretary he must not run counter to the wishes of the man on whom the royal favour was permanently concentrated. At regular intervals he had supplied the favourite with information of the progress of the case and he could not allow Salisbury to affect his judgment.[2]

[1] Cecil MSS., vol. 129, f. 168.
[2] The letters from Calvert apparently addressed to Buckingham and dated 13 October, 23 October, 15 November and 15 November, appear to deal with this matter. They were printed in 1753 in Leonard Howard's *Collection of Letters*, pp. 53–61.

And Calvert exercised a wise discretion for, through this trial, Lord Chancellor Verulam was writing to Buckingham and had these letters been conveyed to Suffolk House or Hatfield, the former Treasurer must have abandoned all hope of escaping condemnation. "We all conceive," wrote the Lord Chancellor on 14 October in describing the conference concerning the Suffolk cause,[1] "the proceedings against my Lord himself to be not only just and honourable, but in some principal parts plausible in regard of the public; as namely those points which touch upon the ordnance, the army of Ireland and the money of the cautionary towns." A fortnight later Verulam had become still more explicit. "This day," he wrote on 27 October,[2] "the evidence went well, for the Solicitor did his part substantially: and a little to warm the business, when the misemployment of treasure which had relation to the army was handled, I spake a word, that he that did draw and milk treasure from Ireland, did not *emulgere*, milk, money but blood."

The last letter sent by Finet during the course of the proceedings, is marked by a certain bitterness caused by the fact that my Lord's counsel made so poor a show. This comes through clearly in the description of young Mr. Finch's speech to the third charge of misemployment of treasure. "He said," wrote Finet,[3] "that these detainings, transferrings, antedatings, and the like, charged upon my Lord under the title of 'the mystery of iniquity now to be reached' proceeded either of necessity or election without intent of fraud & were but mists of cloud hanging over my Lord's head with a little wind to be blown away. Many like passages fell from him and also from Sergeant Bawtry to

[1] Letter from Lord Verulam to the Marquis of Buckingham, dated 14 October, 1619. Gibson Papers, vol. viii, f. 112.
[2] Letter from Lord Verulam to the Marquis of Buckingham, dated 27 October, 1619, Gibson Papers, vol. viii, f. 113, printed in Stebbing, *Life and Letters of Sir Francis Bacon*, ii, p. 53.
[3] Letter from Sir John Finet to the Earl of Salisbury, dated 4 November, 1619. Cecil MSS., vol. 129, ff. 135-6.

my Lord's justification." There was little hope from such verbiage with Calvert's letter lying upon the table with its calm discussion of the sentence.

Within ten days this "great business," as contemporaries loved to call it, had swung to its conclusion with that grandiloquent and consciously high-minded phrasing which the age required from its State causes. "To sum up," began Finet,[1] "the last of the account I owe you touching my lord of Suffolk's great business in the Star Chamber. On Friday, Mr. Attorney made his reply to the defendants' answer and began by magnifying the lords' moderation and inclination to qualify faults, though enormous, and rather to grieve at than desire the punishment of offenders, such as was the Earl of Suffolk a great star fallen out of their own firmament; whose business in hand mainly concerned the King in honour and interest, and the subject in safety and ease, whom if it were a crime to follow with hue and cry up to the seat of justice, he must be said to be guilty of it."

In the same heavy strain the great clauses fell without intermission describing the Earl's issuing of the King's treasure unduly and his many shifts. Her ladyship's letters were arraigned as "impious in style and odious in matter," and it is a relief to come to the less mannered sentence, "if she yielded in anything brought against her, it was but as the mouse would do being in the cat's mouth."

"The next day," continued Finet, "was for the lords' answers which came first from Sir Edward Cooke with these preparatives which I will set down as I caught them long pieces and not with the method they were delivered, too hard a task for my weak observation, especially in such a throng of questioning auditors as were there assembled." And then there came the speeches beginning with Coke's declaration that there were "three loud speaking relators

---

[1] Letter from Sir John Finet to the Earl of Salisbury, dated 14 November, 1619, Cecil MSS., vol. 129, ff. 169–73. The letter with others is given at greater length in the appendix of this volume, pp. 328–31.

that stood up against the defendants, the commonweal, the voice of the oppressed and the cry of the labourer robbed of his hire." It was a high procession. To Lord Coke followed Lord Hobart and then Sir Julius Cæsar, the Lord Chief Justice, the Secretaries of State, Lord Digby, the Bishop of Ely, the Bishop of London "extending himself theologically," the Lord Chamberlain, the Marquis Hamilton the Duke of Lennox, and my lord of Canterbury "his discourse suitable to his profession." "The close," wrote Finet, "was for my Lord Chancellor, which he seldom or never makes, as your Lordship knows without great applause. He fell to discourse how completely happy the King were if the Treasury and state of means were settled, what honour he had obtained above any of his predecessors as to have deserved the title of Uniter of Britain and the Planter of Ireland: how glorious the Church here was like a firmament of stars."

Amid a careful dignity, unhurried and with pomp the trial had drawn to its end. The defendants were found guilty; the Earl and Countess of Suffolk were sentenced to be detained in the Tower of London during the King's pleasure; the Earl was condemned to pay a fine of £30,000. They acknowledged themselves guilty and surrendered to serve their sentence. Within a week they were released and retired to Audley End. Here they spent the winter exploring the possibility of the King's mercy. Lord Howard de Walden lost his court appointment; but the efforts to reduce the fine soon proved successful and by the summer their indebtedness was computed at only £7,000. The Suffolks were able to devote more time to their investments, especially their overseas adventures;[1] Lord Suffolk had more leisure to attend to his

[1] Among the Court Minutes of the East India Company there are two relevant entries, Nos. 785 and 791. On 15 December, 1619: "Concerning the general auditors and the Muscovy business and Lady Suffolk and Sir Thomas Edmondes' adventures." On 31 December, 1619: "Captain Pepwell's accounts; Mr. Featherslye to bring in his notes. £900 adventure in the second joint stock, paid in by Lords Suffolk and Walden."

duties as chancellor of Cambridge University; he practised hospitality at Audley End. His equals gathered round him and Lord Bath wrote to congratulate him on being now[1] "freed from his late troubles." On 20 August following Chamberlain wrote to Carleton[2] that the man who had discovered Lord and Lady Suffolk's courses had been murdered and that Lord Coke was spoken of for Treasurer as also Pembroke, Hamilton and Doncaster. The Earl lived on in his retirement until his death in 1626. There was no intention to penalize him,[3] but only to eliminate the faltering ascendancy of the Howards.

A letter written by Sir Henry Wotton to Sir Edmund Bacon in the midsummer of 1624, is evidence that the scars were healed and the memory of the financial scandals vanished. "The Earl of Suffolk," one reads with some surprise,[4] "is still beheld as a Lord Treasurer, and that conjecture hath never fainted since the very first rising of it. But it is thought that the dignity of Privy Seal shall lie vacant as it did in the Cecilian times."

[1] Letter from the Earl of Bath at Tawstock to the Earl of Suffolk, dated 24 January, 1620. Cal. Longleat MSS., ii, p. 69.
[2] Letter from Chamberlain to Carleton. Cal. S. P. Dom. 1611–8, p. 566.
[3] In this connection the letters from Suffolk to the King and from Buckingham to Suffolk, both written in January 1619, are especially interesting, The Fortescue Papers, pp. 77–9.
[4] Letter from Sir Henry Wotton to Sir Edmund Bacon, dated 24 June, 1624, and printed in the Life and Letters of Sir Henry Wotton, ii, p. 41.

CHAPTER XI

THE VILLIERS FACTION

THERE is a constant tendency among those who deal
with the history of the seventeenth century to read into
the changes of these years that developed political
relationship which had come to exist in the period of New-
castle or Walpole. Too much has sometimes been made of
the domination of particular families in the reign of James I
and there was certainly no dynastic quality in the Villiers.
They were *arriviste* and without roots, amiable and grasping.
Like the Bonapartes around Napoleon, they received what
their brother gave them. At the same time it was the sub-
mergence of the Howards which brought to Buckingham
isolation in authority and drew a hostile attention to his
actions and his relatives.

It was characteristic of the great houses that they did not
yet attain to more than a tentative predominance; but already
the roots of their power were indestructible. The Stuart
sovereigns would encourage or discourage them, but would
never attempt obliteration. That was a medieval method
which had, perhaps for the last time, been successfully
exerted in the destruction of the Duke of Buckingham in
1521. But the peers who had risen through the Reformation
had entered into that secure inheritance which the Elizabethan Settlement had helped to guarantee. The strength
which comes from an established possession had fortified
the notion of a permanent, and indeed inevitable ownership, which is so soon attached to the inheritors of English
land. The great buildings, which they had erected, were

178

pledges that their hold on their wide estates was indissoluble. Slowly they moved forward to their calm domain.

The close attachment which bound Buckingham to the King was in itself a danger isolating him from those who had at first supported his advancement. As King James, and then Prince Charles also, became more devotedly affectionate, the position of the favourite worsened. At Wilton and Audley End and Knole and Hatfield, opinion gradually crystallized against him. The Villiers family followed in their brother's wake imitating as far as possible his splendid if rather hectic progress. Throughout the events of the next nine years the wealthy lords on their estates bided their time. Their latent power was beyond the reach of any favourite; many of them were already hostile; all felt to some extent excluded from their sovereign's counsels. Even those to whom Buckingham showed most friendship could not fail to regard his fresh advancements with a steadily diminishing approval.

It was a natural consequence of the Marquis' solitary eminence that his political actions became drastic. There were abrupt changes among the ministers of State and a general tautening after the long quiet period. For, when left to his own devices, King James had been very reluctant to displace his officers. There is reason to suppose that the political dismissals of his later years seldom took place on his initiative. In the first portion of the reign resignations were of rare occurrence and the health of the great ministers of State crumbled away peacefully in office. The King's complaisant attitude was seen most clearly in the few years which had elapsed between the deaths of Salisbury and Prince Henry and his present favourite's emergence. There had been an element of lassitude at this time in the conduct of government.

But energy was the predominant characteristic of the new favourite and the removal of the Howards from the Treasury and the Admiralty, left his activities untrammelled. It seems most probable that Buckingham's acquiescent good nature would have continued to assist him if only it had been tempered by a reasonable lethargy. Favourites arouse less hostility if they are prepared to tire of giving, but Buckingham was quick to offer advancement and reward, and redeemed these promises with abrupt fidelity. His dealings with the Villiers family is a case in point.

Early in 1619 he had been created Marquis of Buckingham and his mother, who had been given a life peerage with the same title, came out into the foreground. It is worth considering the question of her influence since for the next nine years she was to become increasingly a drag upon his fortune. The favourite was only twenty-seven and still unmarried; his brothers were young; it was inevitable that the Dowager should carry weight with him. She was now in robust middle age; married rather unhappily to her third husband Sir Thomas Compton, who was impoverished and not sober; managing in her disposition; profoundly possessive in her affection. She had the good fortune to please King James and she entered into all his projects for the advancement of her favourite son.

The religious element traceable in her letters was at this time considered an inseparable accompaniment of all manifestations of maternal love. In these matters her approach was still orthodox and Anglican, and she had not yet begun to harm the favourite's prospects. At the same time she had already the beginnings of unpopularity as a comment on one of her pious epistles will make clear. "Many," wrote Bishop Hacket in his account of Archbishop Williams "marvelled what rumbled in her conscience at that time; for, from a maid to an old madam, she had not every one's good word for practice of piety." Now she was worldly wise and bent upon her son's great marriage.

This was a project which King James had for some time had at heart. In January it was rumoured that Buckingham would marry Lord Exeter's daughter, Lady Diana Cecil;

THE DUCHESS OF BUCKINGHAM from a portrait by Paulus
Moreelse in the possession of MR. BRUCE INGRAM

but during the spring negotiations for a more fortunate match were set in motion. The greatest heiress of this generation was Lady Katharine Manners, the only surviving child of Francis, Earl of Rutland. Her mother, now dead, had been a sister of Lady Suffolk and co-heiress with her to the Knevet fortune. The Rutland peerage would pass to a junior branch; but she was heiress to the barony of Roos, which had come to her father on the death of William Cecil. Lady Katharine was young and fair, a little lymphatic, rather slow and simple, but passionately and permanently devoted to this brilliant suitor. There was one drawback : she was a Catholic.

Her father and stepmother had joined this Faith, holding to it with conviction, temperate in their expression of opinion and acting under the guidance of the secular clergy. The King's wishes in the matter were explicit and were prudently supported by Lady Buckingham. It was clear that promotion awaited the divine who could shift Lady Katharine's allegiance; and after some months this consummation was achieved by Dr. Williams, the Dean of Salisbury.

With his marriage in the early summer of 1620 a new stage opened in Buckingham's career for he was freed from his dependent status as a mere attendant upon the King and a recipient of his favours. His position had become solid and he could embark on a process of carefree accumulation. And as he rose so did his family. His mother and sister became devoted to and inseparable from young Lady Buckingham; his brothers flocked around him; there was always a close cohesion among the Villiers. As a consequence of the fantastic prosperity of their elder brother the whole financial plane of the Villiers lifted. They were exposed, laden with their new honours, to the public view; but this serious disadvantage lay in the future.

In addition to the post of Lord High Admiral, a whole host of lesser offices were granted to the favourite. He bought Burley-on-the-Hill in Rutland, and planned there a great mansion. Two years later he acquired Wallingford House in Whitehall, and in the summer of 1622, purchased Newhall from Lord Sussex. Here he designed to transform the Elizabethan palace in accordance with prevailing standards. A short description of the house will give an impression of the Marquis' changed background.

Newhall, for which he was said to have given £22,000,[1] was already an immense building lying out in the fields beyond Chelmsford; a mass of Tudor brickwork with a great hall and high Elizabethan windows. The house had been built by Henry VIII and known as Beaulieu. The lofty gatehouse above the confined entrance way into the forecourt, the chapel so much too considerable for private needs and the plain early Tudor gables all dated from this outmoded period. The Earl of Sussex had reconstructed the mansion in those mid-Elizabethan years when the centre of interest in the house had shifted away from the chapel with its large old-fashioned windows showing the Crucifixion and St. George and St. Catherine with white heraldic roses and pomegranates. Over the entrance Sussex had placed an inscription in honour of his royal mistress, and the element of fantasy in the Elizabethan phrasing found an echo in the mind of King James's favourite. There is still an attraction in the brave words of these verses dedicated to the Virgin Queen.

"*En terra piu savia Regina. En cielo la piu lucente stella.*
Vergina magnanima, Dotta, Divina, Legiadra, Honesta e
Bella."

The present generation of Radcliffes were too poor to maintain this palace.

Buckingham's work at Newhall stands in strong contrast to the building of the great families. His energy of tempera-

---

[1] Letter from Chamberlain to Carleton, dated 13 July, 1622. Cal. S. P. Dom. 1619–25, p. 424.

ment desired an ostentation which should be expensive, striking in the new mode and, above all, rapidly achieved. Here was little of that solid and calm magnificence which went to the planning of Hatfield and Audley End, or to Lord Arundel's wide projects. For the position of the Howards and the Cecils rested on their inalienable landed interests, while Buckingham reflected King James's warm immediate favour. Thus the Marquis showed a certain careless haste as he planned his lime avenues, constructed the bowling greens and tennis-courts and devised the gardens and their statuary. The house was carved open for the new wide staircase which led up to a sea-piece representing Sir Francis Drake in action. A picture of Hymen with a chaplet of roses was painted for the state bedchamber; the grounds were strewn with statues of Harpocrates and Nemesis and the Muses; a labyrinth was laid out and embellished with a figure of Minos. The carts rumbled out of London with his new belongings and everything grew up almost overnight.

The same spirit marked the favourite's construction of his new town residence, York House, of which the watergate alone remains. Two letters of this period will convey a clear impression. "York House," wrote Sir Thomas Wentworth, afterwards the famous Strafford, to his friend Wandesford,[1] "goes on passing fast, another corner symmetrical now appearing answerable to that other raised before you went hence, besides a goodly statue of stone, set up in the garden before the new building, bigger than the life of a Sampson with a Philistine between his legs." Meanwhile Buckingham's collections increased apace, tapestries of the Graces from Mortlake, "a most beautiful piece of Tintoret, another head of Titian, a St. Francis from the hand of Cavalier Bellion, a picture of Our Lady by Raphael."[2]

[1] Letter from Sir Thomas Wentworth to Christopher Wandesford, dated 17 June, 1624, *Stafford Letters*, ed. William Knowler, i, p. 21.
[2] Letter from Balthasar Gerbier to the Duke of Buckingham, dated 17 November, 1624.

At the same time a report from his agent, Balthasar Gerbier, completes the picture. "To conclude," he writes to his great patron,[1] "if your Excellency will only give me time to mine quietly, I will fill Newhall with paintings, so that foreigners will come there in procession; but we must proceed very quietly. Tuesday the paving of the cabinet with marble begins, which will be the grandest thing in the kingdom. . . . Madame has not given orders about the furniture of Persian cloth of gold, nor for matting the other apartments. Half of our Dutch mats have come. Mr. Crow will have the dress with pearl ornaments made at Boulogne."

All that the King had taught his "disciple" seems here reflected, the lavish opulence and easy splendour, the unexacting appreciation of artistic riches. It was only natural that restraint and fastidiousness, and the element of a more personal choice would come with the succeeding generation; but for King James, and those whose taste he formed, the delight in amassing precious objects was wholly satisfying. And in the same way the unexpected purchasing power at his command appears to have entranced the favourite. Pictures, not all appropriate, came in from Holland and from Italy; groups of statuary were brought up on the tide by the Thames barges; away in Constantinople Sir Thomas Roe offered to send a brig to the Ægean to bring back "pillars and tables of marble."

It flowed almost naturally from such display that the Villiers family should have a share in the great fortune. In 1623 the favourite had been created Duke of Buckingham and his brothers John and Christopher, now emerged as Viscount Purbeck and Earl of Anglesea, while his brother-in-law, Sir William Feilding of Newnham Paddox, received a barony and then the earldom of Denbigh. The very close texture of their social life and the way in which they entered

---

[1] Letter from Balthasar Gerbier to the Duke of Buckingham, dated February, 1625, printed from Goodman's papers in the *Court of James I*, ed. J. S. Brewer, vol. ii, p. 373.

into the old King's pastimes, resulted in an inseparable advancement. And it was in keeping with their master's generosity that their rewards should be both inappropriate and lavish.

Quite early, Sir William Feilding had become Master of the Wardrobe, and had gained heavy grants out of the duties laid upon the French and Rhenish wine trade, which was supplemented by an annuity charged against the licence of sweet wines. In the same way the Duke's brother, Edward, was provided for by the lease of customs and subsidies in gold and silver thread. Purbeck, already a little solemn and in time insane, had been given Frances Coke as a bride, and Kit Villiers, who was feather-brained and gay, was married to the young Elizabeth Sheldon after two or three heiresses had evaded him.

Since the Queen's death in 1619, King James had come to rely increasingly upon the favourite's family for his entertainment. Their mutual affection warmed him, and Kit's delightful simplicity. They were unassuming and untalented and thus very soothing to their sovereign's age. A reference in one of the Duchess of Buckingham's letters will suggest the tone of their life together. "Yourself," she wrote to her husband,[1] "is a jewel which will win the hearts of all the women in the world." This was the kind of union which appealed to King James's disposition. But an inevitable effect of this pre-occupied affection was to turn Buckingham's relations with the other courtiers sour.

There was a sense in which the favourite remained very youthful and the closed air of his immediate family circle preserved in him an unreal charm which left him vulnerable. Thus, throughout his life he kept for his mother a most affectionate frolicsomeness, a rare quality both devoted and lighthearted. "Now I say," he wrote, "I dare take the

---

[1] Letter from the Duchess of Buckingham at York House to the Duke, dated 16 July, 1623, printed from Goodman's papers, *op. cit.*, ii, p. 279.

bouldness to tell you with my old free and frolicke stile that the same naughtie boy, George Villiers . . . by the grace of God will caste himselfe at your feete." "Dere Mother," he began on another occasion,[1] "give me but as manie blessings and pardons as I shall make fa(u)lts, and then you make happie your most obedient sonne, G. Buckingham." Delightful as this is, there seems reason to suppose that he was hindered by the love which surrounded him from appreciating the sharpness of political reality. One of the consequences of this failure of perception may, perhaps, be seen in Buckingham's relations with his younger sovereign. How far was he responsible for the fact that King Charles's values were so often those of a dream-world?

[1] These two letters are preserved in the Denbigh MSS. at Newnham Paddox and are calendared under p. 256.

CHAPTER XII

SPAIN AND VIRGINIA

THROUGHOUT the reign there can be traced this conflict, already noted in Buckingham's career, between rooted prejudices and superstitions, and the claims of a calculated commercial and political advantage. Spain and Virginia may be held to typify these two conceptions. For the memory of the Armada had left in the English mind a suffused national antipathy towards the Spaniard which was singularly blurred and imprecise. No satisfactory attempt was ever made to assess the power of the nation's enemy, and even the early literature of the colony in North America is characterized by those denunciations of Spanish barbarity which mark the *Justification for Planting Virginia*. But the actual development of the new plantations brought problems and suggested lines of interest of a wholly different character. These called for a cool and adequate examination remote from the atmosphere of heat and fustian. A new set of forces came into play bringing fresh opportunities and hitherto unknown temptations. A novel sobriety overtook the management of overseas adventures. The break with the carefree Elizabethan values becomes apparent. Possibly it is our knowledge of what was still the future which gives to each event in the American possessions such an air of detached reality. Certainly it is clear that the actual builders of Virginia moved on a plane of ideas which was very far distant from the world of their sovereign's clouded and theocratic rhetoric. By considering first the background of Parliament, the King's speech and the standpoint reflected in the House of Commons, and then the workings of the headquarters of the Virginia Plantation, we can gain some impression of the two outlooks and their profound interior divergence.

An attempt to treat of constitutional development or of the influence of economic factors would be quite outside the scope of the present volume. But there are certain aspects of the House of Commons which must be considered if some effort is to be made to convey the atmosphere of the reign and the interplay of interests and classes. In this matter all students owe a heavy debt to Professor Notestein and his assistants. The seven volumes dealing with the Commons' Debates for 1621, which this historian has assembled, provide a singularly complete ground plan of the speeches and resolutions of that year. The third general election of the reign had just been held and, with the exception of the brief Parliament of 1614, the government had been carried on without the support and embarrassment of the two Houses since the dissolution in February 1611. Then Lord Salisbury had been still alive, and in all five sessions of his first Parliament the sovereign had had the benefit of that statesman's unique experience.

Now the King needed money. His son-in-law had accepted the Crown of Bohemia and had been driven from his new kingdom and his own hereditary states were in grave danger. There was the security of the Palatinate to be considered. The speech from the throne, made under these circumstances, well indicates the King's approach. He had just come from the sermon which Bishop Andrewes of Winchester had preached before both Houses, and the royal words were carefully pondered. One can almost visualize those interrelated phrases as they moved forward, weighty and cumbrous, disentangling in their ordered progress the top-hamper of the Jacobean thought. The King's heavy words could never lack assurance, and his utterance was hardly lightened by his strange and arid pleasantry.

"It is true," he began,[1] "that in many sessions of divers Parliaments before this I have made many long discourses, especially to the gentlemen of the House of Commons, and to them have I delivered, as I myself have said, a true mirror of my mind and free thoughts of my heart. But as no man's actions, be he never so good, are free from sin, being a mortal, sinful creature, so some, through a spice of envy have made all my speech heretofore turn like spittle against the wind upon mine own face and contrary to my expectation, so that I may truly say with our Saviour, I have often piped unto you and you have not danced, I have warned and you have not lamented." The theocratic mood was heavy upon him, and very soon he was in full theology.

"All the world," he declared,[2] "cannot so much as create the least vermin, no more than Pharaoh's magicians could; nor can all the men on the earth create faith, but it is God that must give that. Bishop Latimer said very well: 'The devil is a busy bishop.' If our Church were as busy to persuade the right way as the bold Jesuits and Puritans and other sectaries are to supplant and pervert, we should not have so many go astray in both sides."

"I will not say," the King continued in reference to his own achievements,[3] "I have governed as well as she (Queen Elizabeth) did, but I may say we have had as much peace in out time as in hers. I have laboured as a woman in travail, not ten months but ten years, for within that time have I not had a Parliament nor subsidy. And I dare say I have been as sparing to trouble you not with monopolies but in subsidies as ever King before me, considering the greatness of my occasions and charges."

Then, turning to foreign relations, he explained that he had been reluctant in the matter of the Palatinate. "First," he declared,[4] "for cause of religion for I leave that ground

---

[1] *Commons' Debates*, Anonymous Journal, ed. W. Notestein, ii, p. 2.
[2] *ibid.*, ii, p. 6,   [3] *ibid.*, ii, p. 8.   [4] *ibid.*, ii, p. 10.

to the Jesuits and devil, from whence it came, to cast down crowns for cause of religion, and learn of my Saviour, who came into the world to stablish crowns and not to destroy them and to teach men how to obey." It came naturally to him to drop now into the vein of admonition. He described that "strange kind of beasts called undertakers" which had troubled him in 1614, and he spoke of the ills of his first House of Commons. "I have had," he began,[1] "two kinds of parliaments, the one when I came first into England when I was an apprentice and so inexperienced, governors in the *quondam* time being more skilful by long experience, and so many things might then be amiss which I have endeavoured to amend, considering there are two sorts of speakers which I would inhibit, first, lion-like speakers that dare speak of anything that appertains to princes, secondly, fox-like that seem to speak one thing and intend another, as to bring the King in dislike with his subjects." The sentences become more complex, but how clear the sentiment.

Then Sergeant Richardson was elected Speaker and the notes describe the conclusion of that day's ceremony. "The Speaker," so they run,[2] "replied in a long continued oration, repeating what the King had spoken, and (declaring) that he desired that the dutifull liberty of the House should be given, and that kings were invisible gods and God an invisible king."

In the parish chest in the church at Hatfield Broad Oak, on the edge of that lonely stretch of Essex towards High Easter and the Roothings, there has been discovered the notes of speeches in this Parliament made by Sir Thomas Barrington, the local squire. Here we find the frame of the orations in the Commons set down with a vivid turn of phrase, which the other contemporary annotators lacked. In quality and manner the speakers varied greatly and it is

[1] *Commons' Debates*, Anonymous Journal, ii, p. 12.   [2] *ibid.*, ii, p. 15.

possible to sense the fatigue induced by an array of facts even when sustained by the customary majestic periods.

In this connection a speech on foreign policy made by Sir Edward Coke in the November of that year, is strangely illuminating as the prosy rhetoric ploughs forward with its analyses and subdivisions. The first portion was devoted to an historical survey. "That," so runs Barrington's note,[1] "the Lord hath protected the Queen, King, and nation wonderfully. 3ly That all may conduce to us. I. The Queen made a lawe of 12d for absence Sunday. Then El.2. she established the Common Prayer booke. Pope Pius Quartus sent to the Queen *Incentius Parparia Abus*." It is interesting to speculate as to what these words conveyed to Barrington. It seems improbable that either he or the majority of Coke's hearers could discern the form of Abbot Vincenzo Parpaglia beneath these phrases. The speech moved forward and the term lay embedded in the unfolding rhetoric *Incentius Abus*.

But eventually the prologue would be complete and the speaker would reach contemporary affairs. "The first plauge among our sheepe," he insisted,[2] "was brought by a Spanish sheepe to England and could hardly be cured; and so *Morbus Gallicus* by them from Naples." He was followed on the same subject by Sir Robert Phelips, the owner of the great house at Montacute. "The designes of Spain," began Sir Robert,[3] "are ever accompanied by falsehood, being resting on that greate Roman monster. Theay are reciprocall, and at Rome his religion and in Spain Rome's honour and preservation. I pray God remoove from us that pollituick blaseing starr that hath long hung over us, that we feele not as well the misery thereof as we did of that Celestiall." The day before Mr. Thomas Crew had spoken to the same point in simpler language.[4] "It were excellent that we might crop

[1] *Commons' Debates*, Diary of Sir Thomas Barrington, iii, p. 466.
[2] *ibid.*, iii, pp. 467–8.   [3] *ibid.*, p. 469.
[4] *ibid.*, Anonymous Journal, ii, p. 451.

the House of Austria, and top the Indies from him.[1] Every one would give with a swift and open hand." There is something wonderfully direct and unheeding about such a standpoint.

The question of the new Atlantic colonies could not at that time be considered without reference to Spain, and the attitude towards foreign nations and the vague assured conceptions of colonial geography are both well reflected in this Parliament. The matter of the Virginia Company, which has been mentioned in connection with Lord Salisbury's correspondence, was again before the restricted public of the House of Commons. There had been great developments and it was now seven years since the first shipment of Virginian tobacco had arrived in England. A plan for a tobacco contract was before the House, and the members were brought to consider the question of their sovereign's new possessions.

"Explayne," runs a note made by John Smyth of Nibley which gives the framework of one of his own speeches,[2] "the meaning of the word *Forren*, for Virginia and the somer Ilands are freeholds holden of East Greenwich, etc. Know the care to avoyd the inordinate plantyng of tobacco. To banish all was the desire of Gondemar." A comment made by Sir Walter Cope a little earlier in the session, is equally illuminating. "When," he began,[3] "we made title to certayne mynes in the West Indies, Twelve Millions brought in in one yeare in the Queen's tyme. This great spring is kept from our poole, no marvaile if we want water." Here was the old conception of the Spanish King's jealousies, and the colonies were seen as yet another sphere in which England must remain upon her guard.

---

[1] In common parlance the term the House of Austria was used indifferently to indicate both the Spanish and Imperial branches of the Hapsburg family.
[2] *Commons' Debates*, 1621, Diary of Thomas Smyth, v, p. 334. Mr. Smyth was steward to Lord Berkeley and was a chief adventurer in the Virginia Company.
[3] *ibid.*, Parliament Notes by Sir Nathaniel Rich, v, p. 516.

It may be valuable to go a little further and to attempt to consider what notion the idea of the American dominions then implied. In the first place it is clear that the name of Virginia and the Summer Islands awoke a wide familiarity and came easily upon the lips. Under one aspect they had importance for they were the *locale* of chartered companies for the mainland and the Bermudas.

Investment in these undertakings had been canvassed for some dozen years as a patriotic and religious duty which was calculated to show a profit. Exaggerated notions,[1] encouraged at the beginning of the Virginia Company, had now declined upon a somewhat acrimonious common sense. An Anglican missionary intention and the search for satisfactory dividends, were alike pursued with calm determination. The notion of discovering the South Sea and the passage to India was vanishing under the pressure of more immediate interests, but it was still held in the colony and played its part in the Englishmen's imaginations. In like fashion the early legends of Virginia were quickly changing; the tale of the scent of the pine trees carried out to sea, of the vine "spendinge itselfe even to the topps of the high trees,"[2] of the Pacific Ocean lying close to the West of those deep Virginian woods. These were in their tone Elizabethan. They were in line with that brave prospectus garnished with classical allusions which was characteristic of an earlier day. "Only this I must neede saye," wrote Ferdinando Yate, one

---

[1] An example of this approach is the celebrated sermon preached by the Rev. Daniel Price at Paul's Cross in 1609. North America was held to be a country "not unlike to equalize . . . Tyrus for colors, Basan for woods, Persia for oils, Arabia for spices, Spain for silks, Tarcis for shipping, Netherlands for fish, Pomona for fruit and by tillage, Babylon for corn, besides the abundance of mulberries, minerals, rubies, pearls, gems, grapes, deer, fowles, drugs for physic, herbs for food, roots for colours, ashes for soap, timber for building, pastures for feeding, rivers for fishing, and whatsoever commodity England wanteth," printed in Neill's *Virginia Vetusta*.

[2] Letter from John Pory to John Ferrar, dated 30 September, 1619, in Ferrar MSS. at Magdalene College, printed in *Records of the Virginia Company of London*, iii, p. 221.

of the last adventurers of the old tradition,[1] "that if I had the eloquence of Cesero and the skilfull art of Apellese, I could not pen neither paint out a better praise of the cuntrie than the cuntrie it selfe deserveth." But in the seventeenth century a cooler assessment was now required by this new generation which was at once both more commercial and more religious.

Now men's thoughts were turned to the solid profits of the tobacco traffic, and the strengthening of the King's plantations. In the House both these matters were discussed with calmness. "I would move," declared Sir Edwin Sandys in a debate towards the end of April,[2] "that the poore that can not be sett on worke maye be sent to Virginia. Never was ther a fairer gate opened to a nation to disburden itselfe nor better meanes by reason of the abundance of people to advance such a plantation." The subject was taken up by Sir Peter Frescheville. "Now for the way to have it (tobacco) brought in," he explained,[3] "we see the Spanish way hinders us both in Marchandize and money & then this way of Virginia and the Summer Ilands is a good way for the advancinge of their plantation, so brave and necessary a business, a furtherance to the good and benefitt of our nation, and also a ridding us of that *inutile pondus* of unprofitable members of the Commonwealth." Gravely the question was considered. Men had now freed themselves from Sir Walter Raleigh's grand conceptions. Masts and tobacco had replaced the gold which they had been so often promised. In a rather heated session the projects for Virginia seemed cool and rational. They gave food for reflection and sober thought.

.   .   .   .

It was not, however, in the House of Commons that exact

---

[1] Ferdinando Yate, *The Voyage to Virginia*, 1619, Smith of Nibley MSS., printed in *Records of the Virginia Company of London*, iii, p. 109.
[2] *Commons' Debates*, 1621, The Belasyse Diary, v, pp. 113–4.
[3] *ibid.*, Diary of Sir Thomas Barrington, iii, p. 148.

information about the colonies could be collected. Accurate detail was hard to come by. But such knowledge as any one in London then possessed, would be found among the officers of the Virginia Company as they assembled for the meeting of their Court in the low-panelled rooms in Sir Thomas Smith's house in Philpott Lane, or at Mr. John Ferrar's. Here they could peruse the infrequent and sometimes baffling correspondence brought back from Jamestown in the *Abigail*, while they cast up the expenses of the voyage of the *Bona Nova* or calculated when the *Blessing* would cast anchor in the Downs.

For the benefit of investors the company would set out their declarations, the *Nova Britannia* and *Virginia richly valued* and *Good News from Virginia* and Lord Delawarr's quiet *Relation*. These were in the nature of annual reports and had been issued under the authority of the Treasurer, Sir Thomas Smith "once and for all the Primus moter in the (Virginia) Company."[1] The minutes of the Court meetings suggest the breadth of Smith's experience, his long acquaintance with the Indian trade and all the qualities of that rich and cautious merchant.

The subsidiary Bermuda Company was likewise under his control, and he retained the governorship of the latter enterprise after he had been superseded in the treasurership of the Virginia Company by the efforts of a faction which supported his rival and colleague, Sir Edwin Sandys. Sir Edwin, with Lord Southampton, was in 1621 still the principal director of its policies against a heavy smothered opposition. The detail suggests a later age, and especially the account of how Sir Thomas Smith's opponents compelled him to refuse to stand for re-election. In the efforts and the shifting compromises between Smith and Lord Warwick, on the one hand, and Sandys and Lord Southamp-

[1] Letter of Lord Sackville, *Records of the Virginia Company of London*, ii, p. 259.

ton on the other, and the changing allies of each party, there is already some remote suggestion of the intricate ventures of the capitalistic future with the oil-face on their smooth dissensions and their great bland working.

In private there were difficulties enough, although these were perhaps tempered by the callousness with which the Companies appear to have regarded their employees. The relations of the London Company with the Bermudas, known as the Summer or Somers Islands since Sir George Somers had been wrecked there on a voyage to Virginia in 1609,[1] will afford some illustration. On this subject the *History of Bermudaes*, a contemporary document composed by Captain Nathaniel Butler, who was governor of the island from 1619 till 1621, is most illuminating.

The islands had been placed under the Virginia Company in 1612, and a separate company for their planting and control had come into existence three years later. Butler well describes the effect of the arrival of the different ship-loads of adventurers. In the *Plough* there had come in 1612, "one Mr. Edwin Kendall (a gentleman that had shyp't himself for the voyage upon southerly hopes.)" This phrase is surely interesting and descriptive. "About two months after," he writes of another landing,[2] "arrived the *Blessinge* from England, fraughted with one hundred passengers for the ilands; two dayes after her comes in the *Starre*, and in her one hundred and eightie men; among which were divers gentlemen and men of fashion; as one Mr. Lower, sent ouer (as was sayd) to be marshall; and one Mr. Barrett, takeinge upon him to be an inginier; in her also came over one Mr. Felgate, an old soldier, who hath euer since, for the most parte, bin resident here, and hath done many painefull services for the good of the plantation."

---

[1] *The Historye of the Bermudaes*, ed. from Sloane MSS. and 50, by General Sir J. Henry Lefroy, Hakluyt Society, 1882, and incorrectly attributed to Captain John Smith, p. 21.
[2] *ibid.*, p. 35.

The departure of the first governor, Mr. Richard Moore, is chronicled, and it is explained how he sailed away leaving six men to rule the settlement. One of these, Captain Miles Kendall was the object of Butler's especial animus, and he describes their regime[1] saying "that nowe the bravest and tallest fellowe was he that could drinck deepest, bowle best with saker shott in the governor's garden, and win most loblolly."[2] This account whether accurate or not, is very lucid, and the reader is not surprised to learn[3] that "the company of adventurers in England, haveinge received newes by the *Edwin's* safe arrivall of the revells and the perpetuall Christmas kept in their sommer Ilands, found it more than necessary to make them breake up house: so that truly understandinge that the originall of those gambollinge times proceeded from the miserable insufficiencye of the commandors ther, they resolved to make presently an election of a newe governour. . . . Mr. Tucker, the prime searcher of Gravesend, by meanes of certaine of the custome farmers, who wer of the company, made sute for the acceptance of Mr. Daniell Tucker, his brother, who was lately come over to him from Virginia, wher he had bin for divers yeares Cape merchant."

After Captain Tucker's term, Captain Miles Kendall was again in command, and it is asserted[4] that the discipline was relaxed and that the officers "feasted with store of turkees and great bowles full of loblolly, some drams of hott liquor squezed out of the Governor's celler interlaced with all." And then Nathaniel Butler came out with a new commission.

At this stage the general politics of the Company enter into the matter for Butler was supported by Lord Warwick and Sir Thomas Smith, while Kendall was Sir Edwin Sandys' cousin. Kendall complained to Sandys about his successor

[1] *Historye of the Bermudaes*, p. 481.
[2] It seems that loblolly was a form of porridge made of Indian corn and appears an uninteresting stake.
[3] *Historye of the Bermudaes*, p. 69.   [4] *ibid.*, p. 135.

and the conflict was transferred to Britain. "Your greate care," he wrote in a letter of gratitude to Sir Edwin,[1] "in defendinge my good name and repitatyon the which by that Machavill Butler hath ben sought to deprive me of to the uttermost of his power by Candelus lybells sent." There were charges and counter-charges. Illicit dealings with foreign ships, described alternatively as privateers and pirates, were alleged on either side, and Butler wrote[2] to Sir Nathaniel Rich that Kendall had sold "one murthering piece to the pirate in the Frigate." Against Butler it was asserted that he was a common dicer and robbed the settlers, and he was himself obliged to confess that he had played with dice both for money and tobacco in his own house and the lieutenant's.[3]

Slowly Butler's outlook on the Company itself becomes more jaundiced, and he describes the character of his opponents.[4] With Sandys stood "Medlinge Melling, because the Governor had snibed him to the quick, in an answer to one of his sawcye letters," and then "Mr. Kendall, as being a man mainly marchinge down hill to all dunghill actions; one Carter, a very simple fellowe, but a perfect drunckard; one Grove, a ballad singer, sent over by Sir Edwin Sandys into the Summer Ilands, and made marshall ther by Kendall's wise choice and discretion duringe the miserable yeare of the deputy governorshyp; and lastly one Danby, a most especiall young minion of Kendall's, and a beloved bedfellow of his, God knowes wherfor." Butler's recall was now inevitable and his work was in effect composed as an *apologia*.

But he gives one picture of his life before he left the island which is clear and memorable, and suggests that impression

---

[1] Letter of Captain Miles Kendall in the Summer Islands to Sir Edwin Sandys, dated 15 April, 1623, in Ferrar MSS., *Records of the Virginia Company of London*, iv, p. 119.

[2] Letter of Captain Nathaniel Butler to Sir Nathaniel Rich, dated 30 November, 1620, Cal. Manchester MSS., p. 36.

[3] *Historye of the Bermudaes*, p. 250.   [4] *ibid.*, p. 249.

which a martial captain would wish to convey. It is a reference to the Governor going to the church on the fifth of November, the anniversary of His Majesty's preservation, with a guard of halberds and muskets. The officers and the strangers of fashion, both men and women, dined with him. In the afternoon there was music and dancing and at night "many huge bonfires of sweet wood."[1] All these passages repay a careful study. But it is perhaps the religious overtones which force themselves on the attention, the quality of the references to the drinking and the dicing.

For the work of the principal officers of the Virginia Company was influenced by ethical conceptions, and by a determined missionary spirit. An evangelical quality was apparent in their outlook and a strong dislike for gaming. They understood, in a fashion that the lavish Tudor world could not appreciate, the sin of waste. Close links bound the more substantial London merchants to the Church of England. Sir Maurice Abbot was brother to the Archbishop and there were many ties of friendship between the leaders of the City companies and the clergymen of consideration. The ordered lives of the rich mercantile community gave them a natural sympathy with right action and they entered into the whole doctrine of the sober ministers of God's Word. The instructions given to Sir Thomas Gates,[2] the first Governor of Virginia, contain these words. "You shall take principall order and Care for the true and reverent worship of God that His Word be duly preached and His holy sacraments administered accordinge to ye constitutions of the Church of England. And that Atheisme, Prophanes, Popery and Schisme be exemplarily punished to the honor of God and to the peace and safety of His Church." The same phrases were reiterated in Lord Delawarr's commission.[3]

---

[1] *Historye of the Bermudaes*, pp. 273–4.
[2] Instructions for Sir Thomas Gates, dated May 1609. *Records of the Virginia Company of London*, iii, p. 14.
[3] Instructions for Lord Delawarr, *ibid.*, iii, p. 27.

This was the standpoint which Nicholas Ferrar the elder, then Deputy Treasurer of the Company, held in its completeness. Beyond his care for the commercial policy of the Company, his Virginian interests were concentrated on the projected college at Henrico, where Indian children were to be instructed in "the true knowledge of God and understanding of righteousness." Sir Edwin Sandys, himself the son of an archbishop, and the other Governors of his way of thinking, entered fully into this endeavour. They dispatched bibles, psalters and communion plate to Virginia and the Bermudas. It is not surprising that the funeral sermon preached for Mr. Ferrar at St. Bennet Sherehog by Dr. White, should suggest a Christian assurance closer in its character to Wilberforce than Raleigh. The preacher chose a text in Job v. "Thou shalt come to thy grave in a full age, like as a shock of corn cometh in his season."[1]

This rather authoritarian religious approach, profoundly and inevitably Anglican in its tone, had clearly a marked effect on the development of Virginia. But it is natural that similar influences should also be traceable in the gathering in of one section of the support which was obtained for the Virginia Company of London. Among the adventurers to Virginia were numbered the Archbishop of Canterbury, and the Bishops of London and Bath and Wells and Worcester, and Dr. Donne, the new Dean of St. Paul's.[2] Besides the intimate connection between the greater city merchants and the clerical high tables of the universities seems reinforced by the presence in the list of the adventurers of such names as Duppa, Juxon and the Crashaws.[3]

In their correspondence with the officers of the Company,

---

[1] In Mr. A. L. Maycock's recent biography of Nicholas Ferrar there is an interesting account of the religious background of his early life.

[2] *Records of the Virginia Company of London*, iii, pp. 58–66 and 80–90.

[3] In addition to the names of Rawlie and William Crashaw, the latter apparently the poet's father, those of Jeffrey Duppa and Thomas Juxon suggest a close relationship with Bishop Brian Duppa and the future Archbishop of Canterbury.

the Governors in Virginia themselves take up the tone of a high Christian project. Sir George Yeardley, for instance,[1] referred in a letter to Sir Edwin Sandys to "the spirituall vine you speak of," while he had already recommended a successor in these striking terms:[2] "a most suffitient gent. vertuous and wyse, and one upon whose shoulder the frame of this godley building the government of this whole collony would most fittly sit."

Still, at this period, expressions of a fervent Christian endeavour fell easily from the pen. Even those men of breeding whose interest in religious questions was somewhat casual, would be prepared to use strongly appreciative language in all their references to the King's religion. That class to which the management of Virginia most appealed was conservative and privileged. They would transport to this new soil their loyalties and their strong fixed beliefs; the laws of England; the mental climate; the sober monarchy of the Established Church. The Papists were excluded and the efforts of the sound commercial and landed elements combined in harmony to build an Anglican fortress in Virginia.

On the edge of the ethical and economic considerations lay the problem of the children who would be sent out to the new colony. "The City of London," wrote Sandys to Secretary Naunton upon this subject,[3] "have appointed one hundred children from their superfluous multitude to be transported to Virginia, there to be bound apprentices upon very beneficial conditions. . . . Some of the ill-disposed children, who under severe masters in Virginia may be brought to goodness, and of whom the City is especially

---

[1] Letter of Sir George Yeardley among the Ferrar MSS. *Records of the Virginia Company of London*, iii, p. 128.
[2] Letter from Sir George Yeardley to Sir Edwin Sandys dated 1619, suggesting Captain Thorpe as his successor in the governorship, *ibid.*, iii, p. 123.
[3] Letter from Sir Edwin Sandys to Sir Robert Naunton, dated 28 January, 1620. Cal. S. P. Colonial, 1574–1660, p. 23.

desirous to be disburdened, declare their unwillingness to go."
In this connection the coffer books of Winchester contain
an entry under the date of 30 December, 1625. "60s for the
apparelling of six poor boys that went to Virginia." In the
Barnstaple Account Books there appears[1] an item of
"10s. 4d. paid for shoes for three boys sent to Virginia."
These are interesting glimpses of a section of the youthful
proletariat slowly forced upon the move.

But it was undoubtedly the gentlemen sitting in the stern
cabins of the ships for the plantations, who gave its early
character to the new colony. Articles for a proposed plantation in Guiana, which had been set out a few years earlier,
give a lucid view of the outlook of persons of consideration
upon this matter. "The Planters in generall," it is declared,[2]
"are all Adventurers either in person, or purse." "The
shares," this document then proceeds,[3] "of Commaunders
Officers, and men of place and qualitie, that adventure in
Person are not to be rated according to single shares of
inferiour and common persons that adventure in person; but
according to their place, qualitie and merit, in such sort of
shall be fit to give them content and encouragement to
adventure, their persons in so honourable and worthy an
action." The point could hardly be made with greater clarity.

Under these circumstances it is not surprising to discover
that such Adventurers in person and the more prosperous
squires at home, who financed these private journeys, were
alike suspicious of the sailing masters to whose knowledge
they were delivered. In this connection a letter from John
Smyth to Mr. Berkeley, who together with Sir William
Throckmorton of Clowerwall had sent out the *Margaret* from
Bristol, is most illuminating. The voyage had been made in
ten weeks, an admirable passage, but the promoters of the

[1] *Barnstaple Records*, ii, p. 136.
[2] *A Relation of a Voyage to Guiana*, by Robert Harcourt, Hakluyt
Society, p. 136.
[3] *ibid.*, p. 139.

enterprise soon became suspicious of their ship's captain, Mr. Woodleefe. "I have," wrote Smyth,[1] "sent you Woodlef's joynt letter agayne which gives to us here small content, and the foolery of his contemplative newe magazen (not to be furnished for 1,000 *li.* and of ye newest fashion), lesse.... I cannot for the present but much marvell that you have noe pryvate letters from Rowland Painter, nor I any from John Blanchard who vowed to mee, true and secret advertisement (which I believe because he is honest) especially touching Mr. Woodlefe and his estate, behaviour and usage of our men and other observacyons. I feare the old Virginian trick of surprise of letters (if not counterfeiting also) is cast upon us by Mr. Woodleefe." It is interesting to watch the financial purpose working in a world remote from confidence. Here is a letter all compact of circumspection and cold reason. Out in Virginia the Governor's secretary, Mr. Pory, that old Elizabethan, was composing ornate descriptions to be sent to England in the *Diana*, the official packet about "these Christall rivers and odoriferous woods." But in these matters reason triumphed.

The world descriptions of the last reign, the compendious voyages and the war fever were far away. A more sober presentation was now in fashion. Robert Harcourt's *Relation of a Voyage to Guiana*, which was published in 1613 and by now familiar, indicates the change. The work was intended as propaganda for a plantation in Guiana and is in consequence somewhat hostile to Virginia, but it has that quality of a more scientific interest in sailing directions and in strategy which was to mark the Stuart century.. "And because it may be objected," so opens the passage which is particularly valuable in this relation,[2] "that the Spaniards

---

[1] Letter from John Smyth to Mr. Berkeley, dated 1 January, 1620, preserved among the Smyth of Nibley MSS. and printed in *Records of the Virginia Company of London*, iii, p. 293.
[2] *A Relation of a Voyage to Guiana*. By Robert Harcourt, Hakluyt Society (1927), ed. Sir C. Alexander Harris, pp. 63–5.

inhabiting about Cumana, Margarita and Trinidado, may disturb our Plantation (in Guiana) and indanger the lives of those that shall make the first settlement there; I thought good to resolve all such as have affection to make themselves Conquerors of that goodly Countrey that from the King of Spaines Indies nothing can offend (attack) them, for Guiana being seated in the head of the Brises (Breezes) and to the wind-ward of all the Spanish Indies, the current also of the sea setting to the West maketh it impossible for any Shipping to turne it up from the forenamed places towards us. The Spaniard therefore can no way offend (attack) us, but by a preparation out of Spaine it selfe. . . . But I am perswaded that the Spaniards will take great deliberation . . . before they give any attempt upon us: for we doe not finde that they have yet attempted any thing upon Virginia, which lieth in their way homeward from the West Indies, albeit there have passed many years since the first Plantation there. And surely, if Virginia had not a sharpe Winter, which Guiana hath not (which countrey of Guiana is blest with a perpetuall summer and a perpetuall spring) and that it had that store of victualls which Guiana hath, it would in a short time grow to be a most profitable place."

Still the expressed religious motive was never far distant in this century and its nature is adequately described in the Praemonition to the Reader with which William Strachey prefaced his *Travails into Virginia Britannia*. "For whatsoever," he declared,[1] "God, by the ministration of nature hath created on earth was, at the beginning, common among men; may yt not then be lawfull nowe to atempt the possession of such landes as are void of Christian inhabitants for Christ's sake? Harke, harke, the earth is the Lord's, and all that is therein.

"And all the world he will call and provoke,
Even from the East, and so forth to the West."

[1] *The History of Travails into Virginia Britannia*, by William Strachey, ed. from Sloane MS. 1622, by R. H. Major, Hakluyt Society (1849), p. 21.

"As it is in the 50 psalme, where David prophesieth how God will call all nations by the gospell, and in the 12 verse: "For all is myne that on the earth do dwell, And who shall bar him from his possession?" Many circles in England, and not all religious would re-echo these words. 'And who shall bar him from his possession?'

CHAPTER XIII

THE NATURE OF POLITICAL INFLUENCE

FROM the early days of the Virginia Company there had grown up very understandably an opposition between its officers and the Court. It can well be imagined that the plans for the college for native children at Henrico would be unlikely to appeal to King James's courtiers, and that lucubrations like William Strachey's would appear as positively alarming to those whose negligent interest in America was entirely concentrated on their dividends. There had in the first days of the Company been a speculative appeal in the Virginian investments, which were then held to be capable of yielding gold and silver and precious stones. But by now it was clear that the revenue from the plantation would depend in great part on the tobacco crop, and shares in the Virginia Company had become as relatively uninteresting as most sound investments.

There is no reason to suppose that the courtiers possessed any precise knowledge of the new colony or that their interest had advanced beyond a genuine desire for making easy money in polite company. It is, however, certain that the list of the adventurers and shareholders contains almost all those names which a visit to the Court might make familiar, the leading Cecils, Howards, Sackvilles, Herberts, Bedford, Chandos, Carlisle and Lady Shrewsbury, Paget, Drury, Sir Anthony Ashley, Conway, Calvert, Sir Walter Cope, Cranfield and Sir Baptist Hicks, Bingley and Garraway, Sir John Digby, Sir Henry Carey, Sir John Doddridge, Sir Charles Wilmot, Sir Horace Vere, Sir Drue Drury, Sir

Thomas Chaloner, Sir John Ogle, Sir John Townshend, Calisthenes Brooke and Sir Hatton Cheke, Sir Xtopher Perkins and Phineas Pett, Monteagle of the Powder Plot, Sir Thomas Beaumont, Goring, Fanshawe, Craven, Fleetwood, Finch and Ingram, Sir Thomas Roe, Sir Oliver Cromwell, Sir David Murray and Fulke Greville.

The list in its entirety provides an interesting cross-section of that circle which possessed financial privilege or opportunity. Its ramifications are however confined to London, and to those families which resided, at least intermittently, in the capital. Beyond the names of the courtiers there come those of the richer merchants and the city companies, the Bakers and Barber Surgeons, Clothworkers, Drapers, Dyers, Fishmongers, Grocers, Goldsmiths, Girdlers, Innholders, Imbroderers, Ironmongers, Leathersellers, Mercers, Merchant Taylors, Salters, Stationers and Skinners. There was the Lord Mayor, Sir Humphrey Weld, the Elder Brothers of Trinity House, and three progressive corporations, Chichester, King's Lynn and Dover. The country gentry, as opposed to the courtiers and the Parliament men, were hardly represented. Such squires as Sir Valentine Knightley and Thomas Barrington, sat in the Commons. There were very few women, the only names registered being those of Lady Shrewsbury and Lady Berkeley. Catholics also were very rare; among the peers Petre, Eure and Clanricarde, and among the commoners Robert Stourton, Calvert who became a convert, and possibly two of the Shelleys. Science is represented only by the naturalist John Tradescant.

Yet here it becomes clear how very difficult it is to sift any list of names[1] into its categories for where should one place Lord St. Albans with his ranging interests? Viewed from another angle the members of the Virginia Company seem linked and gathered by the solid prestige of Sir Thomas

[1] For the lists of the adventurers and shareholders, cf. *Records of the Virginia Company of London*, iii, pp. 58–66, 78–90, and iv, pp. 353–6.

Smyth and the zeal and financial courage of Lords Warwick and Southampton. These peers had now little contact with the Court and inspired confidence in their integrity as they sat serious and devoted to this business at the meetings of the Company. With them went Lord Cavendish and the uninterested courtiers followed the guarantee that they provided. On the other hand it was through Sandys and the Ferrars that the episcopal support had been obtained and the city companies in their balanced purchases relied on the great merchants whose business life was linked with them. The Virginia Company was in fact a venture of the official world, which the traders were in a position to appraise. But to the courtiers it must have seemed just one more method of reasonably safe investment for their hard-won gains.

To assess the nature of these gains is difficult, but there is no question of the strenuous character of the effort which the officials at the Court required to reap their profits. They were past the windfalls of the Tudor period. Receipts from contraband had fallen, and men of fashion could only with difficulty keep afloat in a world which every year became more grimly peaceful. There was unlimited competition for each office, a very doubtful security of tenure and not even the vestige of a pension scheme. To attract and retain the royal approval in itself involved much toil for the King's ways were now set and he was weakening slowly. Opportunity for advancement was more restricted than it had been in King James's early days. It was hard for the men with the new faces.

Viewed from some aspects 1621 may be seen as the watershed of the two periods, a date by which the Stuart character of the century had been purged of its immediate Elizabethan influences. The old men were dead or in retirement. This year saw the fall of Lord St. Albans and his deprivation of the great seal. Nottingham, the last of the Elizabethan councillors, had vanished. Those parliamentary

GEORGE, FIRST DUKE OF BUCKINGHAM, from a portrait in the
possession of MR. T. W. FITZWILLIAM

manœuvres which would lead up to the Petition of Right had now begun. Raleigh's last journey to the Orinoco and his death on the scaffold on his return to England after the burning of San Thome had closed an epoch. More characteristic of the new age were the sailing of the *Mayflower* and Courten's West Indian adventures. The tobacco plantations yielded a new and settled trade. Arundel was reaching the apotheosis of his career as a *magnifico*. Over the political and social scene lay the net of Buckingham's influence, so rash and so secure. The King was ailing.

In another field the practices of the reign were well established. And in this respect the position of the favourite makes it easier to focus the play of interest. In the matter of offices and pensions and reversions, there has been a considerable misunderstanding. It seems reasonable to suggest that the whole political structure was in a measure affected by the absence of pension schemes and the ill-defined character of the avenues of promotion. To take one example: the envoys to foreign capitals were well aware that they might soon find themselves without employment. Their eyes would turn to such legal or Court office as might provide a berth for their declining years, while the sharp competition for a post like the provostship of Eton was in part due to the very restricted opportunities open to retiring public servants. The English diplomats were of course often indebted and extravagant; but this extravagance cannot conceal the fact that their indebtedness was frequently incurred on the King's service.

The sale of reversions, which was so characteristic a feature of this reign,[1] was closely related to the same problem and had a certain parallel in the modern purchase of annui-

---

[1] Among the places of profit granted in reversion about this time were the office of a Teller in the Exchequer, a clerkship of the signet, the chief stewardship of Ampthill House and Parks, the office of keeping the King's House at Newmarket, the office of Constable of Chester and the place of Falconer to the King. Cal. S. P. Dom., 1611–8, pp. 128, 99, 102, 152, 226 and 188.

ties. The fact, however, that the profit depended upon the date of the death or retirement of the actual holder, gave a somewhat speculative character to such investments. It was not altogether uncommon for a man in public life to purchase or obtain two or sometimes three reversions to provide against the termination of his employment. Even if the office in question should not fall vacant, it was always possible to re-sell the reversions whose capital value inevitably appreciated in the interval.

In certain cases a reversion might be purchased merely in order to place the reversion-holder in a sound strategic position. As a consequence the avenues of promotion were frequently found to be blocked by quite unexpected obstructions. An instance of this form of transaction is the purchase by Sir Henry Wotton, then ambassador in Venice, of the reversion of the mastership of the Rolls after Sir Julius Cæsar's term. The office was of very considerable importance and never actually fell vacant during the reign, as Sir Julius retained it till his death at the age of eighty-seven. At the same time the possession of the reversion enabled Wotton to obtain a post which he coveted, since he held a substantial asset with which to buy off his nearest rival. These negotiations were, of course, always suave and in general, good-humoured. Reversions were a form of property which a public man of prudence and substance was almost expected to possess, and it is worth noting that in certain offices it was possible to purchase a second or even a third reversion of a place.[1]

Allied to the purchase and re-sale of reversions and very similar in scope was the custom of obtaining by purchase the right to nominate to offices of profit. This practice was

---

[1] For instance on 26 March, 1612, the office of Secretary and Keeper of the Signet in the north of England was granted to Arthur Ingram for life with reversion to four others, and on 12 November, 1613, a grant was made in second reversion of the office of Master of the Toils and Tents. Cal. S. P. Dom. 1611–8, pp. 125 and 206.

especially well-established in legal circles, and the instructions to the Master of the Rolls concerning a grant[1] of the next nomination of a Clerk to the Petty Bag in the Court of Chancery, and the confirmation of the grant[2] of three reversions of the office of one of the Six Clerks, indicate a busy and profitable routine.

If some of these practices were directed to provision for retirement, the same cannot be said of the complex question of the place of the *entrepreneur* in the sale of peerages. But it should be mentioned that in this matter the large sums involved, although not improbable, depend usually upon consistent rumour rather than on any stricter evidence. Thus, in the series of news-letters through which Mr. Chamberlain kept Sir Dudley Carleton informed about affairs in London, there is mention of considerable figures said to have been paid[3] or offered[4] in respect of the creation of baronies or promotion within the House of Lords.

Such profit, however, was in many cases merely nominal. Unlike reversions, which usually involved a straightforward business transaction, the grant of taxes on honours frequently implied the liquidation of a debt. Arrears of pay could be made up from such a source. It seems to have been a situation of this kind which is revealed in an entry in the autobiography of Phineas Pett, then master shipwright at Woolwich. "On the 20th day of November," he wrote,[5] "attending at Theobalds. . . . His Majesty in his princely care of me by the means of the honourable Lord High

[1] Letter to the Master of the Rolls, dated 19 September, 1615, *ibid*, p. 253.
[2] Grant dated 12 November, 1613, *ibid.*, p. 201.
[3] On 29 March, 1617, Chamberlain declared that "Lord Chancellor Ellesmere's son solicits the earldom of Bridgewater, but the £20,000 he offers for it is not enough," *ibid.*, p. 453.
[4] On 15 June, 1615, Chamberlain wrote that "Lord Sheffield has the benefit of Sir Robert Dormer, who pays £10,000 (for his peerage)," and on 15 November, 1616, he asserted that "Winwood has bargained with Sir Philip Stanhope to pay £10,000 to be made a baron." Cal. S. P. Dom. 1611–8, pp. 289 and 398.
[5] *The Autobiography of Phineas Pett*, ed. W. G. Perrin, Navy Records Society, li, p. 121.

Admiral, had before my coming bestowed on me for the supply of my present relief, the making of a knight baronet, which I afterwards passed under the broad seal of England for one Francis Radclyffe of Northumberland, a great Recusant, for which I was to have £700, but by reason that Sir Arnold Herbert (that brought him to me) played not fair with me, I lost some £50 of my bargain."

The episode just related indicates one element which was invariably present in situations of this order. Recourse to the Court was essential, and the royal licence was required for such transactions. There was inevitably a draining away of profit by the *entrepreneur*. Courtiers like Sir Arnold Herbert were always prepared for a consideration to introduce persons of Sir Francis Radcliffe's standing to those whose financial claims the sovereign had decided to liquidate at their expense.

Again, it is only the absence of adequate provision which can explain the intense anxiety which centred around the vacancy of certain posts. So many men could see the opportunity for secure retirement which a position of dignity would offer. From all sides the courtiers converged upon these chosen preferments which in this way received a wholly disproportionate significance. Few episodes illustrate this factor in the situation more clearly than the contest for the vacant provostship of Eton.

The college statute, which required that the provost should be in holy orders, had been dispensed in Sir Henry Savile's case, and as that scholar's life drew to a close, it became apparent how well this office would suit a Court official. Even before Sir Henry's final illness certain tentative proposals for the succession were put forward by Sir Dudley Carleton (who had married Lady Savile's daughter), by Dr. John Hammond and Sir Henry Wotton, and by a rather obscure courtier, Sir William Beecher, who held the clerkship of the Privy Council. Sir Henry died in the opening weeks of 1622, and the King to the general chagrin appointed a Scots layman, Thomas Murray.

Within a year, however, the new Provost was himself in failing health and the matter was agitated once again. In March 1623, the former Lord Chancellor wrote to the Secretary of State with a direct request. "Mr. Thomas Murray, Provost of Eton (whom I love very well)," began Lord St. Albans,[1] "is like to dye. It were a pretty cell for my fortune. The College and Schole I dare not dout but I shall make to flourysh." To this letter Sir Edward Conway replied with courtesy stating that to his regret the place had been already promised to Sir William Beecher. Four days after his first letter, and before receiving a reply, St. Albans wrote once more. "There will," he explained,[2] "hardly fall (especially in the spent howre glass of such a life as mine) anything so fitt for me."

For a fortnight Dr. Murray lingered on and the day following his death the Visitor of the College, Bishop Williams, went down to Eton. It was a complication in the situation that the Duke of Buckingham was out of England and that nothing could be done till his return. "The place," wrote the Visitor to the favourite,[3] "is stayed by the Fellows and myself until your Lordship's pleasure be known." Already the candidates had assembled in some force, and Dr. Williams reported in the same letter that Sir William Beecher, Sir Dudley Carleton, Sir Albertus Morton (Wotton's nephew) and Sir Robert Ayton, Secretary to the late Queen, were among the number. In regard to Bacon he pointed out that the new provost must be "a careful manager and a stayed man, which no man can be that is so much indebted as my Lord St. Albans."

[1] Letter from Lord St. Albans to Secretary Conway, dated 25 March, 1623. S. P. Dom. Jas. I., cxl, no. 32.
[2] ibid., no. 59.
[3] Letter from Bishop Williams to the Duke of Buckingham, dated 11 May, 1623. Cf., H. C. Maxwell Lyte, History of Eton.

Very soon afterwards three other candidates were added, Sir Robert Naunton, Sir Ralph Freeman the Master of Requests, and Sir Henry Wotton. But in the summer of this year Wotton was unexpectedly recalled from the embassy at Venice and his interest at once became acute. "That which doth touch me," he wrote to Buckingham who had by now returned,[1] "is that after seventeen years of continued employment, either ordinary or extraordinary, I am left utterly destitute of all possibility to subsist at home, much like those seal fishes, which sometimes, as they say, oversleeping themselves in an ebbing water feel nothing about them but a dry shore when they awake."

The situation now became entangled for, while some sort of promise had been made to Sir William Beecher presumably in return for a money payment, Wotton was pressing for his substantial arrears of salary and allowances. It was fortunate for him that these had been permitted to accumulate until the Government had removed him from his post. The governing factor seems to have been the reversions in Wotton's possession which he could now dispose of to advantage. To Buckingham himself he offered the reversion which he had purchased to the mastership of the Rolls, while he satisfied Sir William Beecher's claims by the gift of the reversion to half a Six Clerk's place in Chancery. In the summer of 1624 the late ambassador to Venice was rewarded by the appointment to the provostship of Eton.

It is worth glancing for a moment at the fate of the other candidates. The Master of Requests and the Clerk of the Privy Council went forward in their endowed appointments. Sir Albertus was young and thus not qualified to ask for such a post of retirement as the provostship, but came in time to be a Secretary of State. Sir Dudley Carleton's desire for repose had been but transient and his ambassadorial

---

[1] Cf., *The Life and Letters of Sir Henry Wotton*, by Logan Pearsall Smith, ii, p. 284.

career went forward until he returned at last to the Secretaryship and a peerage. Lord St. Albans must have realized how far this modest appointment lay from his grand and embarrassed living. Each of these developments was explicable and governed by a sober reason. The whole affair rippled away into contentment. In that world the rich were not sent away empty.

CHAPTER XIV

DONNE AND PRINCE CHARLES

AT the disordered Court of James I there was one figure who always appears most inappropriate, Charles, Prince of Wales. A dour or buoyant opposition to their father's circle has been a commonplace among heirs-apparent, but it was characteristic of Prince Charles that he possessed the power of accumulating and concealing disapprobation. His childhood had been isolated; his family relationships very barren; from an early age he is seen as at once both nervous and rigid. Throughout his life he was by nature very secret.

He was only twelve when his brother, Prince Henry, died, and he is credited with maintaining a childish hostility directed against both Ker and Villiers. The complete dependence upon Buckingham which developed later is, perhaps, most accurately seen in relation to his former isolation. For, when the Prince's guard was lowered, he gave once and for all his utter confidence. Possibly it was the profound effort which this involved that helped to bind Charles so closely to his friend, and the gravest result of this attachment lay in the exhaustion of the King's capacity for perfect trust. More than most sovereigns King Charles I stood in need of the power to give his entire confidence, but this faculty suffered atrophy when Buckingham was murdered.

There was eight years difference in age between them and the splendour of the Duke's vitality, the ease and candour of his courage, the physique and vigour, and the open and ingenuous charm contrasted with the Prince's impeded adolescence and his lonely mistrustful reticence. Again it is the slow rate of the latter's mental growth which explains the fact that their companionship appears so equal. They were the King's two "scholars" and thus learned together: it was only much later that Charles I developed those perceptions in artistic matters which were to be of such a different quality from the Duke's cheerful reliance on King James's canons of magnificence.

They were united, too, on the question of religion: side by side they absorbed the old King's teaching. In this sphere they followed with an equal eagerness the expositions of their royal master, while their strongly nationalist confidence led them to support each external manifestation of that *Ecclesia Anglicana* which was inextricably interwoven with the Stuart kingship. King James had come in his maturity to his doctrine of the monarchy, but his son had from youth the consciousness of an inviolable right which was linked with the sense of the Divine guardianship over their God-given inheritance. This conviction, and the comfort which could be drawn from it, was imparted fully to George Villiers with his malleable and uncritical mind, so innocent of previous training.

The interior confidence, which seems to have guided both Buckingham and King Charles, appears to be related to this doctrine. In the Duke's case a consistent hopefulness, spontaneous and rather attractive, marked his whole outlook. Even in the last journey to Portsmouth he was to feel himself assured of protection and success. King Charles, also, had throughout life the same belief in his own eventual good fortune, secure in his tranquil knowledge that the destinies of Kingship were committed to the Good Providence of God. Surely King James had a great share in instilling this sense of well-being, a content which emanated in his case from the peaceful exercise of his royal authority. Yet for the old King it was, perhaps, a static contentment, a relief at deliverance from the Kirk and from the shadow of Gowrie.

On the other hand there was a dynamic element in the faith of his favourite and his son. In Buckingham's case it was more conventional in its expression, closer to the surface and less real, while King Charles's belief was more subdued, but very permanent, hidden and unyielding. Both men were in their different ways instinct with energy, and the presence of this active force behind their religious and political convictions was ultimately fatal. There are few doctrines which may not be held with impunity in indolence.

The difference between the Jacobean and the Caroline standpoint appears to be reflected in the distinction between the theological approach of Laud and Donne. For the sermons preached by Donne at the Court, and at St. Paul's, after his promotion to that deanery in 1619, had a profound effect both in their spoken and later in their printed form. In the earlier series delivered at Lincoln's Inn in the years after he had taken holy orders, he was still finding his way in the new medium, and it was some time before he came into possession of his high and unstrained eloquence; so clear and ordered and processional; so firmly sunk into the rock of the world-order of the seventeenth century.

This last point is significant because at no stage did the Dean abandon altogether his mundane values. Rank and the hierarchy of learning were alike so evidently immutable, and from this basis the range of his speculation soared, and his thought formed itself gravely and serenely. It was, in fact, in the sermons and devotions, in these set pieces, that he could attain most easily to serenity.

A passage from the *Devotions upon Emergent Occasions*, first printed in 1624, gives in its manner and material the perfection of what may be called the Jacobean faith. "In Heaven," wrote Dr. Donne, in the fifth section of this treatise, "there are Orders of Angels, and Armies of Martyrs, and in that house, many mansions; in Earth, Families, Cities, Churches, Colleges, all plurall things; and lest either of these should not be company enough alone, there is an association of both, a Communion of Saints, which makes the Militant and Triumphant Church, one Parish; so that Christ, was not out of his Dioces, when he was upon the Earth, nor out of his Temple, when he was in our flesh."

There was likewise in his sermons a singular power by which he brought a devotional tranquillity out of the over-stately conceptions of his rich period. The familiar passage in Sermon LXXIX is worth quoting in this connection, to mark the transition from an euphuistic background to doctrinal statement. "There are Indies," he here concludes,[1] "at my right hand, in the East; but there are Indies at my left hand too, in the West. There are testimonies of God's love to us, in our East, in our beginnings; but if God continue tribulation upon us to our West, to our ends, and give us the light of his presence then, if he appeare to us at our transmigration, certainly he was favourable to us all our peregrination, and though hee shew himselfe late, hee was our friend early."

Much that was traditional received expression. "There then," he declared in Sermon XLIV at St. Paul's Cross, "in heaven I shall have *continuitatem intuendi*. It is not onely vision, but Intuition, not onely a seeing, but a beholding, a contemplating of God, and that *in Continuitate*, I shall have an uninterrupted, an un-intermitted and un-discontinued sight of God."

Yet in 1623 in one of his letters of courteous piety, Donne could write to Buckingham from the Deanery of St. Paul's on an altogether different level. "The hardest Autors in the world," he began, "are Kings; and yor Lordship hath read over the hardest of them. Since you have passed from the Text of the King of Kings, the booke of God, by the Commentary of the wisest Kinge amongst Men, the Counsayls of our Soveraigne." It is possible that to Donne there was

[1] *Sermon LXXIX*, preached at St. Paul's, ed. 1640, p. 810.

little incongruity between his statements. We cannot now recapture the seventeenth-century attitude to kingship or that awe in face of the unassailable fact of royal sovereignty. The courtiers, the King, the Prince and Buckingham, listened to the Dean's great sentences. It was not in the pulpit that he manifested his hesitations or his searing doubts. Here he was calm and his thought proceeded clearly, past his pre-occupation with death and his conceits; he was mature and had no equal. But in one respect Donne was at a disadvantage; he had none of Laud's rigidity, nor the hammering Puritan vehemence; he was so unexacting.

It was this quality of thought at once wide and urbanely beneficent which marked the divergence between King James's theologian and the severer divines of the succeeding reign, with their more orderly and less fluid processes. These men would have scant sympathy for the Dean's mind as it swung round on its great circles so diligent and so un- assertive. "You know," he wrote in a letter printed in his son's collection,[1] "I never fettered nor imprisoned the word Religion; not straightening it Frierly, *ad Religiones factitias* (as the Romans will call their orders of Religion) nor immur- ing it in a Rome, or a Wittemberg, or a Geneva; they are all virtuall beams of one sun, and wheresoever they finde clay hearts they harden them, and moulder them in to dust; and they entender and mollifie waxen. They are not so contrary as the North and South Poles; and that they are connaturall pieces of one circle."

It is not altogether easy to explain why certain aspects of Donne's thought found in his time so little echo. But it is perhaps accurate to suggest that the old King's dream of a calm sphere where the bearers of sovereignty would exist far beyond the accidental divergences of religious doctrine perished with him. All his writings suggest how strongly he

[1] *Letters to severall persons of honour,* written by John Donne sometime Dean of St. Paul's and published by John Donne, Dr. of the Civil Law, 1651, p. 29.

desired to penetrate to a secular peace where the Kings of the earth would commune with their Divine Exemplar. Thus the strain of one of Donne's reveries was appropriate only to King James's circle. "The elements of God's mercies," the Dean begins in a letter on religious differences to Sir Henry Goodere,[1] "run through both fields, and they are sister teats of his graces, yet both diseased and infected, but not both alike. And I think that as *Copernicisme* in the Mathematiques hath carried earth farther up from the stupid Center; and yet not honoured it, nor advantaged it, because from the necessity of appearances it hath carried heaven so much higher from it: so the *Roman* profession seems to exhale and refine our wills from earthly Drugs, and Lees, more than the Reformed, and so seems to bring us nearer heaven; but then carried heaven farther from us, by making us pass so many Courts, and Offices of Saints, in this life, in all petitions."

This elaboration dated quickly. It was too indefinite for the compass of Prince Charles's mind, or for his plainer preferences. The next generation of divines would turn away to the cool and decorous world of Laudian Cambridge or to the freshness of Little Gidding. The insular matter-of-fact outlook of Charles I was ill fitted to comprehend the hot spiced winds of John Donne's charity.

In this connection sufficient allowance is seldom made for the divergent outlook and reactions of adjacent generations. The heavily laden metaphor was to find no echo among those who moved out into the more sober atmosphere of the early Carolines. The burdened elaborate approach, so closely linked to the Renaissance world, would inevitably repel those like Ferrar and George Herbert who were to meditate upon the countryside and its ordered rather formal pastoral scene. Thus the manifestations of Donne's high talent seem

[1] *Letters to severall persons of honour*, written by John Donne sometime Dean of St. Paul's and published by John Donne, Dr. of the Civil Law, 1651, p. 112.

conditioned by his never carefree thought, and by a way of life profoundly civilized and urban. Through his later years there came swinging down into the silence of Donne's study that sound of the Bells of Paul's which well suggested the nature of his duty; the ties that bound him to the unquiet city; the ethical and secular environment that encompassed the sweep of his great generous sentences.

It was clear that a certain simplicity of expression would follow close upon this unrelieved magnificence. In this at least Prince Charles resembled his contemporaries for his own likings lay very far removed from that webbed Jacobean verbal splendour. George Herbert, whose mother was so distinguished a friend of Dr. Donne, is in this connection typical of the later taste for his poems with their pastoral quality suggest an approach which is deliberately insular and simple. And with this line of thought a new light fell on Anglican devotion which the Prince himself was soon to share.

It was to this generation that the Church of England seems first to have appeared with that character of the inevitable which has always a soothing influence on all those who possess a tranquil attachment to tradition. To the younger men of a religious temper the country churches with the dusty heraldic hatchments and the hard and clean oak pews, and the fresh air through the open doorways, seemed the natural abode of quiet devotion and the symbols of a wholly English peace. It is for this reason that in Herbert's work is first reflected a world alien to the Jacobean, unagitated and swayed by reason, conservative and religious, sensitive and moderate.

With this there went a certain spirit of confidence, very far either from Donne's attitude or from that of the first Reformers, which was in time to become a specific mark of Anglican devotion. It was a confidence based on trust, and accepting unquestioningly the settled order. It was fresh

and peaceful and brimming quietly with an immense conviction of the decency and honesty of one's English neighbours.
Such a confidence was very appealing and direct; conservative
in each implicit sentiment and biblical in its expression.

In Herbert's case the effect of his early poems is to conceal
this innate simplicity; but he soon came to a certain rough-
ness of expression and slipped out from the coiled thought
of the old King's generation. "I have always observed," he
wrote in the single letter to his mother which has come down
to us,[1] "the thread of life to be like other threads or skeins
of silk, full of snarles and encumbrances. Happy is he whose
bottom (spool) is wound up, and laid ready for work in the
New Jerusalem." There is a positiveness in these expressions
which was to be re-echoed in the English Christian background for two hundred years.

To quote from *The Pearl* is to anticipate the developments
of thought; but the well-known lines have an especial value
as indicating that religious approach which was to appeal
to Charles I in his later years.

> "That through these Labyrinths
> not my groveling Wit,
> But thy silk-twist, let
> down from Heaven to me,
> Did both conduct, and teach
> me, how by it .
> To climb to thee."

Anglican thought is here seen grounded on its rock-like
certainties, and the whole feeling of Herbert's work suggests
how strong was the structure of the Church of England.
George Herbert was born in 1593 and his character was
forming through King James's reign. He had experienced
the Court and was to turn from his secular ambitions. His
knowledge of certain facets of English life was instinctive and
profound, and was not concealed by his decorous humour.

[1] Printed in the different editions of Izaak Walton's *Lives* and also with
Herbert's other letters in G. H. Palmer's edition of his Works.

He was innocent of the Church of Rome and kindly scornful. "And having conquered did so strangely rule," he wrote of the Papacy in the *Church Militant*,[1] "that the whole world did seem but the Pope's mule." It was characteristic, too, that he should say that Rome[2] "hath kiss't so long her painted shrines" and should be hesitant of the element of mysticism in Juan Valdes.

In the year before Donne's death Herbert took Orders and accepted the benefice of Bemerton. A passage from Izaak Walton indicates the method of his life. "And," writes Walton, "some of the meaner sort of his Parish did so love and reverence Mr. Herbert, that they would let their Plough rest when *Mr. Herbert's Saint's-bell* rang to Prayers, that they might also offer their devotions to God with him; and would then return back to their Plough." This seems to be the atmosphere of the ideal of the early Carolines and King Charles would come to it; but how remote it must appear from the Jacobeans.

These days at Bemerton are here recalled in order to emphasize the very different background of some of the Jacobean prelates. In this connection a study of Bishop Williams is especially valuable since, more than any other man, he represented that commingling of the roles of Church and State which well accorded with King James's hieratic outlook. It is also significant that this prelate, who succeeded Bacon as Lord Keeper and thus held a dominant politico-religious position during the last four years of the old King's reign, should have profoundly alienated the Prince of Wales. Prince Charles's deep and respectful sympathy for the Anglican divines could not in this instance survive the Bishop of Lincoln's opulent processes.

Scrinia Reserata, the biography of Bishop Williams, prepared by his chaplain, Dr. Hacket, gives perhaps the most coherent view of one aspect of the Court life of the

[1] *Works*, ed. G. H. Palmer, iii, p. 373. [2] *ibid.*, iii, p. 103.

dying reign. Its manner is wholly admirable as it traces the rise of one who was born in due time and came by prepared good fortune to his great deserts. A fairly detailed quotation will convey better than any other method the spirit of the time and its attraction.

"Among their copious Stems and far-fetch'd Descents," begins one of the opening passages,[1] "the Pedigree of the House of *Williams* of *Coghwillanne* hath as many brave Strings in the Root, and Spreads as wide in the Branches, as I have seen produced from the Store-House of their *Cambrian* Antiquities. It grows up in the top Boughs to the Princes of *North Wales* in King *Stephen's* days."

"I close it up therefore," Dr. Hacket continues,[2] "that his Pedigree of Ancestors gave a good Lustre to his Birth, but he gave a greater to them. Howosever I receive it for a Moral Truth, as well as a Mathematical, that the longest Line is the least of all quantitative Dimensions."

"All things," we then learn,[3] "fell out happily by Divine Disposition, to bring him (the future Bishop) up from a towardly Youth to a worthy Man. For by that time this Bud began to blow, it fortuned that Dr. *Vaughan*, afterward the Reverend Lord Bishop of *London*, came into Wales and took the School of *Reuthen* in his way, where he found his young Kinsman *John Williams* to be the Bell Weather of this little Flock. Dr. *Vaughan* was exceeding glad to find him in that forwardness: took speedy care to remove his kinsman to Cambridge and commended him to the tuition of Mr. *Owen Guin* of *St. John's* College, well qualified by his Country and Alliance for a Friend and no indigent Tutor. The young Youth was now entring into the 16th year of his Age, much welcom'd to *Cambridge* by the Old *Britains* of

---

[1] *Scrinia Reserata.* A Memoriall Offer'd to the Great Deservings of John Williams, D.D., who sometime held the Place of Lord Keeper of the Great Seal of England, Lord Bishop of Lincoln and Lord Archbishop of York. By John Hacket, Lord Bishop of Lichfield and Coventry, edition of 1692, p. 6.
[2] *ibid.*, p. 6.   [3] *ibid.*, p. 7.

North Wales, who praised him mightily in all places of the University (for they are good at that, to them of their own Lineage)." "I have not added," notes Dr. Hacket[1] at this point, "a Grain to the just weight of Truth, that his Sails were filled with prosperous Winds, which blew from the Cape of Nature, yet that he plied the Oar with main might to make it a Gaining Voyage."

The author then continues his account of Williams' progress during his Cambridge years, and refers to the opposition which he met with from those who had belonged to the former Brownist faction. "They were," he writes,[2] "of the old stock of *Non-Conformitants,* and among the seniors of his College, who look'd sour upon him, because he was an Adherent to and a Stickler for the Discipline and Ceremonies of the Church of *England,* these laid their Heads together to exclude him from Preferment, but their Plot would not hit Others that were the most orderly Sons of the Church were not pleased with him, because he frequented Reverend Mr. *Perkins* his Congregation. It is true, he was his constant Auditor, while Mr. *Perkins* lived, so early his well-kneaded Judgment took delight in clear and solid Divinity. And he that is discreet will make his Profit out of every side, or every Faction, if you like to call it so."

A description is then given of the young man's introduction to Lord Lumley through the latter's nephew, Mr. Llwyd. "It fell out luckily to Mr. Williams," remarks Dr. Hacket,[3] "to keep him from incurring great Debts, that he had such an Ophir or Golden Trade to drive with Lord *Lumley's* Purse, who supplied him with a Bounty that grudg'd him nothing, till the year 1609 (for then that aged Baron died)."

Yet the most interesting section of this biography is,

---

[1] *Scrinia Reserata.* A Memoriall Offer'd to the Great Deservings of John Williams, D.D., who sometime held the Place of Lord Keeper of the Great Seal of England, Lord Bishop of Lincoln and Lord Archbishop of York. By John Hacket, Lord Bishop of Lichfield and Coventry, edition of 1692, p. 8.

[2] *ibid.,* p. 9. [3] *ibid.,* p. 11.

perhaps, that portion dealing with Dr. Williams' attainments which can here only be indicated in general terms. "He moil'd awhile in Chronology," we are told,[1] "and because Cosmography is like Eyes unto the Blind, to lead a diligent Man in all the journeys of the earth, through which divers Authors carry him he took such light to walk by as Ortelius held before him. . . . *Chronology* and *Chorography* were his Bladders to swim with. Now suppose him launch'd into the Main Ocean for Historicall Traffiick."

"He carried in his Mind," we are informed,[2] "an Universal *Idea* of all synods and Convocations that were ever held in our Land, of all of our Cathedrals, their Foundations, Conditions of Alteration, Statutes, Revenues, etc. As he had spared for no travel to purchase this skill; so, to fill his Vessel brim full, he received all that Sir *Harry Spelman*, Sir *Robert Cotton* and Mr. *Selden*, his dear Friends could pour into him. . . . The issue of his Life bewrayed his End therein; for he made his study pay with Wages for all his Labour: For he discerned his own Abilities to be fit for Public Employment; therefore he search'd into the notable Particularities of all Kingdoms, Republicks and their Churches, with all the Importances that hung upon them. And he guessed right, that King *James* would give all he could ask for such a Minister."

This is indeed an admirable view of that Jacob's Ladder by which he mounted to be chaplain to the Lord Chancellor, to receive the rich benefices in the latter's gift, to pass through the deaneries of Salisbury and Westminster to the Lord Keepership and the Bishopric of Lincoln. He is next seen in the household of Lord Chancellor Ellesmere. "He was now," writes Dr. Hacket,[3] "in the House of *Obed-Edom*,

---

[1] *Scrinia Reserata*. A Memoriall Offer'd to the Great Deservings of John Williams, D.D., who sometime held the Place of Lord Keeper of the Great Seal of England, Lord Bishop of Lincoln and Lord Archbishop of York. By John Hacket, Lord Bishop of Lichfield and Coventry, edition of 1692, p. 13.
[2] *ibid.*, p. 14.   [3] *ibid.*, p. 27.

where every thing prosper'd, and all that pertain'd to him. The Chaplain understood the Soil on which he had set his Foot, that it was rich and fertile, able with good Tendance, to yield a Crop after the largest Dimensions of his Desires. To be well then was but to be well now. His fore-casting Mind thought of the Future, how to stock himself with Experience, with Wisdom, with Friends in greatest Grace with other *Viaticum* for the longest Journey of his ensuing Life."

The reader is well prepared by these descriptions for the consummation of each laden paragraph. "He never," declares Dr. Hacket of his patron,[1] "met with any before, no not the Lord *Egerton* (Ellesmere), much less after, that loved him like King *James* at the full rate of his worth." "The Chaplain understood the Soil on which he had set his Foot, that it was rich and fertile." Williams was many-sided; he was to be Buckingham's enemy and Laud's rival, and Nicholas Ferrar's remote diocesan. Still, it is not difficult to imagine the effect of the approach which these thick suffocating phrases so well suggest on that uneasy inhibited idealism which marked the rigid mind of Charles I.

Bishop Williams was to be present at King James's death-bed and would preach his funeral sermon. Here the manner of the old reign was to be for the last time displayed. The whole sermon has been preserved for us printed under the title of *Great Britain's Salomon*. "From his *Sayings*," proclaimed the Bishop in relation to his late master's virtues,[2] "I am come to his *Doings, all that he did* a vast wood, and world of matter, fitter for the *Annals* and *Historie* of the Time, than for a fragment of a *Funerall* Sermon. Every *Action* of his sacred Maiestie was a *Vertue* and a *Miracle* to exempt him from any parallel, among the modern Kings and Princes." "And surely," he went on,[3] "*Actions* of

---

[1] *Scrinia Reserata*, p. 38.
[2] *Great Britain's Salomon*, p. 43.   [3] *ibid.*, p. 56.

Peace (what ever debauched people say to the *contrarie*) set out a *Prince* in more orient colours than those of *War*, and great combustions."

As he came to the fall of the peroration the Bishop did not forget to pay a tribute to the Duke of Buckingham, and introduced a simile from the life of Christ. "How did he thrust," he declared[1] in reference to King James's magnanimity, "as it were into his inward bosom, his *Bishops*, his *Judges*, his neare *servants*; and that *Disciple of his whom he so loved* in particular." How strongly do these words suggest the courage, the doubtful taste and the flamboyant cracking imagery? On the chair of state beneath the pulpit sat the Princes of Wales, now King. Like the stage machinery of a finished masque the Court scenery of King James's period was rolled away.

---

[1] *Great Britain's Salomon*, p. 68.

CHAPTER XV

THE CATHOLIC MINORITY

THIS secure, and in some respects complacent Stuart background, can never be neglected in a consideration of the outlook of the English Catholics. Socially they were inextricably mingled with their Protestant fellow countrymen, but in devotional and doctrinal matters they had developed their own special ethos which was far removed from that of the Anglicans and Puritans. Their writings were characterized by a perfect self-subsisting confidence and their life was marked by a certain uneasy contentment; a sense of strain induced by the external and internal stresses; a strong devotion to the monarchy breeding a loyalty to the Stuarts which was to prove incapable of disappointment.

That section of the Catholic community which was concerned with church politics, had been troubled by the series of conflicts between the Jesuit and secular clergy. In these years this continuing controversy turned upon the merits of the establishment of an episcopate. In another section of the field those Catholics who were by temperament Erastian, found themselves opposed to the theologians, and to the Holy See which had condemned King James's Oath of Allegiance on doctrinal grounds. At the same time there was always a proportion among the descendants of the wealthier recusant stocks who were passing beyond the reach of Catholic influence; men who hardly adverted to the ancient doctrines, and had abandoned the sacraments, while remaining strongly conscious of and troubled by their isolation. Like all politically ostracized minorities, the Catholic community was constantly dissolving at its edges.

This process was hastened by the presence throughout the country of large groups, particularly among the labourers and farmers, which were gradually being starved of the knowledge of the Old Religion. Except in the North of England the tenants of a Protestant landowner had little opportunity for the instruction of their children in the Catholic doctrines. As the recusant squires of the south and Midlands gradually abandoned their ancestral faith, they each broke a chain of contacts among their Catholic tenantry which had only been preserved through the Mass centres in their manors. In the North the Catholics were too numerous and independent to suffer serious loss through the defection of the privileged; but it was a defect of the Tridentine organization that the missioners in Southern England should have concentrated so much attention on the noble patron and have taken such satisfaction in the conversion of the *generosi*. Nevertheless, it is easy to over-estimate the contemporary effect of these conflicts and difficulties and failures. For, on the whole, the impression made by seventeenth-century English Catholicism suggests a remarkable firmness and consistency.

A careful consideration of some of the contemporary ballads and devotional writing, will throw a light upon the Catholic thought of the period, and thus reveal its interior gaiety and perfect confidence. A tranquil conviction of the unassailable truth of their own doctrine seems to have possessed all those Catholics who held to their religion against the pressure of the times. In general, the religious life of these Catholics was marked by characteristics which appear to be the natural consequences of such a standpoint; a light-hearted and determined constancy, a casual indifference to the nature of the beliefs held by their neighbours, and a certain resolute assurance which could turn to arrogance.

Two of the ballads of this reign show forth these qualities.

In *True Christian hearts, cease to lament*[1] their attitude to the State prosecutions, is defined in words which are attributed to John Thewlis, the Lancashire priest, who is represented as speaking to the justices.

> "Christes passion oft before your face,
>   I have declared plaine;
> How for our sinns he suffered death,
>   and how he rose againe;
> And how the twelve Apostles, eike,
>   were put to death for preaching,
> The Catholike faith which Christ did teach,
>   Christ send us happie rysinge!"

The historical background, as the Recusants conceived it, is well described in the opening stanzas of *Winter cold into summer hot*,[2] a ballad which carried with it not only the determination, but also the lightness and delicacy of touch which marked that earlier composition, *The Wreck of Walsingham*.

> "Winter could into summer hoate
>   well changed now may bee;
> For thinges as strange doe come to passe,
>   as wee may plainlie see:
> *England* priestes which honour'd hath
>   soe manie hundred years,
> Doth hange them up as Traytors now,
>   which causeth manie teares.
> She doeth condemne her elders all,
>   as all the world besyde,
> Religion ould, which longe hath beene
>   in landes both farre and wyde.
> A gospell new she hath found out,
>   a bird of Calvin's broode,
> Abandoninge all memorie
>   of Christe his holie roode."

These two last lines have an especial significance, since it

[1] British Museum Add. MS., 15, 225, ff. 22–5. It is printed in *Old English Ballads*, 1553–1625, ed. Hyder E. Rollins.
[2] British Museum Add. MS., 15, 225, ff. 33–5. It is printed in the same volume.

was the doctrine of the Crucifixion which appealed most strongly to the Recusants. Resolvedly they bent their minds to the thought of Christ's Passion and the stirring lines of *Calvary mount is my delight* reflect their prayer. The wayside crosses had been broken, and the Puritans would destroy those representations of the Saviour's sufferings which had assisted their ancestors as they knelt and prayed to God in their temptations. The histories of the Old Testament meant little to the adherents of the Ancient Faith: as a community they were not so much righteous as suffering. In England in the seventeenth century they were not embarrassed by those grave difficulties which surround a spiritual body which is triumphant. The lives of the kings of the House of David failed to stir them; they had not the actuality of Calvary.

Nevertheless, the bitterness with which they were assailed was always incomprehensible to the Recusants, and time and again they were taken by surprise. In this connection the terms of a broadside, issued by Martin Parker in the last years of King James's reign, are very instructive. The robust title, *Famous Britanny, give thanks*, is followed by four explicit lines.

> "Farewell, Masse-monger,
> With all your juggling tricks;
> Your puppet plaies will not
> here be allow'd."

The character of King James is then introduced, and he is praised in these terms.

> "The Pope he excludeth:
> Though oft he intrudeth,
> Yet, like zealous Judeth,
> His head he will crop;
> Like good Hezekias,
> And fervent Iosias,
> He serves the Messias,
> and hateth the Pope."

The broadside was on sale at John Trundle's shop in Smithfield, and was intended for public singing. From time to time the Recusants would hear these raucous phrases. Surely they must have felt that the good honest men who raised that chorus were living in a very different world.

If these ballads represented popular reactions, it was the solid histories which nourished those among the wealthy Catholics who felt impelled to take a view of their religion. In the version of history there presented to them lay the seeds of that separate outlook which was to distinguish them from their fellow countrymen. The opening of these folios in their strong calf bindings would disclose heroic descriptions of the deeds of Catholic princes. As the recusant gentlemen of polite tastes and assured position sat conning over these massive volumes, their flowing periods would sink into the mind forming there a rich deposit. And in addition the effect of such great tomes was much increased since the private libraries were still so small. The subject matter of each book would be chewed and digested through successive winters. A short account of two contemporary chronicles, translated from Italian and French and Catholic in their tone, will suggest the nature of this influence.

Both volumes were in circulation at this time; the *Historie of the Uniting of the Kingdom of Portugall to the Crowne of Castill* had been printed in London in its English translation in 1600, and the *Historie of George Castriot, surnamed Scanderbeg, King of Albanie*, by "Jacques de Lavardin, Lord of Plessis Bourrot, a Nobleman of France," had appeared four years earlier in its English dress. The latter book contains an instructive catalogue of the authorities consulted in the preparation of the Albanian history. "Martin Barletius," the list begins, "*Priest of Scutarie in Epire: from whom the most part of this Historie is drawn word for word. Æneas Silvius alias Pope Pius the Second. Isidore Ruthenian Cardinall.*"

The chronicle moves slowly and heavily, stuffed with orations; the central theme is the action of united Christendom against the Turks in the fifteenth century; there are lengthy and courageous speeches, thick with devotion to the Papacy; Pope Pius II is described, "his birth and commendation."[1] It is an old-fashioned and unexhilarating volume but well calculated to fortify a prosy man in his opinions.

"We may see in *Scanderbeg*," runs a passage in the peroration, "a pure worke of the finger of God, and the evident assistance of his divine hand and power, for the succor and reliefe of his Church and chosen people. . . . So will God still doe the like, and he will provide our *France* of another *Pucell*." In the copy of this work now in the library of St. Edmund's College, Ware, there are various marginal corrections in a seventeenth-century hand. They were made by an attentive reader and serve to render the ecclesiastical phraseology more exactly.

The other book is a very different proposition. It is a sympathetic and flowing history in the grand manner recounting the events of the reigns of the last two kings of the House of Aviz, and the accession of Philip II to the Crown of Portugal. Politics and geography and genealogy, are treated turn by turn urbanely and with dignity. "Lisbone," we read in the introduction,[2] "is the best and chiefest of all their Cities, on the which the whole Realme dependes: It is populous, yea many beleeve that of all the cities of Christendom (except Paris) it contains the greatest number of people. The aire is verie wholesome and temperate; distant from the Equinoctiall nine and thirtie degrees; and with the ebbing and flowing of the salt water (which is great upon that coast) there bloweth alwaies a temperate winde, which doth refresh it."

---

[1] *The Historie of George Castriot, surnamed Scanderbeg, King of Albanie*, by Jacques de Lavardin, translator unknown, p. 450.
[2] *The Historie of the Uniting of the Kingdom of Portugall to the Crowne of Castill*, by G. Conestaggio, translated by Edward Blount, p. 3.

Again, a description of the deathbed of the Duke of Alva shows how different was the impression here created from the view taken by Protestant opinion of that able general. "Hee shewed in dying," declared the author,[1] "the magnanimitie he had in his life, and that which is of great moment, has shewed tokens of a religious Christian, beinge happie that Friar Lewes of Granata, that famous preacher (whose divine writings are pleasing to the worlde) was present at his death."

A final passage dealing with the campaign of Alcacerquibir reveals an element of fantasy and a strange overwrought reverence, that south wind which was to disturb the Cavaliers. "All that time, which was the ninth of November," so runs the narrative,[2] "there appeared in the Zodiaque, in the signs of *Libra*, neere unto the station of *Mars*, the goodliest and greatest Comet, that hath beene seene in many ages, the which happening in the progresse of this war, amazed many, who looking to examples past, said it was a signe of unhappy successe, and that coming from a corrupt aire, it did endomage the delicate bodies of Princes."

Improbable as it now appears to us, this element of obsequious and almost faery reverence, is seen as a constant factor through the early Stuart reigns. The language of hyperbole cannot wholly mask the awe with which the office of those whose duty it was to show forth God's Majesty on earth was then approached. It was, perhaps, this almost spiritual devotion to the fact of kingship which enabled those who took a providential view of the King's authority to sacrifice themselves so generously for Charles I. Such an attitude is reflected clearly in the dedication and epistle to the King which form the prelude to *A Survey of the New*

---

[1] *The Historie of the Uniting of the Kingdom of Portugall to the Crowne of Castill*, by G. Conestaggio, translated by Edward Blount, pp. 301–2.
[2] *ibid.*, p. 27.

Religion, a work written by Matthew Kellison, Doctor and Professor of Divinity and printed at Douai in 1605.

"Your Majestie wil mervaile peradventure (most dread soveraigne)," begins this preface,[1] "how a priest . . . . dareth to be so bold, as to appeare in the presence of so mightie a Prince, sitting in a throne of Majestie and terrour, crowned with a Diadem of greater glorie than hitherto hath stoode upon the King of England his head, and holding in his victorious hand a new Scepter by which he commandeth al the Britaigne Ilandes and, like a Neptune, is Lord of the Ocean Sea." The epistle to the King changes the subject matter, but not the manner. The author has here brought himself to speak of the one thing that is lacking to the realm. "And if your Majestie demand of me what this is," he continues,[2] "I answere: not gold, nor Ivorie of India, nor rich and orient Pearle, for with such treasures your Albion, eike and India, aboundeth: but it is that which is more worth and which your India only wanteth: It is Religion."

This combination of a high royalism with an entire confidence in the strength of the case for the Old Religion is apparent in many Catholic writings. Already the Tridentine leaven was in ferment. There was a satisfaction to be derived from clinching argument and ringing phrases. It is just this mood which is reflected in the "Epistle to the most Noble and renowned English Nation my most deere countrimen" with which Dr. Richard Smith, later Bishop of Chalcedon, prefaced *The Prudentiall Ballance of Religion* which was first printed in 1609. "I have also," wrote the author,[3] "in this parte shewed that the Romane religion of Saint Austin hath continued ever since unto our time in all our Bishopps, Prelats, Pastors, Devines and Cleargie (except Wiclif and his small crue) by the example of their heades the Archbishops of Canterburye, whom I shew to have bene in

---

[1] *A Survey of the New Religion,* p. 3.   [2] *ibid.,* p. 6.
[3] *The Prudentiall Ballance of Religion,* p. 16.

number sixty nyne, and in religion perfect Romane Catholiques."

And in the course of his narrative, Dr. Smith returns to this lament. "But with her," he writes of Queen Mary Tudor,[1] "in the year 1558 ended all the glorie of Catholick Princes of England. Who (except King Henrie 8 for a few yeares, and King Edward 6) had continewed from the yeare 598 till the foresaid yeare 1558 the space almost of a thousand yeares."

Beyond books like *The Prudentiall Ballance*, and all the works of specific controversy which dealt point by point with apologists upon the other side, there stretched the range of devotional literature. Yet it is difficult to determine the effect of such volumes on the mind of the Catholic community, and it is essential not to exaggerate the influence of books.

In this connection a declamatory passage in an account of the execution of Swithin Wells, who had been condemned for relieving priests, must give one pause. It appears in a little work printed at St. Omer in 1614 under the title of *A brief relation of the life and death of Mr. Swithun Welles, Gentleman*. "O blessed life! O happy death!" declaims the anonymous author in recounting these sufferings, "The whole Church Triumphant in heaven rejoyceth in your victories: the whole Catholic Church militant on earth exulteth in your triumphs. Let then," he continues in an outspoken fashion, "our Catholic Nobility. and Gentry emulate, & imitate this rare example."

It is always interesting to trace back the origins of a phrase, and it seems likely that this is one of the earliest cases of the use of a collective description which was to become in the next century very familiar. But what, indeed, in face of all this literature were the reactions of "our Catholic Nobility and Gentry"? It is worth while to begin

[1] *The Prudentiall Ballance of Religion*, p. 412.

by making a brief examination of this already very homogeneous body.

Even at this early stage in the development of the post-Reformation Catholic community, a very close connection linked together the leading families. In the case of the peers this network of relationships was unaffected by those great divisions, the North Country, the Midlands, East Anglia and the western shires, within which the squires were accustomed to maintain their kinship and alliance. For the acquisition of a peerage was in itself evidence of wealth and of some contact with the Court; it implied in most cases at least the occasional tenancy of a London house. The tendency which was to make the old Catholic squirearchy a close corporation in the eighteenth century was already discernible among the peers.

The Howards in their Catholic branches, were not at this period linked by blood relationship to their co-religionists, nor was Lord Shrewsbury, an old man who had come into the title late in life. With these exceptions the recusant peers were nearly all involved in a very complicated network of recent inter-marriage. The emergence of the Catholics as a wholly distinct community, was in great part responsible for the development of such alliances. It was only in this generation that the Catholics drew away from their cousins among the "Church Papists" of the former reign, whose children had by now become absorbed in the general body of the wealthy Anglicans. The religious allegiance of the Recusants had been annealed by the long endurance of the fines and they sought their brides among those of their equals who shared this temper. When the criss-cross of relationship had been completed, the Catholic peers were found in the third decade of the century, in three main groups.

Thus Lord Montagu was linked by the marriages of his children with Lords Worcester, Winchester, Arundell and

Petre. Lord Worcester's sisters were married to Lords Windsor and Petre and to Lord Arundell of Wardour's eldest son, whose sisters in their turn were the wives of the heirs of Lords Eure and Baltimore. Lord Teynham's wife was Mary Petre. It was a real cat's cradle.

Similarly the Paulets had intermarried with the Savages, and Lord Savage with the Monteagles who were related to the Brudenells and Stourtons. The Teynhams were linked with Lords Vaux and Abergavenny, and the Dormers with Lords Worcester, Montagu, Molyneux, Dunbar and Fairfax; while Dunbar's daughter had married Lord Brudenell's son.[1] The converts Rutland and Aston were outside these groupings, but nearly all the avowed Catholic peers in England were caught within this narrow mesh.[2]

At the same time there were strong internal conflicts chiefly turning upon inheritance. The Vaux-Morley suit of the previous generation had left its scars; the new line of the Shrewsburys had been disinherited in favour of Lady Arundel and her sisters, the female heirs; a series of disputes lasting over twenty years had arisen between Lord Arundell of Wardour and the Earl of Worcester.

It is interesting to consider what were the characteristics which determined the outlook of these families. It is quite

---

[1] It is worth indicating briefly the close nature of these relationships. Lord John Paulet, who became the Marquis of Winchester of the siege of Basing House, married Jane Savage. Her brother the second Viscount Savage, who succeeded his grandfather as Earl Rivers, married Catherine daughter of the fourth Lord Monteagle. The three daughters of Sir Thomas Tresham of Rushton married respectively the fourth Lord Monteagle, the tenth Lord Stourton and the first Lord Brudenell. George Vaux, whose mother was a Tresham, married Elizabeth daughter of the first Lord Teynham and left Edward fourth Lord Vaux of Harrowden and Catherine wife of the ninth Lord Abergavenny. The eldest son of the first Lord Dormer married Alice Molyneux. Lord Dormer's sister married Henry Constable of Burton Constable and left Henry first Viscount Dunbar and Katherine wife of the first Viscount Fairfax of Gilling. Sir Charles Smith of Wootton Wawen, later first Viscount Carrington, married their first cousin Elizabeth Caryll; Richard first Viscount Molyneux of Maryborough married Mary Caryll.

[2] The exceptions appear to have been Lords Stafford (whose estate was utterly decayed), Powis, Lumley and Castlehaven.

incorrect to suppose that they were for the most part peers of ancient lineage and decayed estate since only Stourton and, perhaps, Vaux, could be held to answer to this description. It seems accurate to suggest that the Catholic lords were in general rich and that the new peers like Petre, Dormer, Brudenell, Rivers and Teynham, were quite exceptionally wealthy. Such men had risen to the peerage in spite of their religious affiliations, and were for the most part tenacious and worldly wise, profoundly loyalist and with that peculiarly English gift for friendship with their adversaries.

In many cases, no doubt, their religious perceptions had been blunted by success, but they were deeply attached to the point of honour which has done so much to keep minorities faithful to their tradition. In a very real sense the exercise of their religious preferences seems to have appeared to them as a private privilege for which, like other privileges, they were if necessary prepared to pay. Still the question of such payment would not arise until after a conviction for recusancy and it was often possible by the judicious employment of official influence, to stave off this recusant status[1] for many years.

An example will serve to indicate the situation. Sir Henry Constable of Burton Constable, had inherited great estates in Yorkshire in 1607, shortly before he came of age. He was suave, determined and extravagant. A skilful handling of the Court had brought him a Scottish peerage, and the Lord President of the North, Lord Scrope (who was himself half a Catholic) had put him into the deputy lieutenantcy for Yorkshire. His approach to Buckingham was admirable for he knew how to play the constant but not subservient

---

[1] In this connection it is interesting to compare the recusancy assessments of different Yorkshire and Lancashire families. Thus Thomas Waterton of Walton paid £80, Thomas Meynell of Kilvington £100, Stephen Tempest of Broughton £60, Gilbert Stapleton of Carlton £64 and Sir John Thimbleby of Irnham £160.

supporter. Like all his class, he made an almost unconscious profit from his ease of manner. His successful claim to wreck cast by the North Sea gales on the shores of his liberty of Holderness, formed a point of contact with the Lord High Admiral.

In 1630, but not before that date, he found himself obliged to pay heavily as a Recusant. The extract from the Book of Composition is illuminating. "The Right Honourable Henry Viscount Dunbarr," so runs the entry, "to pay unto his Majesty the yearly Rent of three hundred pounds for the Recusancy of him the said Viscount Dunbarr, to begin att the feast of Saint Martin the Bishop, in Winter in the year of our Lord one thousand six hundred twenty nine as by the said composition sett down in the first Book of Entries, and in fol. 64 of the same Book may appear." And then, after further reciting that on Lord Dunbar's humble petition this rent would be reduced to £250 a year, the note concludes with the statement that the payment would be reckoned from Pentecost 1630, since Viscount Dunbar was not convicted before the midsummer of that year. There are several points of interest in this matter; the courtesy like some heavy oily sea; the great almost carefree payment whose very sum seemed dignified; the detached air of magnanimity. The shadow of Rome still hovers over the legal phrasing of these Erastian documents, and it is strange to find "the feast of Saint Martin the Bishop in Winter" put to such a use. Even from the Catholic angle it could thus be seen that the peers moved in their own orbit separated from the gentry by their privileges and their suave treatment.

Less concerned with the Court there stood that body of the wealthy Catholic gentry whose strength can be assessed from the figures for the first creation of baronetcies in 1611. In that year the price of this new dignity was exacted from the heads of the recusant families of Shirley of Staunton Harold, Gerard of Bryn, Shelley of Michelgrove, Bellasis of Newborough, Tresham of Rushton, and Englefield of Wootton Basset. These were joined between 1615 and 1622, by the two North Country stocks of Radcliffe of Derwentwater and Tempest of Stella in the Bishopric, and by the Tichbornes, Jerninghams and Gorings, the Yates of Buckland and the Sussex Gages. Within a few years, Mr. Mannock of Stoke by Nayland, and Mr. Vavasour of Haslewood, would be compelled to purchase this new honour and the earlier Catholic baronetcies would be complete.[1]

In a circle which had now been linked for over fifty years to this group of families, were such Catholic houses as the Throckmortons, Sheldons, Plowdens, Stonors, Blounts, Mores, Fitzherberts, Abingtons, Gascoignes, Stapletons, Langdales, Widdringtons, Swinburnes, Fenwicks and Sherburnes; the Carylls of Harting, Webbs of Odstock, Poyntz of Iron Acton, Bedingfelds of Oxburgh, Arundells of Lanherne, Hunlokes of Wingerworth, Chamberlaynes of Shirburn, Giffards of Chillington, Smiths of Wootton Wawen and Waldegraves of Chewton Magna.

All these stocks possessed a solid foundation of prosperity and took a rank among the greater squires which would have brought them to a place of political significance had they not been hindered by their attachment to the Old Religion.[2] A close inter-relationship was developing; they were conservative and maintained their chaplains; soberly they matched their sons and daughters. Dowagers played their part in the life of this community, spending their wealth for the maintenance of the practice of their Faith, pious in widowhood, Pauline and determined. They moved forward

---

[1] Among the Catholic holders of Jacobean baronetcies were Lords Aston, Brudenell and Dormer, who were almost immediately raised to the peerage, and Sir Richard Molyneux of Sefton and Sir John Savage of Rock Savage whose sons became respectively Viscount Molyneux and Viscount Savage.

[2] On the other hand one of the most complete records of the gradual impoverishment of a landed family through the recusancy laws is that relating to the Sulyards of Wetherden preserved among the Swynnerton MSS.

en échelon in their piety, old Lady Montague; her daughter, Lady Dormer; her son's widow, Lady Gerard; her niece, the Dowager Countess of Arundel; Lady Stonor; Lady Lovell. The Stonors, indeed, were harassed; but the power of wealth lay over these great devout households; a factor well suggested in the Bishop of Chalcedon's Latin life of Lady Montague. She is pictured at Battle, with eighty retainers in the house and its dependencies, as she lay in the state chamber dying in the hard winter, with her chaplains around her before the rich carved altar, and, on the wall, a high crucifix of silver gilt, which had come from a private oratory in the old Catholic days.[1]

Through all these allied circles there could be an assured (to the Puritan mind far too assured) contact with the Stuart Court, even in those cases where rare use was made of such an opportunity. To the increasing Protestant opinion, the Recusants' right of access to the sovereign was unwelcome, and the attraction of their Faith inscrutable. With the new reign a mystified suspicion deepened, since Queen Henrietta's world was wholly alien to the great mass of those who leant towards the godly practices. To the Puritans the ways of the Court were as remote, but unfortunately as imaginable as those of Jezebel.

And in the North there lingered a tough confidence which in its own way was equally disconcerting. The great families, whose heads rode south to London, might weigh the difficulties of the royal policy; but the remoter country gentry and the yeomen in Lancashire and the other northern counties, took no heed of evasive shifts or half-concessions. They held to their ancestral Faith with a conviction of its stubborn and unarguable truth, and an assurance of its triumph.

This matter-of-fact determination comes out most clearly

[1] Bishop Smith states that this crucifix had been inherited from Lady Montague's grandmother Anne Countess of Shrewsbury who died in 1510.

in a paper preserved among the Eyre MSS. at Ushaw College. It is a note of the terms of a trust formed in the early years of the reign of Charles I by John Malling and Elizabeth Tarleton, who wished to preserve Mass vestments and other property. "But," runs this note,[1] "if Catholick times come upp, the black suit of church stuffe shall goe to Harkerk Chapell if one be, or else to the parish church of Sefton, & the silver guilded chalice shall go into Sefton Church so shall the white suite also goe with the chalice." "And for the performance of all this," the draft continues after describing trusts for Masses and other benefactions, "the testators doe appoint twoe of the auncientest Secular Clergie which shall life on Walton & Sefton parish during this or any other schisme." It would be interesting to speculate how far the southern Catholics ever shared this determined belief in victory.

[1] Eyre MSS., f. 78, Ushaw College Papers.

CHAPTER XVI

THE BAROQUE APPROACH

A GRAVE and lasting source of weakness to the Duke of Buckingham, resulted from his mother's conversion to Catholicism in 1622. This had been a slow process, and for her son singularly disastrous, since it provided a focus for all that latent animus which could only find expression when cloaked beneath the forms of loyalty. The consideration of the position of the English Catholics has not yet taken into account that current in the life of the Court which was to lead a number of those in the King's circle to accept the Old Religion with its grandeur and its consolations, but without its trammelling hardships and its penalties.

It seems on the whole likely that the Tridentine mood made a very widespread appeal to those who in the early seventeenth century lived close to the Throne, and were not debarred by their nationalist sentiment from yielding to this attraction. The apotheosis of sovereignty and the approach suggested by Rubens' work, would incline those who took long draughts of monarch-worship to toy sympathetically with the high and stringent claims put forward by the Tridentine Church. For those to whom the Baroque "glory" would appeal, Geneva must seem repellent and the Lutheran heavens meagre. In the case of nearly all the men and most of the women in the English Court circle, the nationalist feeling was so strong as to prevent even the possibility of secession. The small minority who became Catholics were affected by habits of thought which were

246

almost equally remote from the mental background of the Anglican and the Catholic squires. The technique of approach to the question was as novel as it was ornate and in consequence uncongenial to the plain-thinking gentry. Some of the writing of the time may make this clear.

One of the first Catholic works in which this trend becomes apparent is the tract known as *The Bishop of London, his Legacy*. It was issued by an unknown hand shortly after the death of Bishop King, and was a description of imaginary writings which were composed on the unfounded assumption that this prelate had submitted to Rome secretly before his death. The author seems to have believed that the fact of this conversion was assured and proceeded to develop the lines along which he felt that the argument would have been put forward.

"And thus," begins the preface in its reference to King James, "his Majesty (whom God long preserve) following in part the like methode (as Xenophon) doth delineate, and draw with his learned Pencil, the trewe portraiture of a Good Prince in his *Basilicon Doron*, a worke of eternall memory, and worthy to be written in letters, not of gould (too base a metall), but even in letters of Diamonds, if so they could be melted and resolved."

The argument then moves forward through a net of grandiose allusion very pleasant to those whose mental life was nourished on high-sounding phrases. "As easily may we believe," declared the author,[1] "that the Arke and the Idol Dagon could be placed together; or dreame with Copernicus that the heavens stand still and the earth moves. O Delphick and Aenigmatical! or other childish, idle and false since if we believe S. Augustine: *Nihil prodest esse in Ecclesia, nisi sis cum Ecciesia.*" The book was dressed with reasons in favour of the claims of Rome, and included pleasant paragraphs headed, "Prismata or Resultancyes."

[1] *The Bishop of London, his Legacy*, p. 83.

It is not suggested that such a work had any widespread influence. Still the introduction of these quotations serves to show that there was a line of controversial writing which could only appeal to those who relished a certain artificial phrasing and sophistication. It seems, however, to have been treatises of just this character which came to influence the ladies of the Court. Those into whose orbit John Donne swam, would rest unsatisfied with plainness of expression. Far removed from his talent or from an appreciation of his mind, the patrons who toyed with *An Anatomie of the World* would always fumble for the ornamented.

At this point it is worth considering the career of Sir Tobie Mathew, the priest who for more than twenty years served to represent Catholicism to the Court circle, and especially to the ladies of the favourite's family. He was at this time forty-five, slender and very quick, with an intelligence at once brittle and penetrating. His character had great persistency, but less judgment; in temperament he was mercurial; "littell prittie Tobie Mathew." He was best known as a friend, and perhaps the chief intimate, of Lord St. Albans, following with sympathy the vast sweep and the profound imprudences of Bacon's mind. He had become a Catholic when just on thirty, and had then renounced the light conduct of his fashionable youth.

In 1614 he had been ordained a priest, but this fact remained a secret. After periods of exile he had now come back permanently to England through Buckingham's assistance. He had gone with the Prince to Spain, and had been knighted on his return; his father, who combined the archbishopric of York with the lord presidency of the North, once more received him. He had the prudence of an exaggerated diplomacy, but his judgment was often at the mercy of his wit. His flowers of speech served to emphasize rather than disguise his iron acceptances and resolution. In every way he was a man of the new age.

It was with such advantages that Tobie Mathew's work appeared, and if he lacked the fastidiousness and the metaphysical subtlety of Dr. Donne, there was certainly a hint of the world of Crashaw. Very many, even among his contemporaries, would find his work distasteful, but it is surely safe to say that he had no rival. Quotations will give an impression of his style and indicate how he became so great a figure.

The dedication page of his translation of the Confessions of St. Augustine, which appeared in 1620, will very well suggest his quality. "Most gracious and most glorious Queen of Heaven," begin the linked sentences with the heavy even roll of the seventeenth century, "the joy of Celestiall spirits, &, under thy sonne, the highest hope of humane creatures: Behould this Prodigall Child of thyne, who thus presumeth to approach towards thy presence. Instead of a glasse of flowers, I laye upon the Altar of thy goodnesse, a booke of Pictures, which have the fame to be wel limned."

Very slowly he moves[1] into the manner of the epistle dedicatory and the paragraphs go forward warm and hammering and balanced. "Take therefore, this Book, O Sacred and all-immaculate Virgin Mother of God, under the mantle of thy protection. . . . And as for me, I humbly beg that in the sight of God, thou wilt still be pleased to assist my soule. And that neither the mist, or fog of sensuality may deteyne me; nor the syde-wind of vanity divert me; nor the contrary wind of impatience tosse me, as now, by the great goodness of God, the Pyrate of heresy doth no longer threaten to drowne me. But that I may proceed in my navigation towards that country of peace, and joy that *Heaven of Heavens*; whereof Christ our Lord is the neversetting *Sunne*, & thy selfe the sweet, but never-changing or waning *Moone*; and this glorious Saint a most radiant and

[1] *Confessions of St. Augustine*, ed. 1620, p. 3.

resplendent *Starre,* which shall moove in that *Orbe,* after an immoveable manner, for all Eternity."

In the preface to the pious and courteous reader, it is stated[1] that "the Beauty of a person consisteth much in fayre *complexion*; but yet more in good *proportion,* and decent *motion,*" while the Saint's obscurity is explained,[2] "because by his most significant and sententious soule, his pen is thrust into so little roome," and then there comes the translation of Augustine's work. Two brief quotations will serve to illustrate different facets of Mathew's appeal. One displays a delightful panel well-fitted to the understanding of the period, with the new stress upon spiritual direction. He is describing[3] the Saint's coming to the city which was to be his bishopric. "At the end of those three years, being drawn to *Hippo* (which now is known by the name of *Bona*) by a Principall Cavallier who offered to depend upon his advice, in the way of the spirit, & of serving God exactly."

The second passage is still more illuminating. "Against the *Arians* of *Afrike,*" he wrote of St. Augustine,[4] "he obteyned, by the mercy of God, many famous victoryes. He decyphered and discovered (but it cost him the travail of ten continued years) that subtile and sly *Pelagius,* who being a Divel incarnate would needes go for a Saint illuminate. And it seemes, he was expressly ordeyned for the destruction of that heretyke; since upon the very day whereon that Cocatrices egge was hatched in *England,* this *Phenix* rose from the spicy bed of *S. Monica's* blessed wombe in Afrike." Here is all the warmth of the Tridentine world, the certitudes so magnificently deployed and around them the seraphim and the cherubs billowing.

Although the passages just considered undoubtedly present that element in English life which was most penetrated by

---

[1] *Confessions of St. Augustine,* p. 3.   [2] *ibid.,* p. 11.
[3] *ibid.,* p. 28.   [4] *ibid.,* p. 40.

the continental spirit, they nevertheless serve to indicate how remote the specialized Court preferences could become from the commonplace national reactions. For eighteen years more Sir Tobie Mathew was to remain in contact with the circle of the Government. After his more serious political endeavours in the days of Count Gondomar and Francis Bacon, he would decline in time upon the ladies around the throne; first Lady Buckingham and her daughter, Lady Denbigh and then the Villiers' cousins, Olivia Porter and Lady Hamilton and Lady Newport. He, who in politics had been a "Spaniard," could still understand better than other men the French aspects of Queen Henrietta's background. With Lady Carlisle he was to share a valuable and didactic intimacy.

Constant among the lesser figures of the Vandyck era moved Sir Tobie Mathew with his slowly churned out compliments and the careful fantasies and flowers of speech, and above each decorous change of manner the metal canopy of his doctrinal thought. It was the Long Parliament which secured his banishment. The whole episode has its own significance, for it shows that neither Buckingham nor yet King Charles could sense the nature of an opposition. They did not admit the right of the Puritans to their prejudices, nor did they perceive the especial popular hostility to Popery in its decorated guises and to the "Cocatrice's egge."

It is obvious enough that the relationship between Buckingham and the King was not one which, on any interpretation, would find wide sympathy; but it was their mutual close absorption which really emphasized the gulf which separated them from the Englishmen of property. The Statutes were not tolerant and yet they were much more popular than the royal courses. And it was not only that the idea of tolerance was ill-received, but that it aroused acute antagonism when exercised in favour of individuals whose canons of behaviour were sophisticated and urbane.

The King and his minister were alike open to so many influences from which their countrymen were still immune, and there was no one to check the Duke's sense of magnificence or his princely generous indulgence. Both men were little affected by their contemporaries, and it would seem that Buckingham never lost his fundamental simplicity, although arrogance in time would overlay it. In this connection few paintings can convey so great a sense of ostentatious splendour as Rubens' portrait of the favourite riding on the seashore with the ribbon of the Garter on his armour, and around him allegorical figures, and beneath his horse's hoofs the starfish and the shells.

Under these circumstances it is not surprising that Buckingham never seems to have felt that his mother's change of Faith could be a proper subject of public interest, or that there was any ground of criticism in Sir Tobie Mathew's conferences or in the submission of the Villiers brothers[1] to the Holy See. "The Countess of Buckingham," complains a contemporary, "was the cynosure that all the Papists steer by"; but the favourite's mind was insulated from his peers.

Yet it has a bearing on the history of the reign that it appears to have been the King who alone felt the full strain of what he conceived as a perfect friendship, first in the effect worked by the Duke when living upon his friend and master, and then in the years in which he suffered the bitter wounding memory of Buckingham dead. It was the period following King Charles's accession to the throne which saw the fulfilment of the promise of this high-keyed friendship, and much of the subsequent personal divergence between the Court and the leaders of the opposition can be traced to the fact that an English sovereign could with difficulty afford either these rare tuned-up emotions or the indulgence in the mutual obligations of an equal and deeply sensitive relation.

[1] Lords Purbeck and Anglesea.

At the same time the whole approach of the Court was calculated gradually to alienate those whose lives were passed outside its special circle. Queen Elizabeth had possessed the power of popularizing her own magnificence, and until Salisbury's death the art of managing opinion had received attention. But, as King James's reign progressed, it becomes increasingly manifest and it can be observed particularly in one department in the relationship resulting from the development of the masque.

In this connection the old pageant-wagons of the Elizabethan period had been part of the public property of relaxation shared alike by Court and city. Yet the new elaboration of the masques and of the great entertainments staged in the Banqueting House at Whitehall, necessarily tended to remove such specialized production from the general view. It was not that the conceptions became more difficult to follow, but that the whole range of the masque and its new mechanism of wave machines and cloud machines were outside the citizens' experience.

For the privileged it all unfolded tranquilly. In Chapman's masque for the Middle Temple, the chief masquers arrayed themselves in Indian habits, cloth of silver embroidered with gold suns, gold plate and white ostrich feathers, and spangled ruffs of pearl and silver. "On their heads high sprigg'd feathers, compast in Coronets, like the Virginian Princes they presented." In the first scene was set an Artificial Rock "in the undermost part craggy and full of hollow places, in whose concaves were contriv'd two winding paire of staires by whose greeces the Persons above might make their descents and all the way be seene. All this Rocke grew by degrees up into a gold-colour, and was run quite through with veines of golde." This was surely not over-sophisticated as an entertainment; but a barrier was growing between Court and citizens.

The scenes of a former time had stood at the street corners

in the progresses. The familiar parables were re-enacted, the magician of China coming down out of his "heaven" and comparing the country from which he came with ours in a long sleepy speech. But this comforting ritual had vanished with the Tudor epoch. It was the fashion of the age to regard this new vast expenditure on masques for a limited audience as princely and magnanimous. But if that adjective may apply it is also clear that James I, and still more his son, paid for that magnanimity with the nation.

In the field of architecture no influence connected with the Baroque was yet perceptible as the filtered Palladian manner developed in the last period of the reign. But, indeed, the whole question of Baroque variants in England must be approached with caution. Much of the sophisticated writing of these years bears rather the marks of *manierismo*, as Dr. Mario Praz has defined that style. The intricacy of the word play and the elaboration of the ornament derive in part from the Elizabethan Euphuism, while the effect of successfully calculated metaphor suggests the pragmatic approach of English Jacobean writers. Nevertheless, the position is complicated by the fact that so much of the inspiration is derived, if not immediately then at second remove, from sixteenth-century Italian models. In this connection the couplet of Robert Southwell

"Why did the yeelding sea, like marble way
    support a wretch more wauering than the waues."

although so manifestly Elizabethan and foreshadowing so much which seems characteristically English in the early seventeenth-century scene description, very successfully conceals a direct dependence upon the 1560 edition of Tansillo's *Lagrime*.

At the same time that "synthesis of dynamically contrasting elements" recognized as a tendency of the Baroque, is already emergent in the sixteen-twenties. In Mathew's translation of *The Confessions* there are several passages which can only be appreciated in terms of Crashaw. The Jacobean period was catholic in its taste and found the act of rejection difficult. But among the many elements in the writing of that time there are those which foreshadow that perfection of Baroque, the last stanza of the Weeper in Crashaw's *Steps to the Temple*.

> "We go not to seek
>   The darlings of Aurora's bed,
>   The rose's modest cheek,
>   Nor the violet's humble head:
> No such thing; we go to meet
> A worthier object, our Lord's feet."

Still it was only very gradually that *manierismo* was to be left far behind. The static element of patronage has an influence on the career of a *littérateur* which has not yet been studied carefully. Relatively popular taste can change so much more rapidly than the nexus between a poet and his ring of patrons. It was part of the courtesy of this relationship that a patron should not abandon those who had acclaimed him. And this patronage must in turn be repaid by verse composed in the accustomed manner. How much was there of use and wont in the encouragement given to the last years of Drayton?

Yet when even the development in the circle of mannered writing was so complex and retarded, it is clear that the various elements were not discernible by such contemporaries as King James and still less by his favourite. The mass of the literate public wished for something very different. It is only necessary to consider the volumes of *Purchas his Pilgrims*, which were issued at this time, to note the gulf between the two conceptions.

Here there were those direct recitals which were so much favoured. A combination of declared literal accuracy with a pleasantly contemptuous attitude towards the foreigner characterized those accounts of travels which circulated in the *milieu* of potential investors in the chartered companies. The description of Constantinople given by John Sanderson is well worth quoting in this respect. The first passage explains[1] the nature of the Seraglio "so replenished with faire pallaces, brave gardens, marble cisterns, faire fountaynes, sumptiouse *bagnos* . . . and particularlie with two faire lodginges, or as we may say banquiting howses, which they caule Chousks (Kiosks); the top coveringes of lead, but underwrought with curiouse wourke of bossinge, pantinge, and gildinge; built of fair marble pillers of perfido and serpentino, ritchlie laid with gould and inestemable expense."

This is a very simple method of presentation with its jejune uncalculated adjectives, and is a prelude to a description of the old Seraglio.[2] "The virgins of the Grand Signor remaine ther. Thether he (the Sultan) goeth many times uppon pleasure," and then comes that recitative litany of fair lodgings, great orchards, many banias and clear fountains. But behind this there lies the quality of the trade prospectus as Sanderson sat in his brother's house in St. Lawrence Jewry assessing the mohairs and watered camlets[3] with the "Turkie painted books"[4] upon the tables and rich carpets strewn across the "siprus chests."

It would not be fair to omit these passages since they seem to have represented a form of writing which was inevitably popular. This was very far from that cultivated world in which the influence of Spain and Italy were mirrored in a prose, sometimes labyrinthine in its intricacy, loaded with conceits and the careful posed allusion and always sophisticated, a conscious architecture.

[1] *Travels and Correspondence of John Sanderson*, Hakluyt Society, 1930, ed. Sir William Foster, p. 72.
[2] *ibid.*, pp. 72–3.
[3] John Sanderson to the Agent at Constantinople, letter dated 10 May, 1604, *ibid.*, p. 226.
[4] *ibid.*, p. 33.

CHAPTER XVII

SECRETARY CONWAY

THROUGH these years and past the change of sovereigns the Duke of Buckingham's position remained unaltered. Only their somewhat ludicrous optimism could have led the courtiers to suppose that King James's death might bring a change of fortune. For in fact the disappointment which the old King had suffered in the breakdown of the Spanish Marriage project only served to bind the Prince of Wales more closely to his chosen friend. "The great Duke," wrote Sir John Leake in August 1624, in one of the innumerable letters dealing with the favourite's status,[1] "is as gratious as ever and most like to continue having anchored deeply in the Prince his love."

In the first few months of the new reign the strength of the Duke's position became apparent and it is interesting to compare the manner in which the various correspondents at the Court inform their friends and patrons that the favourite's position appeared impregnable. Sir Dudley Carleton was among the first to learn[2] that "His Grace was never in better estate for will or power than at this present." Down at Penshurst Lord Leicester, who held aloof from the Court, received advices. His nephew, Pembroke,[3] stated that "my Lord of Buckingham . . . carries all Businesses in his Brest,"

[1] Letter from Sir John Leake to the Earl of Cork, dated 15 August, 1624, *Lismore Papers*, iii, p. 125.
[2] Letter from Sir George Goring to Sir Dudley Carleton, dated 8 September, 1624. Cal. S. P. Dom., 1625-6, p. 100.
[3] Letter from the Earl of Pembroke to the Earl of Leicester, dated 19 October, 1625. *Sydney's State Papers*, ed. Arthur Collins, p. 365.

while Sir John North complained[1] in reference to Sir James
Fullerton's loss of influence that "neither hee, or any in the
Court, but the Duke only have much Power to pleasure
themselves or their Friends."

The removal of Bishop Williams from the lord keepership
which occurred in the first months of the reign, and the
disgrace of Lord Arundel on account of his son's marriage,
certainly emphasize the favourite's power. "Another good
friend of yours," wrote Sir Arthur Ingram to Sir Thomas
Wentworth in this connection,[2] "which is my Lord Marshal
(Arundel), hath the hand of the Great Duke upon him, who
by his means hath brought the King, that he will hardly
speak with him. . . . The Duke's power with the King for
certain is exceeding great; and who he will advance shall be
advanced; and who he doth frown upon must be thrown
down." The knowledge that only some great catastrophe
would avail to unseat the Duke must have been at the root
of this increasing bitterness. The King and his friend were
young, and their joint rule stretched before them. Under
the circumstances there was accuracy in this grim estimate.

It is true that the new Queen Henrietta Maria, whom
Charles I married on his accession, was an opponent of the
Duke; but in the early stages of this marriage the King was
only influenced to irritation by the prejudices of his child
wife from France. And Charles's mind with its rigid and
censorious delicacy was hardened against all those who might
attack his friend through jealousy. It was these circumstances
which gave an adventitious importance to the already
powerful position of Secretary of State, an office which
pivoted upon the secretaryship to the Privy Council. Since
the Kings and their favourite have been studied, it will
complete the picture of one aspect of the Jacobean Age in its
last phases to consider the official through whom the

---

[1] Letter from Sir John North to the Earl of Leicester, *ibid.*, p. 364.
[2] Letter of Sir Arthur Ingram to Sir Thomas Wentworth, dated 7
November, 1624, *Stafford Letters*, ed. William Knowler, p. 28.

sovereigns could be approached. And of the Secretaries, Sir Edward Conway is in many respects the most typical and, besides, held office at a crucial period.

The position of the Secretary of State[1] increased in significance as the need for an interpreter between the Crown and the great body of the landed gentry became more evident. The marked isolation of the royal entourage and the almost vice-regal standing of the Duke of Buckingham, contributed to throw into relief the question of the relations between the Court and the mass of the conservative country gentlemen. It is difficult to determine the precise nature of that bond which linked the old-fashioned squires to the distant King, but its most evident quality was strength.

In 1625 the senior officials were men who had grown up beneath Elizabeth and come to maturity under King James; but the following generation, that of King Charles's contemporaries, had also now reached manhood. Many from both groups would survive into the Civil Wars. The habits of thought of those who were to be the elder Royalists were formed or forming. The condition of affairs had changed considerably since the Elizabethan period when the ministers had hardly been susceptible to unofficial pressure, except when this had been applied by persons of great political consideration. The commoners who rose to be the principal servants of the Tudor monarchy, lost many of their class contacts in the process and, however diverse their social origins, Cecil, Hatton, Walsingham and Bacon, moved in circles to which the ordinary country gentry did not attain.

In the years of peace the situation altered gradually as the prestige of the Lower House increased, and a squirearchy came eventually to control the solid phalanx of the county representation. Inevitably the line of demarcation became less rigid, now that the great landowners were so often

[1] A valuable examination of the history of this post is contained in *The Principal Secretary of State*. A survey of the office from 1558 to 1680. By F. M. G. Evans.

tempted to acquire a peerage. This increasing influence became apparent when gentlemen of considerable property were appointed to the two principal Secretaryships of State. During the ten years following Lord Salisbury's death, this office had ordinarily been held by those who had been bred to the profession of Court politics and had graduated from the secretarial offices of the great ministers. Thus Winwood and Calvert had been *protégés* of the Cecils; Lake had risen through the Howards; Naunton had come unscathed from Essex's entourage. Most of these men either inherited or acquired a landed property; but the soil meant little to them. Henry Wotton, Albertus Morton and Isaac Wake were equally remote from estate management. The Court was the centre of gravity of the whole political and diplomatic grouping.

The appointments of Sir Edward Conway in 1623 and of Sir John Coke in 1625 made a break with this tradition since both men were closely linked to different sections of the landed gentry. They were both, and especially Conway, bound up with rural property and knew the land. This change in personnel was wholly accidental due partly to the exhaustion of the professional talent, now that the Cecilian training-ground had been twelve years closed, and partly to Buckingham's own preference. Nevertheless, Conway's coming did under one aspect foreshadow the ultimate domination of the squires. He was in blood and also to some extent in spirit the progenitor of the Harleys and the Pelhams.

Not only the new Secretary's qualities, but also his failings tend to make a study of this career rewarding. His limitations of outlook and the absence of political foresight only served to link Secretary Conway more closely to the general body of the rural gentry, while absence of personal distinction or of marked individual ability brought him nearer to the common outlook of those whose ideas on religion and politics he shared. For seven years he stood as intermediary between the vocal sections of the people and their ultimate rulers. His humdrum career is a fitting prelude to the powerful movement of Wentworth's mind or to the rather exotic achievements of Cottington and Windebank. But the surface greyness of Conway's period of office is quite misleading. Once his letter books are examined he appears in his writings and conversation as the typical country squire of the elder generation with all the features of his class; wealthy and fond of field sports, a sober decided Anglican, conservative, devoted to the Crown.

It was on 14 January, 1623, that Sir Edward Conway of Ragley in Warwickshire, was appointed one of the two principal Secretaries of State at the age of fifty-eight. He had been made a privy councillor six months earlier,[1] and rumours of this new promotion had been rife throughout the autumn.[2] The appointment was of course made by the King in person, and was therefore influenced by Buckingham. It had been necessary to find a successor to Sir Robert Naunton and to arrange about the latter's pension.[3] After Sir Dudley Carleton's claims had been once more noted, the chances of Sir Francis Cottington were canvassed for his abstruse erudition at times attracted the old King's wavering sympathy.[4] But rumour soon settled upon Conway who was recognized as the favourite's nominee. Besides, the appointment was in every way suitable and the King himself singled out for commendation Sir Edward Conway's birth and soldiership,[5] his sufficiency and honesty and knowledge of languages. It is not inconsistent with the possession of

[1] Letter from Chamberlain to Carleton then at The Hague. Cal. S. P. Dom., 1618–23, p. 418.
[2] Cf., Chamberlain's letters, *ibid.*, pp. 418 and 461.
[3] A letter from Chamberlain to Carleton, dated 16 November, 1622, states that Sir Robert Naunton was to have £500 a year. Cal. S. P. Dom., 1618–23, p. 461.
[4] Referring to Conway's appointment as Secretary the Venetian Ambassador Valaresso stated that "the favourite obtained the office for him." Cal. S. P. Venetian, 1621–3, p. 557.
[5] Letter from Chamberlain to Carleton, dated 16 November, 1622. Cal. S. P. Dom., 1618–23, p. 484.

these qualities that Sir Edward should have proved a heavy man, slow and prosy in his speech.[1]

His early career had been passed in the military service, a fact which he was accustomed to refer to with suitable pride.[2] His laurels were plain enough. He had been knighted at Cadiz by the unfortunate Earl of Essex, and at the turn of the century had held the Lieutenant Governorship of Brill,[3] a post in which he served for sixteen years. Unlike his predecessors in the Secretaryship he was not within that circle of inevitable interlocked acquaintance which bound those who had attended upon the Cecils and the Howards. But he had by chance been acquainted all his life[4] with Sir John Coke who was to be his colleague, and Robert Coke, a younger brother, had been killed in action[5] serving under him in the Dutch garrison. The appointment at Brill had terminated in 1616 on the occasion of the opportune surrender of the town to the Dutch military authorities and the government of the United Provinces had guaranteed to Sir Edward the very generous life pension of £500 a year.[6] These monies enabled him to spend more freely on the development of his property at Ragley for his primary interest lay in country life. He at once showed himself ready to take his share in those administrative burdens which were falling increasingly upon his class. Like so many of the greater squires he had entered the House of Commons sitting in the Parliament of 1610–1 as member for Penrhyn, a seat which he abandoned at the next election preferring to represent Evesham, a parliamentary borough seven miles

[1] Despatch of the Tuscan Envoy dated 19 August, 1625. Salvetti Correspondence, p. 29.

[2] Conway seems particularly typical of his class when envying the gentlemen of his troop setting out for the wars. Cal. S. P. Dom., 1627–8, p. 182.

[3] He was actually at Brill as late as 1611, Letter Book of Sir John Holles. Cal. Portland MSS., ix.

[4] Cf., Letters in Cal. Coke MSS., p. 22.

[5] In 1600, Cal. Coke MSS., p. 26.

[6] Lord Carew. *Letters to Sir Thomas Roe*, p. 35.

ride from his home. He rented a house in London in St. Martin's Lane;[1] but he devoted a great deal of his time to improving his father's estate which he had inherited in 1603 and had left to the management of his uncle.[2] On returning to England he had established his cousin, Fulke Reade, as his agent in Warwickshire, and between them they had made purchases which considerably increased his landed property.

Sir Edward had lost his first wife, while on military service in Holland, and he now fortified his fortune by a second marriage with the widow of a City of London grocer, a Flemish woman. Such references to Lady Conway as survive[3] show her as mercenary and rather flighty, keenly anxious for a social success to which she was unaccustomed; a difficult woman.[4] As a native of Ghent she was a subject of the Archdukes and was only naturalized in 1626. There does not seem to be any evidence to indicate her religious standpoint.

In spite of the comparative failure of this second venture Sir Edward Conway's family life reflected that assured and patriarchal domesticity which went with the conscious self-respect of the old school of country gentlemen. He was indulgent towards his extravagant wife[5] and distant towards the children of her first marriage who had scant claims upon his company. In his dealings with his son Edward Conway, a man close on thirty, he exercised parental firmness;[6] but the lack of sympathy between this son and Lady Conway was veiled by a mask of courtesy. "I fear," wrote the younger

---

[1] He retained this house until the end of his life. Cf., the Conway Letter Books.

[2] A letter preserved among the Domestic State Papers and written by Francis Conyers to his nephew Sir Edward Conway on 20 June, 1616, throws light on their relations.

[3] See the correspondence preserved in Conway's Letter Books.

[4] Cf., a letter from Robert Dixon among the Montagu papers and calendered in the Buccleugh and Queensberry MSS., iii, p. 319.

[5] Letter from Fulke Reade to Conway, dated 8 December, 1625. Cal. S. P. Dom., Add., 1625–49, p. 74.

[6] A typical instance is the letter from father to son. Cal. S. P. Dom., 1627–8, p. 434.

Conway to his brother-in-law,[1] "I shall have a great question with my stepmother, which I would be as loth to fall upon as a rock at sea." It was a part of the family tradition that the Conways must not lose their bearings.

In fact amid the various difficulties of his private life Sir Edward conducted himself with prudent dignity. Towards his grown-up daughters he indulged a heavy and playful affection, while little practical jokes and humorous turns of speech appealed to him. He was deeply affectionate towards his daughters' small children. The sons-in-law whom he had chosen continued to receive his warm approval, and with one of them, Sir Robert Harley, he formed the closest friendship of his later life.[2] He even spoke to him about religion.

It is a simple matter to fill in the further detail. Sir Edward Conway was hospitable; as a soldier a good disciplinarian; a shade pedantic. He considered himself a sound judge of horse flesh and some of his difficulties arose from backing his own opinion on this matter.[3] He enjoyed all forms of country life and had a gentleman's interest in the construction of pedigrees, while with this there went a sharp appreciation of money values. His general attitude was strongly patriotic; English food appealed to him; his appetite for country fare was good. In the evenings he refreshed himself with a mead posset.[4] Such were Sir Edward Conway's characteristics, typical of his class, a trifle dull, in later years rheumatic. One unusual circumstance, however, raised him to power.

A close friendship had sprung up between Sir Edward and Villiers, then the new young favourite. His final return from

[1] Letter from Sir Edward Conway the younger, to Sir Robert Harley dated 27 February, 1631. Cal. Portland MSS., iii, p. 29.

[2] The series of letters among the Harley Papers, now part of the Portland MSS., describes the progress of this friendship.

[3] In 1626 a dispute arose touching the soundness of a coach horse, a bay gelding purchased out of Conway's stable. Cal. S. P. Dom. Add., p. 186.

[4] According to a letter of his daughter Lady Brilliana, dated 5 October, 1627. Much of this personal detail is derived from the family letters in the Portland MSS., and from the Letters of Lady Brilliana Harley (ed. Camden Society).

Brill coincided with the establishment of the latter's fortune, and it is possible that in its early stages the association may have seemed of benefit to the younger man. Conway had considerable wealth and a certain prestige;[1] he was on the most cordial terms with his first cousin, Sir Fulke Greville; he had a solid backing in Warwickshire. These were matters with which Villiers was familiar and could appreciate. Besides, Sir Edward was first and foremost a soldier and the military virtues always exercised a fascination over George Villiers. But very soon all parity between their positions vanished as the favourite soared to his great eminence. Yet it appears from their letters that Conway attuned himself to each fresh change in their mutual station as Buckingham rose to his ascendancy. Into his attitude there came affection and then reverence, and throughout he showed a perfect loyalty to the youth who had become so suddenly his protector. Sir Edward's ideas on politics were few, and Buckingham flowed over with vitality and energy; perhaps he dazzled him.

Conway has been charged, and notably by S. R. Gardiner, with the vice of sycophancy, but this would seem to involve a superficial reading of his character, and hardly appears to be consistent with his unvarying defence of Buckingham during all the troubles of his final years. And after the Duke's murder, when almost all the courtiers gave expression to their understandable and pent-up malice against Felton's victim, Lord Conway mourned him. On a more careful consideration it seems probable that his attitude and even the strange rodomontade of his exalted phrasing were alike the fruit of Conway's inherited high Royalism in its practical application.

In a humdrum existence, passed in maintaining local law, each thread of the squire's duty led upwards to the apex of his system, the monarchy. The pragmatic Elizabethan

[1] A country gentleman in Devonshire described him as "Sir Edward Conway, an auncient commander in the war," *Diary of Walter Yonge* p. 66.

emphasis on the sacredness of kingship, was the natural prelude to this theorizing. To the elder Cavalier mind the phrase the fount of honour seemed most real when applied to the Crown and its sovereignty, and the refractions of the kingship would appear like the heavenly train which filled the Temple. When discussion could almost look like blasphemy Passive Obedience was present in the germ. Royalists of this school were confident that the English kingship was as secure from examination and as motionless and immutable as the sun. There was, of course, a very different attitude among squires who were to form the opposition, throughout the merchant classes, and among all those in whom the Genevan leaven slowly worked. Again, the lawyers with their reverence for the King's authority had a more careful and exact approach, and there was to be found within the palace circles a half-concealed and sophisticated scepticism. Yet it seems reasonable to regard Secretary Conway's outlook as an example of the old royalist approach with its tortuous and almost obsequious expression and its deep interior simplicity.

This dichotomy can alone explain the contrast between the manner in which Sir Edward approached the Duke, and the whimsical and sometimes crotchety self-reliance which marked his handling of all other situations. One letter is typical. "Your servant," wrote[1] Secretary Conway to Buckingham in 1625, "hopes to kiss Your Grace's hands with as much humbleness and more constancy than ever he did his mistress's and with a faith not to be exceeded of." Such an epistolary style makes it easy to follow the line of thought which led to Gardiner's strictures;[2] but the rest of Conway's career supplies valid reasons for the belief that this attitude was not essentially servile, but arose from doctrine. The reason given[3] by the letter writer Chamberlain to account

[1] Letter dated 25 July, 1625, Cal. S. P. Dom. Add., 1625–49, p. 37.
[2] Cf., S. R. Gardiner, *History of England*, iv, p. 410.
[3] In a letter dated 16 January, 1623.

for his appointment, "his courtiership in trying to fasten the title of excellency upon the Duke," is consonant with both interpretations of his character, nor can any evidence be gathered from the statement that he was King Charles's confidant.[1] But a spontaneous tribute to his honesty has been preserved, and a letter written in the spring of 1626 further elucidates his point of view.[2] It should be explained that Sir Edward had been raised to the peerage as Lord Conway in the previous year, and that the patent had passed the great seal four days before the old King died. "I will, all respects set apart, be in the Upper House on Wednesday," he wrote to the Duke who was then subjected to attack,[3] "and see through whose eyes honour looks and in whose faces envy and unworthiness have fixed the clouds of unsensibleness and mixture of base thoughts with honourable titles." It is an euphuistic statement of his essential position; but like declarations stand at the base of all legitimism.

He was to have ample opportunity to show the sincerity of his attachment. In the autumn of 1627, when the news reached England of Buckingham's failure in the expedition to La Rochelle, the Secretary of State wrote[4] "to offer Lord Conway's humble faith and duty to his gracious patron whose pain he feels by his own." During the next few weeks, when the popular fury against the favourite rose to great heights, he laboured on his behalf. "Lord Conway," wrote Sir Edward Nicholas,[5] "most industrious of all men

[1] Letter from the Earl of Kellie to the Earl of Mar, dated 11 November, 1625. "He (Kairlile) is now all in all with the King in the absence of that great man (the Duke), and onlye Connowaye and he is his confidante of all both counsellours and curteours," Cal. Mar and Kellie MSS., Suppl. p. 237.

[2] Letter from the Earl of Kellie to the Earl of Mar, dated 11 June, 1623. "Secretary Connowaye, whoe is my Lord of Bukkinghame's confident and I think a verrye honest man." Cal. Mar and Kellie MSS., p. 177.

[3] Letter dated 12 March, 1626. Cal. S. P. Dom. Add., 1625–49, pp. 107–8.

[4] Letter from Lord Conway to the Earl of Holland, dated 18 October, 1627. Cal. S. P. Dom., 1627–8, p. 394.

[5] Letter from Sir Edward Nicholas to the Duke, dated 14 November, 1627, ibid., p. 434.

there." "We owe," declared the Secretary of State in summing up his own position,[1] "to the excellent Duke's favour all we are and all we can be." In these generous and explicit words Conway seems to reflect that magnanimity which was to characterize the country Royalists. In some ways he was their fit interpreter, rigid in home politics, with a loyalty determined in action and rather fantastic in expression, robust and insular. His mind, like theirs, was clear and simple and full of sense and prejudice.

Whatever may be thought of his sincerity, it will hardly be disputed that in his ideas Conway represented the general outlook of that class which possessed authority derived from inherited position and untempered by precise political knowledge. He fully shared their lack of literary interests and their casual training.[2] Each prejudice or prepossession embedded in that stratum of English life is found again in Conway's expressed ideas on foreign policy.

In the first place he displayed a marked anti-Spanish trend[3] and he was too bluff and, perhaps, in European matters too little educated to be susceptible to Gondomar's elaborate approaches. His generation had been young men at the Armada and from the accumulated bitterness of forty years a hearty dislike of Spain had taken root, and he was ready to support Spain's enemies. "The Secretary Conovel," wrote the Venetian Ambassador,[4] "spoke strongly in favour of breaking away at once and for all from the Spanish artifices." At the same time, and as an inevitable corollary, Conway had a strong sympathy for the Dutch alliance, and

[1] Letter from Lord Conway to his son Sir Edward Conway, dated 24 November, 1627. Cal. S. P. Dom., 1627–8, p. 434.

[2] In corroboration of King James's jest about "a Secretary who could not write his name" the Venetian Ambassador Alvise Valaresso described Conway on 5 February, 1623, as "an honest man who knows more about the sword than the pen." Cal. S. P. Venetian, 1621–3, pp. 557–8.

[3] Letter from Alvise Valaresso to the Doge and Senate, dated 8 September, 1623, "But the Spaniards hate him (Conway) extremely." Cal. S. P. Venetian, 1623–5, p. 106.

[4] Letter from Alvise Valaresso to the Doge and Senate, dated 2 February, 1624, ibid., p. 208.

was reported to have promised them "great things."[1] Meanwhile the annual pension of £500, which he received from the Government of the United Provinces for his services at Brill, was a suitable reminder of their probity.

Yet, when he was first brought into touch with these high matters, he appears to have supported the project of the Spanish Match.[2] Its completion was King James's personal wish and it seems that Conway's prejudice was overborne by his deference. But he detested the "audacity of the priests"[3] and welcomed Buckingham's decision to urge a breach with Olivares. One phrase will serve to indicate the distaste which he felt for the proposed connection with Madrid. In the course of the correspondence between Conway and his cousin Greville, there is reference[4] to the hope of "bearding the King of Spain in that mystical Court of Pope and Conclave." The Secretary was to a lesser degree anti-French;[5] he came to dislike Queen Henrietta's French attendants; he detested the foreign clerics; all Protestants abroad met with his favour. His was a workable, comprehensive and above all popular standpoint.

Still, it was in home affairs that Conway's personal influence can be detected, and here he could put before his younger sovereign's rigid mind the commonplace reactions[6] to the shifting religious trends and policies. Fortunately, the Secretary's own views are crystal clear. He appears to have

---

[1] Two reports sent to Venice by Valaresso on 3 February and - September, 1623, respectively, bear on this subject. Cal. S. P. Venetian, 1621–3, p. 558 and 1623–5, p. 106.

[2] According to a letter dated 10 October, 1623. Cal. S. P. Dom., 1623–5, p. 91.

[3] This fact, referred to by the Venetian Ambassador, is also mentioned by Chamberlain in his correspondence with Carleton under 31 January, 1624.

[4] Cal. S. P. Dom. Add., 1625–49, p. 53.

[5] Letter from the Earl of Kellie to the Earl of Mar, dated 10 January, 1625. Cal. Mar and Kellie MSS., p. 217.

[6] Lord Montagu of Boughton's Journal of the proceedings of the House of Lords and his notes on the Parliament of 1625 describe the effect produced by Secretary Conway on the Commons and the peers, Cal. Buccleugh and Queensberry MSS., iii, pp. 283–4 and 302–3.

remained uninfluenced either by the Andrewes school of thought or by the preferences of the new High Churchmen. Like so many others of his class and generation, he had received that Erastian upbringing which, during the 'seventies of the previous century, had been the lot of those whose parents lacked sympathy with the traditions of Rome and Geneva. In Conway's case the effect of this training had been modified by the religious experience of his later life. It is also probable that his sympathy for the Dutch and his long residence in Holland, were in part responsible for the Evangelical trend of his preferences.

His orderly slow mind yielded an adequate respect for the bench of bishops, and he seems to have favoured a form of undogmatic peace within the wide frontiers of the Established Church. A letter, written to the Bishop of London in 1624 in defence of the vicar of St. Lawrence, Old Jewry, summarizes attractively his point of view. "It is a malicious artifice," Conway declared,[1] "to call those persons puritanical who by their gifts and graces and acceptance with the people can do most good." The feeling which was to run counter to Archbishop Laud is already perceptible in this choice of phrasing, "gifts and graces . . . acceptance with the people."

In later life the Secretary was accustomed to express his Christian sentiments more freely,[2] especially after the change which came over his outlook through the growth of his intimacy with his son-in-law Harley. In this connection it is worth considering the effect of his favourite daughter's household upon Lord Conway. Certainly these contacts between Ragley and Brampton Bryan take their place among the indications of the strength of Puritan feeling in the Church of England, and serve to stress the closeness of the links which bound the Court party to those who were so soon to be the opposition squires.

[1] Cal. S. P. Dom., 1623–5, p. 355.
[2] Cf., Correspondence with Sir John Ogle who was desirous of taking Holy Orders. Cal. S. P. Dom., 1623–5, and Conway's Letter Book.

To this incipient opposition, Sir Robert Harley did not yet himself belong; in fact he held government office as Master of the Mint. Nevertheless, his religious outlook was of so definite a character that it would in time inevitably carry him into the ranks of the Parliamentarians. He was already a man of fifty-four; a wealthy landowner, in religion a Puritan, twice a widower, when in 1623 he became Lord Conway's son-in-law. As with the generality of marriages of this rank in the seventeenth century, the connection between the two families was in no way fortuitous, and a letter among the Harley Papers indicates that some cousinship existed between them.[1]

The real difference lay in the religious distinction which was to divide the Harleys and the Conways in the struggle that followed; for the Harleys of Brampton Bryan in the Welsh Marches had passed directly from Catholicism to a Puritan feeling.[2] Oriel under Cadwallader Owen had formed Robert Harley's ideas, and the living of Brampton Bryan was held by a clergyman of strong Calvinist views, and in that remote western countryside the personality of the rector could be of great importance. "Mr. Gwallter Stephens of Bishop's Castle," so runs an entry in MS. notes on the rectors of the Harley living, "had lighted his candle at famous Mr. Pierson's. . . . Never a preacher between him and the sea one way." At Brampton Bryan, isolated on the edge of Wales, Mr. Pierson in his Geneva gown preached on the duty of iconoclasm. Into this atmosphere Brilliana Conway came to Sir Robert as a young bride. Her name had been given from her birthplace Brill, following the then fashionable Dutch custom.[3] She was always known as "Brill" for short and had domesticated tastes and a talent for making

---

[1] Cal. Portland MSS., iii, p. 17.
[2] Sir Robert's father Thomas Harley had been a Catholic in his youth.
[3] As in the case of William of Orange's daughters, Charlotte Flandrina, Charlotte Brabantina and Emilie Antwerpiana, and Charles I's niece Louise Hollandina of the Palatinate.

preserves.[1] She accepted her husband's Puritanism completely.[2]

Lord Conway took something of the colour of this household, for a cold relationship with his son perhaps forced him back on Brampton Bryan. His letters to Sir Robert Harley pass from an elaborately stilted manner to a tone of intimacy in a way that is attractive and rather unexpected. "My good sonne" he wrote just before the signature of the marriage contract in a letter which was as stiff and worked as a bride-cake,[3] "for so methinkes it is your good pleasure that the stile runn and methinkes it is as rich an embrodery to mee as it can bee silk lace to you." But this was not his natural expression and the simplicity must soon assert itself as he came to know his daughter's house and his thought turned from London with its tension and disturbance to the coolness of those western shires. A second note written in the summer of 1629 will show the line on which their relations became established: "I have a quarrel with you, son Harley," began the old man,[4] "that you did not kill all the rats, for you left one that bit little Bridget by the nose."

They would thus discuss business and politics, for Harley was concerned with the monopolies for the manufacture of gold and silver thread; then they would come to domesticities; at last religion. The Puritan strain developed slowly, but in time Conway was brought to speak much of prayer[5]

---

[1] Cf., Cal. S. P. Dom. Add., 1625–49, pp. 29–30. Letters in the Harley Papers among the Portland MSS. and *Letters of Lady Brilliana Harley*, *passim* for these personal details.

[2] Her upbringing perhaps made this easier. In referring to her first cousin Lady Fairfax, Clarendon wrote that "having been bred in Holland she had not reverence for the Church of England as she ought to have." *History of the Great Rebellion.*

[3] Cal. Portland MSS., iii, p. 17.   [4] *ibid.*, iii, p. 26.

[5] Contrast. 1623, "Sir Edward Conway was there (at Windsor) gallantly attired in white hat and feather." Letter from Chamberlain to Carleton. Cal. S. P. Dom., 1619–23, p. 576.

1630, "But if you knew the profound leisure I have it might be saide that to pray for my frends did scarce deserve their thankes bycause it wer done as the most men take tobacco." Letter from Conway to Carleton. Cal. Portland MSS., iii, p. 26.

and even to ask for a good preacher. "I would to God," he wrote to Harley in 1627 when he was still in office,[1] "I had a good preacher. Send me one if you can and he shall live with me."

By chance the dating of this last letter is instructive. While Conway was turning to the earnest and grave preachers with their bands and their sad gowns, King Charles was meditating his appointments. The Bishop of Bath and Wells must be promoted, possibly to the great see of London, whose ordinary was dying and certainly to the primacy when that lay vacant. There was here an element of future tension. Throughout England the godly preachers were increasing, they were coming forward and receiving livings. Down at Wells little Dr. Laud pursued the rather hard and clear lines of his thought, the Church seemly and decorous and the high Caroline theology. And the King with the fixed determination of his settled mind was bent on drawing him to Lambeth to that one section of the magnetic field where there must be most disturbance. But these difficulties did not mature in Conway's lifetime. It would seem that right up to his death in 1631 he retained a perfect confidence in the workings of government beneath the Crown and contentment with all the facets of *Ecclesia Anglicana* in those last calm years.

Though it is clear that Conway was sound where Protestantism was in question, his attitude towards the Papists remains to be considered. The Letter Books, which have been carefully preserved, throw much light upon this subject. During his seven years of office the Secretary of State received a mass of correspondence dealing with the routine administration of the Penal Laws against the Catholics, urging their enforcement or pleading for exemption. The laws against Catholic Recusants were upheld with vehemence by Parlia-

[1] Letter from Conway to Harley, dated 16 June, 1726. Cal. Portland MSS., iii, p. 23.

ment: at Court their application was unpopular. Conway stood between these fires.

In the first place the Secretary of State came from a social *milieu* and from a section of the country where bitterness against Rome was tempered by daily intercourse with the adherents of the proscribed religion. He stood remote from the atmosphere of the Court where fanaticism would soon be censured as impolite, but he was also very far in spirit from those West Country circles where a strong zeal fed itself on thoughts of Popery. Catholics were sparse in Devon, and few men there had that personal acquaintance with the Recusants which alone could dispel the worst hostility. In the little seaport towns they were the legendary enemy. And for Conway's career this detestation of Popery was menacing, since in the House of Commons the western members in particular hung on to this subject dourly and grimly.

The diary of Walter Yonge, a gentleman and shipowner of Colyton in Devon, makes this point clear. The diarist was a man of means and well-informed; a friend and neighbour of Sir John Drake of Ash, who had married one of Buckingham's nieces. On this matter of Popery he pondered continually. "There is a report," he noted under 19 August,[1] 1622, "that Papists shall have a toleration here in England, and that the Protestant ministers shall preach but once a Sabbath." While six months after Conway's appointment, which he had received with favour, there came another entry:[2] "the Jesuits and Papists do wonderfully swarm." With an influential section of the country any exemption that Conway gave would injure him.

In the West Country the legend of the Powder Plot had crystallized and Catesby could stand for any Catholic gentleman. But down in Warwickshire men knew the

[1] *Diary of Walter Yonge*, Camden Society, p. 63.
[2] Entry under 26 October, 1623, *ibid.*, p. 70.

character and value of Catesby more exactly; they were familiar with the quiet and unimaginative loyalty of the Catholic landowners; they could understand the distaste with which the Throckmortons had regarded their wastrel cousins long before the mad conspiracy.[1] Indeed throughout Warwickshire and Worcestershire and up into Staffordshire, there was a mutual friendliness between the Catholic and Protestant country gentlemen to which Clarendon was to bear witness.[2] However much one might dislike the priests, few Midland squires would fail in neighbourly courtesy to the priests' protectors.

All the evidence would seem to suggest that Conway considered inherited Catholicism in a man of birth, not as a menace, but rather as a polite and not unamiable weakness. Again his sense of an ordered hierarchy beneath the throne made him very amenable to well-couched requests which reached him from those whom his sovereign favoured. To Conway it appears to have been clear that the King might safeguard any of his subjects from the effects of these recent and penal statutes which he himself had put in operation, and it seemed reasonable that he would so protect the great personages about the Court whom he honoured with his friendship. This point of view was quite consistent with a strong opposition to any general toleration. In the early seventeenth century the right to indulge one's private foibles, was a perquisite of men of influence.

This will perhaps suggest an explanation of the difficulty in which Conway found himself when faced by the demands of the Villiers family. It seemed natural that they should have exemptions each one of which was hateful to the

---

[1] Robert Catesby, Francis Tresham and the Winters of Huddington were all cousins of the Throckmortons of Coughton.

[2] There is an interesting passage in Clarendon's account of the escape of Charles after the battle of Worcester. "Mr. Lane . . . though he was a very zealous Protestant yet lived with so much civility and candour towards the Catholics that they would all trust him," *History of the Great Rebellion*. Cf., The Boscobel Tracts.

favourite's enemies. Conway strongly supported the Duke and his Protestant policy, but it also fell to his lot to deal with the Catholic relatives and dependents who had risen in the wake of the Villiers fortune. Buckingham in these middle years had heedlessly gathered both friendship and enmity. The enemies for the time concentrated upon his person; but the Secretary of State received the full embarrassment of the Duke's friends.

With the embarrassments there were at first many compensations. Lord Rutland showed himself most friendly and discovered that Conway's son was a distant cousin,[1] while old Lady Buckingham became a determined ally and the Duke's brother Kit, a simple fellow, was full of jovial gratitude. Nor were the requests themselves always open to objection. At the petition of the Duke's mother, the Secretary arranged for the release of a venerable priest, John Colleton, "stated to be 4 score and 18 years of age, who wished to live in peace among his books."[2]

Still very soon favours were asked for Kit Villiers' wife's family, the Sheldons of Beoley whom Conway had known in Worcestershire. Mr. and Mrs. Edward Sheldon and their son and daughter-in-law were given leave to travel on the Continent with eighteen servants and six horses,[3] and then there came the troublesome case of Lady Falkland. This was a family quarrel caused by the conversion to Catholicism of Lucius Falkland's mother, a dispute in which she was supported by the Villiers ladies. Here again the Secretary was determined to fulfil his patron's wishes, and it seems as if he never fully realized how the world was coming to regard the ramifications of the Duke of Buckingham's affections. A protest had already been made in the Commons when the Secretary had granted protection to a Catholic lady in Dorset. He had been over-loyal to his master in these private matters

[1] Letter in Cal. S. P. Dom. 1625–6, p. 406.
[2] Cal. S. P. Dom., 1627–8, p. 3.
[3] Cal. S. P. Dom. Add., 1625–49, p. 23.

and opposition, clarified and embittered by religious animus, gathered about the Duke's chief henchman.

Nevertheless it would be a mistake to exaggerate the effect of contact with the Court upon Lord Conway for his line of approach lay through Buckingham to the King. He had no concern with the Queen's friends, nor intimacy with the ambassadors. The Venetian envoy, who had cultivated his friendship, had been recalled and his successor was unfriendly and referred to the Secretary's "usual crass negligence."[1] It is true that in his old age he was growing sleepy, but he stood as far removed as any in the Court from those who had responded to the influence of Gondomar or the unquiet suggestions of Sir Tobie Mathew. His patriotism was staunchly insular and his dislike for the great foreign nations responded fully to the people's mood.

In his attitude towards the State service and the public finances he was practical without being grasping. A memorandum has survived in which Windebank had noted some trivial dividends of Lord Conway's[2] "from the Signet Office for November; at the Petty Bag after Trinity; at the Hanaper for both terms." When his salary was in arrears he could be sharp-tempered[3] and he exacted the usual perquisites attached to his position.[4] Through the death of his brother Sir Fulke Conway, when trying to save his papers when his house was burned down in Ireland in the winter of 1624, he inherited a considerable property in Irish rents[5] which

[1] This report sent in by Zuane Pesaro is in sharp contrast to the tone adopted by Valaresso, who always regarded Conway as being "of a favourable disposition." Cal. S. P. Venetian, 1623–5, p. 547 and 1621–3, p. 564.

[2] Cal. S. P. Dom. Add., 1625–49, p. 54.

[3] A letter from Secretary Conway to Lord Treasurer Marlborough, dated 18 March, 1628, contains an urgent application for his pay as Secretary which would be three-quarters in arrear at Lady Day. Cal. S. P. Dom., 1628–9, p. 25.

[4] Cf., for Mr. Secretary Conway a fee of £4. Cal. Exeter Corporation MSS., p. 92.

[5] This was set down by Chamberlain when writing to Carleton on 18 December, 1624, as "£2,000 a year in land." Cal. S. P. Dom., 1623–5, p. 412. But this is merely the estimate of a letter-writer.

enabled him to consolidate his already very substantial fortune. In regard to financial transactions of a semi-official character, he accepted the prevailing custom. He inherited the practice of raising money on the sale of peerages and found dealing in monopolies well-established. With these he did not interfere; it was not in his nature to initiate.

As a country gentleman, whose understanding primarily concerned land values, he regarded commercial undertakings with some suspicion. He looked coldly on the second Lady Conway's Newfoundland ventures and regretted that she had been persuaded by a local charlatan, Dr. Meddes[1] into investing capital in an unhopeful scheme for producing an immediate profit from furs and sarsaparilla and iron and silver mines. Similarly he was careful to keep his distance with the financiers like Monsieur Philippe Burlamachi who supplied the King's more pressing needs. The manner in which he maintained a composed aloofness from Burlamachi while suggesting further advances with cold dignity is clear throughout their whole long correspondence. Those of his relatives of no particular standing who approached Lord Conway for assistance, found him generous up to a point and then adamant. He was both short and satisfactory in dealing with his nephew, Mr. Hercules Huncks,[2] and altogether fully deserved his reputation for common sense.

An impression of Conway in his later years is provided by Sir John Oglander who met him in September 1627, when he came to visit the Isle of Wight of which he was Captain. "Concerning his person," wrote Oglander,[3] "he was old, unwieldy, and very sickly, neither fit for employment or command. Certainly he had been a brave fellow as now a courtier: he had excellent gifts of nature, but no art: spoke very well, with many words and compliments, affable and

---

[1] For Dr. James Meddes's correspondence with Lady Conway see Cal. S. P. Dom., 1628-9, pp. 180 and 223.
[2] Cf., *ibid.*, p. 20 and 1624-6, p. 501.
[3] *The Commonplace Book of Sir John Oglander*, ed. F. Bamford, p. 25.

courteous." After declaring that he was unpopular, because he could not make good in deeds the courtesies and favours which he offered, Oglander embarked on an elaborate seventeenth-century characterization which is the less valuable because evidently so meditated. "He was," he wrote,[1] "a very good father and husband, making very much of his wife and children. Although he was a very verbose man, yet he had some qualities that were good. He would use all men with respect and he was an excellent house-keeper, never thinking that he had meat enough at his table, for he would have three pheasants in a dish and six par-tridges. Indeed, he was a very epicure and free at his table, both in meat and wines, and as he spent much that way, so would he gain it any other way. I think he never refused anything that was brought him." This is only one view of him and seen from the angle of casual hospitality and from a standpoint which Oglander's last words make very clear. "He was good enough," he concludes,[2] "if we (of the Isle of Wight) had been so happy as to have known how to make use of him."

In general the first Secretary of State embodied the military tradition among the gentry; courteous from a sense of his position; disinclined for study save for an interest in his family history and in "platts" of Conway Castle; jovial when in good health; keen on experiments as a landowner. In private life an authoritarian he was impatient of the inferior clergy and had been compelled to dismiss the curate at Luddington who had ceased to pray publicly for himself and his family. He was considerate towards the gentlemen in his employment and polite to his fussy foreign wife, accepting

---

[1] *The Commonplace Book of Sir John Oglander*, ed. F. Bamford, pp. 141–3.
[2] *The Commonplace Book of Sir John Oglander*, ed. F. Bamford, p. 145. Oglander makes the very much over-simplified assertion that Conway became Secretary as a result of surrendering his company to Buckingham's cousin Alexander Brett. He also states that "at Brill he was run through the body by a madman with a sword."

from her a plaster for his sciatica in which she had faith.[1] For his own grandchildren he had a deep affection "for secretary Edward and my acquaintance, Robin and my unknown Thomas and my dear Brill."[2] He had the distaste of ignorance for foreign policy, a profound loyalty to the King, a deep feeling for his house and family. He was in fact an English squire.

[1] Cal. S. P. Dom., 1627-8, p. 233. All these details are from the State Papers and the Conway Letter Books. Among Conway's experiments was the planting of vines on his estate in Warwickshire.

[2] This litany occurs in a letter written in 1630, the year before his death, to his daughter and son-in-law and it concludes: "God bless you both and all your boys and wenches." Cal. Portland MSS., iii, pp. 28-9.

CHAPTER XVIII

SECRETARY COKE

AS a pendant to the career of Sir Edward Conway, a brief consideration of his colleague's background will indicate another set of influences at work upon the politico-social scene. It is true that Secretary Coke came to the fullness of his influence under Charles I, but he belonged essentially to that generation whose maturity coincided with the earlier reign, and he was over sixty when the old King died. In some respects he derived from the last Elizabethan period and in the reign of Charles I he filled the role both of the monitor of an earlier standard and the supporter of conservative values.

Sir John Coke was in almost every respect a contrast to Secretary Conway except that he, too, represented the landed interest at the Court. While one came from the army, the other had been bred in the Universities. Conway stood for the military tradition; Coke for the cultivated and academic Royalism. The two men had known each other all their lives and on the death of Sir Albertus Morton in the early months of the new reign, had found themselves colleagues. Lord Brooke, Conway's cousin and Coke's patron, put the situation succinctly in a letter written in the September of 1625. "I congratulate you," he wrote to Conway,[1] "on Sir John Coke's advancement as good for the kingdom and a passing safe and easy yoke fellow for yourself." As the phrase implies, "the passing safe and easy yoke-fellow" had conquered his high position by slow degrees during a career

[1] Cal. S. P. Dom., Add., 1625–49, p. 24.

carefully built up until it had reached the culmination of a Secretaryship of State. He had not depended solely upon Buckingham, and never attained to intimacy with him, as witness the distant style of the Duke's letters.[1] Besides, his promotion had come to him late in life at sixty-two, "he having continued long in the University of Cambridge, where he had gotten Latin learning enough and afterwards in the country in the condition of a private gentleman till he was fifty years of age."[2] In every way his character was fixed.

John Coke did not possess, nor did he ever have the prospect of inheriting, a substantial fortune since he was merely one of the younger sons of a Derbyshire squire. The family had a certain standing in that county; his eldest brother Sir Francis Coke of Trusley busied himself in local administration; their mother had been a Sacheverell. Nevertheless, the family belonged to the minor rather than to the richer gentry. One of the brothers had entered the Church and another was steward to a great peer. It was in keeping with such a *milieu* that Coke should have been sent as a foundation scholar to Trinity, and that he should have kept up his associations with Cambridge. From the time of his marriage until 1623, his wife and children lived at Hall Court, near Much Marcle in Herefordshire, a small country house which he had bought. As a young man he had entered the Naval Department obtaining a post in the storehouse at Deptford and he had been promoted eventually to a Commissionership of the Navy. While a bachelor he could not afford a house in London, but lodged[3] with his patron, Sir Fulke Greville, in Austin Friars, undertaking a certain amount of tutorship and general agent's work[3] for his

[1] Cf., Cal. Coke MSS., i, pp. 314 and 362.
[2] Clarendon, *op. cit.*
[3] Letters addressed to him at the store house are preserved among the Melbourne Papers. Cal. Coke MSS., pp. 34 and 43 and at Austin Friars, *ibid.*, p. 91.

official chief and the latter's brother-in-law, Verney.[1] He was fortunately sober in his tastes and very careful about money. A letter from his sister, Mrs. Fulwood,[2] throws light upon his trait. "Let me," she wrote, "send down a beaver hat either black or some sad colour near it, either shorn or unshorn which you think best." Without the burdens of an estate he devoted his spare time in middle life to the then undistinguished pursuit of market-gardening. "It is now," wrote his elder brother a little patronizingly,[3] "full time for your artichokes. I have also sent you five more." So much for a first impression of his background.

Meanwhile a draft letter to Buckingham, which was never sent, adequately presents Coke's own view of his situation. It was written in 1622 shortly before he established himself in London on his appointment as Master of Requests. At this date he had just entered on his sixtieth year. "Howsoever I am valued," the draft runs,[4] "my descent is not base. I was not bred in servile or illiberal trades, the University was my nurse. I have travelled many countries, where I saw peace and war. . . . I am acquainted with books and no stranger to the Courts and affairs of the world. . . . My Lord Brooke (Greville) now telleth me that you require me forthwith to fetch up my family, that I shall have his Majesty's fee for my service in the Navy continued to me, and secure from your lordship £200 a year." Few letters could better describe the man.[5]

[1] Two items will indicate the type of service. Letter from Fulke Greville to John Coke, "I wrote to you about my Lady Baskerville's horses," *ibid.*, p. 27. Letter from Sir Richard Verney to John Coke, dated 28 July, 1604, "I find ther (at Cambridge) the influence of your good affections towards my poor imps," *ibid.*, p. 47.

[2] Letter from Mrs. Mary Fulwood to her brother John Coke, dated 18 April, 1610, *ibid.*, p. 30.

[3] Letter from Francis Coke at Trusley to John Coke, dated 18 April, 1610. Cal. Coke MSS., p. 70.

[4] Draft dated 12 October, 1622, *ibid.*, p. 121.

[5] A biography of Sir John Coke, *The Last Elizabethan* by Dorothea Coke was published in 1937. It contains a considerable amount of information, but the author takes a very roseate view of her subject's influence and abilities.

From his youth Coke's manner had been grave and his judgments pondered and weighty. This solemnity rather emphasized than concealed his closeness in financial matters and a certain cautiously suspicious outlook, perhaps traceable to his early poverty. This attitude comes out clearly in a letter written to his wife Marie, after the sale of Hall Court in mid-October 1623, on the occasion of his family's transference to London. "You shall do well," he wrote,[1] "to thrash out and sell your wheat and put as many of your oxen and kine to feeding as you may conveniently and buy no more stuff or stock; also make haste to work upon your hemp and flax: but publish not your intent." His wife, in addition to her strong capacity, had intellectual tastes and instructed her children in their lessons. "I doubt," she wrote to her husband in March of the same year,[2] "if John have not some more help of a master he will never be a good Grecian. I do hear him construe half a chapter a day in the Greek Testament and I help him with Bèza's Latin Testament and likewise Joseph."

The sons were brought up strictly in the country with journeys to Gloucester[3] to buy their clothes and the expectation of Cambridge. Their father's frame of mind was equally studious and pious. As a young man he had written stiff counsels on religious conduct to his brother who held a Fellowship at Pembroke Hall. "I have received from you," the note began,[4] "three several packets of your theological exercises: and with my kindest and heartiest thanks for them I acknowledge that I have received by them both comfort and profit." It was a great contrast to Buckingham's circle. Down at Hall Court the Coke family sat severe and practical. Across the dresser lay the cloak from Gloucester, the

---

[1] Cal. Coke MSS., p. 121.
[2] Letter from Mrs. Marie Coke to John Coke, ibid., p. 132.
[3] ibid., p. 131.
[4] Letter from John Coke to George Coke, ibid., p. 29.

sound of threshing drifted through the windows, open upon the table lay the Bèza Testament.

One useful friend had been gathered in John Coke's days at the University, Sir Robert Naunton, and one *idée fixe* implanted, a hatred of Popery. This friendship between Coke and Naunton marks the divergence between their "worlds"; for the latter, attractive, known for his polished Latin, the heir to considerable estates, was carried off from Cambridge by the Earl of Essex. He thus came early into the circle of the Court and was impregnated from his youth by that light and sceptical outlook which characterized the late Elizabethans. The cleavage between their modes of thought is clearly seen in their outlook on religion. "It is to be hoped," wrote Naunton to his friend,[1] "the painfuller sort will not ... expose their flocks *ingruenti lupo qui nimis in diis invalescit, Papismum dico.*" This phrase is excellent conveying as it does in its brief image all that gay mockery and disdain of the Essex grouping, *Papismum dico.* In contrast to this sophistication Coke's words appear to come from another country and generation. In a letter composed in 1615[2] he closes with this sentence, "and all the depths of Hell in that Roman gulf." There were many streams which came to feed the Puritans.

Still if Naunton's friendship was an asset, and he was singularly staunch in this relation, Greville's patronage was in some respects a drawback. The whole system of patronage placed a man in a position of intimacy from which it was difficult to advance. In the Coke–Greville relationship there was none of that ease which enabled Naunton to write[3] of "Sir Foulke Greville ... neither illiterate ... and

[1] Letter from Sir R. Naunton to John Coke. Cal. Coke MSS., p. 90.
[2] Letter from John Coke to Sir Fulke Greville, *ibid.*, p. 58.
[3] A series of letters from Lord Shrewsbury to Thomas Coke written between 22 November, 1612, and 13 January, 1614, show the latter's position, while details of his duties are to be found in the same collection. Cal. Coke MSS., pp. 77 83; and 108. Coke's reports during his Italian journey in 1620 are preserved in the Arundel Castle MSS., autograph letters, Nos. 247–9. He died in 1621.

there are now extant some fragments from his pen." It was a grave initial hindrance to be thus dependant.

These employments were customary in the family, for John's brother, Thomas Coke, occupied a similarly difficult position in the Earl of Arundel's great household. Such work was the penalty of talent when unsupported by private means. In this case it was Lady Arundel's father, the old Earl of Shrewsbury, who had negligently introduced the young man to his son-in-law's service, for Trusley Manor was only a short ride from Tutbury and within the circle of the wide Talbot influence. The post involved travel with the Arundels' children, some mild bear-leading, the more serious duties of an agent and courier and the writing of Italian letters when required. He was, above all, a confidential secretary; seeing to alterations in my Lord's carriage and its shipment to Rotterdam; exchanging the household money into pistoles; receiving bills of payment for large sums. The Arundels rewarded him with a close domestic intimacy and placed reliance on "Good Mr. Coke." But there was nothing in this situation likely to contribute to the brothers' advancement.

The actual opportunity for John Coke's promotion came as the direct result of good fortune. It happened that the culmination of his quiet civilian career was reached with his appointment as Naval Commissioner in 1618. That winter the Howards sank from power and Buckingham himself took over the duties of the Lord High Admiral. By another lucky chance Sir Robert Naunton, faithful through all these years, had just received the Secretaryship of State. Naunton brought the favourite and Coke into contact; his industry and despatch were observed, and he was given the task of supervising the suppression of pirates.[1] He met with a reasonable success, his routine work was most orderly and

---

[1] Cf., Correspondence in S. P. Dom., 1621–3 *passim*, and letters dated 1623, Cal. Coke MSS., i, pp. 130–9.

he seems to have managed his subordinates with some tact. The only enemy whom he appears to have made in the course of his naval administration, was Sir Guildford Slingsby, an intemperate officer, who threatened to kill him "unless he is restored to his place before Lady Day."[1] His reasonable success and the methodical qualities he developed, brought him with Naunton's aid the considerable office of Master of Requests. As Master he was used in Parliament;[2] for he had lately entered the Commons, and in return for his services he was given Morton's office as Secretary. He was lucky, too, in the timing of this vacancy. King James might hardly have given the office to one so uncompromisingly godly; but Charles I in the early months of his reign already laid emphasis on the public servants' private morality. And Sir John Coke as Secretary could speak for the high tables at Cambridge, and the lesser squires of a Royalist complexion. His rise had made him, as far as the Court was concerned, their sole representative.

He maintained his old associations settling up his affairs in Herefordshire with his wife's family, the Powells of Preston, near Ledbury, and disposing of Hall Court to Doctor Fell of Christ Church, the Lady Margaret Professor of Divinity. Soon after establishing his household in London at Tottenham High Cross, Marie Coke died and he remarried with a City Alderman's widow. His new position had enabled him to make a sound alliance and Lady Coke brought him a fortune of £10,000 in addition to considerable sums from her husband's money-lending business, which he wound up. Sir John showed a patient acumen in this matter dividing the sums due into hopeful, doubtful and desperate debts.[3] Among the hopeful debtors were

---

[1] Cal. S. P. Dom., 1623–5, p. 181.
[2] An account is given in Lord Montagu's Journal of Proceedings in the House of Lords in the Buccleugh and Queensberry MSS.
[3] Among the Coke MSS. there is a very carefully drawn-up table dealing with all these matters and dated 10 June, 1626.

Lords Falkland and Wentworth, and other gentlemen of standing with whom a reasonable composition was effected. At the same time he kept a sharp watch on his own son's expenses at Cambridge.[1]

Nevertheless, his solid unfashionable associations were themselves an asset during his long tenure of office as Secretary of State, which was to continue until the eve of the Long Parliament right through the eleven years of the King's unfettered rule. Standing for the country gentlemen of small means, and for the opinion of the Universities, he was most familiar with those classes which were only represented to a very limited extent in the House of Commons. He was fifty-eight before he became a member of Parliament, and, but for the accident of his promotion, would have remained outside the House; for his private means were insufficient to warrant that career. In the coming struggle the class from which he sprang formed the backbone of the Royalist party. It is not unreasonable to see in Secretary Coke's career the reflection of a great unvocal body of opinion, that of the lesser gentry, armigerous, poor, Anglican, often strongly anti-Catholic, uninterested in the fortunes of Parliament, not greatly affected by the incidence of new taxation, devoted to that idea of authority which the monarchy expressed.

Secretary Conway's circle was entirely distinct, since he belonged to that section of the country gentry which was already accustomed to the control of local government and to whom the representation of the counties and the rural boroughs fell as the normal privilege of their by now inherited wealth. From his town house, situated fashionably in St. Martin's Lane, he kept in touch with those among his equals whom business or pleasure brought to the capital. The very names of his sons-in-law are suggestive; Sir Robert Harley and Sir William Pelham. Harley and Pelham:

[1] Cal. Coke MSS., i, p. 191.

the eighteenth-century domination could hardly be fore-shadowed more clearly. But it was typical of the rich squires that they were much less unanimous than their poorer Royalist neighbours. There was to be hesitation. They had more to gain and more to lose, and there were to be changes of policy even among those who were closely identified with the Court party. In the Civil Wars the Conways and Harleys were to fight on opposite sides; but even at Conway's retirement the war was still thirteen years away.

Meanwhile the two Secretaries conducted official corres-pondence and sent the answers of Government, and were thus identified with the Crown as its servants. While the life of the Court continued on the surface of public affairs, they kept in touch to some extent with the general feeling in England. The so-to-speak official opposition, with the parliamentary manœuvring at its command, was their firm opponent. Insufficient as they were, the Secretaries yet formed some kind of link between the humdrum country gentry and the increasingly divergent ways of the Court which was for the moment lavish, over-chivalrous and eager for adventure, a little fantastic and out of touch with common life, the Court which mirrored Buckingham.

CHAPTER XIX

THE DUKE'S DEATH

URING the early months of 1628 there was discernible a hardening of the profound antipathy with which Buckingham was regarded in those circles of English life concerned with government. He alone was seen to block the avenues of promotion and the normal exercise of conflicting influence. Men had almost ceased to manœuvre about a sovereign who seemed deaf to every voice except the favourite's. And wherever the Puritan influence was felt the opposition to the Duke took on the quality of a bitter integrity which could not be placated.

The surviving memoirs and letters are full of this sentiment. Thus young Thomas Raymond, who had only lately been "consigned to a lawyer in London," relates how[1] "this lawyer (with whom he lodged) did much frequent the howse of a rich widow, a Puritan." Here they were all prepared to await with determination the inevitable removal of the minister since they knew that God was not mocked. Passing over the great suave preface to the new Bible they considered deeply upon the Word of God. They could not be unconscious of the sinfulness of their own country as they read in Judges that "the Lord strengthened Eglon the King of Moab against Israel, because they had done evil in the sight of the Lord. So the children of Israel served Eglon the king of Moab eighteen years." It was twelve years now since the Lord had given their countrymen into the hands of Eglon, and the generation was delivered up to lechery.

[1] *Autobiography of Thomas Raymond*, Camden Society, 1917, p. 23.

"Long hayre," continues Raymond, "was much condemned, particularly the locke worne on the left side." This was the same mood in which Mr. Nathan Walworth, sitting over Lord Pembroke's accounts in the steward's office at Baynard's Castle,[1] turned over in his mind the question of the Duke and "the many fowle matters . . . alleadged agaynst him."

Those of the strict persuasion bent their thought, which was freed alike from subterfuge and tolerance, upon the Duke's activities. It was evident that he toyed delicately with idolatry. In the little market town of Santon Downham, the vicar, John Rous,[2] noted the rhymes which were circulating in East Anglia among the people about the favourite's ill-fated journey.

> "Could not thy mother's masses, nor her crosses,
> Nor sorceries, prevent those fatall losses."

It was seen that he made no effort to destroy what Simonds D'Ewes forcibly described[3] as "the most gross and feculent errors of the Romish synagogue." There could be no true peace with those who "served Baalim and the groves." There is little doubt that D'Ewes reflected the standpoint of his own godly party when, soberly and in his later years, he stated[4] that "most men execrated the name and memory of George Villiers, Duke of Buckingham, whom they conceived to be the bitter root and fountain of all their mischiefs."

In this connection it is worth noting a reinforcement which the Puritans received during these years; for there came to them all those old men of position who turned to religion in their age. That vague half-political Protestantism which had so often marked their prime became purified as they listened to the preaching ministers with their strong

---

[1] Cf., *Correspondence of Nathan Walworth and Peter Seddon*, Chetham Society, 1880.

[2] *Diary of John Rous*, Camden Society, 1857, p. 20.

[3] *Autobiography of Sir Simonds D'Ewes*, ii, p. 113.

[4] *ibid.*, i, pp. 377–8.

comfort. The Bible was now their sustenance and a study of the Old Testament would not dim their clear censorious judgment.

The case of the Guises was typical. It has been described in some detail by Sir William Guise's grandson Sir Christopher, who wrote with that rather naïve and yet ironic detachment which characterizes the Restoration squires when they discuss the Puritan phenomena.[1] Sir William Guise is seen sitting in his manor house at Elmore below Gloucester, a man of over sixty in this spring of 1628, patriarchal and determined, a careful squire. The scene is built up with much detail;[2] the parlour with the portrait of his mother-in-law, Lady Stallenge, and her daughters; the new chambers at the east end of the house which he had constructed in the Cotswold freestone; the row of elms beyond the orchard and those around the horse pool which had been planted early in King James's reign. And then there comes the description of his spiritual condition. "Sir William Gise att this time," runs the account,[3] "was growne a greate folower and favourer of silent ministers and non-conformists with abundance of zeale."

While the presence of those who objected to Buckingham on religious grounds must be remembered, it is obvious that this sentiment would have little direct effect upon the favourite's political fortunes. It was rather the operation of mundane motives which were universal in their appeal and easily avowed that was likely to be brought to the notice of the Government. Whatever their political outlook or ethical standards, men would unite in protest against the continual "pressing" of soldiers for the war; while distaste for Buckingham would sharpen the fears of a denuded countryside.

A few miles north of Elmore the deputy-lieutenants of

---

[1] *Memoirs of the family of Guise*, Camden Society, 1917, pp. 109–15.
[2] *ibid.*, p. 113.
[3] Sir Christopher Guise was born in 1617 and Thomas Raymond, who takes the same standpoint, in 1616.

Gloucestershire, gathered in the county town were at this time addressing an appeal to the Privy Council for a reduction of the burden of finding soldiers. "The husbandman," they wrote,[1] "is much discowraged by reason of one wett harvest, the ill-ripening and ruining of corne. . . . Lastly, the distance of this place from Portsmouth (is), as we are informed, above six daies march." It was part of the weakness of the Duke's position, and that of the foreign policy which he fostered, that the opposition had interlocking elements, some secret and some explicit.

In these western parts news of the doings in Parliament came down from London by post and carrier, and the newly engaged soldiers for the wars were the chief reminder of the Duke's policies. During the summer there were fifteen hundred most unruly soldiers come to Bristol[2] whose very presence fomented discontent.

Nevertheless, such elements of friction would hardly disturb the profound and slumberous peace of the market towns and ports. The brisk activity of a state of war, which yet did not impede the free movement of sea-borne commerce, would be sufficient to offset all inconvenience and that curious pre-occupation with rank was always present. Thus the mayors and corporations of the towns watched the occasional visits of the greater peers attentively, like the place of the shadow on a sun-dial. There had been difficulties at Bristol when Lord Arundel had come, because no public entertainment had been offered and the civic courtesies were insufficient. Discussion turned upon these matters, and it was decided that the next time an Earl paid an official visit of this nature, he was to be received with peels of ordnance.[3]

---

[1] Letter dated 8 January, 1628. Cal. Gloucester Corporation MSS., pp. 480–1.
[2] Bristol Calendars under date, July, 1628.
[3] The relevant passages from the Bristol Calendars relating to Lord Arundel's visit and to that of the Earls of Essex and Clanricarde in 1631, are printed in Samuel Sayers' *Memoirs historical and topographical of Bristol and its neighbourhood*, ii, pp. 264–71.

Although affected by the spirit of routine, loyalty to the Crown was reflected in every civic action, and there was a desire to honour those whom the sovereign honoured. It is necessary not to exaggerate the hostility shown outside London to any minister. In Bristol the greatest disturbance in recent years had been that of the bells ringing in the steeples for His present Majesty's Coronation.

The same characteristic of methodical and lethargic calm, which remained unbroken save by some ceremonial passage, is found in the market towns of southern England. To some places the troop movements of this year brought news and profit. Thus Basingstoke, where the road from London to Winchester joins those from the Midlands to the Hampshire ports, lay on the line of route for those riding down to Portsmouth where the soldiers and the fleet were now assembling.

The surviving documents give a clear view of the life in this little town. The local landowners were four in number, the Marquess of Winchester, Lord Sandys of the Vyne and two Oxford colleges, Merton and Magdalen. The place was distinguished by the possession of a lecturership founded in the previous reign by Sir James Deane and now fallen, since 1624, into the gift of the corporation. Mr. Crake furnished Bishop Montagu's chaplain with a description of this foundation which enhanced in a measure, the dignity of the local town councillors.[1] It is worth quoting as providing yet another example of that vigilant approach to Popery which every year was becoming more common. "There is," he wrote,[2] "a lecture lately created by means of Sir James Lancaster in Christian love and compassion to the place of his nativity (having been till this time blind with ignorance and superstition) and in zeal for the propagation of the

[1] Tanner MSS. in Bodley, vol. 75, f. 318.
[2] This lecturership was founded in 1608 under the will of Sir James Deane who gave to his cousin Sir James Lancaster the right to nominate the lecturer.

Gospel. . . . It is a place which requireth a man not only learned (even in controversies to encounter the spirit of Popery which here haunteth), but also of gravity and integrity."

And yet the Papists here were indeed pacific. Lord Winchester[1] contributed his share of timber for the building of a new Anglican chapel, and the town lay under the shadow of Basing House. The Paulets were in a quiet way national figures. A vague sycophantic publicity beat upon them and they were to be a target for verse and epitaph. At this date Sir John Beaumont's lines on Lucy, Lady Winchester, which were to be printed in the following year, were already circulating in manuscript; but he had had the privilege of her friendship. When Jane, Marchioness of Winchester died in 1631 strangers composed elegies, Ben Jonson, William Davenant and young John Milton. Under one aspect this seems an early instance of personal tragedy considered as news-value. In these first months of 1628 Basing House represented a great and compact wealth bent to no political end; a purely social force supported neither by politics nor by the mind; an influence which its inheritors were disqualified from exercising. Since the Winchesters were Recusants, a quietness, as of some almost famous backwater, had settled down upon the lodges at Basing Park.

Outside in Basingstoke a chief excitement seems to have been the passage of distinguished strangers, the bells rung for the Queen's passing,[2] and then the long succession of mourning tolls and dirges. In the Churchwardens' Accounts there is record of the moneys paid to the ringers for Lord Southampton's funeral day and of the sums received for the passage of the Bishop of Bath and Wells' corpse, a resting

---

[1] Cf., The Warden's Accounts for the Chapel of the Holy Ghost, Basingstoke, for 1635–6.

[2] Churchwardens' Accounts of Basingstoke printed in the *History of the ancient town and manor of Basingstoke*, by Francis Joseph Baigent and James Elwin Millard, 1889, ii, p. 513.

place for the body and rooms for the attendants, and again money for the ringers as the party set off westward to bury Dr. Lake in the choir at Wells.[1] Later Dr. Laud rode through with little ceremony to take possession of his new see.

Four entries from these same accounts will give an impression of the movements of humbler people in 1628.

> "Paid Mr. Bander, a preacher, for making a sermon 10/–.
> Paid man to Mr. Hodges, a preacher 1/–.
> Paid to a Turkeyman in distress being turned a Christian, 6d, and to Richard Moore for carrying the return of the recusants to Winchester, 2s 6d."

The entry relating to the Turk is most attractive, and it is pleasant to think of this conscientious man coming in with the stream of the sober travellers.

But in this same year the public disquiet and the detestation of Buckingham became manifest, and were confirmed by each successive episode; the arrival of the weekly carrier from London in the remoter villages of the Home Counties; the stray travellers arriving at the inns; the messengers about this martial business. The feelings of the Puritans were in a measure shared by the "pressed" men and by the farmers who grappled with the coming harvest.[2] Unlike the quick hard opinion of the towns, the countryside was more slowly stirred against the favourite.

Up in London the tension about the Duke's person was always increasing and the difficulties of the country came before his buoyant and uncalculating mind. In his palace of York House negligently and without experience, he would cast about in order to discover some more sure basis of support. Thus the idea of gaining the Howards came to him and he toyed with it, and then sacrificed Lord Treasurer

---

[1] All these details are set out in the Churchwardens' Accounts, *History of the ancient town and manor of Basingstoke*, ii, pp. 513–4.

[2] The Letter Book of Sir Richard Norton, Bart., Deputy Lieutenant of Hampshire, 1625, gives a number of details concerning those troubles. British Museum MSS., 21,922, ff, 132–147.

Marlborough so that he might carry through this new-formed plan. But he was ever too sanguine.

A letter sent to Secretary Coke at Portsmouth gives a vivid impression from one angle of these weeks of the favourite's life. "It is not sparingly spoke," wrote Mr. Fulwood,[1] "that the old Lord Treasurer hath £10,000 in lieu of his office and his countess £5,000 and his daughter hath the preferring of two viscounts. My Lord Duke did yesterday part with the Lord Wardenship of the Cinque Ports to the Earl of Suffolk. . . .[2] Some think the Lord Conway will be removed and the Lord Carleton to succeed him in his post as secretary."

The resignation of the Cinque Ports is thus seen as a gesture in that policy of rapprochement with the Howards which was continued half-heartedly by allowing the Earl of Arundel to come back once more to Court. But this was a niggardly concession, since neither Arundel's place at the Council Board nor his emoluments were restored. And few men were more unwilling than he was to accept half-forgiveness from George Villiers. The treasurership, removed from Marlborough on such easy terms, passed to the Chancellor of the Exchequer, Lord Weston, a prudent man who knew how to bide his time in that failing combine.[3]

Meanwhile the Duke pressed forward with his preparations, now utterly reliant on his sovereign. There were fresh disputes between his sister and the Queen, and no attempt to reduce the prevailing enmity or to gather fresh elements of support had proved successful. The fatalist strain in the King's temperament had developed. The sense of his divine

[1] Letter of Humphrey Fulwood to Sir John Coke, dated 17 July, 1628, Cal. Coke MSS., p. 359.
[2] For an adverse judgment on Suffolk see the account given by the Venetian envoy. "Suffolk a mean spirited man, his (the Duke's) creature and humble servant." Cal. S. P. Venetian, 1628–9, p. 213.
[3] A comment of Clarendon's gives an impression of the current instability. "Many," he writes, "who were privy to the Duke's most secret purposes did believe that if he had outliv'd that Voyage in which he was engaged he would have removed him (Weston) and made another Treasurer," History, ed. 1705, p. 47.

commission and that aloofness which always so fatally protected him, had already settled upon the favourite's royal master. Each factor served to bind King Charles yet closer to the minister whom he alone could now appreciate. The King's fastidiousness and his sense of solitary dignity, seem to have given him a confidence in his power to discriminate. This made the Duke's position in the royal favour quite impregnable; but it was the only part of his situation which was well-defended.

In mid-August amid a continuous rumour of Court changes he eventually left London,[1] only too anxious to forget the shifting difficulties of politics in the planning of a military campaign. Sir John Coke was already at Portsmouth, and Buckingham rode down to Hampshire to join him and supervise the preparations for the Fleet. Phineas Pett, the master shipwright, and his son Richard had ridden down from Lambeth a week before, and on paper all was in good order.[2]

Some notes from a view of Portsmouth at that date prepared for the benefit of the Lord High Admiral, will indicate the superficial assets of this harbour. "The depth of water," so runs the document,[3] "sufficient, the ground very good . . . if it do not overblow the great ships may warp out all winds, and the less may kedge out. It is a very convenient place, if need require, to careen a ship in; beside the river of Hamble is within two or three hours sail. The harbour not given to mussels and foulness so much as at Chatham. All kinds of victuals better and both cheap and more convenient to be boarded than at Chatham. A great commodity for all seafaring men that are pressed out of the western ports."

This last factor was indeed most relevant, and the "great commodity" was overstrained. There was a dangerous

[1] On 8 August, 1628, the Duke wrote to Sir John Coke from Buckingham House, "I set forth from here on Monday next." Cal. Coke MSS., p. 36.
[2] Phineas Pett, *Autobiography*, p. 140.
[3] S. P. Dom. Charles I, xiii, 62.

ÆTAT SVÆ 43

PHINEAS PETT from a portrait attributed to Jan de Critz in the
NATIONAL PORTRAIT GALLERY

element of discontent among the seamen. And the town was crowded with the sailors from the warships and the daily gathering military levies. From the moment of his arrival the Duke moved surrounded by a press of officers and in his wake there followed those sober Huguenot exiles who were bent on securing the sailing of the expedition to La Rochelle. The ordnance of the fleet and the guns at Southsea Castle and the bells pealing in St. Mary's tower welcomed the great commander. All the lodgings in the town were filled with courtiers, for the King had been staying for the past few weeks at Sir Daniel Norton's house at Southwick, five miles away in the cup of the valley beyond Portsdown. Buckingham himself had decided that, until he was ready to go aboard his flagship, he would lodge at Captain Mason's house in the High Street, close to the King's Steps in Portsmouth Harbour.

He had already risen on the morning of 23 August, a few days after taking over his command, when a false rumour was brought in to him that the Huguenots in La Rochelle had been relieved. The Duke's house opened out on to the main street of the seaport town and as the rumour spread the ground floor was soon filled with those who had some right of entry. The uneasy crowd of soldiers of fortune and place hunters, some seeing their chances of employment vanish at this news, eddied about the favourite. It was in keeping with his rather scornful pride that there was no one at hand to guard him from this dubious but more or less distinguished company.

As he passed from the lower parlour into the hall, while the servants held back the hangings, John Felton, an unemployed lieutenant, drove a knife with a white haft into his breast. The knife penetrated to the heart and the Duke staggering through the doorway died in the crowded hall across the table beneath the clock. His sister-in-law Lady Anglesea, who was standing in the gallery looking down upon the movement in the rooms below, saw him collapse and told the Duchess who had not yet risen. A courier was sent to tell the King who was found attended by Secretary Conway at morning prayers with Sir Daniel's household. On hearing of the tragedy the King remained until the prayers were finished in the chapel, motionless.

King Charles withdrew for some days to the privacy of his apartments, and then his outward life recovered slowly from the shattering of this devoted friendship. The expedition was pressed forward as an act of piety. The King turned to his own family and to his religious counsellors. In too many quarters there was an ill-concealed rejoicing. "I remember," wrote Sir Philip Perceval years later,[1] "I was in England when the Duke of Buckingham fell whom many men thought the only cause of all the evils." And it is remarkable that even in loyal Oxford in the private diary of Thomas Crosfield, a Fellow of Queen's College, there occurs this entry,[2] *Auspicata mors Ducis Buckingham peracta.*

Experience and loyalty were what the King would henceforth seek for, and not affection. The channels of his spiritual life and his deep reserve, were now strengthened by an element of bitterness. But surely it was very natural that the courtiers' minds should hover in hopeful meditation around the spoils left by the murdered Duke. Yet few episodes indicate more clearly the remoteness of the sovereign and the apparent lack of knowledge of his character possessed at Court, than the course of his chief servants' speculation. The next twelve years were to bear the marks of this personal disaster. The King became less happy, more self-reliant and more secret, and in such interior isolation there began to develop those characteristics, some disquieting and some distasteful to the English, which were to complete the portrait of the Royal Martyr.

[1] Letter dated at Dublin, 15 March, 1641, Cal. Egmont MSS., I, i, p. 131.
[2] *The Diary of Thomas Crosfield*, ed. Frederick S. Boas, Oxford University Press (1935), p. 30.

CHAPTER XX

EPILOGUE

IT was, indeed, an unprecedented situation which the more influential politicians and courtiers were now called upon to enjoy. The favourite had perished; and he was the first of his class to die in office, abandoning to his supporters and opponents an immensely rich succession. Even in the material sense it was a splendid inheritance of great offices all suitably endowed and carrying with them a stream of patronage. But overshadowing such definite appointments was the new and ill-defined position of first minister to which the seventeenth-century mind recurred; for in the chief monarchies it was now almost usual for some great officer of state to hold a predominance of power and favour. In Spain the Count-Duke of Olivares and in France the Cardinal de Richelieu, acted as interpreters of their sovereigns' will, and as refractors for the monarchic power, not yet raised to the hierarchic splendours of the *Roi Soleil*.

It would seem that the reserved English King was held by those about his Court almost to need the services of some interpreter. And in this connection few contrasts are more curious than that between the widespread feeling against Buckingham and the immediate efforts made by the court party to find a successor who would almost certainly raise up against himself the same hostility. It seems reasonable to consider the pursuit of this line of policy as one of the early instances of the cleavage between the courtiers and the country party. Meanwhile, leaving the problem of ultimate control to the future, there were the offices to divide;

301

for by a fortunate chance Buckingham's heir the little Earl of Coventry, was a child of seven months and all the perquisites were thrown, so to speak, upon the open market.

Among the consequences of the manner of the late favourite's rise, was the fact that the offices which he held were in the strictest sense personal, and were not attached to estates or zones of territorial influence. They were thus the more easily transferable, and it was clear that in the present instance rich rewards would be obtained by those who could display the necessary dexterity and courage.

A proportion of the possessions would go to the child heir; the titles of course, the dukedom and marquessate of Buckingham, the earldoms of Buckingham and Coventry, the viscountcy of Villiers, the barony of Whaddon, the great estates, Buckingham House and Newhall, and with them that little perquisite, the keepership of Whaddon Park and Chase, one of the earliest of King James's gifts to his "disciple and scholar." The inheritance was embarrassed and included art collections, much elaborate unfinished building, half-completed marble pavements, a great quantity of jewellery, both free and in gage, and £61,000 of debts. That, however, was the King's affair and the Villiers': the offices were vacant; no reversions had been sold; they were entirely unpledged and free.

During the preparations for his expedition, the Duke had been the Lord High Admiral of England, Master of the Horse, Lord Warden of the Cinque Ports, Lord Lieutenant of Buckingham and Middlesex, Chancellor of the University of Cambridge, Constable of Dover Castle, Chief Justice in Eyre south of Trent, High Steward of Hampton Court and Westminster and Constable of Windsor. In one direction the aggregate had been diminished by a grant to the Earl of Suffolk, hardly a month before the favourite's death, of the lord wardenship and its satellite office of Constable at Dover. Still this action eliminated the claim of the Suffolk Howards to a share in the division of the spoil, and all awaited the development of a situation of such hopeful profit.

The fact that many peers about the Court considered that Lord Carlisle was likely to succeed the Duke of Buckingham in his great offices and the royal favour comes as a rather surprising discovery. It is one among many indications that the King's character was in no way understood. For, while it is true that Carlisle was in a lazy courteous way opposed to Buckingham, and that his wife was now the Queen's chief friend, it was surely a fantastic supposition that this ageing opulent luxurious peer, who had drifted magnificently through so many embassies, should now return to Court to rule them all. Again, when the Duke was murdered and the King left desolate, Lady Carlisle was in Sussex ill with small-pox while her husband had just arrived in Venice, coming on a special mission from King Charles out of Lombardy with a great train. Possibly the incapacity of those about the King to penetrate his lacerated confidence or to break through his iron reserve, gave men a confidence in the Carlisles as the only personal combination which had not so far been brought in play. An examination of the position of the last of the Scottish favourites would seem to be appropriate to the close of a study of the Jacobean Age.

The exact date of birth of James Hay, first Earl of Carlisle, Viscount Doncaster and Baron Hay, has never been determined, but he must have been in the early twenties when he came south with his royal master. He had never been in the technical sense a favourite and he had, in fact, been Robert Ker's first patron. From Buckingham he had held himself a little distant, acquiescing with the exaggerated courtesy of that period in his predominance. Salisbury had been his mentor,[1] and he was lavish and circumspect. In

---

[1] A letter to Lord Salisbury shows that Sir James Hay had early developed an urbane manner. "I send your Lordship," he wrote, "this enclosed with many wishes that you may so study Galen as hereafter your Lordship may never have occasion to become his scholar." Cecil MSS., vol. 197, f. 3.

foreign politics he was anti-Spanish;[1] he had always succeeded with the French; he cultivated Queen Henrietta. His unpopularity had been due to King James's money grants. Chamberlain writing to Carleton[2] gives what was probably the current opinion in 1620: "Viscount Doncaster, a bountiful and complete gentleman, yet some wish England had never seen him." Yet this dislike evaporated. There is little evidence that Carlisle was gifted with marked capacities, but few politicians have possessed his talent for making his own ways smooth.

He had been married twice, first very prudently to the only daughter and heiress of Lord Denny, and secondly to Lady Lucy Percy who was many years his junior. The marriage which had taken place in 1617, had been opposed by Lord Northumberland who objected to his daughter "dancing Scottish jigs." In the succeeding years there had been difficult, and at times stormy, relations with the Percys, but at this date Carlisle was on excellent terms with Lord Leicester,[3] who had married his wife's sister, and with Algernon Percy, the son and heir.

The politically significant portion of Lady Carlisle's career belongs to the period of the Long Parliament when her influence over the Queen had increased still further, and she was Strafford's ally and coquetted with the Parliamentarians and with Pym. She had that ringleted fairness which was now the fashion; vivacity; a dangerous temperament. She appears to have possessed a tolerance bred from religious and political indifference, and she charmed the Queen by

[1] In a private letter to Sir Edward Herbert Carlisle write in 1620: "I have heard from Master Gresley of the passage of His Highness into Spain. I am sorry for it from my very soul." Cal. Powis MSS., p. 388.
[2] Letter from Chamberlain to Carleton, dated 25 January, 1620. Cal. S. P. Dom., 1618–23, p. 116.
[3] Cf., for these earlier troubles a letter sent on 31 August, 1622, to Sir Roger Townshend by his son Roger. "From thence," wrote the latter, "they went to Pettworth to my Lord of Northumberland where ther hapened a difference betweene his two sonnes in law, my Lord of Doncaster and my Lord Lisle. I cannot tell you the particulars, but they were at blowes and partes taken." Cal. Townshend MSS., p. 21.

aiding Catholics.[1] There is reason to suppose that the Duchess of Buckingham was acutely jealous of her;[2] but she never put her suave and ageing husband in a position in which he might be compelled to disavow her. He had set out alone on his present journey.

It was on 22 August, the day before the death of Buckingham, that Lord Carlisle came in the State gondolas to the house at San Antonio belonging to the Procuratia de Ultra, which the magistracy of the Rason Vecchie had been instructed to prepare.[3] The fourteen coaches in which he and his suite had travelled since leaving the Albergo della Torre at Verona two days before, had been abandoned at the quayside at Mestre. At Padua he had been received by two companies of cuirassiers, a company of Capelletti from the Levant and by Stradiot infantry and gunners. At Venice an elaborate reception had been staged;[4] he had replied in French; he was very tired.

Relations with the Serene Republic were a little delicate owing to the recent attack by Sir Kenelm Digby on some French ships under Venetian protection in a Turkish port. At Turin Carlisle had been testy to the Venetian envoy;[5] but now he had recovered and as the gondolas moved

[1] Lady Carlisle interceded with the King on behalf of Lady Falkland, *The Life of Viscountess Falkland*, ed. 1862, from a contemporary MS., p. 30.

[2] The following letter written by the Duchess of Buckingham to her husband and dated 10 October, 1627, seems to refer to Lady Carlisle. "Your great friend," she writes, "that you believe is so much your friend, uses your friends something worse than when you were here and your favour has made her so great that she cares for nobody." Cal. S. P. Dom., 1627–9, p. 381.

[3] Report of secret deliberations of the Senate, 19 August, 1628. Cal. S. P. Venetian, 1628–9, p. 227.

[4] The details of Carlisle's journey through Venetian territory are contained in various papers, *ibid.*, pp. 248–53.

[5] Letter from Francesco Corrier, Venetian Ambassador to the Court of Savoy, to the Doge and Senate. "The Earl of Carlisle came to see me when I had barely arrived at Turin. . . . I now see, he remarked, that the Republic thought I was a charlatan or mountebank, who wished to climb into St. Mark's Square in that character. I soothed him somewhat, as owing to the esteem he enjoys in England I should be sorry for him to go back there in an ill humour," *ibid.*, pp. 220–1.

down the Grand Canal "the Earl dilated in praise of the city and its architecture, especially the Cornaro Palace."[1] Nevertheless, the situation presented certain difficulties, for it appears that Carlisle's instructions were only of a very general character, and that he had been in doubt as to whether he was wise to leave England at this time.[2] Amerigo Salvetti, the Tuscan envoy, had reported[3] to his home government that it was anticipated that the results of this English embassy would be more showy than substantial. Then shortly before reaching Venice the ambassador had received two letters of a disquieting character. His fellow-countryman, Sir Robert Aiton, who acted as his private intelligencer for court affairs, wrote to inform him that it was commonly believed that either his Lordship's employment tended towards peace or else that it was slight and perfunctory.[4] Were the former rumour to prove correct Sir Robert had heard that Mr. Porter of the Bedchamber was to be despatched to Venice to reinforce him and thence sent forward, perhaps to Spain. The alternatives were somewhat chilling, and then by the next messenger came a letter of depressing courtesy from his moneylender. Mr. Allsop[5] thought it the fitting way to take the burden of the debt for the robes from the Earl, since it now amounted to the figure of £8,000.

Carlisle had always lived in the grand manner,[6] with his

[1] Report of Carlisle's reception. Cal. S. P. Venetian, 1628–9, p. 256.
[2] On 5 April, 1628, Salvetti had reported that "the Earl of Carlisle ought to leave soon, but it is believed that he is waiting to see what turn Parliamentary affairs will take." Salvetti Correspondence in Cal. Skrine MSS., p. 144.
[3] Report dated 9 May, 1628, ibid., p. 149.
[4] Letter from Sir Robert Aiton at Denmark House to the Earl of Carlisle, dated 18 July, 1628. Cal. S. P. Dom., 1628–9, p. 218.
[5] Letter from Robert Allsop at the Inner Temple to the Earl of Carlisle, dated 24 July, 1628, ibid., p. 230.
[6] A convincing testimony is that of a young attorney's clerk, Thomas Raymond. "I have often seene," wrote Raymond of Lord Carlisle, "his dyet carryed from his kitchen crosse the Courte at Whitehall, 20 or 25 dishes covered, most by gentlemen richly habited, with the steward marching before and the clerke of the kitchen bringing up the reare, all bare head." Autobiography of Thomas Raymond, Camden Society, p. 24.

clothes of ceremony sewn with diamonds, staving off insolvency with grant and perquisite. He had his saws that "a generous man is like a good conscience a contynual feast" and "Spend and God will send." Twelve months before, in reply to this latter maxim, his father-in-law had said to him:[1] "Send, what will he send?' and the King had given him quite suddenly the Caribbee Islands. This grant, registered in the *Colonial Entry Book* under date of 2 July, 1627, is typical of his abrupt good fortune. "To the Right Hon. James Earl of Carlisle," the entry runs,[2] "the first grant of the following islands called the Caribbees, viz. St. Christopher's, Granada, St. Vincent, St. Lucia, Barbadoes, Dominico, Guadaloupe, Antigua, Montserrat, Nevis and twelve other islands hereinafter named Cariola or the islands of Carlisle Province, reserving a yearly rent of £100 and a white horse when the King, his heirs and successors shall come into those parts." It was a kingdom and might be leased to companies or sold or mortgaged.

Dissatisfied with the character of his mission and caught in an intricate financial situation, which had yet never yielded him to actual embarrassment, Carlisle succumbed to the unaccustomed heats and lay at San Antonio in a fever.[3] To him in this condition there came the news of the Duke's murder and gradually post by post the accumulated correspondence of the English courtiers. So improbably, this middle-aged and lavish man on his sick bed in Venice became the centre upon whom the converging hopes of men of influence about the King had come to rest.

The very first private letter that seems to have reached Carlisle was conveyed by a special messenger to Paris two days after Buckingham's death. Sir Francis Nethersole, the agent of the Queen of Bohemia in London,[4] wrote urging him

---

[1] *Autobiography of Thomas Raymond*, pp. 24–5.
[2] Colonial Entry Book, v, pp. 1, 2, printed in Cal. S. P. Colonial, 1575–1660, pp. 85–6.
[3] Report of 16 September, 1638. Cal. S. P. Venetian, p. 299.
[4] Letter from Sir Francis Nethersole to the Earl of Carlisle, dated 24 August, 1628. Cal. S. P. Dom., 1628–9, p. 268.

to hasten home and a letter from Lord Pembroke followed[1] in the same sense. Henry Percy, writing to his brother-in-law,[2] enclosed the usual list of competitors now swollen by the number of the vacant offices; for the mastership of the horse, Hamilton, Holland and Salisbury,[3] for the chancellorship of Cambridge, Suffolk, Berkshire, Montgomery and the Bishop of Lincoln. But it was Sir Robert Aiton who first mentioned the King's unwillingness to take action. "The general news," he wrote from the Court at Farnham ten days after the catastrophe,[4] "which is the assassination of the Duke of Buckingham includes all. The state of things as yet is so raw that no discourse can express it to your Lordship. Your absence and the sickness of your lady do infinitely perplex your friends, and none more than that incomparable princess our Queen and mistress. . . . The King seems not to be wishing to bestow in haste any of the Duke's charges. I hope you may come in time to the dividing of them and, howsoever the Earl of Holland would fain have the world think that he shall be the Duke's heir, that you may have your share." It was this fear of Holland which was at first uniting them and led the old Scots to make an effort for their countryman.

The King was now at Hampton Court and Lord Dupplin, the Lord Chancellor of Scotland, had written urgently to Carlisle,[5] "But come to us and come speedily"; while Sir Robert Ker, who was of His Majesty's Bedchamber, had

---

[1] Letter from the Earl of Pembroke to the Earl of Carlisle, dated 31 August, 1628. Cal. S. P. Dom. Add., 1625–49, p. 290.
[2] Letter from Henry Percy to the Earl of Carlisle, dated 3 September, 1628, *ibid.*, p. 292.
[3] Actually Algernon, Lord Percy, raised the question of the rumour of Salisbury's appointment to this office in a letter sent to Hatfield on 27 August. "I cannot believe," he stated, "that he (the Duke) was ever friend to anything but his own ends and so I leave him as yet unlamented." Cecil MSS.
[4] Letter from Sir Robert Aiton to the Earl of Carlisle. Cal. S. P. Dom. Add., 1625, pp. 192–4.
[5] Letter from Viscount Dupplin to the Earl of Carlisle, dated 25 September, 1628. Cal. S. P. Dom. Add., 1625–49, p. 337.

sent word[1] that he had not forgotten to wish the Earl at the helm as earnestly as those of his friends in whom he placed greater confidence. For, as the weeks passed by, it became clear that the King was not accepting Holland, nor indeed any man. In another letter mention was made of the Lord Steward's resolve to urge the King to recall his special envoy since Carlisle could not return without a summons.[2]

In the King's numbed state, it now occurred to the Queen's friends that Carlisle and his wife might in combination rouse the sovereign. Business went forward and he had been left with Lord Weston as his Treasurer; but Her Majesty's entourage naturally hoped for some one more amenable to their interests. "This blessed Queen," wrote Lord Goring to Carlisle,[3] "is your Lordship's really and after such a manner hath she expressed her trust and value of you to the King as deserves your acknowledgment for the same in a high degree. Here is yet a calm in your affairs at home; no place of consequence disposed of nor resolution therein, save only for the admiralty which shall be governed by commission. . . . As you love yourself, honour and substance or both, hasten home with all diligence and let no foreign consideration detain you one hour."

And then there came another letter from Pembroke. "We are now," he wrote,[4] "all busy at this place about settling the clock, as our old master was wont to term it. Your wife is now well at Penshurst; the smallpox hath but kissed her face." In a postscript, he added: "I pray leave your 'trittle trattle trollilollies' and come to us." But still no command was sent to Venice by the King.

The next day, 28 September, Sir Robert Aiton sent a

[1] Letter from Sir Robert Ker, to the Earl of Carlisle, dated 31 August, 1628. Cal. S. P. Dom. Add., 1625–49, p. 278.
[2] Letter from James Hay to the Earl of Carlisle, dated 1 September, 1628, *ibid.*, p. 310.
[3] Letter from Lord Goring to the Earl of Carlisle, dated 16 September, 1628, *ibid.*, p. 295.
[4] Letter from Earl of Pembroke to the Earl of Carlisle, dated 28 September, 1628, *ibid.*, p. 295.

fresh report urging his patron to hasten home. "All things," he wrote,[1] "Are in suspense and it seems that he (the King) will have need of one to prompt him, and to take him off of these impressions of the man that is gone. . . . Your lady hath recovered both her health and beauty beyond expectation. She is still the only woman in the Queen's affections, and I am persuaded that you are the man about the King that her Majesty doth wish best to." Only a day elapsed before Goring was again writing[2], and then Nethersole[3] with whom he was in consultation[4]. Yet the King made no move and Carlisle himself was thus becalmed.

It would seem that various factors had influenced the growth of this disquiet, and the appeals for Carlisle's aid. For Nethersole and perhaps, for Pembroke the desire for an aggressive foreign policy was uppermost, and the ambassador had always had the reputation of a friend of Protestant policies and a man of experienced if negligent common sense. To others some return to the easy contacts of King James's reign had seemed essential; for should the King prove himself too unapproachable there would be an end to that quiet drift of patronage on which their careers were insecurely built. Some feared Lord Treasurer Weston and detected a tendency towards Catholicism in his new influence. But most of all, perhaps, there was a dread[5] of the paths which

[1] Letter from Sir Robert Aiton to the Earl of Carlisle, dated 29 September, 1628. Cal. S. P. Dom. Add., 1625–49, p. 296.

[2] Letter from Lord Goring to the Earl of Carlisle, dated 29 September, 1628, ibid., p. 297.

[3] A letter written much later on 24 November by the Earl of Dorset, Lord Chamberlain to the Queen, gives support for Carlisle from another angle. "If I could have wrought miracles," he declared, "you then should have been transported hither in the instant after that deplorable murder committed on the person of the late Duke," Cal. S. P. Dom. Add., 1625–49, p. 302. It is interesting to note that one of the few friendly references to the dead Buckingham came from the political detachment of Knole.

[4] Letter from Sir Francis Nethersole to the Earl of Carlisle, dated 28 September, 1628, ibid., p. 297.

[5] An instance of old-fashioned opposition to ecclesiasticism is seen in a letter written to Carlisle on 2 September, 1628, by the father of his first wife the Earl of Norwich. "Arminius," he declared, "is grown as famous as ever Arius was. Piety may go beg in rags if adorned by never so sound a learning . . . unless policy and Arminianism put on the rochet and the robe." Cal. S. P. Dom., 1628–9, p. 311.

the King might take should he fall completely under the guidance on which he had come so unexpectedly to rely, the Bishop of London.

In the month before the Duke's assassination, Bishop Laud had taken up his residence of Fulham after he had been translated from the unembarrassed quiet of Bath and Wells. He had had no part in recent politics, and his orderly mind had been wholly occupied by the affairs of his new diocese. There had been, too, a tiresome matter of charges against the Bishop-Elect of Chichester which he had taken his part in overcoming. While Buckingham rode out of London on his last journey, the Bishop had been engaged in drafting answers to a series of queries[1] placed before him by Dr. Cosin about the placing of the Communion Table, the custom of standing and singing the Creed after the Gospel, the use of wax lights and tapers, and a specific request for a decision about the altar which Mr. Burgoyne had set up. Later in the month, his work completed, Dr. Laud had crossed the river and ridden down to the Archbishop's country house at Croydon to assist at the consecration of Dr. Montague to the See of Chichester. During the ceremonies he heard of his penitent's murder.[2]

It is an evidence of the callous false calculation of the courtiers that the very day that he learned of the Duke's death Lord Holland had written to the King,[3] agonized beyond bearing, not to express his sympathy, but to ask for one of Buckingham's minor offices either the constableship of Windsor Castle or the keeping of Hampton Court. Then there came Laud to help his master to face the future. Is it

---

[1] Letter from Dr. Cosin to Bishop Laud, dated 19 August, 1628. Cal. S. P. Dom., 1628-9, p. 259.

[2] "And Bishop Laud had advertisement of his (Buckingham's) death the 24th of August being there at Croiden with Bishop Neal, and other bishops consecrating Bishop Montague for Chichester," Rushworth *Historical Collections*, p. 635.

[3] Letter from the Earl of Holland to the King, dated 24 August, 1628. Cal. S. P. Dom., 1628-9, p. 267.

surprising that the King made no attempt to put some courtier in his friend's place, that he did not seek out the relics of his father's reign or give his confidence to the Duke's milder enemies, or send to Venice for Lord Carlisle?

It is always difficult to find any dividing line between two periods except in those cases where changes appear to be bound up with the fall of a dynasty or the outbreak of some great conflict. It is only from the point of view of the Court that the year 1628 appears significant. The religious currents and particularly the growth of Puritan feeling, which has not been considered in this study, were wholly unaffected by such an event as the favourite's murder. It was naturally without repercussion on the spirit or method of the Universities or on that country life whose details are reflected in the *Oxinden Letters*. But as far as the kingship is concerned, there was surely a unity in that period of fourteen years of King Charles's personal rule between the killing of his friend and the beginning of the Wars.

With Buckingham there vanished from the neighbourhood of the government of England, those whose lives had been bound up with the Jacobean outlook. The Duke was the last of King James's legacies. The men of the former generation were disappearing. Bacon and Lancelot Andrewes were now dead and Donne was failing. Archbishop Abbot's declining years were without influence and Bishop Williams, though he would reappear, was now removed from active politics. The vestiges of the old King's reign were passing. Such survivors from an earlier epoch as Ker and Cranfield could find no place at King Charles's Court where the characteristics of Van Dyck's world were taking shape.

Gradually the Caroline spirit was emerging. It was very far from the Court atmosphere, but it depended upon the maintenance of the King's rule. The Jacobean Age was giving place to a more taut decade, alike restrained and ornamental, consciously orthodox and regalist after the later manner. It was a period in which the Monarchy and the frame and doctrine of *Ecclesia Anglicana* were to be intertwined under the rigid sovereign and his new archbishop. An increasingly delicate and careful taste prevailed in a state of society which was not durable. The old easy Jacobean spirit and its coarse and homely splendour, went out with Buckingham.

There was no portion of the English world in which the news of the assassination did not produce a deep impression. It seems to have come last of all to Sir Kenelm Digby's ships which were in the Mediterranean privateering. They had provisioned at Zante where the Proveditore "at every woord called King of England's shippes of war *ladroni e corsari*,"[1] and on 30 October they had stood out north across the eastern waters of the Ionian Sea for Cephalonia. There in the harbour of Argostoli they had found and captured a small French sailing vessel, a *sattia*, whose master had told Sir Kenelm that the Duke was dead. In England this news was already two months old. The Jacobean Age had passed away.

[1] *Journal of Sir Kenelm Digby*, Camden Society, 1868, p. 70.

APPENDIX

THE following confession, which is contained among the Cecil MSS. at Hatfield House, vol. 118, f. 67, gives a remarkable impression of the religious life of a Catholic family in Yorkshire. There seems no reason to doubt the accuracy of the deposition and the young servant, who was suddenly introduced to knowledge of his master's worship, appears as candid as he is at times confused. The description of the Requiem Mass by one who, presumably, had never seen priests vested is particularly convincing. On reaching his home it seems clear that he suddenly realized the perils to which his actions had exposed him.

21 December, 1606, 118/67. The confession of John Nicollson son of William Nicollson of Winston in the county of Duresme, and late servant to Mr. Ambrose Pudseye of Barforth within the county of York, where he hath been notably abused with popish delusions, etc.

First, he said that he hath heard much talk against our religion many times, and that the papists' religion was the true religion, and that none ought to come to our churches, etc.

Item, he confesseth that one William Walker sometimes used for the butler in old Mrs. Pudseye's house, did give him a cross to wear about his neck to sign himself withal, and also a picture of Christ nailed upon the cross to set up, etc.

Item, he confesseth that all the last year a Jesus Psalter did lie open in Mr. Ambrose Pudseye's house for him and others to read on, and his master, Mr. Pudseye, did lend him a Jesus Psalter to read on and another cross and certain beads to say his prayers by, etc.

Item, he saith that the said William Walker did carry him upon Wednesday was a sennet early in the morning into a chamber at Barforth Hall, where a popish priest was, who

315

did there shrive him, telling him that his soul should be for his, if he would confess his sins to him, if he did not absolve him. And then he made his confession after which the priest made him sit down upon his knees and then did absolve him in Latin words and enjoined him his penance, which was to say every day three Ave Maries, three Paternosters, and one creed, and every Friday to say five Ave Maries, five Paternosters, and one creed, and to give three pence to three poor folks.

Item, he saith he was there with that priest, both that morning and the morning after, having the like conference and talk.

Item, he confesseth that he was resolved to go no more to our churches, and that the first night after he talked with the priest he was greatly troubled in his sleep, and thought he saw the ill man and that somebody was turning the leaves of his Jesus Psalter all night, and that he should see visions and martyrs; and also he saith that his crucifix was loosed from his neck and after in the morning he found a little paper in the chamber window, which he saith was not there in the evening before, wherein was written that he should see visions and martyrs, which he thinketh now was but the priest saying mass which he saw after.

Item, he confesseth that his master, Mr. Ambrose Pudseye, talked with him the Sunday after, which was Sunday last, and told him he might go down to his mother's upon Monday or Tuesday if he doubted of his right christendom or any other point of his faith. Whereupon he went upon Monday in the morning and William Walker carried him into his chamber, where the priest was an ancient man with white hair with two or three garments upon him, the uppermost was of fine black stuff with a white cross in the back, and there said mass in the presence of old Mrs. Pudseye, another gentlewoman that came out of Northumberland, William Walker and himself. There were wax candles burning upon the table, where stood the chalice which he did see the priest lift up at Mass.

Item, the said John Nicollson delivered unto me both the above named crosses, the pictures, the beads and the Jesus Psalter, although he had thrown the picture and one of the crosses in the dunghill at his father's house, and kept the other things to send to Mr. Pudseye, as he saith he promised to do.

Lastly, talking of the papists he said they rested much upon the end of this Parliament, longing to know the event thereof, not much regarding what was done already still hoping for favour.

(Signed) By me Hen. Thurscros, parson of Winston.

The following memorandum was submitted by Viscount Cranborne to his father, and is dated 1611. It is among the Cecil MSS. at Hatfield House, vol. 197, f. 3.

1611. The names of sundry knights and gentlemen that were in Italy in the time whiles I was there and have been likewise at Rome to my knowledge.

Sir Charles Moryson
Mr. Wray
Mr. Askeworth with two or three servants. } These were in the company of Sir Charles Moryson.

Sir George Peter   Alone.

Sir William Dormer
Mr. Anthony Tracy
Three servants of Sir Wm. Dormer } These were in company with Sir W. Dormer.

Sir Robert Chamberlain
Sir Edm. Hampden
Sir Thomas Crompton
Mr. Baskervyll
Mr. Boughton
Mr. D. Moore and a servant of Sir R. Chamberlain's } With these I kept company at Rome and at Naples, never being out of their company, night nor day.

Mr. Gyffard, a servant of my Lord of Shrewsbury's } This man was alone. In his return from Rome met me at Padua, presently after my first arrival in Italy.

Mr. Barrett
Mr. Leveson, and
Mr. Fitzwilliams with
three servants. } These were Mr. Barrett's company.

Mr. Froome   Alone. He is a vintner's son about Newgate Market and hath lived long abroad specially at Rome.

Mr. Partherydg, a Kentish gent. allyed to Sir H. Wotton his Majesty's ambassador at Venice.

Mr. Fynche, son to Sir Moyle Fynche
Mr. Duncombe } These two travelled together, and Mr. Fynche wrote to Persons to have leave to come to Rome, having shewed his letter to divers, and Persons' answer.

Mr. Toby Mathew
Mr. Easton } These travelled together.

Mr. Rooke, a servant of Sir Henry Wotton's.
Mr. Hunt, an organist, servant to my Lord's Grace of Canterbury.
Two sons of Sir Edward Moore of Odiham Hants with their tutor.
Mr. Fryer, son to Dr. Fryer the physician.
Mr. Mychell, secretary to My Lord's Grace that now is.
Mr. Raynells, nephew to my Lord Chamberlain's secretary.
Mr. Gorg, son of Mr. Wm. Gorg, near Plymouth.

Mr. Gage and Mr. Wenman. } These were another company.

Mr. Chalcroft	} This is a servant of his Majesty's of the Scottish nation.
My Lord of Mar's son Mr. James Colvyll	} These were another company.
My Lord of Murray Mr. Mongo Murray and Another Scottish gent. whom I know not.	} These three kept together.

THE EARL OF SUFFOLK'S CASE

IT has seemed simpler to deal with this specialized matter in an appendix rather than to incorporate it in the body of the book. Among the Hatfield House transcripts at the Record Office there are a number of letters from Sir John Finet, the Master of Ceremonies at the Court, to the Earl of Salisbury at Hatfield. They are written at various dates between 22 October and 14 November, 1619, and they give a vivid impression of the trial of Salisbury's father-in-law, Lord Suffolk. It is probable that the series is incomplete.

"This day's work," wrote Sir John Finet on 22 October, 1619,[1] "which we judged would have made riddance of the greater part of my lord of Suffolk's business in question, that deceived our expectations, and so may my letter your lordship's, since of five parts whereof the bill brought against his lordship consisteth only two were handled, which were touching ordnance and the alum works.

The part first in question of deceit of trust committed about the Jewels was not so much as mentioned, since my lord and lady's pleading of their discharge under the great seal expressly freeing them from ever being molested, impeached or sued to that purpose, served them for an armour of proof (which as Mr. Attorney said the other day the King had given them and they had now put on) and kept them from all further question. The two last parts of misemployment of the King's treasure and of extortion from the subject

[1] Cecil MSS., vol. 129, ff. 160, 161.

remain to be handled the next day. So the first that was fallen upon this day was concerning the Ordnance, wherein few examinations were read or proofs produced (being such as Mr. Sergeant Crewe,[1] who spake most, called for) yet tending strongly to the confirmation of a double hand in the disposition of the £6,000 allotted yearly by His Majesty for the payment of officers and other charges belonging to the Ordnance.

This was made to appear in my lord's not bringing in of books into the Exchequer in their due seasons and in making of orders antedated, in not discharging the necessary charges of the office nor paying the officers their wages; in having in the meantime disbursed to Sir Roger Dallison in two years and a half nine thousand pounds, whereof 2200 pounds were charged as paid a year after Sir R. Dallison was out of his place and the like, wherein my lord your deceased father[2] (to me & all honest men of happy memory), had by the way an honourable mention while it was delivered there in Court that in the precedent Treasurer's time Dallison was not to be found in arrearages; but while my lord of Suffolk was Treasurer he grew in the space of two years and a half above £9,000.

This point thus left (wherein Mr. Attorney scarce ever interposed one word but the Solicitor sometimes and to no light purpose) Sergeant Crewe fell to handling the charge of the Alum works: wherein was extolled the King's good husbandry, who while he kept them in his own hands made in two years and two months above £22,000, and my lord's undertakings decried who (howsoever he pretended a greater profit that should be his endeavour accrue to His Majesty) he was occasion to him of above £13,000 loss in the two first years; whereas there should have been bond of £12,000

---

[1] Sir Randolph Crewe, 1558–1646, Serjeant-at-Law, 1615.
[2] Robert first Earl of Salisbury was Lord Treasurer from 1608 until 1612 and the Earl of Suffolk from 1614 until his resignation in the year preceding his trial.

(taken of the contractors in the aid two years) it was neglected to the loss of such advantage as might have been taken by the King of the contractors, and when in the beginning of the third year a new contract was made, Mr. Chancellor refusing to join, there was but £6,000 bond taken for the King's security. And of three contractors formerly bond Angell was omitted (at the pronouncing of which name and words my lord Chancellor interposed with a smile these words, "I doubt not their angels were omitted"). After which the Sergeant proceeded to aggravate by bringing in Turner, one of the first contractors, his offer to my lady (and her acceptance) of £2,300 for the procuring of £20,000 debt out of the custom house, together with her returning part of the £2,300, when my lord seemed to be offended at it, and Turner's repayment of it again to her. All which was brought forth upon the reading of Humphrys' Examination and 2 or 3 of my lady's letters to him, which so plainly expressed her fears and shifts that the corrupt double carriage of that business should be discovered as there needs little matter else to condemn her ladyship howsoever my lord may (I pray God he may) escape his dangerous part of it.

Mention was made likewise of £300 a year to come from the contractors for 21 years to Sir Thomas Howard; but no proof following that it was ever paid that charge past no farther.

I will only add that I find the weather grows more and more foul for this unhappy lord's business, and if the sun of the King's grace or the wind of his gracious favour dispel or blow not away the storm threatened there is nothing but ruin to be expected, which God turn away." So concluded the first of the surviving letters and five days later Finet again resumed his story.

"To continue," he wrote to Salisbury on 27 October,[1]

[1] Cecil MSS., vol. 129, ff. 162-7.

"the account of the great business. This day was handled by the Solicitor General the 4th part of that five fold division of the bill against my lord of Suffolk and others in proving the accusation brought against him for misemployment of the King's Treasure, and this was subdivided into 3 parts.

Misemployment	of money paid the King upon surrender of the cautionary towns to the States. Of assignments for the service of Ireland. Of treasure unduly taken out of the Receipt of the Exchequer.

For the first it was alleged that whereas the King had received for the said towns £213,000, whereof was paid into the Exchequer £173,000 (and a privy seal granted for distribution of these moneys with a schedule annexed specifying the particulars) £3,000 was found to have been taken out and no mention made of it in that schedule."

Sir John then describes Lord Suffolk's complicated explanation.

"In the meantime," he adds, "the money was proved to rest in my lord's hands and after two years rest there was sent to Mr. Burlamachi with caution that it might be secretly returned into the Exchequer, as if it had been till then remaining in his hands unpaid: whereas Burlamachi affirms he never expected such a return, having paid it into the Exchequer two years before; and Vandeput, his partner, being also examined, addeth that the reason (as he thought) why this money was brought back was that there having been no tally struck all that time it might seem never till then to have been paid into the Exchequer.

Hereupon wanted not invectives against the disorders of issuing moneys without express order, according to the prescribed form, or with blank orders (termed so because instead of an order they set a blank) whereby orders might be supplied at the pleasure of Sir John Bingley, as it was proved they were, long after moneys had been issued to other particular uses, and might be transferred whither and to what uses they will to the extreme wrong both of King and subjects. Here was Sir John Bingley also taxed (besides many other charges which this day brought him into deeper and more dangerous question than hitherto) for directing all such orders as were of little or no profit to which of the Tallies pleased him least, whereby he held them in awe with the fear of their loss if they would not show themselves serviceable unto his turn.

Upon which occasion Sir Ed. Warder, having been examined, confessed that which Mr. Attorney called the other day "the mystery of iniquity," discovering what moneys had been charged, some upon the Navy (which, Sir Robert Mansfeld disclaiming the receipt of, was thereupon transferred to the Wardrobe), some upon particular persons as lord Stanhope, Sir Gervase Elwyse, Sir Baptist Hicks, and many taken out in other men's names; and much charged upon the old debt of Ireland, for which Sir J. Bingley had a privy seal in 8. Jas. I. & which as an *abissus* or gulf swallowed store of treasure never in danger to be accounted for by Sir Jo. Bingley till he were called to it (and that by likelihood never) for all together.

In all these charges it was enforced that my lord of Suffolk could not but be as faulty as Sir Jo. Bingley and with him *particeps criminis* in regard the weekly examination of the Exchequer accounts could not pass without his knowledge and consequently must be with his connivance and to his benefit. Amongst other charges two were brought upon my lord of £100 and of £40 taken out of the Exchequer and paid to Mr. Carter, the first for his building at Newmarket and the latter for his stable at Charing Cross. Whereupon Mr. Solicitor (in the rest of his speech little or nothing tart) took occasion to ejaculate, "Thus the great foundation of the Exchequer must be subverted for the building up of my lord's stables." But when they came to Ireland there fell a storm of aggravations for transferring of moneys upon that country's service (though said to be employed to my lord's and other private uses) for the mischiefs that might follow it by mutinies of the soldiers for want of pay, and for the wrongs done to particular officers and commanders there by drawing from them consents to give large yearly allowances for assurances of good and certain payment. In sum, Humphrys' book and confession was there produced to prove many of the allegations but more of his own having in betraying his master; whom misfortune still attends with the world for speaking of his ruin if His Majesty's goodness prevent it not." This concluded Sir John's letter and only one day was to elapse before the next message.

"The next day," he wrote to Salisbury on 28 October, "Mr. Sergeant Finch spake to the first and last remaining part of the bill concerning extortion exercised against the subject, saying at his entrance that the 'mystery of iniquity' spoken of by Mr. Attorney was now to be revealed in her own colours; and having delivered the circumstances offering themselves, as he said, in the bill, viz.,

"The nature of the business.

"The means used for extortion, and

"The proportions of the extortions—he insisted upon their ways of taking and drawing in of profit, by bargaining, delaying, persuading, threatening, etc., saying no door could be opened without a golden key, and if charms would not serve they would use conjurations: as when Cortin sued for his debt of £18,000 from the King, Sir John Townsend demanded of him £3,000 and sayd 'What is it to give £3,000 to such a man as my lord be it but to purchase his favour?'"

Sir John Finet then continued the recital of several similar charges brought forward on that day. "And," he relates, "for £10,000 borrowed of the farmers upon the leases of Oswestry, when they grew to a treaty, what should be given to my lord yearly to assure his favour, of £2,500 first demanded next of £2,000, they agreed at last to give £2,500 *per annum* conditionally it should be towards the settling of every year of so much of the main debt."

The next charge concerned 3,000 pieces taken from the Merchant Adventurers for confirming or renewing their charter, then Sir David Murray's composition for £3,000 which resulted in an offer of £1,000 to Lord Suffolk. "Sir Miles Fleetwood followed this for £500 given for the transferring of 500 marks pension to the Court of Wards, and for £100 more that himself had given to smooth the way against checks in his office.. . . Sir John Spilman of a debt of £3,000 was owed £2,000, took a bond for the third thousand at year's day of payment, delivered the bond into Sir John Bingley's hand (with a ring of £110 value), from his hand to my lady's; there detained."

With other like these which had the parties' depositions or Sir John Townsend's or else Humphrys' book to confirm them. Besides another letter was produced under my lady's hand complaining of Sir Arthur Ingram that could not procure her but five in the hundred, and extolling Sir John Bingley that could help her to far better bargains.

Again she writes to Humphrys' that he should keep himself from being examined and from swearing to anything and upon his objection that he should then be punished for contempt she bid him not fear, for she would defend him from all charges.

In the last place came the question of £2,800 paid Bingley to distribute amongst certain pirates to keep them honest men after their reclaiming. Of this money one Captain Boghe should have had £1,100: he never could get but £40, was imprisoned for debt, died there of discontent.

A man named Randall was employed to induce another pirate, Captain Millington, to take a less sum than the £666 due to him. "The like proceeding," continued Finet, "or worse was with the rest of the pirates who could never obtain but little and some nothing of the King's bounty."

"Paul Fore, a lodger of strangers, had long entertained in his house a Duke of Saxony, and for all his charge of diet and otherwise was content to accept of a privy seal of £1,000 due to the said Duke from his Majesty's gift; for which contracting with Sir John Bingley he gave him £100 to procure it, had a tally struck, and, being put over to the custom to receive it, fell thence into the little less merciless hands of Sir P. Garrowey and Mr. Johns, who took of him £50 for composition."

Sir Allen Apsley being examined confessed that for a new year's gift he gave my lord every year a hundred pounds or plate to that value, but that being often plunged for want of due payment he had given to Bingley at several times above six hundred pounds.

All the while these charges were there in Court laid upon Sir John Bingley was present, and with open face outstood them, at last spake himself out loud (which is not as you know used there unless in an *ore tenus*) saying: "My lords, I have ever hated the name of a deceiver, and if I prove not against all these accusations that I have done the part of an honest man I desire no favour. The world in the meantime wonders at his confidence and little believes that he will make good his profession of innocency." Thus concluded Sir John Finet's third letter and his fourth was sent to Hatfield the next day.

"This day," wrote Finet on 29 October, "the defendants came to their answer, which was taken first in hand by Sergeant Richardson, and carried with that strength of wit and argument as hath shaken much of the world's opinion concerning the guilt of my Lord in the two charges of the Ordnance and the alum business." Finet then proceeded to explain that Lord Suffolk's counsel took the line that in regard to the Ordnance the Lieutenant and not the Lord

Treasurer was chargeable for the payment of the offices. The responsibility in his opinion rested on Sir R. Dallison. He also brought forward arguments in regard to the alum contracts and succeeded in clearing the matter of Sir T. Howard's gratuity. "Many other reasons," continued Finet, "passed *pro* and *contra* to prove and disprove the differences of gain and loss to the King in time of the agency and of the contract, which was intricate to me to conceive, and out of my distance to hear by reason of the tempestuous noise of my lord Mayor's shot, drums, and trumpets at his landing at Westminster. Only I could apprehend that whereas in 3 years space of the agency of Johnson the King was not answered above £4,000 as the Sergeant affirmed, he made after his disbursement of only £10,000 to the contractors more than £9,000 yearly clear gain. Which the King's counsel and some of the lords taking in hand to disprove, strong arguments were brought against it and the sergeant's so in certain points convinced as we might see how the world inclineth and how that lord is like to suffer, if not in these in the other wounds he is like to receive through his lady's sides, against which the world and its prejudging conceit (much less the lords in their searching wisdom) will admit no hope of defence. And so God send him patience and your lordship health."

Sir John Finet then added a postcript of a more personal character. "I thank you," he wrote, "for your so noble offer of venison and will be bold to accept it, beseeching you will be pleased to send me a doe on Thursday or Saturday to welcome Mr. Secretary Calvert to my nearer neighbourhood together with Will Ashton and other friends to bear him company, when your health shall be heartily remembered."

It was in connection with this matter and possibly on Finet's advice that Salisbury wrote to Secretary Calvert who had had a long contact with his family. Calvert's reply is inserted in the midst of the Finet letters. "God forbid," he wrote in the conclusion to a note of compliment, "I should, though I must deal plainly with your lordship in this that if it comes to sentence howsoever Sergeant Richardson did as much for my lord's defence as possibly the cause would bear, yet in good faith my lord, *bona fide*, I do not understand that the discharge is so clear as you have heard it be." These sentences are an admirable example of caution and procrastination.

Two days later came Sir John Finet's next letter. After describing the continued defence made by Sergeant Richardson and Sergeant Bawtry he gave an account of young Mr. Finch's speech to the third charge of misemployment of treasure. "He said," wrote Finet,[1] in describing Finch's summing-up, "that these detainings, transferrings, ante-datings and the like, charged upon my lord under the title of 'the mystery of iniquity' now to be reached proceeded either of necessity or election without intent or fraud, were but mists of cloud hanging over my lord's head with a little wind to be blown away. Many like passages fell from him and after from Sergent Bawtry to my lord's justification. But the confidence that I hear Mr. Attorney professeth to some of his inward friends, that in his reply he will make all clear for the King against the defendants makes me doubt of some strength in reserve for the last that may prove to my lord's overthrow if not from himself from his lady and Sir John Bingley."

Ten days elapsed, and then Sir John Finet wrote his final letter to his patron. "To sum up," he began,[2] "the last of the account I owe you touching my lord of Suffolk's great business in the Star Chamber. On Friday, Mr. Attorney made his reply to the defendant's answer and began by magnifying the lord's moderation and inclination to qualify faults though enormous, and rather to grieve at than desire

[1] Cecil MSS., vol. 129, ff. 135–6.   [2] *ibid.*, ff. 169–73.

the punishment of offenders, such as was the Earl of Suffolk a great star fallen out of their own firmament; whose business in hand mainly concerned the King in honour and interest, and the subject in safety and ease, whom if it were a crime to follow with hue and cry up to the seat of justice, he must be said to be guilty of it.

It was true, he said, they had made the best of every poor occasion like those in peril of drowning, who to save themselves take hold of every reed. But accusations were to be made good by proofs, proofs by reply, wherein he would follow them the nearer because at the bar, he said, they had so braved it.

It was apparent the Earl had issued the King's treasure unduly to a man (Sir R. Dallison) that had shifted himself out of the place and His Majesty out of his money, and that they laboured by their arguments to draw men's eyes from the wound and to blear them that they might not see the depth and danger of it. . . .

After Mr. Attorney . . . proceeded to spare no plainness of terms in taxing her ladyship as for her letters that some of them were impious in style and odious in matter, that she made show to esteem no friends but money, that her subtleties, thrown out upon several occasions, had made my lord's house a snare for the subject; that she did angle with several hooks upon one line, that the sundry sums given for the bribery were landed at her stairs under the conduct of Bingley and employed to my lord's use: that if she yielded in anything brought against her it was but as the mouse would do being in the cat's mouth.

The next day was for the lords' answers which came first from Sir Edward Cooke with these preparatives which I will set down as I caught them long pieces and not with the method they were delivered, too hard a task for my weak observation, especially in such a throng of questioning auditors as were there assembled. He said there were loud speaking relators that stood up against the defendants, the commonweal, the voice of the oppressed, and the cry of the labourer robbed of his hire.

Then Mr. Chancellor of the Exchequer "how my lady was joined in my lord's faults, how Bingley was not only a tempter but a moulder of frailty in my lord." Then Lord Hobart, Sir Julius Caesar, Lord Chief Justice Montague, Mr. Secretary Calvert, Mr. Secretary Naunton. "He tells first a note the world had taken of that family (the Howards) that in their best light of sunshine were seen ever to set suddenly in a cloud; glanceth upon the Tower, whereof though they were not guilty they were glad to lay both their hands upon their pardons, condemneth Bingley for a player under board, and like a partridge retrieved from hedge to hedge, for an unworthy servant hanging upon the train of his lord and lady." Sir Thomas Edmonds, Lord Digby, the Bishop of Ely, the Bishop of London 'He extended himself rather and delivered (theologically) his reasons and instructions to all great men to make use of this great example," my lord Chamberlain, my Lord Marquis Hamilton the Duke of Lenox. My Lord of Canterbury's discourse suitable to his profession was of the abuse of extorting officers who like ill shepherds did tear and not shear the sheep." The close was for my Lord Chancellor, which he seldom or never makes, as your lordship knows, without great applause. He fell to discourse how completely happy the King were if the Treasury and state of means were settled, what honour he had obtained above any of his predecessors as to have deserved the title of Uniter of Britain and the Planter of Ireland: how glorious the Church here was like a firmament of stars.

Then he went through each state and element in the nation glorious and beneficent. Finally "he descended to the aggravation of the several charges against my lord, my lady and Bingley, concluding that my lady kept the shop, Bingley was the prentice that cried 'What do you lack?' but all went in to my lord's cash. And so assenting to Lord Hubbard's preparative the Court rose from longer sitting, as I now willingly do from writing to easy a drowsy head and a wearied hand." A postscript to this last letter closes the correspondence. "ps.," wrote Sir John Finet, "I beseech your lordship not to forget to burn this hasty and ill-digested relation intended to no man's reading but your lordship's."

BIBLIOGRAPHICAL NOTE

A list is appended of a number of primary printed auuthorities which have been consulted in conjunction with this study. This note is not intended to be exhaustive and only those sources are mentioned from which sidelights on the life of the period can be easily obtained.

I. HISTORICAL MANUSCRIPTS' COMMISSION REPORTS

Calendar of Ancaster MSS. including the papers relating to John Cotton of Warblington.

Calendar of Bouverie MSS. including William Ayshcombe's autobiographical fragment.

Calendar of Buccleugh and Queensberry MSS., vol. iii.

Calendar of Coke MSS. containing the correspondence and *memoranda* of Secretary Coke.

Calendar of Denbigh MSS. for the personal detail of the Villiers family grouping.

Calendar of Drummond Moray MSS., including a correspondence between Winwood and Buckingham in 1617.

Calendar of Edmonstone MSS.

Calendar of Eglinton MSS. including a curious list of expenses at the English Court, dated 1603.

Calendar of Franciscan MSS.

Calendar of Gawdy MSS.

Calendar of Hastings MSS., vol. ii.

Calendar of Hothfield MSS. containing notes left by Anne Countess of Dorset.

Calendar of House of Lords MSS.

Calendar of Kenyon MSS.

Calendar of Kilmorey MSS.

Calendar of Manchester MSS. including letters dealing with the Summer Islands.

Calendar of Mar and Kellie MSS. including the Kellie-Mar correspondence.

Calendar of Middleton MSS.
Calendar of Muncaster MSS. including certain letters from
Lord William Howard.
Calendar of Portland MSS., vol. iii, including the Conway-
Harley correspondence.
Calendar of Powys MSS. including certain letters from Sir
John Danvers and a short correspondence between Sir
Edward Herbert and Secretary Calvert.
Calendar of Rutland MSS., vols. i, ii.
Calendar of Stafford MSS. containing a detailed inventory
of Costessey Hall in 1622.
Calendar of Stewart of Alltyrodyn MSS.
Calendar of Stonyhurst MSS.
Calendar of Talbot MSS.
Calendar of Townshend MSS.
Calendar of Westmorland MSS. containing a relation of
Lord Salisbury's last days.
Calendar of Wingfield Digby MSS. including the corres-
pondence of Sir John Digby in 1610–12.
Calendar of Wells Chapter MSS.
Calendar of Bishop's Castle Corporation MSS.
Calendar of Bridgnorth Corporation MSS.
Calendar of Exeter Corporation MSS.
Calendar of Gloucester Corporation MSS.
Calendar of Plymouth Corporation MSS.
Calendar of Salisbury Corporation MSS.
Calendar of Wenlock Corporation MSS.

II. Collections of State Papers

Calendar of State Papers, Domestic.
Calendar of State Papers, Venetian.
Calendar of State Papers, Colonial.
Acts of the Privy Council.
Register of the Privy Council of Scotland.
Sir Ralph Winwood's State Papers.
Clarendon State Papers.
Strafford Letters, ed. William Knowler.
Journals of the House of Lords.
The Lords Debates in 1621, Camden Society.

Diary of John Smyth of Nibley, Parliament Notes by Sir Nathaniel Rich, Belasyse Diary, Barrington Diary and the other accounts of the transactions of the Parliament of 1621, ed. Wallace Notestein, F. H. Relf and H. Simpson. State Trials.

III. LETTERS, DIARIES AND CORRESPONDENCE

Sources still in manuscript and referred to in the preface or the text or footnotes are not referred to here.

Fortescue Papers, Camden Society.
Lismore Papers, vols. ii and iii, ed. Rev. A. B. Grosart.
Tixall Papers, ed. Arthur Clifford.
Trevelyan Papers, vols. ii and iii, Camden Society.
Egerton Papers, Camden Society.
The Oxinden Letters, vol. i, ed. D. Gardiner.
Letters, ed. Sir Henry Ellis, Camden Society.
Letters of Lady Brilliana Harley, Camden Society.
Diary of Thomas Crosfield, ed. F. S. Boas.
Diary of John Southcote, C.R.S., vol. i.
Diary of Walter Yonge, Camden Society.
Diary of John Rous, Camden Society.
Journal of Sir Roger Wilbraham, Camden Mjscellany.
Correspondence of Nathan Walworth and Peter Seddon, Chetham Society.
Correspondence of Amerigo Salvetti.
Sir Kenelm Digby's Journal, Camden Society.
Carew-Roe Correspondence, Camden Society.
Correspondence of Jane Lady Cornwallis.
Letters in James Spedding's *Life of Bacon*.
Letters in John Nichols's *Progresses of James I.*
Correspondence in R. F. Williams's *Court and Times of James I.*
Correspondence in G. Goodman's *Court of King James the First.*
Letters to severall persons of honour written by John Donne, ed. John Donne, D.C.L.

IV. AUTOBIOGRAPHIES, MEMOIRS, MEMORANDA, ETC.

Autobiography of Sir Simonds D'Ewes, vols. i, ii.
Autobiography of Archbishop Laud, ed. Henry John Park.

Autobiography of Lord Herbert of Cherbury.
Autobiography of Phineas Pett, Navy Records Society.
Autobiography of Thomas Raymond, Camden Society.
Memoirs of Sir George Courthop, Camden Miscellany, xi.
Memoirs of the family of Guise, Camden Society.
Memoirs of the Holles Family, Camden Society.
Letter Book of Sir John Holles, Cal. Portland MSS.
Letter Book of Sir Edward Conway, Cal. S.P. Dom.
Memoirs of Anne Lady Fanshawe, ed. H. C. Fanshawe.
The Life and Death of George Villiers, Duke of Buckingham,
    by Sir Henry Wotton.
The Conversion of Sir Tobie Mathew, ed. A. H. Mathew.
Brief Lives, notes by John Aubrey, ed. A. Clark.
Lives, by Izaak Walton.
Life of Lady Anne Clifford, Roxburgh Club.
Diary of Lady Anne Clifford, ed. V. Sackville-West.
Life and Works of Sir Henry Mainwaring, Navy Records
    Society.
Life of the Lady Falkland.
Life of Anne Countess of Arundel and Surrey, ed. Henry
    Duke of Norfolk.
Memoir of Robert Cary, Earl of Monmouth, ed. G. H.
    Powell.
Works of William Drummond of Hawthornden, ed. L. E.
    Kastner.
*Original Unpublished Papers illustrative of the life of Sir Peter
    Paul Rubens,,* ed. W. Noel Sainsbury.
Historical Collections, ed. John Rushworth.
Historicall Discourses, by Sir Edward Walker.
Scrinia Reserata, by John Hacket, Bishop of Lichfield.
Relation of the death of Prince Henry, ed. John More, Bishop
    of Ely, printed in *Desiderata Curiosa*.
Observations, by the Rev. John Bowle, chaplain to the Earl
    of Salisbury, printed in *Desiderata Curiosa*.
Notes from the Household Books of the Rev. John Bowle,
    Dean of Salisbury, *ibid.*
Sir Lewis Stukeley's *Petition* printed in Harleian Miscellany,
    iii.
The Discovery of the Jesuits' College at Clerkenwell in March,
    1627–8, narrative of Sir Robert Heath, Attorney-General
    Camden Miscellany, ii.

The Montagu Musters Book, ed. Joan Wake, Northampton-
shire Records Society.
Robert Loder's Farm Accounts, 1610–20, Camden Society.
Memoirs of the Verney Family, vol. i, ed. Frances Lady
Verney.
The Commonplace Book of Sir John Oglander, ed. Francis
Bamford.
The Loseley manuscripts, ed. A. J. Kempe.
Naval Songs and Ballads, Navy Records Society.
Old English Ballads, 1553–1625, ed. H. E. Rollins.
Records of the Virginia Company of London.

INDEX

Members of a family are grouped around a chief to whom their relationship is shown. Cross references indicate the various marriage alliances and the changes of title which are so confusing at this period. The considerable amount of genealogical detail is inserted in the index to enable the network of connections to be traced.

ABBOT, GEORGE, d. 1632, Archbishop of Canterbury, 23, 94–7, 102, 104, 106, 111–13, 176, 200, 311
Sir Maurice, d. 1642, his brother, 96, 199
Abercrombie, Robert S.J., 22
Abergavenny, Henry (Neville) d. 1641, ninth Lord, 240
Catherine (Vaux), his wife, Lady, 240
Abington, William, d. 1654, 243
Lucy (Herbert), his wife, 243
Aldersbroke, 45
Aleppo, 146
Alicante, 90
Allsop, Robert, 306
Althorpe, 35
Alva, Duke of, 236
Ampthill House, 209
Amsterdam, 106
Andover, Viscount, *see* Berkshire, Earl of
Andrewes, Lancelot, d. 1626, Bishop of Winchester, 10–1, 76–8, 96, 176, 188, 312
Anglesea, Christopher (Villiers) d. 1630, first Earl of, 184–5, 252, 276
Elizabeth (Sheldon), his wife, Countess of, 185, 276, 299
Anne (of Denmark), Queen, 22–3, 111, 112, 113
Anstey House, 31
Anstey, manor of, 29
Anstruther, Sir William, 47
Anthony, John, 88
Mrs. Mabell, 88
Antigua, 307
Apethorpe, 108
Apsley, Sir Allen, d. 1630, 326
Aquaviva, Claudio, S.J., 126
Aquila, honour of, 104

Argostoli, 313
Arundel, Philip (Howard), d. 1595, Earl of, 103
Anne (Dacre), his wife, Countess of, 125–31, 244
Thomas, d. 1646, his son, Earl of, 56, 124–47 *passim*, 258, 286, 293, 297
Alathea (Talbot), his daughter-in-law, Countess of, 131–9, 286
Henry Frederick, d. 1652, his grandson, Earl of, 258
Elizabeth (Stuart), his grand-daughter-in-law, Countess of, 258
William, his grandson, *see* Stafford, Viscount
Arundell of Lanherne, John, d. 1633, 243
Anne (Jerningham), his wife, 243
Arundell of Wardour, Thomas, d. 1639, first Lord, 28–34, 56, 63–5, 239
Mary (Wriothesley), his wife, Lady, 56
Sir Matthew, his father, 29–31
Charles, his uncle, 64
Anne, his daughter, *see* Baltimore, Lady
Catherine, his daughter, *see* Eure, Mrs.
Thomas, d. 1643, his son, second Lord, 35, 240
Blanche (Somerset), his daughter-in-law, Lady, 240
William of Horningsham, d. 1653, his son, 239
Mary (Browne), his daughter-in-law, 239
Ash, 274
Ashdown Forest, 104
Ashley, Sir Anthony, d. 1627, 36; 49, 206

Aston of Forfar, Walter, d. 1639, first Lord, 240, 243
Atkinson, Thomas, 43
Aubrey, John, 117
Audley End, 160–2, 175, 177
Audley of Walden, Thomas, Lord, 160
Audley, ninth Lord, see Castlehaven, second Earl of
Ayton, Sir Robert, d. 1638, 213, 306

BACON, FRANCIS, see St. Alban's, Viscount
Sir Edmund, his nephew, 160, 177
Baiae, 135
Baker, David Augustine, O.S.B., d. 1641, 104–5
Baltimore, George (Calvert), d. 1632, first Lord, 172–5, 207, 260
Cecil, d. 1675, his son, second Lord, 240
Anne (Arundell), his daughter-in-law, Lady, 27, 240
Banbury, William (Knollys), d. 1632, Earl of, 159, 168
Elizabeth (Howard), his wife, Countess of, 129
Bancroft, Richard, d. 1610, Archbishop of Canterbury, 43, 71
Bander, Mr., 296
Barbados, 307
Barforth, 315
Barforth Hall, 315–16
Barkworth, Mark, 96
Barnet, 67
Barnstaple, 202
Barolo, 102
Barret, Mr., 196
Barrington, Sir Thomas, 190–1, 207
Basing House, 295
siege of, 65, 240
Basingstoke, 294–6
Baskerville, Lady, 283
Bath, 74–5
Bath, William (Bourchier), d. 1623, third Earl of, 177
Bawtry, Serjeant, 328
Baynard's Castle, 291
Beaulieu, 182
Beaumont, Sir John, d. 1627, 295
Beaumont, Sir Thomas, 207
Beaumonts of Cole Orton, 109
Bedford, Edward (Russell), d. 1637, third Earl of, 206
Lucy (Harington), his wife, Countess of, 105

Bedingfeld, Sir Henry, d. 1657, 243
Elizabeth (Howard), his wife, Lady, 243
Beecher, Sir William, 212–13
Bellarmine, Robert Cardinal, 155
Bellasis, Sir Henry, d. 1644, 242
Ursula (Fairfax), his wife, Lady, 242
Sir Thomas, d. 1652, his son, 242
Bemerton, 224
Beoley, 276
Bergen-op-Zoom, 46
Berkeley, George, d. 1658, thirteenth Lord, 192
Berkeley, Maurice, 202
Berkshire, Thomas (Howard), d. 1660, first Earl of, 125, 171, 308
Charles, d. 1679, his son, second Earl of, 129
Dorothy (Savage), his daughter-in-law, Countess of, 129
Bermuda, 6, 192, 193–9
Bermuda Company, 195–7
Beza, Theodore, 284
Billisdon, school at, 109
Bindon, 129
Bingley, Sir John, 163–76 seq., 206
Bishop's Castle, 163, 271
Bishopthorpe, 41
Blackwell, George, d. 1613, 127
Blanchard, John, 203
Blandford, 85
Red Lion at, 85
Blois, 109
Blount of Mapledurham, Sir Richard, d. 1619, 243
Elizabeth (More), his wife, Lady, 243
Sir Charles, d. 1644, his son, 243
Anne, his grand-daughter, see Swinburne
Bodley, Sir Thomas, d. 1613, 78–9
Boghe, Captain, 171, 325
Boteler, Sir Henry, 40
Boules, William, 30
Boulogne, 184
Bowle, John, d. 1637, Bishop of Rochester, 74
Brackley, Viscount, see Ellesmere, Lord
Brampton, Bryan, 127, 270–2
Bramshill, 97
Brenta, the, 141, 151
Brest, 46
Brett, Alexander, 30, 279

Brickhill, 67
Bridgéwater, John (Egerton), d. 1649, first Earl of, 102, 211
Brill, 60, 262
Bristol, 202, 293
Bristol, John (Digby), d. 1654, first Earl of, 176, 206
Brome, Cornwallis of, 34
Brooke, Fulke (Greville), d. 1628, first Lord, 207, 265, 269, 281-3
Brooke, Henry, see Cobham, Lord
Sir Calisthenes, 207
Brooksby, 108
Broughton, 241
Browne, Anthony Mary, see Montague, second Viscount
Mary (Dormer), his mother, see Gerard
Mary, his aunt, see Southampton
Elizabeth, his aunt, see Dormer
Brudenell, Thomas, d. 1663, first Lord, 12, 240, 241, 243
Mary (Tresham), his wife, Lady, 240
Robert, his son, second Lord, 240
Mary (Constable), his daughter-in-law, Lady, 240
Bruges, 32
Brussels, 55, 63-5, 133, 165
Brydges, Grey, see Chandos, Lord
Bryn, 242
Buckeridge, John, d. 1631, Bishop of Ely, 77
Buckhurst, Lord, see Dorset, first Earl of
Buckingham, George (Villiers), d. 1628, first Duke of, 1, 9, 19, 22, 24, 50, 77, chap. vii, x-xi, xvi-xix passim
Katharine (Manners), his wife, Duchess of, 181, 300, 305
Mary (Beaumont), his mother, Countess of, 180-1, 186, 246, 251, 252
George, d. 1687, his son, second Duke of, 302
Buckland, 243
Burghley, William (Cecil), d. 1598, first Lord, 1, 37, 73
Burghley House, 5, 167
Burgoyne, Mr., 34
Burke, see Clanricarde, Earls of
Burlamachi, Philip, 136, 278, 322
Burley-on-the-Hill, 182
Burton Constable, 240, 241-2
Butler, Nathaniel, 6, 197-9
Buxton, Robert, 128

CADIZ, 35, 262
Cæsar, Sir Julius, d. 1636, 176, 210
Calvert, Sir George, see Baltimore, Lord
Calvin, 93
Cambridge, 52, 97, 106, 111, 177, 225-6, 282, 288
Chancellorship of, 51, 160, 177
Stewardship of, 51
Emmanuel College, 19, 107
Magdalene College, 193
Pembroke Hall, 284
St. John's College, 51, 225
Trinity College, 133, 282
Camden, William, d. 1623, 15, 81
Candia, 157
Canterbury, 176
Canterbury, Archbishops of, see Bancroft, Richard ; Abbot, George; Laud, William
See of, 94
Capel, Sir Gamaliel, 62-3
Cardigan, Earl of, cr. 1661, see Brudenell, Lord
Carew, Sir George, 30
Henry, 30, 31
Cariola, 307
Carleton, Sir Dudley, see Dorchester, Viscount
Carlisle, James (Hay), d. 1636, first Earl of, 48, 75, 149, 177, 206
Lucy (Percy), his second wife, Countess of, 251, 303, 304-10
Carlton, 241
Carrara, 72
Carrington, Charles (Smith), d. 1664, first Viscount 240, 243
Elizabeth (Caryll), his wife, Viscountess, 240
Carter, Mr., 170
Cary, Sir Henry, see Falkland, Viscount
Caryll, Sir Edward of Harting, d. 1609, 243
Philippa (Gage), his wife, Lady, 243
Sir John of Warnham, d. 1613, his brother, 243
Mary (Cotton), his sister-in-law, Lady, 243
Sir John of Harting, his nephew, 243
Mary (Dormer), his niece, Lady, 243
Cashel, Thomas (Somerset), d. 1651, Viscount, 110
Casse, Edmund, 52

Castlehaven, Mervyn (Audley), d. 1631, second Earl of, 240
Cavendish, Lord, see Devonshire, Earl of
Caversham, 74
Cecil, see Exeter, Earls of; Salisbury, Earls of; Burghley, Lord; Roos, Lord
Sir Robert, see Salisbury, first Earl of
Elizabeth (Brooke), his wife, Lady, 38
Lady Frances, his daughter, 38, 51, 73
Cephalonia, 313
Chalcedon, Richard Smith, d. 1655, Bishop of, 237–8, 244
Chaloner, Sir Thomas, d. 1615, 207
Chamberlain, John, 153, 304
Chamberlaynes of Shirburn, 243
Chambord, 135
Chandos, Grey (Brydges), d. 1621, fifth Lord, 206
Chapman, George, d. 1634, 253
Chardstock, 84
Charles I, King, 21, 82–3, 97, 107, 110, chap. xiv, xvii–xx passim
Charlton, 128, 160, 161
Chatham, 298
Cheke, Sir Hatton, 207
Chelmsford, 182
Chester, 67
Constableship of, 209
Chewton Magna, 243
Chichester, 207
See of, 10
Chillington, 243
Chillingworth, William, d. 1644, 117
China, kingdom of, 58
Chioggia, 151
Chiswick, 11
Christian IV, King of Denmark, 67
Clanricarde, Richard (Burke) d. 1635, fourth Earl of, 207, 293
Frances (Walsingham), his wife, Countess of, 293
Ulick, d. 1657, his son, fifth Earl of, 293
Clarendon, Edward (Hyde), d. 1674, first Earl of, 5, 130, 131, 136
Clarke, Mrs. Margaret, 60
Clifford, see Cumberland, Earls of
Clifton, 29
Clowerwall, 202
Clun, 163
Cobham, Henry (Brooke), d. 1619, eighth Lord, 38

Elizabeth, his sisters, see Cecil
Frances, his sister, see Stourton
Cockington, 30
Coke, Sir Edward, d. 1634, 28, 114, 175–6, 177, 191, 260
Lady Elizabeth, his wife, see Hatton
Frances, his daughter, see Purbeck
Coke, Sir John, d. 1644, 262, chap. xviii passim
Marie (Powell), his first wife, 282–4, 287
Joan (Gore), his second wife, 287
Sir Francis of Trusley, his brother, 282
Robert, his brother, 262
Thomas, his brother, 137–9
Cole Orton, 108
Coleshill, 67
Colleton, John, 276
Colville, James, 319
Colyton, 274
Compton, 31
Compton, Sir Thomas, 180
Constable, Henry, 240
Mary (Dormer), his wife, 240
Katherine, his daughter, see Fairfax
Henry, his son, see Dunbar, Viscount
Constantinople, 55, 139, 144–6, 184, 256
Castle of the Seven Towers, 146
Mosque of Ahmed, 144
Mosque of Rustem Pasha, 144
Mosque of the Yeni-Valide, 145
Porta Aurea, 146
Conway Castle, 279
Conway, Edward, d. 1631, first Viscount, 206, 213, chap. xvii, xviii, passim, 300
Dorothy (Tracy), his first wife, Lady, 263
Catherine (Hueriblock), his second wife, Lady, 263, 278–80
Edward, d. 1655, his son, second Viscount, 263–7
Brilliana, his daughter, see Harley
Frances, his daughter, see Pelham
Sir Fulke, d. 1624, his brother, 277
Conyers, Francis, 263
Cope, Sir Walter, d. 1614, 58, 68, 69, 73, 192, 206
Copernicisme, 221
Coriton, Scipio, 30

Cornwallis, Lady Catherine, 62
Coryatt, Thomas, d. 1617, 106
Cosin, John, d. 1672, Bishop of Durham, 311
Cottington, Sir Francis, d. 1652, 261
Cotton of Warblington, John, 84, 86–8, 91
Mary, his sister, see Caryll
Cotton, Sir Robert, d. 1631, 138, 227
Coughton, 275
Courten, Sir William, d. 1636, 170, 209
Coventry, 67
Cowper, Richard, 88
Coxden, 82, 84, 85, 91
Crake, Mr., 294
Cranborne, Viscount, see Salisbury, Earl of
Cranborne Chase, 2
Cranborne Manor, 36
Cranfield, Sir Lionel, see Middlesex, Earl of
Crashaw, Rawlie, 200
Crawshaw, Richard, 200, 248, 255
William, 200,
Craven, Sir William, d. 1618, 207
Crewe, Sir Randolph, d. 1646, 320
Crewe, Sir Thomas, d. 1634, 191
Cromwell, Sir Oliver, 207
Crosfield, Thomas, 300
Croydon, 311
Cumana, 204
Cumberland, George (Clifford), d. 1605, third Earl of, 40
Lady Anne, his daughter, see Dorset
Francis, d. 1641, his brother, fourth Earl of, 162
Henry, d. 1643, his nephew, fifth and last Earl of, 7
Cwchwillan, 225

Dallison, Sir Roger, 171, 329
Darcy, Lord, see Rivers, Earl
Davenant, Sir William, d, 1668, 295
Daventry, 67
Davis, Captain, 30
Davys, Sir John, 26
Deane, Sir James, 294
Delawarr, Thomas (West), d. 1618, twelfth Lord, 195, 199
Delphi, 146
Denbigh, William (Feilding), d. 1643, first Earl of, 184–5
Susan (Villiers), his wife, Countess of, 184, 251, 297
Dene, 12

Denny, Lord, see Norwich, Earl of
Deptford, 282
Derby, William (Stanley), d. 1642, sixth Earl of, 113
Derwentwater, 243
Devereux, see Essex, Earls of
Devonshire, William (Cavendish), d. 1628, second Earl of, 59, 208
D'Ewes, Sir Simonds, d. 1650, 82–3, 84–6, 111, 291
Digby, Sir John, see Bristol, Earl of
Sir Kenelm, d. 1665, his cousin, 304, 313
Dirleton, Lord see Kellie, Earl of
Ditchley, 25
Dixon, Robert, 263
Dobbinson, Ralph, 69
Doddridge, Sir John, d. 1628, 206
Dolman, Alban, 69
Dominica, 307
Doncaster, Viscount, see Carlisle, Earl of
Donhead Andrew, 30
Donhead St. Mary, 30
Donne, John, d. 1631, Dean of St. Paul's, 77, 97, 100–4, 107, 200, 248–9
Dorchester, 85, 133
Dorchester, Dudley (Carleton), d. 1632, first Viscount, 107, 121, 139, 140, 143, 157, 163, 211, 212–14, 257, 297
Dorset, Thomas (Sackville), d. 1608, first Earl of, 3, 37, 65, 70, 71, 95, 102–5
Robert, d. 1609, his son, second Earl of, 103
Lady Jane, his daughter, see Montague
Lady Mary, his daughter, see Abergavenny
Richard, d. 1624, his grand son, third Earl of, 102–5, 113
Anne (Clifford), his grand-daughter-in-law, Countess of, 4–5, 105
Edward, d. 1652, his grandson, fourth Earl of, 102–5, 113
Dorye, William, 88
Douai, 237
Dover, 67, 207
Dover Castle, constableship of, 302
Downing, James, 86
Drake, Sir Francis, 183
Sir John, 274
Drayton, Michael, d. 1631, 105–7, 255

Drummond, William, 105
Drury, Sir Drue, d. 1617, 206
Sir Robert, 100, 206
Dugdale, Sir William, 108
Dunbar, George (Home), d. 1611, first Earl of, 48, 96, 163
Lady Elizabeth, his daughter, see Suffolk
Dunbar, Henry (Constable), d. 1645, first Viscount, 240, 241–2
Mary (Tufton), his wife, Viscountess, 240
John, d. 1668, his son, second Viscount, 240
Mary (Brudenell), his daughter-in-law, Viscountess, 240
Mary, his daughter, see Brudenell
Duncombe, Mr., 318
Duppa, Brian, d. 1662, Bishop of Winchester, 200
Jeffrey, 200
Dupplin, Viscount, see Kinnoull, Earl of
Durham, 42
Deanery of, 42–3

EAST GREENWICH, 192
Edmondes, Sir Thomas, d. 1639, 55, 65, 110, 165, 176
Effingham, 129
Egerton, Sir Thomas, see Ellesmere, Lord
Elizabeth, Queen of Bohemia, 80, 96, 99, 133
Ellesmere, Thomas (Egerton), d. 1617, first Lord, 55, 66, 100, 102, 112, 227, 228
Elmore, 292
Elwes, Sir Gervase, d. 1615, 323
Ely, Bishops of, see Andrewes, Lancelot; White, Francis
Emden Coach, 74
Englefield, Sir Francis, d. 1631, 243
Jane (Browne), his wife, Lady, 243
Sir Francis, d. 1656, his son, 243
Errol, Francis (Hay), d. 1631, ninth Earl of, 68
Ersfield, Anthony, 59–60
Erskine, see Kellie, Earl of; Mar, Earl of
Escrick, 125, 160
Essex, Robert (Devereux), d. 1601, second Earl of, 1, 4, 27, 46, 130, 260, 262, 285
Frances (Walsingham), his widow, see Clanricarde

Robert, d. 1646, his son, third Earl of, 98, 293
Frances (Howard), his daughter-in-law, Countess of, 98
Lady Dorothy, his daughter, see Shirley
Eton, provostship of, 209, 212–14
Eure, William, d. 1646, fourth Lord, 207
Ralph, d. 1640, his son, 240
Catherine (Arundell), his daughter-in-law, 240
Evelyn, John, 147, 161
Evesham, 262
Exeter, 66
Exeter, Thomas (Cecil), d. 1623, first Earl of, 38, 166–7
Frances (Brydges), his second wife, Countess of, 167
Lady Elizabeth, his daughter, see Hatton
Lady Lucy, his daughter, see Winchester
Lady Mary, his daughter, see Norwich
Elizabeth (Manners), his daughter-in-law, see Roos
William, d. 1618, his grandson and heir, see Roos
Lady Diana, his grand-daughter, see Oxford
Eyston, Mr., 150

FAIRFAX OF CAMERON, Thomas, d. 1640, first Lord, 28
Fairfax of Elmeley, Thomas, d. 1636, first Viscount, 240
Katharine (Constable), his wife, Viscountess, 240
Thomas, d. 1641, his son, second Viscount, 240
Alathea (Howard), his daughter-in-law, Viscountess, 240
Falkland, Henry (Cary), d. 1633, first Viscount, 207, 288
Elizabeth (Tanfield), his wife, Viscountess, 276, 305
Lucius, d. 1643, his son, second Viscount, 117, 276
Fane, Sir Thomas, 67
Fanshawe, Sir Henry, d. 1616, 81
Sir Richard, d. 1666, his son, 81, 207
Anne (Harrison), his daughter-in-law, Lady, 81
Farnham, 86
Farnham Castle, 77

Farringford, 168
Fawkes, Guy, 12
Faygate, 90
Feilding, see Denbigh, Earls of
Felgate, Mr., 196
Fell, Dr. Samuel, d. 1649, 287
Felton, John, 265, 299
Fenton, Viscount, see Kellie, Earl of
Fenwick, of Fenwick, Sir John, d. 1658, 243
  Catherine (Slingsby), his wife, Lady, 243
Ferdinand II, Emperor, 156
Ferdinand I, Grand Duke of Tuscany, 152-3
Ferne, Sir John, d. 1610, 41-2, 44
Ferrar, John, 193, 195, 208
  Nicholas, the elder, 200, 208
  Nicholas the younger, 200, 221
Finch, Sir Henry, d. 1625, 174, 324
  Sir Moyle, 207, 318
Finet, Sir John, d. 1614, 164-75
Fitzherbert of Swynnerton, William, 243
  Bridget (Caryll), his mother, 243
Fleetwood, Sir Miles, 170
  Sir William, 207
Fletcher, Phineas, 106
Florence, 136, 139, 153
  Pitti Palace at, 153
Fontana, Annibale, 147
Fontana dei Serpi, 139
Fontmell, 31
Fore, Paul, 326
Frederick, Elector Palatine, 80, 96, 99, 188
Freeman, Sir Ralph, 214
Frescheville, Sir Peter, 194
Fryer, Dr. John, 318
Fulham, 311
Fullerton, Sir James, 258
Fulwood, Humphrey, 297
  Mrs. Mary, 283

GAETA, 139
Gage of Firle, Sir John, d. 1633, 243
  Lady Penelope (Darcy), his wife, 243
  Edward, 30, 31
  Mr., 150
Garnett, Henry, S.J., 65
Garradon, 62
Garraway, Sir William, 206
Gascoigne of Barnbow, Sir John, d. 1637, 243
  Anne (Ingleby), his wife, Lady, 243
Gates, Sir Thomas, 199

Geneva, 76, 230
Gerard of Bryn, Sir Thomas, d. 1621, 242
  Mary (Browne formerly Dormer), his wife, Lady, 242, 244
  Sir Thomas, d. 1630, his son, 242
  Frances (Molyneux), his daughter-in-law, 242
Gerard, Thomas, d. 1618, first Lord, 122
Gerbeir, Balthasar, 183-4
Gerrard, George, 165
Ghent, 152, 263
Giffard, of Chillington, Walter, d. 1632, 243
Gilling, 240
Gloucester, 284, 292-3
Glover, Sir Thomas, 55
Goa, 133
Goadby, 109
Godalming, 86, 88
  King's Arms at, 88
Gogar, 48
Gondomar, Diego Count of, 92, 119, 192, 268
Goodere, Sir Henry, d. 1627, 105, 107, 221
Goodman, Godfrey, d. 1656, Bishop of Gloucester, 24
Gorell Gate, 25
Gorges, Sir Ferdinando, d. 1647, 59
  William, 318
Gorhambury, 117
Goring, Sir George, 207, 257, 309-10
Goring of Burton, Sir William, 243
Gorthy, 51
Gosnold, Bartholomew, d. 1607, 56
Gowrie Conspiracy, 14
Gratz, 156
Gray, Patrick, d. 1612, sixth Lord, 23
Greene, William, 69
Greenefield, Barnard, 30
Greenwich, 140, 163, 172
Greenwich Park, 163
Grenada, 307
Grenville, Sir Richard, 160
Greville, Sir Fulke, see Brooke, Lord
Guadaloupe, 307
Gudgen, Peter, 43-4
Guiana, 203-5
Guise, Duke of, 63
Guise, Sir William, 292
  Sir Christopher, 292
Gunpowder Plot, 12-13, 14, 20, 37, 92
Gwyn, Owen, 225

HACKET, JOHN, d. 1670, Bishop of Lichfield, 11, 76–7
Hague, The, 133, 134
Hall Court, 282, 284
Hamilton, James, d. 1625, second Marquis of, 176
James, d. 1649, his son, third Marquis of, 308
Hammond, Dr. John, d. 1617, 212
Hampden, Sir Edmund, 150, 318
Hampton Court, 45, 134
high stewardship of, 302
Hampton Court Conference, 20
Hanley, 29
Harcourt, Robert, d. 1631, 203
Harington of Exton, John Lord, d. 1613, 105
Harington, Sir John, d. 1612, 75
Harkerk Chapel, 245
Harley, Sir Robert, d. 1656, 264–73
Brilliana (Conway), his wife, Lady, 264–72
Harting, 243
Hartingfordbury, 172
Harvey, William, d. 1657, 116–17
Harwood, Sir Edward, d. 1632, 165
Haslewood, 243
Hastings, Henry, see Huntingdon, Earl of
Hatfield, parish of, 60
Hatfield House, 1, 37, 60–3, 76
Hatfield Broadoak, 190
Hatton, Sir Christopher, 259
Hatton, Lady Elizabeth, 172
Hawthornden, 105
Hay, Sir James, see Carlisle, Earl of
Honora (Denny), his first wife, Lady, 304
Francis, see Errol, Earl of
George, see Kinnoull, Earl of
Heidelberg, 134
Hengrave Hall, 34–5
Henrietta Maria, Queen, 5, 251, 258, 297, 304–10
Henry, Prince of Wales, 42–3, 50–1, 79–83
Henry III, King of France, 155
Henry IV, King of France, 155
Herbert, see Pembroke, Earls of
Herbert of Cherbury, Edward, d. 1648, first Lord, 107
Magdalen, his mother (Lady Danvers), 97, 221
George, his brother, d. 1633, 97, 221–4
Herbert, Lord, see Worcester, fifth Earl of

Herbert, Sir Arnold, 212
Sir John, d. 1614, 113
Sir Thomas, 133
Hexham, 123
Hicks, Sir Baptist, 6, 206
High Easter, 190
Hillyarde, Nicholas, 68
Lawrence, his son, 68
Hitchcock, George, 90
Hobart, Sir Henry, d. 1625, 176, 330
Hobbes, Thomas, d. 1679, 117
Hodges, Mr., 296
Holde, Christopher, 90
Holland, Henry (Rich), d. 1649, Earl of, 123, 308–10
Holles, Sir John, 262
Home, Sir George, see Dunbar, Earl of
Honthorst, Gerard, 143
Hooker, Richard, d. 1600, 20
Horsham, 89, 91
Howard, see Arundel, Earls of; Berkshire, Earls of; Norfolk, Duke of; Northampton, Earl of; Nottingham, Earls of; Stafford, Viscount
Thomas, see Norfolk, fourth Duke of
Lord Henry, his brother, see Northampton
Lady Jane, his sister, see Westmoreland
Philip, his son, see Arundel
Lord Thomas, his son, see Suffolk
Lord William, his son, 30, 31, 125, 128
Elizabeth (Dacre), his daughter-in-law, 128
Elizabeth, his grand-daughter, see Bedingfeld
Lady Margaret, his daughter, see Sackville
Howard of Bindon, Thomas, d. 1610, third Viscount, 129, 160
Howard de Walden, Lord, see Suffolk, second Earl of
Howard of Escrick, Edward, d. 1675, his brother, first Lord 125
Howby, 109
Huddington, 43, 275
Humphreys, Mr., 164
Hunloke, Sir Henry, d. 1648, 243
Huncks, Hercules, 278
Huntingdon, Henry (Hastings), d. 1643, fifth Earl of, 26
Hutton, Matthew, d. 1606, Archbishop of York, 41

Hyde, Edward, *see* Clarendon, Earl of

INGLEBY OF RIPLEY, JOHN, 43-4
Lady Anne (Neville), his mother, 44-5
Anne, his niece, *see* Gascoigne
Ingram, Sir Arthur, d. 1642, 207, 210, 258
Irnham, 241
Iron Acton, 243
Isle of Rhé, 291
Isle of Wight, 23, 59, 278-9

JAMES I, KING, chap. ii, iii, vii, ix and *passim*
James, William, d. 1617, Bishop of Durham, 42
Jamestown, 195
Jenman, William, 87
Jerningham, Sir Henry, d. 1646, 243
Eleanor (Dacre), his mother, Lady, 243
Eleanor (Throckmorton), his wife, Lady, 243
Anne, his sister, *see* Arundell
Jerusalem, 126
Jessop, Dr., 30
Jones, Inigo, d. 1652, 99, 100, 107, 120, 134-6, 138
Jonson, Ben, d. 1637, 100, 119, 295
Junius, Francis, 142
Juxon, Thomas, 200

KELLIE, THOMAS (Erskine), d. 1639, first Earl of, 48-9, 267, 269
Kellison, Dr. Matthew, d. 1642, 237
Kendal, Edwin, 196
Captain Miles, 197-8
Kensington, 58
Kent, Elizabeth (Tabot), Countess of, 131
Ker, Robert, *see* Somerset, Earl of
Ker, Sir Robert, 308-9
Keyneston, 29
Kiddington Pond, 241
Kilvington, 241
King, John, d. 1621, Bishop of London, 200, 247
King's Lynn, 207
Kinnoull, George (Hay), d. 1634, first Earl of, 308
Kitson, Sir Thomas, d. 1602, 34
Elizabeth (Cornwallis), his wife, Lady, 34
Mary, his daughter, *see* Rivers
Knaresborough, 43

Knevet, Sir John, 128
Knightley, Sir Valentine, 207
Knole, 5, 102-5, 143
Venetian room at, 28, 103
Green Gallery at, 31
Knollys, Lord, *see* Banbury, Earl of
Knollys, Sir Thomas, 45-6

LACHIE, EDWARD, 87-8
Lake, Arthur, d. 1626, Bishop of Bath and Wells, 295
Lake, Sir Thomas, d. 1630, his brother, 113, 165, 168, 172, 260
Elizabeth, his niece, *see* Roos
Lambeth, 71, 96, 298
Lancaster, Sir James, d. 1618, 294
Lane, John, 86-7
Langdale, Sir Marmaduke, 243
Lanherne, 243
La Rochelle, 267, 297
La Tremouille, Duchesse de, 166
Laud, William, d. 1645, Archbishop of Canterbury, 107, 228, 296, 311-12
Lavardin, Jacques de, 234
Laycock, 75
Leake, Sir John, 257
Ledbury, 287
Lee, Sir Henry, d. 1610, 25
Leghorn, 72
Leicester, Robert (Dudley), Earl of, 4
Leicester, Robert (Sydney), d. 1626, first Earl of, 257
Robert, d. 1677, his son, second Earl of, 304
Dorothy (Percy), his daughter-in-law, Countess of, 304
Lennox, Esme (Stuart), d. 1583, first Duke of, 23
Ludovick, d. 1624, his son, second Duke of, 176
Ley, Sir James, *see* Marlborough, Earl of
Leyden, 73, 106, 143
Lichfield, 67, 95
Limbury, 29
Lincoln, 95
Lisbon, 235
Lisle, Lord, *see* Leicester, Earl of
Little Gidding, 221
Lockum, 46
London, *passim*
Arundel House, 127, 137, 140-4
Austin Friars, 282
Bishopsgate Street, 90
Mouthe Tavern in, 90

London, Bridewell Dock, 87
Charing Cross, 161, 170, 323
Charterhouse, 161
Denmark House, 306
Drury House, 100
Fleet Street, conduit in, 87
Eagle and Child in, 87
Gray's Inn Hall, 117
Jewel House, 168
Lincoln's Inn, 87
Middle Temple, 253
Newgate Market, 318
Northampton House, 134, 160
Philpott Lane, 195
St. Bennet Sherehog, 200
St. Dunstan-in-the-West, 103
St. Lawrence Jewry, 256, 270
St. Martin's Lane, 173, 263, 288
St. Mary Overies, 87
St. Paul's, 218
St. Paul's Cross, 219
St. Paul's Deanery, 219
Salisbury House, 2
Shoe Lane, 88
Smithfield, 234
Somerset House, 111
Suffolk House, 174
Tottenham High Cross, 256, 287
Wallingford House, 182
Whitefriars, 87
Whitehall, 15–16, 173
Banqueting House in, 253
York House, 183, 185
Lovelace, Arms of, 85
Lovell, Lady, 244
Lower, Mr., 196
Lucca, 139
Luddington, 279
Luis de Granada, 216
Lulworth Castle, 161
Lumley, John, d. 1609, Lord, 141, 227
Richard, d. 1661?, his cousin, Viscount, 240

Madrid, 133
Malaga, 90
Malling, John, 245
Manchester, Henry (Montagu), d. 1642, first Earl of, 28
Manners, *see* Rutland, Earls of
Sir Oliver, 62
Mannock, Sir Francis, d. 1634, 143
Mansfield, Sir Robert, 57
Mantua, Court of, 120

Mar, John (Erskine), d. 1634, seventh Earl of, 48–9, 267
Margaret Marsh, 29
Margarita, 204
Markham, Sir Griffin, 65
Marlborough, James (Ley), d. 1629, first Earl of, 28
Marlborough, parsonage at, 75, 297
Marwood, 109
Mary, Queen of Scots, 64
Maryland, 27
Mason, Captain, 299
Mathew, Tobie, d. 1626, Archbishop of York, 41–2, 248
Sir Tobie, his son, 97, 102, 150, 248–52, 318
Maupas, Charles, Bishop of Blois, 109
Maximilian, Duke of Bavaria, 153
Meadhole, 59
Meddes, James, 278
Melbourne Hall, 282
Melbury, 30
Melling, Alderman, 198
Melton Mowbray, 109
Mercer, Christopher, 31
Mere Park, 29
Mestre, 305
Meynell, Thomas, d. 1653, 243
Winefred (Pudsey), his wife, 243
Michelgrove, 242
Michell, Sir Francis, 318
Middlemore, Mrs., 87
Middlesex, Lionel (Cranfield), d. 1645, first Earl of, 6, 206
Milan, 134, 136, 147, 152
Duomo of, 147
San Celso, 147
Milbourne, Dr., 81
Millington, Captain, 325
Milton, John, d. 1674, 102, 295
Molin, Niccolo, 63
Molyneux of Maryborough, Richard, d. 1636, first Viscount, 240, 243
Mary (Caryll), his wife, Viscountess, 240
Monemvasia, 90
Monke, William, 30
Monson, John, 166–7
Montacute House, 191
Montagu of Boughton, Edward, d. 1644, first Lord, 28, 168, 269
Montagu, Henry, *see* Manchester, Earl of
Montagu, Richard, d. 1641, Bishop of Chichester, 294, 311

Montague, Anthony Mary (Browne) d. 1629, second Viscount, 12, 239
Jane (Sackville), his wife, Viscountess, 240
Magdalen (Dacre), his grandmother, Viscountess, 244
Jane, his sister, see Englefield
Mary, his daughter, see Wiltshire
Mary, his daughter, see Petre
Francis, d, 1682, his son, third Viscount, 240
Elizabeth (Somerset), his daughter-in-law, Viscountess, 240
Monteagle, William (Parker), d. 1622, fourth Lord, 207
Elizabeth (Tresham), his wife, Lady, 240
Catherine, his daughter, see Savage
Henry, d. 1635, his son, fifth Lord, 240
Philippa (Caryll), his daughter-in-law, Lady, 240
Montgomery, Earl of, see Pembroke, Earl of
Montserrat, 307
Moore, Sir Edward, 318
Moore, Richard (of Bermuda), 197
Moore, Richard (of Winchester), 296
Mordaunt, Lord, see Peterborough, Earl of
More of More Place, Cresacre, d. 1649, 243
Helen (Gage), his wife, 243
More of Fawley, Sir Henry, d. 1633, 243
Elizabeth, his sister, see Blount
More, Sir John, 73
Morley, Lord, see Monteagle, Lord
Morrall, Roger, 51–2
Mortlake, 183
Morton, Sir Albertus, d. 1625, 213–14, 260, 281
Morton, Anne Lady, 120
Much Marcle, 282
Mulgrave, Edmund (Sheffield), d. 1646, first Earl of, 42, 211
Munich, 153
Alte Residenz at, 153
Murray, Sir David, d. 1629, 51–2, 82, 107, 170, 207
Mungo, 319
Dr. Thomas, d. 1623, 213
Mynne, Mr., 213

Naples, 121, 139, 150, 167, 191
Viceroy of, 121
Nantwich, 67
Naunton, Sir Robert, d. 1635, 201, 214, 261, 285–6
Naworth Castle, 128
Neile, Richard, d. 1640, Bishop of Winchester, 311
Nethersole, Sir Francis, d. 1659, 307–10
Neville, Henry, see Abergavenny, Lord
Nevis, 307
Newborough, 242
New England, 56
Newfoundland, 6
Newhall, 182–4
Newmarket, 26, 170, 209, 323
The King's House at, 209
Newnham Paddox, 184
Newport, Anne (Boteler), Countess of, 251
Newton, Sir Adam, d. 1630, 42–3, 50
Nibley, 192
Nicollson, John, 315–17
William, 315
Norfolk, Thomas (Howard), fourth Duke of, 128
Norreys, Sir John, 46
North, Sir John, 258
Northampton, Henry (Howard), d. 1614, Earl of, 4, 7, 31, 45, 125–8, 140, 159–60
Northumberland, Henry (Percy), d. 1632, ninth Earl of, 305
Algernon, d. 1668, his son, tenth Earl of, 304, 308
Lady Dorothy, his daughter, see Leicester
Lady Lucy, his daughter, see Carlisle
Lady Eleanor, his sister, see Powis
North-West Passage, 58
Norton, Sir Daniel, 299, 300
Sir Richard, 296
Norwich, Edward (Denny), d. 1630, Earl of, 304, 310
Mary (Cecil), his wife, Countess of, 304
Honora, his daughter, see Hay
Nottingham, Charles (Howard), d. 1624, first Earl of, 4, 125–6, 208
Charles, d. 1642, his son, second Earl of, 125
Nunwell, 23
Nys, Daniel, 143

ODIHAM, 318
Odstock, 243
Ogle, Sir John, d. 1640, 207, 270
Oglander, Sir John, d. 1655, 23, 24, 278
Olivares, Count-Duke of, 301
Orinoco, the, 91, 209
Orleans, 90
Ostend, 46
Oswestry, 170
Overbury, Sir Thomas, d. 1614, 98-9, 112, 113, 141
Owen, Cadwallader, 270
Owen, Hugh, 64
Oxford, 95, 300
  Christ Church, 286
  Magdalen College, 294
  Merton College, 295
  Oriel College, 271
  Queen's College, 300
  University College, 95
  Worcester College, 134, 135
Oxford, Diana (Cecil), Countess of, 167, 180

PACKINGE, FRANCIS, 30
Padua, 104, 132, 134, 136, 139, 305, 318
  Santa Giustina at, 104
Paget, William, d. 1629, fourth Lord, 206
Painter, Rowland, 203
Palladio, Andrea, 134-6, 157
Parham, Sir Edward, 91-2
Paris, 145, 152, 166, 235, 307
Parker, Martin, 235
Parpaglia, Abbot Vincenzo, 191
Paulet, see Winchester, Marquesses of; Wiltshire, Earl of
Pelham, Sir William, 288
  Frances (Conway), his wife, Lady, 288
Pembroke, William (Herbert), d. 1630, third Earl of, 43, 131, 177, 257, 291, 309-10
  Mary (Talbot), his wife, Countess of, 131
  Philip, d. 1650, his brother, fourth Earl of, 5, 48, 49, 79, 113, 308
  Anne (Clifford), his sister-in-law, Countess of, see Dorset
Penrhyn, 262
Penshurst, 257
Pepwell, Captain, 176
Pera, 55
Perceval, Sir Philip, 300

Percy, Henry, see Northumberland, ninth Earl of
  Henry, his second son, 308
  Thomas, 69
Perkins, Sir Christopher, d. 1622, 207
  William, d. 1602, 226
Pesaro, Zuane, 227
Peterborough, John (Mordaunt), d. 1642, first Earl of, 120
Petre, Sir John, 30
Petre, William, d. 1637, second Lord, 207, 240, 241
  Catherine (Somerset), his wife, Lady, 240
  Mary, his daughter, see Teynham,
  Robert, d. 1638, his son, third Lord, 240
  Mary (Browne), his daughter-in-law, Lady, 240
  Sir George, his brother, 150
Pett, Phineas, d. 1647, 207, 211-12, 298
  Richard, his son, 298
Petty, William, 146
Petworth, 305
Pevensey, honour of, 104
Phelips, Sir Robert, d. 1638, 191
Pierson, Thomas, 127, 271
Pilgrimage of Grace, 61
Pitt, William, 38
Plot, Robert, 90
Plowden, Francis, d. 1652, 243
  Mary (Fermor), his wife, 243
Plumpton, 44
Plymouth, 58, 59, 318
Popham, Sir John, d. 1607, 58
Porter, Endymion, d. 1649, 306
  Olivia (Boteler), his wife, 251
Portsdown, 299
Portsmouth, 59, 60, 293-9
  high stewardship of, 59
  High Street, 299
Pory, John, d. 1635, 193
Pound, Henry, 87
Powis, William (Herbert), d. 1656, first Lord, 240
  Eleanor (Percy), his wife, Lady, 240
  Lucy, his daughter, see Abington
Poyntz of Iron Acton, 243
Preston, 287
Price, Rev. Daniel, d. 1631, 193
Pudsey, Ambrose, 315-17
  Mrs., his mother, 316
Purbeck, John (Villiers), d. 1657, Viscount, 184-5, 252

Purbeck, Frances (Coke), his wife, Viscountess, 185
Purbeck, marble, 146
Pym, John, d. 1643, 80

RADCLIFFE, see Sussex, Earls of
   Sir Francis, d. 1622, 212, 243
   Mary, his daughter, see Widdrington
Ragley, 261, 270
Raleigh, Sir Walter, d. 1618, 2, 15, 16, 56, 79–80, 91–2, 114, 131–2, 158, 209
Randall, Mr., 325
Ratcliff, 56
Raymond, Thomas, 290
Reed, Fulke, 263
Rich, see Holland, Earl of; Warwick, Earl of
Rich, Sir Nathaniel, d. 1636, 6, 198
Richelieu, Cardinal de, 137, 301
Rigby, John, 96
Ripley Castle, 43
Rivers, Thomas (Darcy), d. 1639, first Earl of, 34, 241
   Mary (Kitson), his wife, Countess, 34
   Lady Penelope, his daughter, see Gage
   Lady Elizabeth, his daughter, see Savage
Rivers, John (Savage), d. 1654, second Earl, 240
   Catherine (Parker), his wife, Countess, 240
   Jane, his sister, see Winchester
   Dorothy, his sister, see Berkshire
Robartes, Mr., 141
Rochester, Viscount, see Somerset, Earl of
Rock Savage, 243
Roe, Sir Thomas, d. 1644, 144–6
Rome, 137, 138–9, 145, 150, 154, 167
   Orso del Oro, 139
   Settimana Santa in, 138
   Temple of Vesta, 140
Roos, William (Cecil), d. 1618, sixth Lord, 142, 166–7, 181
   Elizabeth (Lake), his wife, Lady, 166–7
   Katharine (Manners), his cousin, Lady, see Buckingham
Roper, see Teynham, Lords
Rotterdam, 133, 286
Rous, John, 291
Royston, 9, 26, 49
Rubens, Peter Paul, 142

Rudolf II, Emperor, 156
Russell, Edward, see Bedford, third Earl of
Ruthin, 225
Rutland, Francis (Manners), d. 1632, sixth Earl of, 62, 181, 240, 276
   Frances (Knevet), his wife, 181
   Lady Katharine, his daughter, see Buckingham
   Roger, d. 1612, his brother, fifth Earl of, 62

SACKVILLE, SIR THOMAS, see Dorset, first Earl of
   Lady Margaret (Howard), his daughter-in- law, 103
   Thomas, his son, 105
Saffron Walden, 160
St. Albans, 67
St. Albans, Francis (Bacon), d. 1626, Viscount, 32, 54, 113–20, 150, 174–6, 207, 208, 213–15, 248
St. Christopher's, 307
St. Giles', 36, 49
St. Leonard's Forest, 89
St. Lucia, 307
St. Vincent, 307
Salisbury, 9, 91
Salisbury, Robert (Cecil), d. 1612, first Earl of, 1–4, 30, chap. iii–vi passim, 98, 117, 138, 166
   William, d. 1647, his son, second Earl of, 38, 50–2, 122–3, 150, 168–76, 206, 308
   Catherine (Howard), his daughter-in-law, Countess of, 51
Sampford, 69
San Cassiano, 132, 134, 136
Sanderson, John, 256
Sandys, Sir Edwin, d. 1629, 195, 198, 201, 208
Sandys of the Vyne, William, d. 1629, fourth Lord, 294
San Thomé, 209
Santon Downham, 291
Saunders, John, 44
Savage, Sir John, d. 1615, 243
   Sir Thomas, d. 1635, his son, first Viscount, 240, 243
   Elizabeth (Darcy), his daughter-in-law, Viscountess, 240
   John, his grandson, see Rivers Earl
Savile, Sir Henry, d. 1622, 212
Scanderbeg, 235
Scrope, Lord, see Sunderland, Earl of

Seddon, Peter, 291
Sefton, 243
Sefton Church, 245
Selden, John, d. 1654, 134, 227
Semley, 29
Sevenoaks, 103
Shaftesbury, 64
Sheffield, Lord, *see* Mulgrave, Earl of
Sheffield, 131
Sheldon, Edward, 243, 270
  Mrs. Edward, 270
  Ralph, 30
Shelley, Sir John, d. 1644?, 242
Shifnal, 126
Ships,
  Abigail, 195
  Blessing, 195, 196
  Bona Nova, 195
  Destiny, 131
  Diana, 203
  Edwin, 197
  Margaret, 202
  Mayflower, 106, 209
  Plough, 196
  Princess Royal, 133
  Speedwell, 106
  Star, 196
Shirburn Castle, 243
Shireburn, Edward, 142, 165
Shirley, Sir George, d. 1622, 242
  Lady Dorothy (Devereux), his wife, 242
Shrewsbury, Gilbert (Talbot), d. 1616, seventh Earl of, 68, 131-9, *seq*, 142
  Mary (Cavendish), his wife, Countess of, 68, 131, 207
  Lady Alathea, his daughter, *see* Arundel
  Lady Mary, his daughter, *see* Pembroke
  Lady Elizabeth, his daughter, *see* Kent
  George, d. 1630, his cousin, ninth Earl of, 239
Siena, 136
Slingsby, Sir Guildford, 287
Smith, Sir Francis, d. 1629, 243
  Sir Charles, his son, *see* Carrington, Viscount
Sock Durys, 29
Somers, Sir George, d. 1610, 196
Somerset, Robert (Ker), d. 1645, Earl of, 24, 50, 98-9, 109-13, 141, 159
Somerset, *see* Worcester, Earls of; Cashel, Viscount

Southampton, 57
Southampton, Henry (Wriothesley), d. 1624, third Earl of, 62, 96, 107, 193, 208, 295
  Mary (Browne), his mother, Countess of, 62
  Lady Catherine, his aunt, *see* Cornwallis
  Lady Mary, his aunt, *see* Arundell of Wardour
Southsea Castle, 299
Southwark, 86, 88
  King's Head, in, 86-7
  White Horse, in, 89
Southwell, Robert, S.J., 254
Southwick, 299
Spa, 133
Spaldington, 44
Spelman, Sir Henry, d. 1641, 227
Spiller, Robert, 126
Spithead, 60
Stafford, Henry d. 1637, fourth Lord, 240
  William (Howard), d. 1680, his brother-in-law, Viscount, 125, 132
Stallenge, Lady, 292
Stanhope, Sir Michael, 67
  Sir Philip, 211
Stapleton, Lady, 75
Stapleton of Carlton, Gilbert, d. 1636, 241, 243
  Eleanor (Gascoigne), his wife, 243
Staunton, Harold, 242
Stella, 243
Stephens, Walter, 271
Stoke by Nayland, 243
Stone, 67
Stonor of Stonor, Sir Francis, 243
  Cecily (Chamberlayne), his mother, Lady, 244
Stourton, John, d. 1588, ninth Lord, 65
  Frances (Brooke), his wife, Lady, 65
  Edward, d. 1633, his brother, ninth Lord, 30, 240, 241
  Frances (Tresham), his sister-in-law, Lady, 240
Stourton, Robert, 207
Strachey, William, 56, 204
Strafford, Thomas (Wentworth), d. 1641, first Earl of, 183, 258, 288
Strasbourg, 134
Stroud, Sir William, 66
Stukeley, Sir Lewis, d. 1620, 91-2

Suffolk, Thomas (Howard), d. 1626, first Earl of, 4, 50–1, 112, 125, 128, chap. x. *passim*, 319–30
Catherine (Knevet), his wife, Countess of, 51, 128, chap. x *passim*, 329
Theophilus, d. 1640, his son, second Earl of, 125, 163, 176, 297, 308
Elizabeth (Home), his daughter-in-law, Countess of, 163
Lady Catherine, his daughter, see Salisbury
Lady Elizabeth, his daughter, see Banbury
Lady Frances, his daughter, see Essex
Thomas, his second son, see Berkshire, Earl of
Summer Islands, see Bermuda
Sunderland, Emmanuel (Scrope), d. 1627, Earl of, 24
Sussex, Robert (Radcliffe), d. 1629, fifth Earl of, 35, 182
Suttill, Robert, 44
Swinburne, of Capheaton, Sir John, d. 1652, 243
Isabel (Tempest), his first wife, Lady, 243
Anne (Blount), his second wife, Lady, 243
Syston, 6

Tarleton, Elizabeth, 245
Tawstock, 177
Tempest of Stella, Sir Nicholas, d. 1626, 243
Isabel (Lambton), his wife, Lady, 243
Sir Thomas, d. 1641, his son, 243
Isabel, his grand-daughter, see Swinburne
Tempest of Broughton, Stephen, 241
Tesimond, Oswald, S.J., 65
Teynham, John (Roper), d. 1618, first Lord, 241
Christopher, d. 1625, his son, second Lord, 240
Elizabeth, his daughter, see Vaux
John, d. 1628, his grandson, third Lord, 240
Mary (Petre), his grand-daughter-in-law, Lady, 240
Thackwrey, Samuel, 44
Theobalds, 2, 9, 23, 37, 49, 52, 58, 67, 134, 211

Thewlis, John, 14, 232
Thimbleby, Sir John, 241
Thorpe, Captain, 201
Throckmorton, Sir John, 26
Sir William, 202
Throckmortons of Coughton, 275
Thurscros, Henry, 317
Tibbs, Thomas, 85
Tichborne, Sir Benjamin, d. 1629, 243
Sir Richard, d. 1657, his son, 243
Tilbury, 46
Tisbury, 30
Tomkyns, Captain, 57–8
Tournai, 32
Towcester, 67
Townsend, Sir John, 170, 207
Sir Roger, d. 1636, 304
Tracy, Anthony, 317
Tradescant, John, d. 1637?, 151, 207
Trenchard, Sir George, 30
Trent, Council of, 18
Tresham of Rushton, Francis, 275
Sir Lewis, d, 1639, his brother, 243
Elizabeth, his sister, see Monteagle
Frances, his sister, see Stourton
Mary, his sister, see Brudenell
Trevi, 140
Trevor, Sir John, 57
Trinidad, 204
Trinity House, Elder Brothers of, 207
Troy, 145–6
Trumbull, William, d. 1635, 26, 167
Trundle, John, 234
Trusley, 282
Tucker, Captain Daniel, 197
Turin, 305

Ubanke, Prebendary, 42
Upper Tadmerton, 90

Valaresso, Alvise, 17, 261
Valdes, Juan, 224
Vandyck, Sir Anthony, d. 1641, 142
Van Somer, Paul, d. 1621, 23
Vaughan, Richard, d. 1607, Bishop of London
Vaux of Harrowden, William, d. 1595, third lord, 240
Mary (Tresham), his second wife, Lady, 240
George, d. 1594, his son, 240
Elizabeth (Roper), his daughter-in-law, 240

Vaux of Harrowden, (contd.)
 Edward, d. 1662, his grandson, fourth Lord, 241
 Catherine, his grand-daughter, see Abergavenny
Vavasor, Alexander, 44
Vavasour of Haslewood, Sir Thomas, d. 1635, 243
 Ursula (Gifford), his wife, Lady
Venice, 72, 134, 136, 139, 142, 150–2, 214, 303, 305–9
 Canareggio, 150, 151, 156
 Cornaro Palace, 306
 The Giudecca, 152
 The Grand Canal, 306
 Porta degli Ormesani, 151
 Procuratio de Ultra, 305
 Rason Vecchie, Magistracy of the, 305
 San Antonio, 305
Venice, Gulf of, 121
Vercellini, Signor, 143
Vere, Sir Francis, d. 1609, 60
 Sir Horace, his brother, 206
Verney, Sir Richard, 283
Veronese, Paolo, 142
Verona, 305
 Albergo della Torre, at, 305
Verulam, Lord, see St. Albans, Viscount
Vicenza, 134–6, 141
Villiers, George Viscount, see Buckingham, Duke of
 Sir George, his father, 108
 Sir Edward, his brother, 184
 Susan, his sister, see Denbigh
 John, his brother, see Purbeck, Viscount
 Christopher, his brother, see Anglesea, Earl of
Virginia, 16, 27, 56–9, 96
 Virginia Company, 172, 195–201

WABBERTON, 87
Wadham, Nicholas, 30
Wake, Sir Isaac, d. 1632, 260
Waldegrave, Sir Edward, d. 1650, 243
 Eleanor (Lovell), his wife, Lady, 243
 Jeronyma (Jerningham), his mother, Mrs., 243
Waldegrave, Nicholas, 63
Walker, Sir Edward, 130–8
Walker, William, 315–16
Wallingford, Viscount, see Banbury, Earl of

Walmeslowe, Justice, 31
Walsingham, Sir Francis, 64, 259
Walton, 241
Walton (in Lancashire), 245
Walton, Izaak, 97, 224
Walworth, Nathan, 291
Wambroke, 83
Wandesford, Sir Christopher, 183
Warblington, 96
Ward, Captain, 157
Warder, Sir Edward, 323
Wardour Castle, 27, 28–35
Ware Park, 81
Warwick, Robert (Rich), d. 1658, second Earl of, 195, 208
Waterton, Charles, 32
 Thomas, 241
Watson, Sir Lewis, d. 1653, 168
Webb of Odstock, Sir John, d. 1680, 243
 Mary(Caryll), his wife, Lady, 243
 Catherine (Tresham), his mother, Lady, 243
Weld, Sir Humphrey, 207
Weldon, Sir Anthony, 24
Wells, Swithin, 238
Wentworth, Sir Thomas, see Strafford
West, Thomas, see Delawarr, Lord
Westminster, deanery of, 11, 95, 227
Westminster, Steps, 171
Westmoreland, Charles (Neville), d. 1601, sixth Earl of, 45
 Jane (Howard), his wife, Countess of, 45
 Lady Anne, his daughter, see Ingleby
Weston, Sir Richard (later Lord), d. 1635, 65, 297, 310
Weymouth, Captain George, 56
Whaddon, 302
Whaddon Chase, keepership of, 302
Wheelhouse, William, 43–5
 Wiliam, 44
White. Francis, d, 1638, Bishop of Ely, 200
White, Richard, 84
Whytmore, Ralph, 88
Widdrington, of Beaufront, Roger, 243
 Mary (Radcliffe), his wife, 243
Wilbraham, Sir Roger, 159
Williams, Alexander, 165
Williams, John, d. 1650, Bishop of Lincoln, 97, 107, 213, 224–9, 258, 308
Willoughby, Richard, 138

Wilmot, Sir Charles, 206
Wilton, 5, 9, 36
Wiltshire, William (Paulet), d. 1621, Earl of, 239
  Mary (Browne), his wife, Countess of, 239
Winchester, 295
  William (Paulet), d. 1629, fourth Marquess of, 11, 65, 239, 294
  Lucy (Cecil), his wife, Marchioness of, 65, 295
  William, his eldest son, see Wiltshire, Earl of
  John, d. 1675, his second son, fifth Marquess of, 240
  Jane (Savage), his daughter-in-law, Marchioness of, 240, 295
Windebank, Sir Francis, d. 1646, 261, 277
Windesley, Garth, 44
Windsor, 134, 272
Windsor, Thomas, d. 1642, sixth Lord, 240
  Catherine (Somerset), his wife, Lady, 240
Wingerworth, 243
Winters of Huddington, 43, 275
Winwood, Sir Ralph, d. 1617, 113, 120-1, 165, 260
Wittenberg, 220
Woodhall Lodge, 40
Woodleefe, Captain, 203
Woodstock, 9
Woolwich, 211
Wootton Wawen, 240, 243
Worcester, Edward (Somerset), d. 1628, fourth Earl of, 11, 239

Elizabeth (Hastings), his wife, Countess of, 239
  Henry, d. 1646, his son, first Marquess of, 240
  Elizabeth (Dormer),his daughter-in-law (Lady Herbert), 240
  Thomas, his second son, see Cashel, Viscount
  Lady Blanche, his daughter, see Arundell of Wardour
  Lady Catherine, his daughter, see Petre
  Lady Catherine, his daughter, see Windsor
Wotton, gardens at, 147
Wotton, Sir Edward, d. 1626, 70
  Sir Henry, d. 1639 his brother, 73, 107, 109, 150-6, 177, 211, 214, 260
Wriothesley, Henry, see Southampton, Earl of

YATE, SIR EDWARD, d. 1644, 243
  Catherine (Baker), his wife, Lady, 243
Yate, Ferdinando, 193-4
Yeardley, Sir George, d. 1627, 201
Yelverton, Sir Henry, d. 1629, 164
Yonge, Walter, 274
York, 41
  Archbishops of, see Hutton, Matthew and Mathew, Tobie

ZANTE, 313
Zizicum, 146
Zouche, Edward, d. 1625, eleventh Lord, 97
Zouche, Sir William, 165